# Diving into the Gospel of John

# Diving into the Gospel of John

*Life through Believing*

BRUCE R. REICHENBACH

CASCADE *Books* · Eugene, Oregon

DIVING INTO THE GOSPEL OF JOHN
Life through Believing

Cascade Books
An Imprint of Wipf and Stock Publishers
199 W. 8th Ave., Suite 3
Eugene, OR 97401

www.wipfandstock.com

PAPERBACK ISBN: 978-1-6667-4207-7
HARDCOVER ISBN: 978-1-6667-4208-4
EBOOK ISBN: 978-1-6667-4209-1

*Cataloguing-in-Publication data:*

Names: Reichenbach, Bruce R., author.

Title: Diving into the gospel of John : life through believing. / Bruce R. Reichenbach.

Description: Eugene, OR: Cascade Books, 2023. | Includes bibliographical references and index.

Identifiers: ISBN 978-1-6667-4207-7 (paperback). | ISBN 978-1-6667-4208-4 (hardcover). | ISBN 978-1-6667-4209-1 (ebook).

Subjects: LCSH: Bible. John—Criticism, interpretation, etc.

Classification: BS2615.2 R454 2023 (print). | BS2615.2 (ebook).

To my grandchildren, Hudson Harvie Mitarotonda, Meyers Warren Mitarotonda, and Weston Thomas Reichenbach. My prayer is that as they grow up, they become great divers, and in their exploring discover not only the riches of the Gospel of John, but of the rest of the Bible, the treasures of great literature, and inspiring ideas everywhere.

To Sharon, my wife of fifty-seven years, whose loving companionship and joyous partnership has richly enhanced my life and work. She read the manuscript many times, noting possibilities and connections, suggesting ideas, pointing out unclarities and errors, checking passages, and encouraging me to rethink and rephrase discussions. The book reads very much better because of her many contributions.

# Contents

# Acknowledgments

ALL SCRIPTURE QUOTATIONS, UNLESS otherwise indicated, are taken from the Holy Bible, Today's New International Version®, TNIV®. Copyright © 2001, 2005 by Biblica, Inc.™ Used by permission of Zondervan. All rights reserved worldwide. www.zondervan.com. The "NIV" and "New International Version" are trademarks registered in the United States Patent and Trademark Office by Biblica, Inc.™

Journal articles provide the opportunity to present ideas before they find their home in a book. The editors of the following journals have kindly consented to allow me to reprint material from my articles that were published in their respective journals.

"Reconciling Disparate Reasons for Jesus' Death in the Gospel of John," *Wisconsin Lutheran Quarterly* 117 (2020) 167–77, is included in chapter 7.

"The Theological Significance of Sevens in John," *Bibliotheca Sacra* 177 (2020) 286–307, is included in chapter 10.

"Soteriology in the Gospel of John," *Themelios* 46 (2021) 574–91, is included in chapter 11.

"Why Does Jesus Use Ambiguous Rhetoric?" which expands chapter 1 by addressing the function of and reason for ambiguity in the Gospel of John, is not included in this volume but is forthcoming in *Bibliotheca Sacra*.

# Introduction

LEON MORRIS WRITES, "I liken the comparison of John's Gospel to a pool in which a child may wade and an elephant can swim. It is both simple and profound. It is for the veriest beginner in the faith and for the mature Christian. Its appeal is immediate and never failing."[1] I invite both waders and swimmers to dive in and explore the Gospel's precious waters in this book. Abundant treasures await the persistent, observant diver. The Gospel is not merely a story. It has a clearly stated purpose, an obvious organization that realizes that purpose, a richness of symbols and literary techniques that advance the purpose, strength of dialogic narrative to communicate the purpose, and provocative discourse emphasizing the purpose. The more I read the Gospel, the more treasures I discover hidden in its language, symbols, ideas, and themes. The Evangelist presents striking characters, bold claims, antagonistic interchange, dramatic scenes, difficult riddles, shocking irony, subtle humor, intriguingly structured discourses, and developed arguments that lend the Gospel an air of linguistic and theological enchantment, subtlety, and mystery.

As more than a literary container of wonderful treasures, the Gospel has a power of its own. George Beasley-Murray writes about the Gospel:

> To pursue the study of the Gospel that seeks to make [confronting God's presence and himself] plain is one of the most rewarding exercises a Christian believer can undertake. And not only Christians. The instinct which leads Christians to hand on a copy of this Gospel to those who do not share the Christian faith is related to that of the dying believer who turns to it in his latest hours, and that of the Christian preacher who expounds it to deepen the experience and understanding of Christ among his or her congregation. The power of this Gospel's testimony to Christ is an experienced fact. Archbishop Frederick Temple attested this from his own experience; writing to his son, who was finding philosophic difficulties in his attempts to grasp the Christian faith, he stated: "I am obliged to confess that from seventeen to five and twenty I indulged largely in such speculations. But I felt all along like a swimmer who sees no shore before him after long swimming, and at last allows himself to be

---

1. Morris, *Gospel,* 3.

picked up by a ship that seems to be going his way. . . . My passing ship was
St. John."[2]

The Gospel is a carefully crafted, complex composite of arguments supporting
the author's overtly stated thesis: that Jesus is the Messiah, the Son of God, and that
through believing in him readers/listeners will find eternal life. In short: life through
believing. As a philosopher of religion, I am deeply interested in arguments. However,
although some have viewed the Gospel using the model of a legal trial,[3] the Gospel
generally has not been approached in a manner that directly focuses on eliciting the
complexity and cohesion of its arguments per se. In what follows, I invite readers to
encounter the Gospel of John in a new way, as containing intentional, multifaceted,
coordinated arguments introduced to achieve the author's goal. The arguments are
couched in four parts. First, the Gospel author introduces readers to symbols and
unique uses of language that hide their significance from Jesus's interlocutors but are
revealed to the readers. We will appreciate the wonderful artistry advanced by the literary techniques the Evangelist uses to portray Jesus. We will come to understand how
ambiguity plays out in the Evangelist's use of double meanings, irony, riddles, significant questions, and rich symbols, and why the author uses this style of communication
to make his case for believing. Second, the author progressively introduces evidence
for his thesis in the form of signs, testimony, self-identification, and relationships. We
will discover how the Evangelist uses stories of personal encounters to persuade his
readers about the nature and function or mission of Jesus as the Messiah. Third, the
author uniquely structures theatrically influenced dialogues and triadic discourse to
convey Jesus's identity and mission. We will explore these dialogues and discourses to
see what they tell us about Jesus, noticing that the Evangelist consciously constructs
dialogues and discourses differently as they function as part of the author's overall
argument. Finally, the author presents important hints throughout the text—Jesus's
appeals to his hour or time, seven as the theological number of completeness, and
discussion of origin or parentage—to portray Jesus's salvific work that provides life
through believing. This way of looking at the Gospel of John though the conjunction
of his arguments affords a fresh and important way of understanding the text.

Along the way, I will share, often in footnotes, some of the many insights I have
gleaned from reading the Gospel and studying what others have written about it. As
the undersea explorer would have great anticipations poking around the fauna of
coral reefs or steering a submersible in the ocean depths, I have come to expect that
around the next verse or next scene I will discover something new. Jesus as presented
by the Gospel writer conceals with double meanings and reveals with irony. The writer
tantalizes the senses—"the house was filled with the fragrance of the perfume" (12:3);[4]

2. Cited by Robinson, *Historical*, 27, in Beasley-Murray, *John*, xxxiv–xxxv.

3. Lincoln, *Truth on Trial*.

4. Biblical references in the text without cited sources are from the Gospel of John.

"you have saved the best wine till now" (2:10)—and makes the reader thirsty (4:15) and hungry (6:34) for more. He paints a Jesus who pushes some away (8:44; 20:17) and brings others into his inner circle (10:3). He touches all social classes and yet is beholden to none; even the uncomprehending disciples fall under his lovingly harsh criticism (16:31–32).

The Gospel author's book and my book are invitations. My hope is that by the time you finish reading this series of thematic essays, you too will feel that you dived into and explored the depths of an ocean of treasures or that you have been picked up by that same ship of St. John and transported with deeper understanding of the Evangelist, the argument he presents, the Jesus he portrays, and the God Jesus reveals. All will not be plain; the waters are at times murky. The author's Jesus is a mysterious, enigmatic figure who revels in ambiguities, ironies, and paradoxes, pointing all the while to something beyond the obvious and at hand. Yet in the end, what Jesus accomplished in personally demonstrating God's love for the world should be both clear enough to stimulate commitment and encouraging to the mind and spirit, yet rich, subtle, and mysterious enough to encourage further study and debate.

## MY APPROACH

Discovering the arguments and insights of the Gospel of John reminds me of Jesus's parable in Matthew (13:45–46) about the jewel merchant who quested for the most exquisite pearls. After much searching, he finally discovered the pearl of great value for which he diligently sought and on finding it sold everything he had to purchase it. Scholars who have spent many fruitful years studying the Gospel of John tell of experiencing the excitement of uncovering inklings about who might have written the book, who might have edited it, or how the editors were related to the Beloved Disciple, John the disciple, the Presbyter John, the School of John, or the John exiled to Patmos. They labor to unravel the layers of the Gospel to discover the source materials the editors may have used, its reliance on or independence from the Synoptic Gospels, and its possible subsequent redactions.[5] Disconnections, uneasy transitions, and aporias (internal inconsistencies that seem irresolvable) purportedly signal editorial reconstructions. Alan Culpepper offers us the literary image of an ancient tell, where archaeologists gradually and arduously peel back layer by layer the accumulated debris to reveal the ancient strata and broken-down walls that hold secrets of past events.[6] Scholarly excavators of John painstakingly pare back the structural and literary layers

---

5. Raymond Brown suggests five editorial stages in the formation of the Gospel (*Gospel i–xii*, xxxiv–xxxix).

6. Culpepper, *Anatomy*, 3.

hoping to locate the primitive fragments embedded in the textual accretions[7] and possibly reconstruct what they consider to be the original order of the text.[8]

I will approach the text differently. Over one hundred years ago Richard Moulton presaged a movement that has had substantial influence in the last half century. Johannine studies had been dominated by what he termed the historic approach: the concern for sources, primitive texts, textual reconstructions, identification of redactors and schools, historical influences, and the like. Moulton argued that "the historic and the literary are theoretically distinct; . . . they must not be undertaken together; for the whole method and spirit of the two are in opposition. Historic analysis must skeptically question the very details which literary appreciation must rapidly combine into a common impression. . . . The existing text cannot be truly interpreted until it has been read in the light of its exact literary structure."[9] One need not advocate a radical separation of the literary approach from the historical, for it has become clear that literary analyses cast needed light on difficult questions about the unity, coherence, and meaning of the text that function in determining answers to historical problems of authorship, audience, integrity of the text, redactions, writing location, etc.[10] This book focuses on a literary understanding of the Gospel of John for the argument about Jesus's identity and mission that it coherently develops and for the multitude of insights it provides along the way. In doing so, it is "concerned with the level above that of the individual sentence: with intersentential connections and with global rather than local links."[11] In this it goes beyond the attention of commentaries that atomize the text, by emphasizing the larger, interconnected structures and coherence of the stories, dialogues, discourses, and narrator contributions, to ascertain the meaning that arises from seeing how the parts relate to the whole tapestry of the book and how the whole enlightens the parts—without losing the significance of the author's careful choices of words, phrases, and sentences.

Accomplishing this requires attending to the literary style of the author. Sang-Hoon Kim notes that although the vocabulary of John is relatively simple, "no other book in the NT compares to John in its complexity. It is difficult to grasp its styles

---

7. See Fortna's source criticism in *Gospel of Signs*.

8. Bultmann, *Gospel of John*, 10–11.

9. Moulton, *Literary Study*, viii–ix. His application is largely to Old Testament texts. See his Appendix III. Breck (*Shape*, 192) writes, "While the main stream of commentators continues to probe for evidence of multiple underlying traditions and multiple authorships, a small minority has concentrated on the literary structure of the fourth Gospel, and in particular on the chiasmic patterns that recur throughout. Their conclusions point to the unity of composition that characterizes the Gospel, suggesting that a single hand was in fact responsible for shaping Johannine tradition into its present form."

10. "One cannot ignore the question of the historical audience or the historical Jesus of John's story without reducing and restricting the functions of narrative" (Stibbe, *Storyteller*, 12).

11. "It has become obvious to a growing number of linguists that the study of the syntax of isolated sentences, extracted without natural context from the purposeful constructions of speakers, is a methodology that has outlived its usefulness" (Brinton, "Historical," 222–23). See Givón, *Syntax*, xiii.

and structure."[12] In taking an argumentative and literary approach to the text, which searches the depths of the interaction between the author and his readers, I will treat the text as a unitary narrative developed in defense of a specific thesis. Regardless of the sources the writer used or any editorial layers, the final product has a purpose and a thesis in terms of which the author structured the text. In this it is "a coherent text that is inherently meaningful in its own right, regardless of the processes and situations that produced the story as we have it today."[13] Thus, I will address how the author constructs and narrates the argument of the text, how the intended or implied reader might best understand this argument, what that author wants the readers to take from the text, and hence what the text means as it stands, not only to the original readers but also to us. I will not focus on or discuss the historical sources of the text. This topic can be pursued in the many good critical commentaries on the Gospel. My approach will be to explore the themes and wonderful insights present in the Gospel in argumentative support of its fundamental conclusion, to polish the pearl to reveal in diverse lights its true value as it aims to inculcate believing in Jesus as Messiah, the Son of God.

It is not that the historical-critical approach to the Gospel is unimportant or does not yield interesting finds. However, I will not read the text as a patchwork of sources, strategically rearranged and editorially modified, inserted into the work of what to some seem to be inept editors, where beauty and wholeness is replaced by the fractured and fragmentary. Rather, I intend to treat the Gospel as a literary whole cloth, whether the work of one writer or of editors. I want to discover and understand what ideas, themes, and messages the writer desires this book to convey in a defended development of its thesis and to discern how the author communicates these to his readers, both ancient and modern. Read this way, "[p]rimarily at least, it is the literary creation of the evangelist, which is crafted with the purpose of leading readers to 'see' the world as the evangelist sees it so that in reading the gospel they will be forced to test their perceptions and beliefs about the 'real' world against the evangelist's perspective on the world they have encountered in the gospel."[14] I will look for the beauty, architectural and theological integrity, richness of thought and characters, symbolic ideas, and penetrating themes and insights the Gospel expresses. I will search out

12. Kim, *Sourcebook*, 1.

13. Thatcher, "Anatomies," 1–2.

14. Culpepper, *Anatomy*, 4–5. I will not presume that the text does not reflect the teaching, style, or ministry of the historical Jesus. "If we are to honor the literary (and theological) integrity of the story, we must recognize and consider it as a historical story set in a historical context" (Horsley and Thatcher, *John, Jesus*, 103). John is a book of both memory and history (Thatcher, *Why John Wrote*, 167). Paul Anderson concurs: "Therefore, just as John's material includes the most elevated and theological presentations of Jesus among the four canonical Gospels, John also is the most mundane and grounded among them. John's empiricism is thus an empirical fact. So, until an alternative view is established, the Johannine editor's claims that the Johannine narrative reflects an individuated memory of Jesus's ministry must be taken seriously as a narratival attestation with implications for understanding more about its subject, Jesus of Nazareth" ("Why the Gospel," 26).

the subtleties, the plays on language, the use of numbers, riddles, ironies, double meanings, metaphors, and allusions to other writings the Gospel uses to present its message. I will highlight the way the author dramatically sketches the dialogues and triadically structures the discourses. In effect, I want to discover and interpret the text as the author bequeathed it to us, and in doing so work with the strong unity of argument, thesis, and narrative that courses through the Gospel of John. Thus, with C. H. Dodd, although excluding his bracketed caveat, "I shall assume as a provisional working hypothesis that the present order (of the Gospel) is not fortuitous, but deliberately devised by somebody—even if he were only a scribe doing his best—and that the person in question . . . had some design in mind, and was not necessarily irresponsible or unintelligent."[15] Indeed, the result of our study will demonstrate the high artistic ability of the author, the multiple ways he invoked his considerable literary skills in constructive defense of his thesis, and his realization of his singleness of purpose in creating an effective, unitary testament of testaments to Jesus.[16]

## THE PURPOSE OF THE GOSPEL

My approach takes seriously the author's explicit purpose for writing the book.[17] Whether it is written to nonbelievers who are open to investigating what they might have heard about events some years ago in Roman-occupied Israel, or whether it is written to people who already are part of the believing community in a distant land but need to be strengthened in their faith and understanding, or to both, is unclear.[18] What is clear is that the Evangelist writes with a purpose: "that you may believe that Jesus is the Messiah, the Son of God, and that by believing you will have life in his name" (20:31). And since what he writes is given in defense and development of that thesis, what he includes is not happenstance. Rather, all is part of a multifaceted argument. Since the Gospel is a book about believing, we will explore in the chapter 1

15. Dodd, *Interpretation,* 290.

16. "[T]he gospel is an understanding of Jesus artistically expressed in the language of story" (Stibbe, *Storyteller,* 13). For a critical discussion of other possible purposes, see Painter, *Quest,* 93–105.

17. Alan Culpepper writes, "The implicit purpose of the gospel narrative is to alter irrevocably the reader's perception of the real world" (*Anatomy,* 4). I suggest that it is not merely implicit; it is explicit. He goes on, "The narrative world of the gospel is therefore neither a window on the ministry of Jesus nor a window on the history of the Johannine community." This is much too strong, for insofar as John wants us to believe something about the Son of God, it is the Son of God come in the flesh in Jesus who also is relevant in identity and function to the community to whom the author writes. In its selectivity and testimonial character, it tells us both about the Jesus of the believing community written to and the Jesus who did signs, who discoursed with seekers, disciples, and antagonists, and who suffered, died, and was raised.

18. Textual variants in 20:31 leave the matter unclear. Some manuscripts read πιστεύσητε ("These are written that you come to believe") while others read πιστεύητε ("These are written that you keep on believing"). Denaux ("Twofold Purpose," 526–28) discusses the possible grammatical interpretations of "believe" that underlie the discussion. Carson ("Understanding Misunderstandings," 87–88) suggests both believe and keep on believing are intended.

the literary tools the author intentionally employs to accomplish his purpose. Understanding these tools is challenging but necessary to open the book to us, assisting us to see more clearly how the Evangelist carefully crafts his important message to bring about believing.

## THE GOSPEL'S NARRATIVE

The Fourth Gospel is a narrative, preceded by a Prologue and ended with an Epilogue, that contains stories about Jesus's interaction with diverse persons, dialogues that enlighten us about the significance of these encounters, discussions, and discourses about signs, symbols, metaphors, and relationships, and an extended passion story. The Evangelist engages these elements to argue for and to help his readers understand Jesus's identity and function or mission.[19] The *author* of the Gospel constructed the text utilizing a specific architecture for the particular purpose of bringing readers to believing. Both the author, who is anonymous but whom we will term John (for reasons of tradition[20]) or the Evangelist and the original readers stand outside the text. However, the presence of both is integral to the text.[21] We would have neither the

19. "Contemporary narrative approaches to the Gospels attempt to enter into the process of communication between an author and a reader whom we do not know, and who are long since dead, so that the contemporary reader might be moved and inspired by the passionate convictions of the author" (Brown, *Introduction to John*, 33).

20. All agree that the author is anonymous, but that has not prevented much speculation about his identity. John 21:20, 24 identifies the author as the Beloved Disciple but introduces a further "we" that leaves open questions about the Beloved Disciple's identity and whether that person was the actual author or a source (among other sources) of information for the author (Schnackenburg, *John*, 3:383). By the end of the second century Irenaeus, Clement of Alexandria, and Tertullian all held that the Beloved Disciple, who authored the Gospel, was John the son of Zebedee, and this view generally held until the last century. Leon Morris thoughtfully defends this view (*Gospel*, 4–25; also Köstenberger, "Use of OT," 41–45). The probable differentiation of John, the son of Zebedee, and the Beloved Disciple in 21:2, 7, provides a counter-perspective. Recent authors, noting that earlier external evidence questions this identity, emphasize that Papias's apparent distinction between John the apostle and John the Elder, who was a disciple but not an apostle, allows for more than one John. Bauckham (*Testimony*, chs. 1 and 2) suggests that tradition conflated the two Johns and argues that the latter is the Beloved Disciple who is the author. Beasley-Murray (*John*, lxx–lxxv) rejects the thesis that the Beloved Disciple, although an eyewitness, authoritative interpreter of Jesus, and source of much of the material, is the author because no author would self-reference in this manner. R. Brown suggests that while John the apostle was "a source of the underlying historical tradition," his disciples "played a role in the composition of the Gospel, . . . preaching and developing his reminiscences even further, according to the needs of the community to which they ministered." Ultimately, from this community one principal disciple, "marked with dramatic genius and profound theological insight," was responsible for the later stages of editing (Brown, *Gospel i–xiii*, c–ci). My use of "John" or "the Evangelist" is not meant to take sides in the debate regarding the identity of the author, authors, or Beloved Disciple.

21. "Although the real author and the real reader(s) do not play an active role in the events of the narrative, they leave their traces. Narratives have deliberatively contrived plots and characters that interact throughout the story along a certain timeline, through a sequence of events. An author devises certain rhetorical features to hold plot and character together so that the reader will not miss the author's point of view. These rhetorical features are *in* the narrative" (Brown, *Introduction to John*, 32).

Gospel of John nor the specific structure that the Gospel presents to us were there not an author who had a purpose in writing the text and readers for whom he wrote. Although we don't know his name, we can learn something about him from what he has written. He is a believer in Jesus since he tells us that he wants us to become believers also. He is a Palestinian Jew[22] literate in Greek in which the current Gospel was composed but also familiar with Hebrew and Aramaic terms that he transliterates (1:42; 5:2; 19:13). He knows the Old Testament (1:23; 2:31, 45; 7:41–42; 10:34; 12:13–15; 13:18; 16:25; 19:24), the geography of and buildings in the land of Jesus's ministry (4:4; 5:2; 6:1, 16–24; 10:23; 11:18), the relevant religious beliefs, customs, and laws (2:6; 5:1, 18; 6:4; 7:2; 10:24; 13:1; 18:39; 19:7, 14), and the Jewish leaders (11:49; 18:13–14). He seems to know intimately Jesus's band of followers, identifying what they say to each other (4:33; 16:17; 20:25), places they frequented (11:54; 18:2), and what they were thinking (2:11, 17, 22; 4:27; 6:60–61).[23]

The author does not intend the Gospel to be a comprehensive biography of Jesus, although it is biographical.[24] The actual events and discourses the author presents cover only a very small fraction of the days and years (traditionally three) of Jesus's ministry. The author has carefully selected what he gives us with his purpose and goal in mind, omitting much else to which he did or did not have access. In fact, the author or final editor notes its incompleteness: "Jesus did many other things as well. If every one of them were written down, I suppose that even the whole world would not have room for all the books that would be written" (21:25). Thus, while we must read the Gospel from the perspective of the author, we also must read it from the perspective of the *intended readers*, for the author wrote with them, their situation, deep needs, ongoing concerns, and their possibly precarious situation in mind, carefully choosing and crafting from materials he has and his experiences what he considered would be relevant and meaningful to them. The author deliberately selected and fashioned his stories, dialogues, signs, and events as parts of an argument for his intended readers.

Since we have only indirect evidence about the intended readers, we can only make educated guesses about them based on inferences from the text. Since the Gospel is written in Greek, we can infer that the intended readers/listeners were

22. Morris, *Gospel*, 11–12. Brown (*Gospel i–xii*, 500) writes that "the primary influence on John was Judaism, and not Gnosticism nor Hellenistic thought."

23. Morris, *Gospel*, 12.

24. "John should be understood as an ancient biography and the gospel's author incorporates features of other genres, especially literary and thematic features of revelatory writings" (Carter, *John*, 17). For a description of the features of ancient biography, derived from Richard Burridge (*Gospels*) and which are not the same as being primarily history, see Carter, *John*, 9–12. Bauckham, however, contends that one should "place John's Gospel squarely within the part of the spectrum of types of ancient biographies where the genre of biography overlapped with that of historiography." That this is "a highly theologically interpretative telling of the story of Jesus is not at all an obstacle to recognizing the biographical genre of the Gospel, for all ancient biographies, to one degree or another, were interpretative projects that present the writer's convictions about the significance of his subject" (*Testimony*, 19, 18).

fluent in Greek.[25] Probably many in the Gospel's audience were illiterate, since only a minority of people in that day were literate.[26] Thus, for some, at least, the Gospel was to be presented orally. Since one contemporary form of oral presentation was drama, some have suggested that the stories, consciously or unconsciously, take on the form of Greek drama.[27] We will say more about this in chapter 7. Although the Evangelist tells us that he is writing so that his audience will believe, as we already noted it is unclear whether they are already believers, perhaps needing reinforcement for their believing, or people seriously considering this new faith.

Characteristics that we might infer from the stories and themes the author has chosen suggest that at least some readers fall into the category of believing Jews. The Pharisees view Jesus as breaking Sabbath laws (5:9, 16; 9:14), while Jesus expresses concern about the distractions occurring in the temple precincts (2:14–17). The Evangelist worries about believers being expelled or excommunicated from the synagogue (9:22, 34; 12:42; 16:2).[28] This emphasis on Jesus's conflicts with Jewish leaders over cultic practices intimates that the readers may be facing similar problems, so that indirectly the author provides guidance and encouragement for converted Jews who find themselves in conflict with their religious community. Numerous subtle allusions to the Old Testament and wisdom literature further support the view that Jews are among the intended readers.[29]

That the intended readers also include gentiles is reinforced by several considerations. The author translates the Hebrew terms rabbi (1:30) and Messiah (1:41), and the Aramaic terms Cephas (1:42), Bethesda (5:2), and Gabbatha (19:13), into Greek. He explains Jewish customs and beliefs (2:6; 4:25). For example, in 4:9 John explains why Jews did not associate with gentiles, while in 10:22 John informs his readers that Hanukkah occurred in winter, facts that Jews would know. In 19:40 John explains the Jewish burial custom of wrapping a body in spices and a linen cloth. In 11:52, John comments that Jesus would die for all people, both the nation (ἔθνος) and the "scattered children of God" (although for Caiaphas this would be the Jewish Diaspora).[30] Finally, some of the early converts reported in the Gospel were not Jews (4:4–54), a welcoming idea for gentile readers.

The intended audience also apparently was concerned about the purity or authenticity of the prior information they had received about the identity and ministry of Jesus. Thus, the Gospel promises that the Spirit will remind about Jesus's teachings (14:26; 16:7–14), perhaps using this Gospel as a ready tool. Finally, the intended

25. Bultmann writes that "the Gospel of John was undoubtedly written in Greek. But the author's Greek is dyed with a Semitic colour" (*Gospel of John*, 3).

26. Harris, *Ancient Literacy*, 13, 22.

27. For a brief discussion of this trajectory in the literature and her own view, see Brant, *Dialogue*.

28. Martyn, *History*, chapter 2.

29. Brown, *Gospel i–xii*, cxxii–cxxv.

30. Morris, *Gospel*, 505.

readers may have wondered about the absence of Jesus. Although the Gospel contains no departure scene, Jesus frequently reminds his disciples in veiled terms that not only will he return to the Father, but he will return to them (14:3; 16:10, 16–24), although the details are ambiguous at best.[31]

While the author and intended readers stand outside the text in that they are not part of the text itself, the narrator and those narrated about are located within the text.[32] The *narrator* is identified as the Beloved Disciple (21:20, 24), who appears several times at the end of Jesus's ministry: at the last meal, at the cross, at the tomb, and at Peter's commissioning (13:22–25; 19:26–27; 20:2–9).[33] The Beloved Disciple is anonymous, and as a result his identity and name are the object of much speculation. The Gospel portrays the narrator in the third person as a detached but not unbiased observer who transcends the limited perspectives of the characters about whom he writes. He is semi-omniscient in that he knows and more deeply understands what the various characters think, feel, or intend (5:16; 7:12–13; 12:10). He is influenced by the Old Testament and omnipresent in that he can report what occurs even if he (as a character in the story) is not present (7:35, 40–52; 11:49–53; 19:23–24). His knowledge even penetrates Jesus's thoughts (6:64, 71; 7:39; 18:4) and dialogues. He tells us about Jesus's conversation with the Samaritan woman even though the two are alone at the well, about the searching crowd moving across the lake after Jesus and the disciples have departed (6:22–25), and about the conversation between the formerly blind man and the Pharisees (ch. 9). He knows the past as well as the future (from the perspective of the narrated events) (2:22; 7:39; 12:16; 13:7).[34]

"In John, the narrator is undramatized and serves as the voice of the implied author. Since the narrator shares the author's point of view, the two are not usually distinguished. . . . In fact, there is no reason to suspect any difference in the ideological, spatial, temporal and phraseological points of view of the narrator, the implied author, and the [real] author."[35] The narrator provides essential information that is not contained in the dialogues and helps the readers properly understand and interpret statements made by the characters and events presented (2:11, 17, 22, 24–25; 4:8–9, 44; 5:18; 6:64, 71; 7:30, 39; 8:20, 27; 9:7; 11:2, 51; 12:4–6, 16, 33, 37–41; 13:28–29; 18:9; 19:24, 36–37; 20:9; 21:12, 23). He sees events from the post-resurrection perspective

31. For a discussion of the eschatology in John, see Brown, *Gospel i–xii*, cxv–cxxi.

32. "Communication between a real author and a real reader who are *outside* the text takes place through an implied author, a narrator, a narratee and an implied reader who are *inside* the text. . . . Via the literary features of the storytelling, narrative critics trace the communication taking place *in the narrative* between an author and a reader" (Brown, *Introduction to John*, 33). Also, Culpepper, *Anatomy*, 6.

33. Some (Brown, *Gospel xiii–xxi*, 822–23) also see him in the house of the high priest (18:15), although this is speculative.

34. For a thorough discussion of the narrator, his knowledge, role, and contributions, see Culpepper, *Anatomy*, ch. 2.

35. Culpepper, *Anatomy*, 16, 43.

and comments on or explains their significance—their role in the overall argument—in that light. For our purposes, we assume that the author also functions as the narrator of the text, in that he speaks or writes through the narrator.[36]

*Those narrated about* are the persons found in the Gospel, most centrally Jesus. "There is a striking similarity in the language and ideological perspective of the narrator and Jesus. Jesus's point of view . . . corresponds remarkably to that of the narrator. Both Jesus and the narrator are omniscient, retrospective, and ideologically and phraseologically indistinguishable."[37] Thus, either the narrator deeply imbibed the linguistic and structural persona of Jesus, or else what we have is a reconstruction of what Jesus said, using the linguistic and possibly ideological framework of the narrator.

Some of the narrated characters—John the Baptizer, Nathanael, Nicodemus, Martha, Mary, Lazarus, Joseph of Arimathea, some of the Twelve—have names and thus assume special importance. Others play a significant role in the drama but remain anonymous. Still others, such as Jews[38] and Pharisees, are treated corporately. We will look more closely at some of these persons in chapter 6 and elsewhere.

Communication between the Gospel's author and his readers extends beyond first century readers to you and me today. Although we are not directly part of his implied readership, that is, the specific readership John had in mind when he constructed the book, his witness message to believe and have eternal life applies also to subsequent readers. This takes seriously the purpose of the author as he tells it to us, that "you may believe that Jesus is the Messiah, the Son of God, and that by believing have eternal life" (20:31). I will explore, elucidate, and reflect on the Evangelist's intentions in writing the Gospel, the unique ways in which he crafts his argument and text, his use of language that creates ambiguity found in irony, repetition, and metaphor and symbol, and his structures of narration, dialogue, and discourse to further develop and argue for his message. I invite the reader to explore along with me the central *themes*, *arguments*, and associated *insights* of this Gospel. In presenting this thematic study, I will refer to the Fourth Gospel as a Book of Books, where each of the "books" adopts and elucidates an important viewpoint, theme, or diverse perspective that not only supports the ultimate purpose for which the Evangelist wrote but courses its way

36. For a detailed defense of the thesis that the author/narrator is the eyewitness, the Beloved Disciple, see Bauckham, *Eyewitnesses*, chs. 14–17, and *Testimony*, chapters 1–2.

37. Culpepper, *Anatomy*, 36.

38. As often noted, the term "Jews" (Ἰουδαῖοι) has a variety of (possibly overlapping) referents in John, including the people (2:6; 7:15, 35), source of salvation (4:22), committed followers (12:11), temporary followers (8:31), the curious (2:18), antagonists (5:16, 18), Judeans (7:10), Jewish religious leaders (1:19; 3:1; 5:10), and characters present in the Gospel (Zimmermann, "Jews," 71–75). Thus, the term "is not a blanket appellation for the inhabitants of a region" but often refers to people or authorities who are hostile toward Jesus (11:36–37, 45–46; 12:9, 17, 34) (Koester, *Symbolism*, 58). "The Jews make their first appearance asking questions, and most of the time when their speech is reported in the first ten chapters they are asking questions. Thereafter, they ask only a few questions. The questions, of course, challenge, generate confrontation, and eventually demonstrate that the Jews cannot accept the answers they are given" (Culpepper, *Anatomy*, 126–28).

through the text. The stories, signs, dialogues, and discourses contain multiple themes that eventually create the argumentative tapestry that the Evangelist wants to weave to bring out Jesus's identity and mission. Historical critics have highlighted what they perceive as flaws in the tapestry and have used these to identify sources and multiple weavers.[39] We, on the other hand, will treat these "flaws" as part of the warp and woof of the tapestry and ask how they further development and recognition of the overall pattern.

## THE JOURNEY

The number of publications on the Fourth Gospel is staggering. In the Luther Seminary Library in St. Paul, Minnesota, the books devoted solely to the Fourth Gospel occupy six large bookcases six shelves high. Gilbert Van Belle's *Johannine Bibliography 1966–1985* runs to over five hundred pages for this time frame. Commentaries are plentiful, thick, multivolume, detailed, varied in their approaches and conclusions, thoughtful, and excellent. A plethora of scholarly monographs explore and highlight specific themes in John. Journal articles examine in exquisite theological and linguistic detail and speculate about its manifold features. However, much of the material is not directed to or accessible by laypersons who want to explore the Gospel for group or personal Bible study or a Christian education class or to clergy preparing sermons. Since Johannine themes and insights are scattered throughout the literature, I want to make these and my own available and accessible to the reader. However, above all, I want readers to appreciate the careful, detailed argument the author develops in defense of his thesis.

I write for both laity and clergy. This volume is not a commentary, but a thematic, argumentative exploration of the Fourth Gospel. Through this exploration, I will engage the reader in the excitement of exploring the subtle and profound ideas, insights, and themes the author of the Gospel presents. I distill ideas found in research and add to them treasures that I personally discovered in the text. For those who want to plunge more deeply into John's challenging waters or explore alternative explanations, I provide additional footnotes.

The reader will find eleven snapshots of the Gospel, eleven books as I will call them. These "books," although treated separately, stand interrelated. They trace the author's overall argument and themes through the Gospel, each supporting the author's primary purpose of identifying Jesus in order to bring about our believing in him. My goal is to convey the reader into the enjoyment of discovery of the Gospel's arguments and insights. To this end I invite you to dive with me, to open the eleven "books" of the

---

39. Two of numerous examples include Anderson, "Dialogue," 96–108, and Stibbe, "Magnificent," 149–65.

Book of John to personally explore and experience in this "literary, theological, and religious masterpiece"[40] the incredible journey to believing and thereby to eternal life.

## QUESTIONS FOR REFLECTION AND DISCUSSION

1. What purpose does the author give for writing the Gospel? Do you find this purpose important in your life?

2. After reading this chapter, what did you discover about the characteristics and situation of John's audience?

3. In what ways were the characteristics and situation of John's first-century audience similar to and different from your situation today? How might what you look for or value about the Gospel differ from that of the first readers?

4. Suppose the author was one of the disciples or the Beloved Disciple. Why do you think that the author wrote the Gospel in the third person rather than in the first person? What difference would it have made if he had written in the first person?

5. The narrator is only identified in John chapter 21 and seems to know many things about private feelings and dialogues and events where he was not present. How do you think the narrator (or the author, since they have the same perspective) acquired or knew the material he put into the Gospel?

6. This book takes a literary approach to the Gospel, rather than an historical-critical approach. How do you understand the difference between these? For example, what different kinds of questions would each approach ask of the Gospel?

40. Painter, "Prologue," 40.

CHAPTER ONE

# Book of Ambiguity

GOOD BOOKS REVEL IN words, their medium of communication. The Gospel of John is a book about the word—the living Word, the spoken word, and the written word. The words of the Word, which are the revealing words (8:28) of the God who sent the Word (17:6), are to be heard (5:24), remembered (15:20), followed (8:31), kept and guarded (8:51–52). They shock, mystify, and so astound that those who encounter the words of the Word audibly struggle to comprehend both the words and the Word. To illustrate this, John tells the story of the temple guards sent to arrest Jesus when he was teaching in the temple courts. They, along with the people in the temple, hear Jesus's words, "Believe in me, and the Scripture (writings; words) that says that streams of living water will flow within you will be fulfilled." Both guards and temple attenders puzzle not only over his words but also over the identity of this person whose words make strange claims. The guards return empty-handed to the chief priests and Pharisees who sent them. "Well, why didn't you bring Jesus in," the Jewish leaders inquire. "No one ever spoke like this man," the guards reply (7:46). The deeply ambiguous words of the Word, the baffling teaching of the Rabbi, the confrontational style of the Riddler, all simultaneously attract and repel his audience. For us, then, to begin to penetrate this mysterious Gospel and the teachings of its central character—to understand the identity of the Word—we must comprehend something of the nature and structure of the Gospel's presentation of the words of the Word.

## PRESENTATIONAL TECHNIQUES

On the one hand, the vocabulary of John is so simple that the Gospel often is used as a primer for teaching students Koine Greek. On the other hand, the fertility of language, diverse uses of literary techniques, and employment of poignant symbols and double meanings makes the Gospel a source of both exploratory delight and rich understandings and misunderstandings.[1] "In John, the reader finds that the evangelist says a

1. Carson ("Understanding Misunderstandings," 59–60) notes the importance of literary devices

great deal without actually saying it. Having drawn readers to his side by means of the Prologue, the evangelist trusts them to pick up the overtones of his language, the irony of conversations and events, the implications of the misunderstandings into which various characters blunder, and the symbolism of the places, things, and abstractions which serve as more than stage props for his story."[2]

How does the author pull off his argument in this Book of Books? How does he carefully but subtly construct his argument to defend his thesis? To fully appreciate the Gospel, we first need to penetrate the author's style. Throughout this book I will explore his stories, dialogues, and discourses, identifying diverse unifying themes and insights present in the Gospel, all in service of his stated thesis. Here I want to focus on the wealth of the literary techniques the Evangelist employs to elicit the responses he encourages from his readers. One cannot fully grasp the treasures of this Gospel and the ways that Jesus as envisioned by John communicates his message without recognizing the author's overt and subtle techniques. Put more succinctly, unless readers pay attention to the stylistic features and how the message is conveyed, they often will miss the author's point entirely—which is just what happens with the contemporaries who listen to Jesus. And even if they get his point, the subtilties and insights often go unrecognized. The content is at the service of the style, for through the style of Jesus's teachings the Evangelist brings the readers into Jesus's person and mission.

The characters in the Gospel, whether individually or part of the audience, frequently cannot understand this rabbi and what he says. They are trapped by his ambiguous language and indirect discourse. "What seems clear and simple on the surface is never so simple for the perceptive reader because of the opacity and complexity of the gospel's subsurface signals. Various textual features, principally the misunderstandings, irony, and symbolism, constantly lead the reader to view the story from a higher vantage point."[3] Readers of the Gospel come from a privileged position; having read the Prologue, they have an advantage in trying to understand the ironies, linguistic subtleties, and symbols.[4] Yet, "traffic on the gospel's subterranean frequencies is so heavy that even the perceptive reader is never sure he or she has received all the signals the text is sending."[5] Since the Evangelist's methods are critical to understanding the text, I will identify here a few examples of these narrational techniques to prepare the reader for the riches to follow in this book.

At the outset it must be noted that there are no clear lines differentiating some of the following characteristics of style. They interpenetrate as a web. Irony and riddles presuppose ambiguity and misunderstanding. Misunderstanding and sarcasm rely on ambiguous language and double meaning, as does the communicative success of

---

but reminds against reducing misunderstanding to a literary device.

2. Culpepper, *Anatomy*, 151.

3. Culpepper, *Anatomy*, 151.

4. Painter, "Prologue," 39.

5. Culpepper, *Anatomy*, 151.

using symbols and images. We will distinguish the following features of style more by their nuances than by clearly distinctive sets of criteria. Since all the styles used by the author involve Jesus's use of double meanings, we begin with John's presentation of this prevalent stylistic feature of Jesus's teaching.

## DOUBLE MEANINGS

The language Jesus uses in speaking to the crowds, Jewish rulers, and disciples draws from their common, ordinary experience. He speaks of birth, life, and death; of water, food, bread, wine, and flesh; of houses with rooms and ways to travel; of work, servants, shepherds, and thieves; of holding a banquet and washing feet; of fields, vineyards, seeds, and harvest; of light and darkness. He speaks of origins (where he is from) and destiny (where he is going); of his Father, fathers, and ancestry; of the cult in the temple, the Law, the Sabbath, and circumcision; of sin and healing; of being lifted up, disappearing, and returning. The natural way to understand these words is to take them in their ordinary meaning growing out of the listeners' daily life experiences of eating and drinking, home life and work, values and worship. However, when the disciples, crowds, and Jewish rulers interpret what Jesus says in this ordinary way, they completely misunderstand Jesus's point, for the common or ordinary meaning is from below, from human experience. Since Jesus is from above, he brings understanding from that dimension to the terms he uses. Jesus thus continually trades on this linguistic complexity of meanings—using the "from below" to transport to the "from above." One might accurately report that the Gospel *celebrates* double or multiple meanings.[6]

The Evangelist's story about the lonesome Samaritan woman abounds with double meanings. It begins with Jesus's offer of water that leaves a woman drawing water from a well puzzled: how can this man give her water when he has nothing to draw water with and the well is deep? What Jesus understands by the water of life possesses a deeper meaning than the Samaritan woman comprehends. The water of life for her and her family encompassed what she could laboriously draw each noon from Jacob's ancient well; for Jesus it is the water of eternal life, sprung up in him, that when given to her changes her orientation (4:11–14). The woman never gets beyond the literal meaning of "water," a commodity that she desperately wants in abundance because it would free her from both the daily drudgery of coming to the well and the constant reminder that she must come at noon because she is a social outcast in her community. The Evangelist reminds us that the water Jesus speaks of is not the temporally satisfying liquid found in the well but Jesus himself. When Jesus comes into her life, revealing her past and enlightening the present, the spiritual thirst she experiences by the tragedy of her multiple marital experiences ends. Forgiveness substitutes for blame; acceptance replaces being shunned by her villagers; thirst for meaning is quenched.

6. For further discussion of double meanings and the resultant ambiguity, see Richard, "Expressions."

When the disciples rejoin him after their foray into the village to purchase gro-ceries, Jesus speaks to them about food. The disciples, who encourage Jesus to eat by offering him food, take him to mean the physical food that they purchased, but Jesus goes on to tell them that the food he talks about is the nourishment he gets from doing the Father's will and completing his Father's work (4:34). It is realized in the people of Samaria responding to the woman's fervent invitation, "Come, see," and streaming from the village to meet, hear, and ultimately believe in him. Similarly, the agricul-tural term "harvest" comes with a double meaning. The agricultural harvest was four months off, but the harvest of the crop for eternal life was pouring out of the village at the woman's behest to meet the man who told her everything she did. Whereas farmers in harvesting distinguish between wheat and tares, Jesus's spiritual harvest makes no distinctions between Samaritans and Jews, for the worshipers will not wor-ship especially here or there, for place matters not, but will worship in spirit and in truth (where both terms have double meanings). The eschatological age, prophesied in Amos 9:11, arrives with the Samaritans coming to Jesus and believing in him. None of the participants in this drama ever fully comprehend the double meanings that lie at the heart of Jesus's conversation.

A particularly pertinent example of double meaning is found in John's account in chapter 6 of Jesus's expansion of a boy's lunch to feed the large crowd and the subse-quent extended discourse. The narrative begins with Jesus using bread and fish to feed five thousand people. When the crowd pursues him to make him their king and food provider, Jesus at first disappears and then reappears elsewhere to respond to their quest. The bread they want given to them is physical bread, and Jesus builds on this desire to say that he is the bread provided by the Father that brings not physical but spiritual nourishment. The crowd seeks an unending supply of bread but completely misunderstands that to obtain the bread they really need, their work must not be grain threshing, oven baking, or bread gathering, but believing in him, for he is the sustain-ing manna come from heaven, sent by the Father. Jesus says that they must feed on his flesh, again words with radical double meaning that leave Jews both skeptical and aghast (6:41–42, 52).

Among the words rich with double meanings are "truth" and "free" (8:31–36). Jesus proclaims that one result of knowing or experiencing truth is freedom. Truth—not just propositional truth, but Jesus himself as personal truth—sets us free. Jews re-spond with their understanding of freedom in terms of physical enslavement, leading to their incredible, historically mistaken contention that they "have never been slaves of anyone" and hence do not need to be set free. The freedom of which Jesus speaks is spiritual freedom from sin, in which his listeners who are attempting to kill him are currently engaged. They are slaves to sin, hence not true sons. Thus, although they long to be free from the Roman yoke, they really need to be set free from the bondage of sin. Double meaning is further developed in terms of their father (8:38–44). The Jews claim descent from Father Abraham, but Jesus responds that their father is the

17

one whom they obey and emulate. Since they are trying to kill him, they are obeying and emulating the one who was "a murderer from the beginning, not holding to the truth, for there is no truth in him" (8:44). Jesus directs their attention away from earthly, genetic descent to heavenly, spiritual descent by his double meaning of "free" and "father." True freedom is found not through biological descent from Abraham or anyone else but through believing in and becoming disciples of Jesus, who dwelt in the Father's presence.

Later, Jesus ambiguously says to Peter that "you (plural) are clean, but not all" (13:10). "Not all" (οὐχὶ πάντες) has an ambiguous referent; it could mean "everyone there," for as the narrator points out, Judas was there, or it could mean "their entire self" as in "not wholly clean" since Peter with whom he is dialoguing is present and, despite his earlier protestations, will deny him, and the other disciples present will abandon him. "Clean" also has a double meaning of being physically washed (Jesus had just washed their feet) or morally purified (Matt 23:25). The ambiguous dialogue leaves the disciples still ignorant of the upcoming betrayals.

This is just a small taste of Jesus's use of double meanings. We will return often to this theme in the subsequent chapters. In chapter 2 we consider the symbols John introduces in his Prologue and their subsequent employment throughout the book. Most, if not all, of these symbols realize their fruitfulness through double or multiple meanings.

## AMBIGUITY AND MISUNDERSTANDINGS

Jesus's frequent use of double meanings creates ambiguity, which in turn leads to recurrent misunderstandings of what he says and to his curious audience's extreme puzzlement.[7] Ambiguity and its consequential misunderstandings underlie many of the presentational features that we will discuss.[8] The Evangelist constructs his Gospel around the theme of knowledge and ignorance. The goal of the author is to bring readers/listeners to knowing and believing, which suggests that to a lesser or greater extent he believes that they are ignorant of Jesus's identity and what he does and will do. To assist readers in the quest for understanding, he provides inside knowledge even before they read the details of the story. The Prologue produces keys to the text and to Jesus's true source and identity, which allow readers some advantage to properly interpret the narrative. However, the Johannine narrative is constructed around the ignorance of those with whom Jesus dialogues and what it takes to end ignorance through knowing and believing.

Jesus believes that the Jews do not know who God really is and thus comes to reveal God (1:18; 7:28). They do not know or understand about God's concern for the

---

7. For a detailed discussion of misunderstanding, see Culpepper, *Anatomy*, 152–65.

8. Köstenberger (*Theology*, 144–45) finds misunderstandings in every chapter except 1, 5, 15, and 19. For a list, see Culpepper, *Anatomy*, 161–62.

temple, his house (2:16), and that this structure will someday prove to be irrelevant (4:22–24). They are ignorant of the Law of God (7:19) and hence not only wrongly interpret the Sabbath laws but fail to comprehend who really is lord of the Sabbath (7:22–24).

However, not only is God hidden from them, so is Jesus who reveals the Father (8:19). They are ignorant of his identity, where he is from, and what he is about. He is an enigma. Some say he is a good person (7:12); others a deceiver (7:12) and demon-possessed (7:20; 8:48, 52). Some claim he is the prophet (4:19; 7:40), others the Messiah (7:26, 41), others are just doubtful (7:40–43). Some Pharisees view Jesus as a Sabbath-breaker and sinner (5:16; 9:16); a blind man sees him as his healer and prophet (9:24–34). Some consider him as insane (10:20); others note that mad men cannot make the blind see (10:19–20). Although Jesus attempts to set them straight through his signs and words, the majority refuse to recognize his relationship to his Father (8:58), his heavenly source and destiny (8:19), or the mission or purpose for which he came. Because the listeners, whether Jews, Pharisees, the crowd, or disciples, fail to understand the double meanings of Jesus's teaching, they take what Jesus says literally rather than spiritually (from above) and miss his deep symbolism. The presentational techniques Jesus (and the Evangelist) employs create overwhelming ambiguity that leads to confusion.

When Jesus tells the Jews, "Destroy this temple, and I will raise it again in three days" (2:19), the perplexed Jews naturally understand "temple" to refer to the magnificent Herodian structure in front of them, "destroy" to tearing it down, and "raise" to rebuilding it. In an aside the narrator provides the information that the Jews lack: that Jesus was really referring to his body and the death and resurrection that he would undergo. When Jesus tells Nicodemus that he must be born ἄνωθεν, Nicodemus understands the word to mean "again," whereas the author, using Greek to convey the ambiguity, has Jesus mean "anew" or "from above" (from heaven or God).[9] From his misunderstanding, mystified Nicodemus is led to rhetorically ask the (seemingly silly but genuine) rhetorical question, "Surely one cannot enter a second time into his mother's womb to be born?" (3:4). When Jesus tells the Samaritan woman that he can give her living water, she takes "water" literally and politely puzzles how he can draw the water since the well is deep and he has no bucket (4:11). When the disciples return from their grocery shopping in town and urge Jesus to eat something, he replies that he already has food to eat. The narrator informs us that the confused disciples wonder whether someone had brought him physical food (4:33), whereas Jesus's food was doing the Father's will and bringing the Samaritans to believing. When Jesus invites people to come to him and drink, the narrator helps the readers to know that he is referring to "the Spirit that had not been given because Jesus had not yet been glorified" (7:37–39). When Jesus says that he has come so that "the blind will see and those who see will become blind," the confounded Pharisees wonder whether they are

9. Michaels, *Gospel of John*, 188n16.

blind in the way that the sighted man was once blind (9:39–40). When Jesus tardily informs his disciples that Lazarus "sleeps," the baffled disciples misunderstand and inquire whether "he will get better" (11:11–12), and the narrator must set the record straight that Jesus really was referring to Lazarus's death. And when Jesus says that "it is finished" (19:30), it is likely that the listeners think that this only refers to his life and fail to see that it refers to his spiritual mission of finishing God's work (4:34; 5:36; 17:4). Clearly, ambiguity and the resulting misunderstanding are central features of Jesus's interactions with his contemporaries.

## IRONY

Perhaps the most common literary device in which the Evangelist uses ambiguity is irony.[10] Since irony has diverse structures, instances of it are difficult to pin down with precision. Paul Duke notes three characteristics of irony, which may not be present in all cases. *First*, ironical statements often are "a double-layered or two-storied phenomenon."[11] Irony trades on a multiplicity of meanings of the same term. We already have seen how multiple meanings characterize the style of the Gospel. *Second*, irony is present when a statement seems to be true at the surface level but "in reality the opposite is true."[12] In creating irony there might be (and often is) a clash of meanings or incongruity between levels of meaning. One level might exist in tension with another, contradict the other, or transcend the other. In an ironic statement the speaker might say one thing but really mean something else. Or again, speakers might say something that is very self-deprecating while at the same time demonstrating that they possess the superior characteristics they denied they had. Appearance contrasts with, if not hides, reality. *Third*, in irony someone involved in the conversation is or claims to be unaware of the higher or deeper meanings.[13] It might be the person who is spoken to, or it might be the person creating the irony who feigns some sort of ignorance. One meaning usually is obvious; on this the audience focuses while simultaneously missing the deeper significance and as a result puzzle over the conversation.

The Jesus of John's Gospel is often frustratingly ironical. A group of Jews believed in Jesus, but he wished to test their newfound faith. "If you hold to my word (λόγος), you are really my disciples. Then you will know the truth, and the truth will set you free" (8:31–32). As we noted above, this saying invokes ambiguity because of its double meanings. First, holding to his teaching is, as the Prologue informs us,

10. Culpepper, *Anatomy*, 165–80. Keener (*John*, 6) suggests that irony was "a common ancient literary technique."

11. Duke, *Irony*, 13.

12. Koester, *Symbolism*, 31.

13. Duke, *Irony*, 16. Duke defines irony as "a literary device [that] is a double-leveled literary phenomenon in which two tiers of meaning stand in some opposition to each other and in which some degree of unawareness is expressed or implied" (17).

holding to Jesus himself, for he is the Word or message from God (ὁ Λόγος). "Word" has a double meaning. What is held to is more than his teaching as seen "from below" or seen "from above"; it is Jesus himself. Second, the word "truth" here refers not only to the propositional teaching of Jesus but also to Jesus himself. Truth is the divine reality that comes to light in the teachings and person of Jesus. If they know, that is, experience, the truth, they will be free. The Jews, however, completely miss the ironical point about truth and instead focus on Jesus's use of "free." Jesus contrasts freedom with slavery (δουλεία), which the Jews interpret as political whereas for Jesus it is spiritual: slavery to sin. They live in spiritual captivity by their failure to keep their covenant with God. Irony is found in that the Jews fail to realize or appreciate that their history has been one of slavery in both of its senses. They lived for generations as slaves in captivity in Egypt. Although not slaves, they lived as captives in Assyria and Babylon, and even now suffer as subjects under Rome's oppressive rule, their liberty severely restricted. They miss the irony because they interpret freedom as embodied in their descent from Abraham, regardless of their actual political circumstances. For Jesus, true freedom from the slavery of sin comes solely through believing in him. By not truly believing, the Jews remain slaves of sin. As they died in their slavery in Egypt and elsewhere, they will die as slaves to their sins because they refuse to accept Jesus's sonship (8:23–24). The dialogue is ironical because the audience neither recognizes, appreciates, nor appropriates layers of meaning. Their missing the deeper point ultimately leads to a clash of understandings in Jesus's rebuttal of their basic contention that they are free because of their Abrahamic heritage and to trading harsh words. As Jesus points out, they are in bondage to their true father, the devil, whose ways they emulate in lying and attempting to kill him. The patriarchal fatherhood of Abraham contrasts, alas, pales, beside their emulation of the devil in their deeds.

The Evangelist also invokes this ironical characteristic of ignorance through the Jews' attempt on Jesus's life. In the ironic passage of 11:49–50, Caiaphas says that "it is better for you that one man dies for the people than that the whole nation perish." In saying this, Caiaphas says "something that anticipates the actual outcome, but not at all in the way he means it"[14] or in the way he would have understood it. Jesus does indeed die, not only "for the people" but for the sins of the whole world so that they do not perish (3:16–17). At the same time, despite Jesus's death and Caiaphas's hand in it, on the earthly and political level the nation of Israel perishes under their own rebellion to Roman authority. Caiaphas looked only to the political, but for John the larger picture was the salvific act of Jesus's death that Caiaphas was ignorant of, advocated, and personally enabled (18:24).

Duke lists over eighty instances of irony in the Gospel. For example, "I have shown you many good works from the Father; for which of these works do you stone me?" (10:32). Jesus contrasts his good works, which emulate those of his Father, with the hard stones Jews have picked up. His good works, which the Pharisees take as the

14. Abrams, *Glossary of Literary Terms,* 80, quoted in Duke, *Irony,* 12.

works of a sinner since some are performed on the Sabbath, are contrasted with the intended evil, murderous deeds of those who see themselves as paragons of righteousness. Again, Jesus says, "You know me and you know where I come from. I am not here on my own, but he who sent me is true. You do not know him, but I know him" (7:28–29). The Jews think they know where he is from, namely, Galilee, and this is partly true from an earthly point of view because he was raised there. However, from the heavenly point of view, they really do not know his origin. Indeed, even more deeply, they assert that they know the Father whom Jesus claims sent him, but in not knowing from where Jesus truly is, they really do not know the Father. They cannot conceive that God would become incarnate out of love for the world. The result is that they attempt to seize him, but "his hour had not yet come." John uses irony regarding knowing and not knowing Jesus and where he is from several times (6:41–42; 8:14, 42–43; 9:29), for one's origin is a key to one's identity.

Again, the author has the Pharisees rhetorically ask whether any religious leaders believe in Jesus, with Nicodemus sitting right there with them. Nicodemus's response shows that their assumptions are wrong; their knowledge is limited and contrasts with reality (7:48–51). In fact, not much later they worry that "the whole world has gone after him" (12:19). John immediately builds on the irony of their worried remark by having some Greeks come to Jerusalem to worship and to ask to see Jesus (12:20–21). The world indeed arrives! What the Pharisees do not understand is that, even within a short period of time, "that the whole world will go after Jesus" will prove to be true and not a slick piece of hyperbole. John also depicts irony when the chief priests plan to kill Lazarus, even though he already died and was raised (12:10–11).

## SARCASM

In the Gospel, irony sometimes manifests itself in sarcasm. Sarcasm is a kind of ironical statement captured in a taut or cutting remark. It is a statement that functions on two levels. On the one hand, it appears to be a straightforward comment. On the other hand, the statement has a bite to it that seeks to place someone in a harsh or negative light. It can be a crude form of aggression that attempts to cause the object of the remark to lose face.[15] It also can be a sophisticated way of showing one's superiority over another, who because of the remark is put on the defensive. The author of the Gospel effectively employs the narrative tool of sarcasm to advance the message of who Jesus is and of the goal of inspiring believing in him.

When Philip approaches Nathanael and announces that they have found the one Moses wrote about in the law, Nathanael sarcastically retorts, "Can anything good come from Nazareth?" (1:46). The rhetorical question does more than make a

---

15. "There is an extremely close connection between sarcasm and irony, and literary theorists in particular often treat sarcasm as simply the crudest and least interesting form of irony" (Haiman, *Talk*, 20).

statement; it negatively judges the value of this person from Nazareth. Philip invites Nathanael to "Come and see," and from his encounter Nathanael discovers that he truly underestimated the object of his sarcasm. Jesus, as all-knowing, was not a simple rustic from Nazareth; he is the all-knowing Son of God from heaven who knew Nathanael even before he approached Jesus.

John also ascribes sarcasm to Jesus's brothers. "When the Jewish Feast of Tabernacles was near, Jesus's brothers said to him, 'You ought to leave here and go to Judea, so that your disciples may see the signs you do. No one who wants to become a public figure acts in secret. Since you are doing these things, show yourself to the world'" (7:3–5). Their suggestion to Jesus that he reveal himself was not made from believing but out of derision. They apparently entertained grave doubts about the reports of Jesus's abilities and signs and wanted to see him embarrassed by showing his ineffectiveness "to the world."[16] What his brothers did not realize is the cosmic dimension of their half-brother. Not only will he reveal himself to the world, he has come to save the world, but in his own time.[17]

Perhaps the most striking (and empathetically enjoyable) use of sarcasm is employed by the formerly blind man in his debate with the Pharisees. When continually pressed by the Pharisees on whether Jesus was a sinner and what Jesus did for him, the formerly blind man finally "loses it." "I told you already, and you did not listen. Why do you want to hear it again? Do you want to become his disciples, too?" (9:27). The Evangelist uses this well-placed piece of sarcasm to raise the issue of discipleship. Whereas the formerly blind man can now see, recognize, and worship Jesus, becoming his disciple, the Pharisees are ignorant of their blindness and inured to becoming Jesus's disciple. The initial setting, where Jesus encounters the man blind from birth and where the Pharisees question him about what he "sees," is reversed. The formerly blind man sees Jesus and worships him; the blind Pharisees understand nothing of Jesus and are willfully guilty, having a hint of but not fully comprehending their self-inflicted blindness.

In another example, in response to Jesus's claim that now he will no longer speak figuratively but will tell his disciples plainly about his Father, the disciples ironically blurt out that now they understand and believe. "Why has it taken so long to speak clearly?" This ironical response, born out of ignorance about the extent of their own questionable understanding and commitment, is met with Jesus's knowing sarcasm,

16. "Many a man faced with cruel opposition in public life has been sustained by the faith and faithfulness of his kith and kin. Jesus was denied this solace" (Morris, *Gospel*, 351).

17. "We have here a striking instance of the characteristic Johannine irony. On the surface, we are reading about a rustic prophet who leaves the obscurity of the provinces to appeal to the great public of the metropolis (Jerusalem). But the words φανέρωσον σεαυτὸν τῷ κόσμῳ (show yourself to the world) have a weight disproportionate to the ostensible situation. In their deeper meaning they are an appeal to the Messiah to manifest Himself to Israel. But if we go deeper still, they speak of the manifests of the eternal logos, as life and light, to the world of human kind" (Dodd, *Interpretation*, 351).

"You believe at last!" (16:31). Jesus knows how the disciples are about to react to his arrest. "You will leave me alone" (16:32), hardly a sign of understanding, lasting trust, and believing. The ironical conflict lies between what they say and what they do. Their believing "will not stand the test of time, and of persecution."[18] Jesus's sarcasm here is gentle but telling. He knows that, despite spending at least three years with him, the disciples neither anticipate nor grasp the significance of what is about to occur and the extent to which they will be tested. His statement affirms the superiority of his knowledge and the disciples' ignorance of what is transpiring in his teaching and action.

The narrator thus incorporates sarcasm into his literary toolbox. When irony is directed at Jesus, he shows that sarcasm does not work. Jesus cannot lose face or be shown to be inferior because he truly is the Son of God, come from the Father with a mission to reveal the Father and bring about believing. If sarcasm requires ignorance, Jesus is not ignorant of what others mean. If it implies inferiority, Jesus's identity affirms his superiority to those who make sarcastic remarks. When Jesus uses sarcasm, it is to show that the claims others make they do not fully understand. They may claim that they understand and believe, but in fact at this stage both are negligible. To understand Jesus's message, one needs access to the Prologue, something the Gospel readers have but those immediately dialoguing with Jesus lack. Because of this additional information, the Gospel readers can recognize the sarcasm that is lost on Jesus's hearers.[19] The tragedy of the irony is that those to whom it is addressed fail to see the irony.

## RIDDLES

Tom Thatcher suggests that the ambiguity that lies at the heart of irony leads us into riddles, which intentionally employ ambiguity as a central feature.[20] Riddles are "intentionally ambiguous statements that challenge the audience to identify which of the several possible things the speaker talks about. The riddler appears to be describing something the wrong way, or her words could potentially refer to so many different things that the audience cannot tell which one is the true subject of the comment."[21] "The riddles in the Fourth Gospel function along the lines of irony because they, like irony, require the reader or listener to know information in advance to understand

18. Michaels, *Gospel of John*, 854.

19. For additional examples, see 8:43–45, where Jesus engages the tentatively believing Jews; 8:57, where the Jews sarcastically taunt Jesus for claiming that Abraham saw his day; and Pilate's sarcastic remarks, "You really are a king?" and "What is truth?" (18:37–38).

20. Thatcher lists thirty-eight riddles in John and suggests that his listing may not be complete (*Riddles of Jesus*, 187).

21. Thatcher, *Jesus the Riddler*, xv–xvi. Elsewhere, Thatcher defines riddle as "*a concise, interrogative unity of language that intentionally and at once conceals and reveals its reference with a single set of signs*" (*Riddles of Jesus*, 179, italics in original). He notes that they occur in riddling sessions, where one riddle leads to another.

them."[22] Thatcher notes different kinds of riddles[23] but is particularly interested in the sage riddle, which "showcases Jesus's remarkable wit and wisdom and . . . establishes his credentials as a rabbi and/or to promote the aspects of his message."[24] He holds that creating riddles is a feature of the Gospels, both in the Synoptic Gospels and especially in John. Jesus, he says, is a riddler; "riddles were a prominent feature of Jesus's repertoire."[25]

According to Thatcher, riddles may be recognized by several characteristics.[26] *One* feature is that the author or narrator might indicate directly or indirectly, as by an aside, that the discourse is intentionally ambiguous. For example, 2:19–21 (what temple can be destroyed and raised in three days); 4:7–11 (how can you ask me for a drink, and how do you get the water); 4:32–33 (what kind of food does he have to eat that differs from what they brought); 11:11–13 (what can be done to a sleeping person); 12:32 (what will I do when I am lifted up); 13:10–11 (are you all clean); also 16:19 and 21:19. The ambiguity of riddles frequently centers on a term with two or more meanings. In the case of Jesus, the listener understands the statement with the common, earthly meaning, and in doing so completely misunderstands Jesus's point. There is an extra layer of complexity behind what appears obvious. This leads to a *second* characteristic: the presence of a riddle may be indicated when the respondents indicate confusion in the presence of the statement (for example, their response to the riddles in 2:19–20; 4:10–12, 32–33; 6:51–52; 7:33–36; 8:51–53; 8:56–57; 9:39–41; 16:16–19). *Third*, a riddle may be indicated when a statement seems inherently contradictory or challenges conventional logic. It brings "together words and/or things that are normally kept apart."[27] For example, in 1:15 John the Baptizer says that the one coming behind me was ahead of me because he was before me. "The tension between the three spatial clauses cannot be immediately resolved at the surface level: if

22. Thatcher, personal correspondence. Also, *Riddles of Jesus*, 191–93.

23. Thatcher classifies four different types of riddles. Dramatic riddles "build suspense and secure the audience's interest in creating the entertainment value of the narrative." They heighten the "dramatic tension of the narrative." Neck riddles, so-called because they are employed to rescue the riddler from foreboding disaster, "demonstrate Jesus's wit and prove his mental superiority over his dialogue partners." Jesus's ability to riddle successfully protects his "public reputation as a sage," which is in jeopardy. Mission riddles, "which play on the Johannine understanding of Jesus's identity and mission, . . . explore the revelation of God through Jesus's signs and death, and highlight the failure of the world to receive that revelation." Salvation riddles, "which play on the Johannine understanding of the relationship between believers and God, . . . develop the unique relationship between God and true believers, a relationship which the world does not enjoy and cannot comprehend" (Thatcher, *Riddles of Jesus,* 210–11).

24. Thatcher, *Jesus the Riddler*, xxiv. Sage riddles are a kind of neck riddle.

25. Thatcher, *Jesus the Riddler,* 45.

26. Thatcher, *Riddles of Jesus*, 183. Thatcher phrases it in terms of four criteria in *Jesus the Riddler* (47–51), three of which we introduce here. The fourth we will consider in the next paragraph.

27. "When a character uses language that seems *calculated to challenging conventional way of thinking and leaves it to the audience to resolve the dilemma*, the statement is a riddle" (Thatcher, *Jesus the Riddler*, 48 (italics in original)).

someone 'was before' and 'has become ahead' of John, how can that person be 'coming behind' him?"[28] (See also 2:19; 3:3; 6:51; 8:56; 9:2; 9:39; 10:34–36.)

Thatcher notes that "riddles are difficult to nail down with any level of certainty, and definitely difficult to nail down with the level of certainty that Jesus researchers typically seek to establish. Simply put, riddles can be very hard to find."[29] However, he goes on to suggest that riddling can be identified when the members engage in a riddling session.[30] What constitutes a riddling session will vary with the cultural tradition in which the riddling is situated, but at the very least it has the above-noted characteristics of intentional ambiguity and deception. The riddler uses language ambiguously to hide which of the possible referents of or answers to the riddle is the "correct" one. Thatcher notes that the culture determines when the appropriate time and place for riddling occurs and what the rules are. "The laws of riddling dictate the appropriate times and places to exchange riddles, the appropriate people to exchange them with, and the appropriate rewards and consequences for the ability or inability to answer."[31] One way to identify a riddling session is to look for certain verbal cues and for a resulting puzzlement on the part of the members.

The following are just a few of the instances in John that Thatcher identifies as riddles. On one occasion, early in his ministry, when Jesus was teaching in the temple, he challenged the authority of the religious rulers on their home turf by driving out from the temple courts those selling animals and exchanging money. When the Jews demanded that he produce a sign to signify his authority, Jesus replied, "Destroy this temple, and I will raise it again in three days" (2:19). Thatcher takes this as a riddling session where a conundrum is posed to the Jews, who puzzle how the Herodian temple could be restored in three days after its destruction, since it took forty-six years to build in the first place. Even the disciples could not solve the riddle until after Jesus's resurrection, when they linked the event with Ps 69:9 (2:17). They then remembered that the temple to which Jesus referred was his body and the restoration after destruction was his resurrection after three days in the tomb. The riddle depends upon Jesus's use of ambiguity in the form of double meaning, which creates the puzzle, conundrum, and misunderstanding by the Jews. On the literal sense, the temple itself would be destroyed, an event unfathomable to those who were standing at this formidable Herodian structure. However, Jesus has a second meaning for "temple," namely, himself. He came from God, who now dwells in him as in his temple. Since a stone-constructed, earthly temple is no longer needed, Jesus removes the sacrificial animals and the special temple currency. He transformed the Sabbath from a time of doing no work to a time of doing good (7:22). The riddling winner in this situation retains his authority.

28. Thatcher, *Riddles of Jesus*, 182.
29. Thatcher, *Jesus the Riddler*, 45.
30. Thatcher, *Jesus the Riddler*, chapter 3.
31. Thatcher, *Jesus the Riddler*, 28.

In the next chapter Jesus dialogues with a Pharisee named Nicodemus. "No one can see the kingdom of God unless he is born again" (3:3). The riddle Jesus poses about birth rightly puzzles Nicodemus, as it would us: "How can someone enter a second time into his mother's womb to be reborn." Jesus explains to him that being born again is not a physical but a spiritual process, but the explanation fails to significantly relieve Nicodemus's puzzlement: "How can this be?" The solution to the riddle again depends on the ambiguity of double meaning, this time on being born either anew or from above. Nicodemus, as would we, takes birth in a literal sense, whereas Jesus means it in a spiritual sense of being born from heaven or from God.

Chapter 4 contains other riddles. Encountering a woman at a well in Samaria, Jesus asks her for a drink (4:7). However, he quickly turns the request into a riddle: "If you know the gift of God and who it is that asks you for a drink, you would have asked him and he would have given you living water" (4:10). The woman is rightly puzzled: How can you give me water when you have no vessel with which to draw water? It is not clear that the woman ever fully solved the riddle, which would have required her to understand that Jesus's giving "water" has a double meaning, but in this encounter she has enough experience with Jesus to realize that here is someone special, possibly the Messiah.

Jesus later engages in riddles with both the Pharisees and his own disciples. One pair revolves around Jesus's assertions about being with them for a short time and then their inability to see him. To the Pharisees he says, "I am with you for only a short time (χρόνον), and then I go to the one who sent me. You will look for me, but you will not find me; and where I am, you cannot come" (7:33–34). The Jews are puzzled about this and come up with several suggestions to solve the riddle, including that Jesus would go among the diasporas.[32] This same riddle is posed in 8:21, where the puzzled Pharisees respond that maybe Jesus is going to commit suicide. The solution to the riddle was not external to them but internal. They did not know his Father, to whom he was going (7:28). Hence, since they did not know where and whom he was from, they could not know where he was going or go with him. "The reason they do not know (know and worship God), he says, is that 'the One who sent me is True' (that is, truly God), so that if they reject the messenger, they are rejecting God, who sent him."[33] Jesus knows the sender and is going to him because he sent Jesus. The solution to the riddle is divine intimacy.

Jesus poses a similar riddle to the disciples. In the first instance, Jesus tells them that they cannot come where he is going (13:33). Simon Peter takes the bait, asking Jesus where he is going, to which Jesus responds with a second riddle: "You cannot follow now, but you will follow later" (13:36). Peter is more confused than ever, for whereas he is looking for a place that will solve the riddle, Jesus is speaking about

---

32. As we will see later, this search for an answer is ironical, for in a nonliteral sense, through his disciples as recorded in Acts, Jesus goes and takes his message to that very diaspora.

33. Michaels, *Gospel of John*, 452.

the experience of dying for him. However, Jesus does not let up on his riddling, but continuing the riddling session, he adds a third riddle, that before Simon dies for Jesus, he will first disown him (13:37–38). It is not until later that Peter personally, painfully discovers the meaning of the third riddle (18:27) and is given a clue to the meaning of the second riddle (21:18).

Jesus continues posing riddles in this vein. "In a little while you will see me no more, and then after a little while you will see me" (16:16). The disciples, the narrator informs us, were puzzled by "a little while" (16:18), perhaps being puzzled by this entire sequence. Jesus does not flat-out respond to their puzzlement but adds to it with a comparison and an analogy. When the world rejoices, they will "weep and mourn," but in the end their "grief will turn to joy" (16:20). It is like a woman who experiences the pain of childbirth who later rejoices to see the fruit of her labor. The riddle is filled with double meaning. The disciples will not see him because they flee in the face of his death, yet they will see him shortly thereafter in his resurrection appearances. This is the immediate dimension of the riddle. The long-term dimension is that Jesus will return to his Father (16:28) where they cannot see him, but he will return to them through the Spirit, who will remind them of everything, and ultimately return eschatologically.

After his entry into Jerusalem, Jesus responds to the crowd that he, the Son of Man, is going to be lifted up (12:33). This puzzles the crowd, for Jesus puts together two incompatible pieces. He is the Son of Man, whom the crowd takes to be the Messiah. However, the crowd believes that the Messiah will live forever (12:34). How then can he die? If Jesus is going to die, he is not the Messiah (Son of Man). What the crowd does not understand is that "lifted up" has the further meanings of being raised from the dead and glorified. As to the former, this would resolve the riddle of the Messiah not dying yet Jesus dying. His death is not final but culminates in the resurrection that provides the eternal life he has promised others. As to the latter, death seems an unlikely way of being glorified. The crowd does not realize that Jesus's (the Messiah's) being lifted up was a glorification or exaltation, for through it he "would draw all men to myself," showing not only the manner of his death by crucifixion but the subsequent establishment of the church that would read these words.[34] Jesus employs multiple meanings on "lifted up/exalted" (ὑψόω) to not only build on but further enrich the concept of messiahship. By being lifted up he conveys a different kind of messiahship (see also 8:28).

Undoubtedly the most striking riddle occurs in the account of Jesus healing the blind man. I came into the world, Jesus says, "so that the blind will see and those who see will become blind" (9:39). The riddle puzzles some Pharisees, who ask Jesus whether they are blind also. To them Jesus provides an enigmatic response. If they were truly blind, they would have an excuse for not believing. However, since they

---

34. For a discussion of the universal implications of "draw all men to myself," see Michaels, *Gospel of John*, 699–701.

claim that they can see (understand), they are guilty of creating their own blindness. The riddle is irresolvable unless one pursues the double meaning of "blind." Whereas the Pharisees understand it as physical blindness with which the account began, Jesus has in mind the spiritual blindness that has clouded their ability to see that he is not only Lord of the Sabbath but also the very Son of Man who is to be worshiped.

Jesus's opponents also use riddles to try to catch Jesus.[35] In John, a Pharisee riddling session occurs in a passage whose authenticity is doubtful (7:53–8:11).[36] The teachers of the law and the Pharisees come to Jesus and ask what he would say about a woman they bring to him. Their goal, the narrator informs the reader, is to trap him. They claim that she was caught in adultery. The problem, however, is that one needs two witnesses to make such a charge (Deut 17:6), and either there are no witnesses and the charge is trumped up, or one or two of their group were witnesses, which would immediately compromise their position. Jesus plays on the latter, without making a direct charge. He quietly writes on the ground with his finger when asked to comment on the Law, which gives credence to those who see this as a subtle but forceful way of asserting that he is responsible for and has authority over the Law, which God wrote with his finger (Exod 31:18). Jesus escapes between the horns of its dilemma, neither denying the law regarding the punishment for adultery (which would put him in opposition to Mosaic orthodoxy) nor approving it (which would end the poor and outcast viewing him as a social reformer). Instead, he refocuses on how the punishment is to be enacted, requiring that the punishers themselves, who would be the first to throw stones and who had to be witnesses, be completely innocent of sin, otherwise the evil would not be completely purged (Deut 17:7). Slowly, knowing their own condition and being known by those around them, the accusing Pharisees move away, first the older who are purportedly wiser, followed by the younger. Jesus masterfully responds to the riddle or testing dilemma with wisdom.

Since it is very obvious that the characteristics of riddles noted by Thatcher correspond with those of irony given by Duke, some question whether riddles add to irony.[37] Both, employing double meaning, have intentionality: the ironist employs double meanings with the intent to move the listener/reader to higher levels of understanding, while similarly the riddler intentionally highlights the puzzle dimension, emphasizing the aspect of the conundrum that requires some creative, ingenious thought to resolve. For our purposes, whether these instances are identified as riddles or simply instances of irony is unimportant. What is critical is to see that Jesus creates and plays on ambiguity in attempting to move his audience from the common understanding

35. E.g., Matt 22:15–23. For a return catch riddle, see Mark 11:29–30.

36. This passage is not found in the best and oldest manuscripts and not commented upon until much later. It is also at times located elsewhere in John (after 7:36; 7:44; or 21:25) and in Luke (after 21:38). However, others have noted that the encounter accords well with other Gospel accounts in its portrayal of Jesus. For a discussion, see Beasley-Murray, *John*, 143. We return to this story in chapter 7.

37. The passages in John that Duke lists as ironic significantly overlap those that Tom Thatcher lists as riddles. Thatcher, *Riddles of Jesus*, 179.

(the earthly) to the higher, spiritual understanding (from above). His message thus is consistent with his repeated assertion of where he is from. He is not merely a Galilean or a Jew; the Father sends him to reveal the Father and to be the medium through whom believers are saved and have eternal life.

## PENETRATING QUESTIONS

According to John, Jesus had the ability both to ask penetrating questions and to take a penetrating question and deftly turn it to his own advantage. When presented with Philip's claim that they had found "the one Moses wrote about in the Law," Nathanael replies, "Can anything good come from Nazareth?" (1:46). Jesus takes Nathanael's rhetorical question and turns it by means of his own claim to the degree of knowledge that only the person Moses and the prophets wrote about could have.[38] He insightfully knows Nathanael's character without ever having met him and has precise foreknowledge of his distant location under the fig tree. According to Isaiah, foreknowledge and the ability to reveal the future were signs that distinguished the authentic God from spurious gods represented by the idols (Isa 41:22–29; 42:8–9; 43:8–13; 45:18–25; 46:9–10; 48:3–8). Nathanael recognizes this sign in the person he meets and declares Jesus to be the Son of God.

The Samaritan woman asks whether Jesus is "greater than our father Jacob, who gave us the well and drank from it himself" (4:12). The question appears to be rhetorical: "Who do you think you are? Someone greater than Jacob himself?" She already assumes the response. Jesus's actual response is to compare the water from Jacob's well to the living water he provides. Those who drink from Jacob's well will thirst for more, but those in whom the living water wells up will have eternal life. Jesus takes the question of greatness and turns it into a statement about the greatness of his water compared to that of others.

The question of greatness again arises when the Jews, out of their presupposition that Jesus is demon-possessed, rhetorically and sarcastically ask whether Jesus is greater than "our father Abraham" (8:53), who although great was mortal. Jesus turns their question about greatness not into his seeing Abraham (which the Jews thought was impossible because Jesus was "not yet fifty", that is, not ancient at all), but about Abraham seeing Jesus's day. The Jews thought that Abraham was great because he preceded Jesus (and all the rest of those from Israel), but Jesus says, if you want to ascribe greatness to precedence, I am greater than Abraham, for I preceded Abraham and he saw my day. Indeed, Jesus is the "I am" himself (8:58). He takes the rhetorical question about greatness and exploits it to bolster his claim to being God.

---

38. John, like Luke (24:27), gives no specific indication of where these writings may be found, perhaps assuming that the readers would have some general background knowledge in the Old Testament.

The Jews wondered not only at Jesus's claims of precedence but also about the wisdom he demonstrated in his teaching. "How did this man get such learning without having studied?" (7:15). Jesus takes this question about his learning and education and turns it into a claim about his authority. His learning and hence authority came from God because he speaks on behalf of God. As the readers of the Gospel Prologue already know, Jesus is the divine Word. He is what God says, revealing the Father to those who should have known him, for they already possessed but did not follow Moses's teachings. For Jews in his audience, Jesus cannot be whom he says he is. His Galilean origin and his appearance as demon-possessed seem to confirm that he is a charlatan. To this Jesus replies, "Stop judging by mere appearances and judge correctly" (7:24).

The questions posed to Jesus are often rhetorical, presupposing a skeptical answer. Rhetorical questions are particularly powerful dialogic tools, for they put the person questioned immediately on the defensive. A specific answer is assumed by the questioner, and the respondent must find a way somehow to escape this assumed negative response nondefensively. Jesus is particularly adept in addressing this kind of question and turning it to his own advantage. He demonstrates his ability to take a rhetorical question that puts in doubt his identity and mission or function and to turn it into a statement that affirms both.

Jesus also tactically employs rhetorical questions. He asks Simon Peter, "Will you really lay down your life for me?" (13:38). Jesus already knows the answer both that Peter will disown him and that eventually he will die for him. However, in the present context the rhetorical question serves to quiet the fervent but misguided ardor of Peter. It recalls an earlier rhetorical question, following the departure of many disciples who found his discourse on being the bread of life to be eaten most problematic, if not distasteful (6:60–66). "'You do not want to leave too, do you?' Jesus asked the Twelve" (6:67). In this case Peter likewise replies impetuously but earnestly, testifying that Jesus is the Holy one of God, the only one who has the words of eternal life. Jesus effectively uses the rhetorical question to bring out the testimony of others.

## SYMBOLS

The ambiguity of double meanings appears again with the Gospel's prolific use of symbols. Koester suggests that for John, "A symbol is an image, an action, or a person that is understood to have transcendent significance."[39] A symbol has a double meaning; it begins from our common experience and generally refers to something that we experience by our senses: an object or action. At the same time, it goes beyond the sensible to have a deeper meaning, often pointing to something intangible. In effect, the common transfers what it stands for to point to something else, either a thing,

39. Koester, *Symbolism*, 4.

action, idea, or metaphysical reality.[40] Symbols trade in ambiguity, for although their origins from human experience are clear, how they connect beyond the ordinary and what they elicit are ambiguous. A heart symbolizes love, but what it tells us about love is quite imprecise—and no less suggestive or useful for that.

Since the Gospel of John is about the identity and mission or function of Jesus, and since Jesus bridges the gap between the heavenly and earthly, the Gospel employs symbols to bridge that gap. Without these symbols we would only recognize Jesus as a rustic, wandering rabbi who performs wonders. We would wonder, as did those who witnessed him, whether his powers come from being a special person or whether they come from being demonic. The symbols Jesus employs often function in contrasts, showing the difference between the heavenly and the demonic. Jesus is life, not death; light, not enveloping darkness; life-giving water and nourishing bread, not death-bringing drought and famine; truth, not falsehood; leading shepherd, not slinking thief; a vine that nourishes, not withers. We consider some of these key symbols in chapter 2 and emphasize others throughout our book.

## CONCLUSION

We have provided a representative taste of the important presentational techniques employed by the Gospel's author and, if John reports accurately, by Jesus as the chief character in the Gospel. This suffices to bring to light both the richness and difficulties of the text and Jesus's teaching. It alerts the reader to look for the many additional examples and their contextual significance. The techniques employed are not ends in themselves but directed to showing the wisdom, understanding, and message of Jesus, in contrast to the ignorance and unwillingness to accept manifested by those in dialogue with him. The widespread use of ambiguity points to the deeper meaning of the Gospel and to our understanding of Jesus. To take him and his words at the obvious level of common experience is to visit with a quick-witted, sharp-tongued, possibly misguided rabbi. Can anything more significant than this come out of Nazareth and Galilee? However, once we penetrate these presentational techniques, we see that Jesus uses them to push, pull, and encourage his listeners to go deeper, while puzzling those whose quick reaction is easy dismissal. Only then will they understand that his source is not Galilee but the Father whom he came to reveal, and his purpose is to bring life to all by being lifted up, first on the cross, then in the resurrection, and finally in his return to the Father from whom he came. These presentational techniques call us to a deeper understanding of Jesus's identity and mission, which is what the argument of the fourth Gospel is about.[41] At the same time, because Jesus's audience fails to grasp

40. "[T]he gospel connects concrete images with abstract meanings" (Stibbe, *Storyteller*, 19).

41. "[T]he Gospel of John fundamentally contains a single theme: the Person of Jesus. The entire Gospel is concerned with the fact of his presence, the nature of his claim, whence he comes and whither he goes, and how men relate themselves to him" (Bultmann, *Gospel of John*, 5).

the ambiguity, the double meanings created from the earthly and heavenly perspectives, they misunderstand, misinterpret, or fail to understand what Jesus says about his identity and mission. Such failures lead to the deathly success of his mission.

## QUESTIONS FOR REFLECTION AND DISCUSSION

1. What kinds of techniques does John use to create ambiguity around the person and teachings of Jesus?

2. What are double meanings? How do they function in creating ambiguity? Do you talk in double meanings, and if so, why? (For example, do you like to make puns on words?)

3. What are irony and riddles? Can you give Johannine examples and non-Johannine examples from your experience of each of them?

4. Why do you think that Jesus so frequently used ambiguity in his teaching?

5. How does Jesus's audience react to Jesus's use of ambiguity in his conversations with them? Why do you think they reacted as they did? How would you have reacted to Jesus's use of ambiguity?

6. Do you think that John's introduction of instances of sarcasm into Jesus's conversations detracts from or adds to the Gospel's portrayal of Jesus?

CHAPTER TWO

# Book of Symbols

Much in this world we don't know; indeed, the more we learn the more we realize what we don't know. As Ralph W. Sockman put it: "The larger the island of knowledge, the longer the shoreline of wonder." This is not only true about our knowledge of people, places, things, and events in the world, it is also true about what transcends this world. About God—his nature and actions—we are very ignorant, for he transcends our limited knowing. Beyond our carefully crafted theologies and analytic philosophies lies confounding mystery. This ignorance makes it difficult for many to believe not only that God exists, but that God loves us and acts in the world for our good.

The Evangelist wrote the Gospel of John to encourage believing by dispelling ignorance. He assumes that God as spoken of in the Old Testament and worshiped by Jesus's contemporaries is hidden, obscured in transcendence. However, the good news of the Gospel is that ignorance of *God* can be dispelled so that we can know God, and the burden of the Fourth Gospel is to tell us how we can know. The way is through Jesus, who from his intimacy with the Father was sent to us by that very Father so that we can see the Father in and through him.

The Gospel also dispels ignorance about *Jesus*. Much is strange about this teacher who appears suddenly on the scene, talking about God as if God were his personal father and identifying himself as his unique son (5:19–23), although we can also be his children (1:12–13). He claims to be in an exceptional position to know the Father, since he has been eternally with and comes from the Father (8:58). He is strange because he does not fit the mold of the anticipated ruler-messiah. He appears not as an anointed Davidic king from the prophesied town of Bethlehem (7:41–42), but a wandering nobody reared in the nobody town of Nazareth of Galilee with his commoner family known to some of his Galilean audience (1:46; 6:42). He performs what to the people who witnessed them were miracles but whose significance is a mystery. He has power to do wonderful things for other people, and yet in the end refuses to exercise that same power to save himself from Roman crucifixion despite the perturbed persistence of Pilate for an answer or the loud mockery of the crowd (Luke 23:35). He engages his opponents in ironic, acerbic arguments filled with double meanings, makes wildly unbelievable claims about himself and his relation to the Father, and openly challenges the religious authorities of his day by the way he treats the temple, the Law, and the Sabbath. He knows the Old Testament and speaks eloquently but apparently has little formal education (7:15). And for our purposes in this chapter, he speaks using symbols that to his hearers are ambiguous and the source of much misunderstanding. The Fourth Gospel intends to inform us who this man was, what he was doing, and why he was doing it (20:31).

The Gospel also dispels ignorance about what is *expected of us*, the actual or potential followers of Jesus. It informs us that it is not so much what we do as whom and what we believe (6:28–29), about whom we should listen to and love (8:31, 42; 15:12). It is about real discipleship and continued abiding in him (15:5–12), about servanthood (13:14) and the Spirit that dwells in his community (16:13–14). It tells us how we are to relate to religious leaders in our community, to other believers, and to the world.

In short, the Gospel conveys *knowledge* through the word. It informs us how Jesus dispels ignorance about God the Father through being his very revelation (14:7–9). It informs us about who Jesus was (his nature) and about what he was doing (his function, purpose, or mission) through the testimony of those he touched and his discourses with friends and foes alike. It informs us that as believers in Jesus we can expect to be disenfranchised from our (religious) community (9:22, 34) and fractured from other believers (17:21–23).

However, this is to get ahead of our story, for the Gospel begins with a Prologue that sets the stage for the rest of the book. The Prologue is filled with symbols and themes that arise repeatedly throughout the Gospel, knowledge of which will advantage its careful readers. To the Prologue and its poignant symbols let us turn.

## THE PROLOGUE

The initial task of the Evangelist was to prepare his readers with important background information so that they know what to look for in the Gospel narrative, how they should read and understand what he has written, and how they should interpret its mysteries and hidden truths.[1] "The prologue is an introduction in the sense of being an overture leading the reader out of the commonplace into a new and strange world of sounds and figures, and singling out particular motifs from the action that is now to be unfolded."[2] It informs about the themes that the author develops in the Gospel

---

1. "The prologue is a directive to the reader as to how the entire gospel is to be read and understood" (Thyen, "Aus der Literatur," 223, in Beasley-Murray, *John*, 5).

2. Bultmann, *Gospel of John*, 13.

around Jesus's identity and enlightens about the meaning of central ideas and motifs.[3] Simply put, it provides the keys to unlock the Gospel that contains the mystery of who Jesus is and what he does.

The scholarly focus of the academic discussion of the Prologue on its possible origin as a separate hymn appended (with commentary) to the Gospel can make it easy to overlook its binding connection with the rest of the Gospel.[4] Some view it as a pre-Christian Gnostic hymn[5] or as having its origins in early Christian hymnody.[6] Others see it as a polemical piece responding to those who claim that John the Baptizer was really the messiah.[7] Some regard it as a later editorial addition to the book.[8] Yet, in content and function it intrinsically and inseparably connects to what follows.[9] At the very least, "[t]he Prologue introduces the first characters to appear and sets the mood of the first scene."[10] Its themes, symbols, and message prepare the way for understanding Jesus, just as John the Baptizer does beginning in 1:19. Both the Evangelist and the Baptizer project their message from an eternal perspective—"in the beginning" and "before me."

Those who engage with Jesus lack the information found in the Prologue. Consequently, the crowd, Pharisees, teachers of the Law, even the disciples fail to understand who Jesus *is*. Is he the Messiah, the prophet, merely a miracle worker, or a demon possessed, insane man? Lacking the keys to unfold the discourses, dialogues, and double meanings, they constantly misunderstand what the symbolizing Jesus *says*, interpreting it on the earthly level—from below—whereas Jesus means it to be understood on the spiritual or heavenly level, from above (8:23). As we saw in chapter 1, Jesus's vocabulary, although apparently simple, is complex with multiple meanings. In effect, the Evangelist provides readers with the Prologue so that they will not misunderstand and make the same mistakes as Jesus's audiences do but will be able to comprehend more deeply what Jesus taught in order to bring about or strengthen their believing.

The Prologue, like the Gospel as a whole, is fundamentally about the identity of Jesus in terms of both his nature and his mission. Symbols provide the core for understanding the overall point that John wants to make, namely, that Jesus is

---

3. Painter, "Prologue," 39.

4. Bultmann, *Gospel of John*, 15–18; Brown, *Gospel i–xii*, 21. For a discussion, see Beasley-Murray, *John*, 3–4.

5. See Bultmann, who sees it as a borrowed and edited hymn from gnostic-Mandaean-Baptist circles ("History," 18–35). For a discussion of this, see Evans, "Prologue."

6. Schnackenburg, *John*, 1:225–31. Brown, *Gospel i–xii*, 20–23.

7. Bultmann, *Gospel of John*, 17–18.

8. Anderson, "Dialogue," 116.

9. "The Prologue prepares the audience to be an audience. . . . It initiates the audience into the privileged realm of knowing that makes irony possible, orients the audience to the broader narrative in which the action is situated and prepares it to enter the action in media res, and calls the audience into being and gives it a role" (Brant, *Dialogue*, 17).

10. Brant, *Dialogue*, 21.

the Messiah, the Son of God. As Messiah, Jesus connects to diverse community expectations (the horizontal); as Son of God, he accentuates his heavenly source (the vertical).[11]

To appreciate the Gospel and its themes, then, we must explore this Book of Symbols to see how majestically the author weaves together the heavenly and earthly dimensions of the symbols. Jesus often introduces the symbols abruptly, which contributes to the audience struggling with their ambiguity. To overcome this for his readers, the Evangelist introduces in the Prologue the central symbols Jesus appropriates to himself and his message. Lest the book's readers miss the point, the author repeats the symbols several times in the Prologue, giving both nuances and in some cases multiple meanings of the symbolic terms.

Interpreters of the Gospel of John have worried at times about the repetitions, variations, and amplifications in the Gospel. Some take them, along with other clues, as part of a case for holding that the Gospel underwent numerous editorial touches, incorporating various sources.[12] However, there is another way of looking at the repetitions. Repetition comes into play when a speaker or writer desires to make or emphasize a point that the audience not only will take special notice of in the remainder of the discourse but will remember.[13] It alerts the hearers or readers to what the author or speaker thinks is important and should engage their attention. In effect, John uses repetition to set the thematic stage for the remainder of his work, telling readers that what he repeats should be noted and remembered.[14] By repeating, varying, or amplifying the same words three or more times in the Prologue he indicates that these are the vital themes and ideas of his Gospel, so that when readers encounter them again in the subsequent narrative they will not only recognize and attend to them but can trace them through the dialogues and discourses.

In this chapter we will highlight the chief symbols that the Gospel presents in the Prologue and note how they get fleshed out in the subsequent narrative. Later, throughout our book, we will address other important symbols not found in the Prologue.

---

11. Denaux, "Twofold Purpose," 534.

12. Bultmann (*Gospel of John*, 6–7) identified multiple sources, including the Synoptic Gospels, a signs source, separately circulating discourses, and a passion narrative independent of the synoptic tradition. Brown (*Gospel i–xii*) developed a five-stage process for composition (xxxiv–xxxix). Others, however, disagree. Van Belle contends that the repetitions and variances argue for the unity of the Gospel ("Theory of Repetitions," 18–22). "J. Gerhard argues that the Fourth Gospel 'was not the work of many but of one author, that it was a unified manuscript from beginning to end, and that it was written according to the laws of parallelism rather than the laws of narrative'" (Van Belle, "Repetitions in Johannine Research," 73).

13. Van Belle, "Repetitions in Johannine Research," 45. He notes other possible literary reasons (67–68). Morris suggests that repetition is "due to a habit of mind," but it seems more intentional than this (*Studies*, 318).

14. James Resseguie (*Narrative Criticism*, 42) notes that repetition is an important stylistic device for emphasizing one's point, adding force or clarity, and for identifying narrative structure and design.

## SYMBOLS

The Evangelist carefully describes Jesus's identity and mission in the Prologue through symbols. Craig Koester explains, "A symbol is an image, an action, or a person that is understood to have transcendent significance. In Johannine terms, symbols span the chasm between what is 'from above' and what is 'from below' without collapsing the distinction."[15] They are revelatory and traffic in the transcendent.[16] This accords with the overarching theme that since God is from above and we are from below, his presence is veiled and his activity elusive (1:18). The Johannine Jesus uses symbols to bridge that gap to reveal this hidden God. It is appropriate for Jesus to do this because he participates in and understands both dimensions; as the Word he came from heaven to be incarnate and is the word of God to all people (3:34; 5:43; 8:28). Koester notes that the root meaning of "symbol" is "to put together." "In John's gospel the symbols help to disclose how apparently contradictory ideas can be brought together. . . ."[17] Thus, Jesus uniquely creates an understanding of the transcendent by drawing it together with the earthly and familiar.

John derives symbols, conveyed in ordinary language, from everyday experience—our earthly life—to help his readers understand heavenly things. The readers and audience already know what water, words, light and darkness, life, to be born, world, and truth are. John and the narrated Jesus take these common words and move them to the heavenly or spiritual level. In this way these words have a symbolic function that often engenders complexity and creates misunderstanding, for whereas their ordinary meaning is usually clear, the extraordinary or symbolic meaning and use are ambiguous. Thus, to understand the use of symbols in the Prologue and elsewhere, we must focus on the double or multiple meanings and the dialectical movement of meaning between them. Only by penetrating this linguistic complexity can one begin to understand John's Gospel.

## WORD

The Gospel begins with "the word" (ὁ λόγος), repeated three times in the first four verses, along with four pronouns ("he," "him") referring to "the word." The term

---

15. Koester, *Symbolism*, 6. This distinction of origins—between being from above and being from this world (below)—is central to Jesus's thought (3:31; 8:23).

16. Akala, *Son-Father Relationship*, 11. She defines a symbol in the Johannine context as "a figure of speech that embodies certain characteristics of its literal meaning, and leads to a transcendent meaning that is significant within its narrative context and transformative in its theological purpose." It "points beyond itself to a referent not explicitly in the text," but at the same time "operates by embodying some characteristics of its literal or primary meaning" (26).

17. Koester, *Symbolism*, 28. "Symbol (Σύμβολον)—as the word itself suggests—is the joining together of two otherwise dissimilar realities" (Coloe, *God*, 4).

appears again in 1:14, along with two pronouns ("his") referring to "the word."[18] Whereas we normally think of words as written or spoken, John treats the word in 1:1–4 as a being rather than as a mere utterance. In the Old Testament, God reveals himself through the spoken word. "The whole idea of revelation in the Old Testament is determined by the analogy of the word spoken aloud. . . . It preserves the ontological distance between God and man, while affirming that God, of His personal choice, approaches men and deals with them in a way they can understand, and expects their response."[19] God's word is separate from God in that it is spoken by him and comes to humans. Yet, as John emphasizes, it is identical with God, for his word is himself as revealed (1:1–2). The word is revelation, creative communication, not a mysterious silence. Thus, the prophets bring God's spoken word to the people and in doing so bring God to them. The divine word, God's message that they speak, is the very basis of their authority.

The word spoken, however, does not disappear once uttered but possesses a "kind of substantive existence of its own."[20] God is a living presence in his word.

> As the rain and the snow
>> come down from heaven,
> and do not return to it
>> without watering the earth
> and making it bud and flourish,
>> so that it yields seed for the sower and bread for the eater,
> so is my word that goes out from my mouth:
>> It will not return to me empty
> but will accomplish what I desire
>> and achieve the purpose for which I sent it. (Isa 55:10–11)

John's "word" has multiple meanings. John speaks of the word not only as an utterance—what God spoke—but as a person: He is the preexistent One, "in the beginning with God" (1:2). The Word (ὁ Λόγος) as a person has both his own identity and an identity with God, with God but not separate from God, not merely divine but in union with God.

John strikingly connects "the word" with the Old Testament. He follows Genesis in seeing God's speaking (his word) as creative, the origin and source of all that is.[21] God speaks, and everything comes to be: light separates from darkness; expanse,

18. λόγος is used nineteen times elsewhere in John.

19. Dodd, *Interpretation*, 263.

20. Dodd, *Interpretation*, 264.

21. "John's Gospel has moved beyond Genesis in its own ways, however, first by its transformation of the refrain, 'and God said' (Gen 1:3, 6, 9, 11, 14, 20, 24, 26, 29), into the noun 'word' or *logos*, and second by its personification of 'word' as 'the Word'" (Michaels, *Gospel of John*, 50).

oceans, and dry ground appear, as do heavenly lights, and living things (Gen 1). It is true that in the Septuagint the Greek for "speak" in Genesis 1 is εἶπεν (utter). However, in Ps 33:6 we find the creative word (λόγος): "By the word (λόγῳ) of the LORD the heavens were made; their starry host by the breath of his mouth." Although Genesis is concerned with cosmic creation, John is interested in the making (ἐγένετο) of creation as it brings God into our human lives. The Word is the origin of life, which, as we will see, John understands not only quantitatively but qualitatively. The Word is both at our beginning and at our end, at our coming to be and at our resurrection or re-creation, for in the Word we have eternal life (11:25–26). The Word is also in our present, for believing in the Word makes a difference the moment one enters into obedient discipleship. Furthermore, this life-giver is the revealer; he brings light as a revelation of God and dispels the darkness of ignorance of the God with whom he is since the beginning.

This Word is also like the word brought to and through the prophets. They could speak boldly: "this is what the LORD says." Their word was not just *their* words, but the message of the LORD. Unfortunately, the covenant people whom God adopted as his own rejected this word. Similarly, when the Word comes to his own, his own reject him (1:11); yet a remnant believes and becomes the children of God (1:12).

Although John begins his Gospel with a metaphysical understanding of "word" (λόγος), it has other meanings throughout the text. In the Prologue the Word is both the preexistent One and the one who becomes incarnate, who "tents" among us (1:14). The Word thus links the divine and human, the critical connection without which we would have neither the saving grace nor truth (1:14) about our sinful condition and the possibility of salvation (3:16–17). Understanding this linkage is crucial to the Gospel that John supplies to the readers but is hidden from those with whom Jesus engages. Jesus tells this linkage to his audience in language about his source and destiny, but it strains their worldview to even imagine that God could be incarnate.[22]

John also uses "word" to refer to the actual words spoken by Jesus (2:22; 4:41, 50; 12:48; 15:20; etc.). The Father's giving of life through the Word is emulated through the Word's life-giving word.[23] In 5:24, λόγος has the broader meaning referring to

---

22. Dodd takes this difficulty of understanding the Word becoming flesh from a Jewish context to expand the meaning-source of the concept of λόγος to include similarities to "Stoicism as modified by Philo, and parallel to the idea of Wisdom in other Jewish writers. It is the rational principle in the universe, its meaning, plan or purpose, conceived as a divine hypostasis in which the eternal God is revealed and active" (*Interpretation*, 280). For a detailed discussion of the concept of λόγος in contemporary cultures, see Beasley-Murray, *John*, 6–10. "The employment of the Logos concept in the prologue to the Fourth Gospel is the supreme example within Christian history of the communication of the gospel in terms understood and appreciated by the nations" (10).

23. Painter, "Prologue," 46.

Jesus's entire message,[24] which if believed brings eternal life. "Thus the λόγος of Christ is the λόγος of God, and that is truth (ἀλήθεια), the ultimate reality revealed."[25]

As we noted in the previous chapter, Jesus is not averse to playing on the double meanings of "word" (λόγος). In 5:38, Jesus says that if the Jews do not believe his testimony (his words), they do not have God's word in them. Not believing in Jesus is rejecting God's word, himself in his revelation. And by rejecting Jesus as the Word, they reject the Torah and the life that they thought they had found in the Torah, which also was God's word given through Moses. To fully understand this monologue, one must have access to the Prologue to see that the message of Jesus (his self-testimony) is himself, the very ontological Word of God.

This same play on "word" occurs in 8:31–32.[26] "If you hold to my word (λόγῳ), you are really (truly, ἀληθῶς) my disciples. Then you will know the truth (τὴν ἀλήθειαν), and the truth (ἡ ἀλήθεια) will set you free." The word is present both in the revealing message that Jesus brings and in himself. True disciples hang not only on Jesus's every word, but on Jesus himself as he hangs on the cross and rises from the grave. We will say more about the play on "truth" later.

John is very concerned to reveal both the nature and the function of the Word. As to its *nature*, John tells us that the Word was in the beginning (eternal), with God (as God's very spoken, revealing, creating word), and was God himself (the mystery of identity and difference) (1:1–2). The *function* of the Word was to bring everything into existence. He created everything (1:3). His *nature* is to be light (1:4–5), and the *function* of that light is to bring about life: to make us living children of God (1:11–12). The nature of the Word is bound up with his function and the function with his nature. Together, the two form the structure of the Gospel.

## MAKING AND COMING TO BE

Making or coming to be (γίνομαι) is a central symbol and theme, not only in John's Prologue but in the entire book; it is often for good (12:36), sometimes for ill (9:39). The creative power of the Word is front and center, occurring three times in 1:3. Everything comes into being through the One who was there before the world was made (1:10; 17:5, 24), who lightens every person who comes (ἐρχόμενον) into the world (1:9), and who then comes (ἐγένετο) as a human so that we might become (γενέσθαι) children of God (1:12, 14). The Gospel is the book of creative making and coming into being. In this it echoes the opening chapter of Genesis, where God speaks

24. See also 8:37, 43.

25. Dodd, *Interpretation*, 267.

26. See also 15:3, where the word cleanses. Possibly also 17:14, where Jesus speaks about giving the disciples "your word," where "word" could mean both God's message and, as is forthcoming, himself in his death.

and things come to be (Gen 1:3, 5, 8, 9, 11, 13, 15, 19, 20, 23, 24, 30), and where God sees that what he makes is good.[27]

John takes the "being made" of creation, using forms of the same verb, and connects it with testimony and the signs that form the basis for Jesus's self-testimony. The first testifier comes to be (ἐγένετο), sent from God (1:6). Jesus remakes (γεγενημένον) the water of purification, detailed under the old covenant, into wine, which symbolizes the death necessary for establishing the new covenant (2:9). He asks the invalid if he wants to become well (γενέσθαι) and proceeds to make him to become well (ἐγένετο) (5:6, 9, 14). Through his presence and power the disciples' storm-tossed ship came (ἐγένετο) immediately to land (6:21). The signs in the Gospel testify not only to who Jesus is (his identity) but also to his creative function. Thus, they align with the Prologue whose function is to inform ahead of time who Jesus is (his *identity*) and what is his *function* or *mission*. Jesus is the original maker, who comes in flesh, and the continual remaker, creating us to be children of God.

## LIFE

John continues to connect the Gospel with the creation account of Gen 1 through life: in the Word is life. "Life" (ζωή) occurs twice in 1:4 and thirty-four times elsewhere in John. As with other terms, "life" has multiple meanings as it functions as an important symbol for Jesus.

In the Prologue, the Word is both life itself and the giver of life through creating whatever began, specifically, living things.[28] On the one hand, the *nature* of the Word is life eternal, life he had from the beginning. However, John also highlights the *function* of this eternal life by alluding to the Word's acts of creating living things in Gen 1:11, 20–26: God speaks, "Let it be," and it is so. All living things have their origin in the speaking of the Word that is life. Thus, the creating functions of the Word flow from the nature of the Word. This anticipates the Word becoming human and announcing that he is the life (11:25; 14:6) and hence the life-giver. The double meaning of life now becomes obvious. It is no longer merely biological life that derives from the creator but the spiritual life we have in Christ. The life-giving water flows from us "to become a spring of water, welling up to eternal life" (4:14). We have real, fulfilling life because we participate in the Life that gives life (3:36). The earthly symbol—our life—participates in the reality of which it is a symbol.[29]

27. Michaels notes that the Genesis account focuses on God's act, not his being, which is simply presupposed, while John's account focuses on God's being (*Gospel of John*, 46–47). However, not only would this be expected since the making in John is transferred to the substantive Word, but John also focuses on the act, where verse 3 repeats "being made" or "coming into being" three times.

28. For a discussion of the syntax of vv. 2 and 3 and how "what comes to be" is connected with "in him was life," see Michaels, *Gospel of John*, 51–54.

29. Dodd, *Interpretation,* 140.

The life that Jesus gives us is both quantitative and qualitative. About half of the usages of "life" in John are coupled with "eternal," but without any apparent difference of meaning from merely "life." *On the one hand*, the life Jesus gives is future (*quantitative*), connected to our resurrection or re-creation (6:54). It is a life anticipated by Lazarus's bodily resurrection from the cave in which he was interred (11:25–26). *On the other hand*, the life Jesus gives is *qualitative*. It is an abundant life that begins here and now (10:10; 4:14), a life that bears fruit by remaining in that which gives life (15:4–6). Indeed, eternal life is "knowing God" and knowing Jesus Christ whom God has sent (17:3). This knowing is not merely intellectual, but the knowledge born from experiencing, of relationship in becoming a disciple. Discipleship can lead to death (21:18–19), but above all it leads to abundant life, now and in the future. The Word incarnate is thus the source of life, in the beginning through creating all living things, in the now in abundance, and in the unending future. To bring his readers to realize, receive, and believe this in an attitude of discipleship is the burden of John's Gospel (20:31). We will return to life as the product of salvation in chapter 11.

## LIGHT

In the Prologue, John quickly moves to a second understanding of life, where the symbol of life is joined with the symbol of light: "the life is the light of men" (1:4). Here and elsewhere (3:16–21; 8:12) the Gospel connects life with light (φῶς).[30] Genesis begins with the creation of a world that is "empty and desolate."[31] Its outstanding features were barrenness and darkness, yet not without the unsettling presence of the wind of God hovering over the water. Light is much more than that emitted by the heavenly bodies, for they are created after God's creation of light. Light is a reality itself, with the causal power to dispel darkness. John reverses the Genesis order and personalizes the light. It is no longer life in general, but *the* Life (ἡ ζωή) that now assumes the function of bringing light into darkness, here the human darkness (1:4–5). The very *nature* of the Word as life is light. Jesus is the light (τὸ φῶς) of the world (8:12; 9:5); this is his *nature*. Light in John assumes a substantive, personal character.

The Word's *function* as the Light is to bring light. Whereas in Gen 1 light precedes life, a picture that would be commonly accepted in an agricultural society, here in John life brings light. John contends that the light given by the Word is revelatory. As the light, Jesus reveals the Father to those with whom he comes in contact (1:18). It is not that the Father is darkness; indeed, "God is light," (1 John 1:5), the "father of lights" (Jas 1:17). However, light can blind (9:39; Acts 9:3, 8), so that what is light is, paradoxically, hidden. Those who have truly seen the Light will have seen the Father (14:9). The Word as the light also exposes the darkness of evil (1:5; 3:19–21). In our

---

30. Light (φῶς) occurs seven times and darkness (σκοτία) twice in 1:4–9. Light occurs sixteen times elsewhere.

31. Reichenbach, "Genesis 1," 57–58.

daily lives evil takes place in darkness; those who do evil avoid the light. Most crime occurs in the hidden or at night, in the secrecy of darkness.

With John's penchant for double meaning, it is clear that not only does Jesus refer to what the listeners would take to be the physical light and darkness that we experience; he also refers to himself as the source of light and truth revealed. In Jesus we find light that leads to our salvation. Employing his double meaning, John takes light to the higher level; those who do evil avoid the Light. Those who do righteousness and love the truth love and come to the Light, so that what they do can be manifest. Jesus is the test case for righteousness (16:10).

Light also functions to prevent stumbling or falling (11:9–10). Again, the double meaning is clear. This obvious function of light in our common experience also occurs in the spiritual realm. However, in this realm the light that we need to have, so that we are not subject to the dangers of darkness, is not external but internal to us. Jesus is that internal light that leads us to walk in proper ways, so that we may become sons of Light (12:35–36). Jesus the Light also functions to reveal the path to where we are going, its rocks and ruts, pitfalls and smooth places, hills and valleys. Finally, Jesus announces that the light that the followers have experienced is about to be extinguished, and those who had the light however briefly will be plunged into walking in darkness.

The symbol light no longer appears after chapter 12. Jesus turns from his public ministry to ministering to his disciples, who presumably have seen the light and no longer walk in darkness. It is not that the symbol of light is irrelevant for them, but they already have internalized the light who is about to be taken from them and replaced with the Spirit who will call to remembrance what the Light has taught and will guide them into all truth. The Prologue, however, informs us in advance that Jesus's revelation will not be comprehended but misunderstood. It will be rejected, for those who hear him will say that he is demon-possessed, that the kingdom of darkness is in him (8:48, 52). Blinded to their own darkness, as to who their real Father is, they project their darkness onto Jesus.

It is obvious that for John the symbols of life and light are tightly interwoven. Jesus is the light of life, the life that gives light, the light that comes into the world, and the life that makes the light. Interweaving these symbols, with their many meanings, creates the richness of Jesus's teaching (word, λόγος). Jesus also connects light with truth (3:21), the symbol which we will address shortly, and with blindness (9:1–5), which we treat in chapter 7.

## WORLD

The final Prologue creation motif or symbol is the world (ὁ κόσμος).[32] The creation story speaks of God creating the heavens and the earth, although "the Hebrew Old

32. "World" appears seventy-eight times in John, over half of the uses in the New Testament.

Testament has no word for the universe. . . . [But] the word is common in the books originally composed in Greek. Indeed, the Jewish Hellenistic writers, especially those influenced by Greek philosophy, seemed to have a liking for the term and brought it into their religious and theological vocabulary."[33] Thus, by the time John writes the gospel, κόσμος is the common term for the world, universe, earth, or humanity, and John incorporates this into his Gospel understanding.

The Prologue links the beginningless Word with the universe or world through creation. Everything (πάντα) that came into being did so by the Word (1: 3).[34] However, John quickly changes his treatment of "world" to multiple meanings. The Word is in the world (the world of humanity), the very world made by him (a place, given in a physical sense), yet the world (the world of humanity) did not know him (1:10). Thus, John uses "world" both as the created heaven and earth and also as the human world (1:29; 3:16–17; 6:14, 33, 51).[35] The third sense of world refers to those who stand opposed to Jesus (17:14). They hate Jesus (7:1–7; 5:18–21), reject the Spirit of truth (14:15–17), rejoice at Jesus's departure (16:20), and fail to know the Father (17:25). Understood in a moral or spiritual sense, the world is governed by "the prince of the world who will be driven out" (12:31). All three of these senses can be found in Jesus's prayer for his disciples in chapter 17. The world as the created universe is referenced in 17:5. The world of humanity is referenced in 17:6 as the place where those given to him come from and in 17:15 as where the disciples are. The world in opposition to Jesus is what we are not of (17:16). This illustrates John's complex usage of "world" and shows why those listening to Jesus would be thoroughly confused by Jesus's conversations on this topic, for in this symbol Jesus transmutes the earthly, physical world into the spiritual through treating it as humanity for whom Jesus was sent by the Father and died.

## TRUTH

As we move through the Prologue, we come upon the symbol truth. John mentions truth as a noun (ἀλήθεια) three times in the Prologue (1:9, 14, 16–18) and twenty-two times elsewhere. By contrast Matthew uses the term as a noun once, Mark and Luke three times. Similarly, whereas John uses the adjectives ἀληθής (truthful) and ἀληθινός (trustworthy, true) twenty-three times, Matthew and Mark do not use them at all and Luke only once. "Plainly this concept [of truth] matters to John."[36] It is also

33. Sasse, "κοσμέω," 881.

34. "The concept of the κόσμος as the totality of all created things, of universal space and everything contained in it, comes to expression in statements concerning creation and the part of the Logos in it" (Sasse, "κοσμέω," 884).

35. "The term [κόσμος] is used to refer to the material reality of the created world, the physical realm into which Jesus has entered, and the object of God's affection and salvific intentions, . . . (as well) as a symbol for humanity" (Skinner, "World," 61).

36. Morris, Gospel, 260.

important to note that he couples it with grace (χάριτος) (1:14). Grace and truth go together; they are not at odds or in competition. Indeed, it may be that truth is what is given in grace.[37]

As he does with other key terms, John uses "truth" in several senses. *On the one hand*, it is propositional, applying to statements or claims. What God and Jesus say is true, reliable, trustworthy: "I tell you the truth" (8:40, 45–46; 16:7).[38] These are features one would expect from the Word (given its double meaning) who comes from and reveals God. Jesus's truth is revelatory. *On the other hand*, "truth" is a term that John applies to persons. "Truth" is transferred to people who make true statements, from veracity to sincerity. John the Baptizer testified to the truth (5:33). It was not merely that the Baptizer told the truth (although that would be affirmed), but that he testifies that Jesus in his person is the truth: trustworthy, reliable, real. Truth thus also has to do with the person of Jesus (14:6), his nature as expressed in his character.

Jesus plays on this double meaning of "truth" in 8:31–32: "If you hold to my word, you are really my disciples. Then you will know the truth, and the truth will set you free." We already noted the double meaning of "word" here as both teaching and the person who is the Word. In addition, both "truth" and "free" have double meanings. *For one thing*, the truth is the word or teaching of Jesus. Truth here has a propositional sense that leads to abiding in or obeying what Jesus taught. If we do this, we experience freedom from error and being misled. The contrast here is with the devil, who is the father of lies. "There is no truth in him" (8:44). Jesus here refers to the temptation of Eve in Gen 3, where the serpent twists the truth to entice Eve into betraying her fidelity to God. "When he lies, he speaks his native language, for he is a liar and the father of lies" (8:44). Jesus, by contrast, "tells the truth" and, by virtue of telling the truth, deserves to be believed. The purpose of truth-telling in John is not truth-telling per se, but to bring persons to believe in who Jesus is, the Son of God, and ultimately to belong to God (8:47). Truth-telling is purposeful.

However, "truth" *also* has a metaphysical meaning; Jesus is not merely the teller of truth, he is in himself the truth. He is real, coming from God, and he is trustworthy.[39] When Jesus speaks about abiding in the truth, he is talking about us living and existing in himself. The meaning of abiding in the person of Jesus who is the truth is brought out in the analogy of Jesus as the vine and his followers who are to abide in him as the branches (15:4). Abiding in Jesus frees us from sin, which holds us as a slave (8:34–36). Ultimately, only in the Truth, through the Word, will we be "sanctified in truth" (17:17, 19).

37. Moloney, *Johannine Studies*, 297.

38. "The adjective ἀληθής is in its earliest and most constant usage applied to statements which correspond to the facts" (Dodd, *Interpretation*, 170).

39. "ἀλήθεια can also mean 'genuineness,' 'divine reality,' 'revelation.' . . . It is the reality of God. . . . " (Bultmann, "ἀλήθεια," 245).

The multiple meanings of "truth" and its symbolic function come to a climax in Jesus's discussion with Pilate. Jesus says that he has "come into the world to testify to the truth" (18:37). "Ἀλήθεια (Truth) here stands for the realm of pure and eternal reality, as distinct from this world of transient phenomena."[40] Jesus goes on to tell Pilate that "everyone who is of the truth (on the side of; imbued with) listens to me" (18:37). The double meaning of this symbol "truth" here is obvious. If one wants the truth about our spiritual condition, we need to listen to the teachings of Jesus. We must attend to the one who tells us about sin and salvation, about the role of the Law and the new commandment to love. At the same time, in our position in the world, we can either be with or against Jesus who is the Truth, on his side as the side of truth or with Satan as the father of lies. This contrast between truth and lies accords with other Johannine dualistic emphases. Pilate seems not to comprehend the multiple meanings of "truth"; indeed, it is not clear that he understands what truth is in the first place. His actions betray his view that might is the maker of truth, for in the end he yields to the threats of the crowd to expose him as no friend of Caesar and condemns Jesus to death, without having any basis for a charge against him, let alone for condemnation (19:6). Truth for Pilate is what preserves his own skin and reputation.

Truth also connects with the Spirit, one of whose functions is to guide all people "into all the truth" (16:13). Thus, John can call the Spirit "the Spirit of truth" (14:17; 15:26; 16:13), who comes from the Father to abide in us, to testify truly concerning Jesus, and to guide us into all the truth (here, again, with the double meaning of propositional, revelatory truth taught to us and to bring us into the reality of the life of Christ).

Of all John's symbols, perhaps truth is the richest, intrinsically linked with the word/Word. It refers to the veracity of what is said or claimed, to the gospel testimony itself. It refers to the person who is completely trustworthy and the purveyor of truth, the very one testified to. It identifies what is real, the one come from the Father, as over against that which is merely appearance. John also uses "truth" to refer to the Spirit whose function is to guide and bring to remembrance the truth in ways that lead to eternal life.

## OTHER SYMBOLS IN THE PROLOGUE

Since the Prologue presages the discussions that follow in the narrative, so that the readers can more fully understand Jesus and his message, I want to briefly comment on four symbolic themes that the Gospel later takes up. The Evangelist tells us that the Word came to *his own* and his own did not receive him (1:11).[41] John uses the symbol of parentage and ancestry to contrast the normal family relationship with the spiritual

40. Dodd, *Interpretation*, 176.

41. Scholars puzzle over the significance of the change in gender between the two "his owns." The first—τὰ ἴδια—is neuter, while the second—οἱ ἴδιοι—is masculine.

family relationship Jesus introduces. The Gospel often raises the issue of origins and paternity, for John asserts that our source or origin tells us something about who we are. John's dualism is manifest here in that there are two families.[42] One traces their ancestry back to Abraham and Jacob, through whom they are children of Israel. However, in fact, as demonstrated by their deeds in trying to kill him, their father is the devil, the purveyor not of truth but of deceit and murder (8:31–46). The heritage of the other is with God; whether they can trace their ancestry back to Abraham is quite irrelevant. As manifested by the respective works, Jesus's Father differs from the father of the Jews. Who one loves and emulates, not genetics, determines parentage.

To be God's own they must be Jesus's own, and to be Jesus's own they must love the Truth, that is, Jesus who is the truth. The Gospel is about becoming children of God, not through natural parentage but through the work of God (1:12–13). The work of God is not labor, such as keeping the Law, but believing in Jesus who was sent from God (6:29). Thus, the Gospel affirms that simply being of a certain heritage, here Jewish but it could be of any heritage or parentage, does not make one a child of God. Becoming God's own is not genetic but results from God's grace where the response is a conscious decision to believe and become a disciple. We will return to the theme of parentage in chapter 11.

This leads to the second symbolic theme: *receive and believe*, which occurs four times in the Prologue (1:7, 12). Believe (πιστεύω), which occurs ninety-eight times in John, is never a noun (πίστις) in John but always a verb. We are to be believing as an action, not have belief as a possession. Believing brackets the book. In the Prologue John tells us that this is the way to become children (sons and daughters) of God. At the end of the Gospel, John tells us that bringing his readers to believing that Jesus is the Messiah, the Son of God, is his purpose (20:31). Believing in Jesus, the Evangelist tells us, is the key to the Gospel's objective: "Whoever believes in the Son has eternal life, but whoever rejects the Son will not see life" (3:36)

On what basis should we be believing? "Witness" or "testify" (μαρτυρέω) is repeated four times in the Prologue and thirty-three times elsewhere. From its beginning, the Gospel testifies to the identity and function or mission of Jesus and to accomplish this relies on the testimony of others. Repetition of "witness" or "testimony" indicates the central importance of this concept. We will devote chapter 4 to discussing testimony.

All of this, John tells us, brings *glory* (δόξα) to God. "Glory" is mentioned eleven times in John. Everything that the Son does is directed to bringing glory to the Father, but in doing so he brings God's glory to himself (1:14; 17:1–5). Jesus asks to have his glory, which he had from the beginning with God, restored, but this will occur, ironically, only when he is lifted up (3:14; 12:32–33). Here again John engages symbolically in double meanings. To be lifted up is, in this context, to be crucified. However, it is more than this, for it is the time when people will realize who Jesus is, the Son of Man

42. Minear, *Christians*, 82.

who is the glorified Son of God (8:28) come from the Father. "Glory" thus connects with Jesus's portending death, his resurrection, and his return to the Father—all central themes in the Gospel. Many who passed by the cross "read the sign, for the place was near the city," and the sign over the lifted-up one was multilingual: The King of the Jews (19:20). We will return to this in chapter 11.

## SYMBOLS LOOKING BACKWARDS AND FORWARDS

John's thought and his use of symbols in the Prologue look backwards to creation and forward to Jesus's ministry, passion, and return to the Father. One must

> understand the divine *befores* if one is to understand the human *afters*. . . . This poet, in crafting the Prologue, had one eye fixed on the Genesis account of creation, where these *befores* first appear, and the other eye fixed on the stories about Jesus. . . . This poet had moved by careful steps from the beginning before all things were made to a human being whom he finally names, Jesus Christ, "God the only Son" (1:17–18). If the first four verses accented the absolute beginnings, the rest of the poem stressed a double focus on relating the *befores* to "the present years" (2 Esdras 6:5). The double role of John the Baptist was the first example of this double focus. Though Jesus came *after* John, John proclaims that he had been sent from God to testify that Jesus was *before* him as a pretemporal light. . . . So insistent was the narrator on this double focus that he repeated [three] times the verbal paradox of "after-before" ("He who comes after me was before me"—1:15, 27, 30).[43]

The Prologue links Jesus and his gospel with the creation and its before ("the beginning").[44] John knew Genesis, as he did other parts of the Old Testament.[45] Not only does he quote Gen 28:12 in 1:51 and elsewhere make allusions to it,[46] but in the very beginning of his Gospel he refers to the title for the book of Genesis, Ἐν ἀρχῇ.

The Prologue also ties the Old Testament with the coming Word and in doing so looks forward. The turning point of the Prologue is 1:14, where the Word moves from

43. Minear, *Christians*, 83.

44. "In the Targums there is further evidence for linking the Prologue with the Genesis Creation story." One problem, however, is that "the text of the Targums may be later than the New Testament era," although it may reflect an earlier liturgical origin. For further discussion see Coloe, *God,* 21–22.

45. "There can be no doubt that the Old Testament played a large part in the author's thinking. He obviously read it well and pondered it long. He quotes it a number of times, sometimes from the Septuagint, and sometimes perhaps from his own translation of the Hebrew" (Morris, *Gospel,* 55).

46. John the Baptizer's identification of Jesus as the Lamb of God may echo Abraham's sacrifice in Gen 22:8. Simon Peter's renaming may echo the renamings in Genesis of Abraham, Sarah, and Jacob (17:5, 15; 32:28; 35:10). Jesus's statement to Nathanael regarding seeing angels ascending and descending recalls Jacob's vision of a ladder from the Lord in heaven (1:51; Gen 28:12). Jesus's mother's statement to the servants at the wedding banquet to do what Jesus tells them echoes Pharaoh's statement to his servants regarding Joseph (2:5; Gen 41:55). 3:16 may echo the Abrahamic sacrifice of Isaac as his only son (Gen 22:12).

timelessness (in the beginning) and a place with God to a time and place with us in history. The relation between Logos and God now becomes personal. The Logos/God relation changes into Son/ Father (1:18).

Mary Coloe sees the parallel this way:

| | |
|---|---|
| 1:1a. In the beginning was the word | 14a And the word became flesh |
| And the word was with God | and the word tented among us. |
| And the word was God.[47] | |

The fact that there is no parallel for the third clause she takes as evidence that Jesus's divinity continues in the incarnation. Not only does the Prologue tell us *that* he came, it also affirms *how* he came, coming in the flesh as a human being (1:14).[48] The Word does not *seem* to be human or *surrender* his divinity, but transforms into flesh, while maintaining his being with God.[49] The Prologue thus transitions from the beginning to the incarnation. God in and as the Word really comes to dwell with us as one of us.[50]

Jesus's dwelling, however, is temporary, not permanent. Jesus does not build a home but tents (σκηνόω) among us, a fellow pilgrim in this desert (Matt 8:20). Yet he is not a mere pilgrim but the one who experiences the vertical coming from and going back to the Father. The tenting motif recalls that God's glory was present to the Israelites in the tabernacle tent and now is present in the incarnate, tenting Word.[51]

The Prologue presents us with a new creation. It is not the coming to be of a cosmos with biological life and an earthly humanity, but a new creation within the cosmos. Jesus brings light to dispel darkness, life to defeat death, acceptance to replace rejection, and grace and truth to surpass or build upon law.[52] The Word enters the

---

47. Coloe, *God*, 24.

48. That the Word comes as flesh connects with the only other use of flesh in John, namely, in chapter 6, where "flesh" anticipates Jesus's death (Coloe, *God*, 25).

49. John 1:14 does not deny continuity of being God in v. 1. Harner ("Qualitative," 87) suggests that v. 1 be translated, "the word had the same nature as God. By this structure it expresses the nature or character of the Word."

50. John "alludes to the Sinai tradition by using such terms as dwelt/tabernacles, glory and gift." "The law was understood to be God's gift to Israel; '. . . *they told Ezra the scribe, to bring the book of the law of Moses which the Lord had given to Israel*' (Neh 8:1). The Law is linked with other gifts of bread and water given in the wilderness (Neh 9:13–15)." "[T]he evangelist uses these traditions in a polemical manner, for the Gospel presents God's dwelling in the midst of humanity not by way of Israel's Torah, but in the humanity of Jesus. . . . The evangelist reinterprets Israel's traditions and institutions in the light of a new situation brought about in the life, death, and resurrection of Jesus" (Coloe, *God*, 62 and 62n101; italics in original).

51. Gench, *Encounters*, 4. "[T]he tabernacle expresses the impermanent, transitory nature of tent dwelling in a way suggestive of the transitory and itinerant life of Jesus" (Painter, "Prologue," 56).

52. There is significant debate about how to understand 1:16–17, and in particular "grace upon grace" (χάριν ἀντὶ χάριτος). Is ἀντὶ a word of opposition between Law and truth, indicating replacement, or is it a word of addition, indicating that truth is a further gift in addition to the Law? See Moloney, *Johannine Studies*, 299–300, who makes the case that one gift does not replace another but adds to it.

world not as a stranger but as having created it and making a covenant with "his own." Unfortunately, Israel's rejection of the covenant and the Lord of the covenant is repeated anticipatorily also of the Word. The cosmos people (his own) do not recognize and receive the creator. Thus, the Prologue sets the stage for the mission of the Word made flesh: to make whoever receives him by believing in his name to become his own, children of God (1:11–12). Jesus accomplishes this by manifesting God's glory (1:14), which is God himself, in grace and in truth (1:17), and by his revealing God in the personal, familial light of the Father (1:18). In this way the Prologue introduces the theme of believing, the realization of which constitutes the goal of Jesus's ministry and John's Gospel.

To reveal God, Jesus must reveal himself. Thus, the Prologue leads again to the purpose of the Gospel. The question that runs throughout the Gospel is, Who is Jesus? To receive and believe in him Jews (and whoever hears) first need to know who he is. John anticipates this in the Prologue, highlighting the role of testimony (1:6–8, 15). Believers also need to know his mission. The purpose is stated in the Prologue—to enable us to become children of God—but the author leaves the details to develop in the book, with hints given early by the Baptizer (1:29) and by Jesus through the symbol of being lifted up (3:14–17).

> If Mark's Gospel be viewed as a passion narrative provided with an introduction, it may be said that John's is all passion narrative. And we do not forget that a passion narrative includes the resurrection of the crucified. Accordingly, in John the lifting up of the Son of Man on his cross reaches to the throne of heaven; and as the shadow of the cross marks the entire story of Jesus, so the glory of the Resurrection event suffuses every hour of his ministry, and even reaches back to the morning of creation. The eschatological glory for which creation was made was brought to actuality in the deeds and words of Jesus.[53]

## CONCLUSION

The Prologue thus sets the stage and delivers the interpretative keys for the remainder of the Gospel. Readers now can follow the symbols, double meanings, central concepts and themes, and lines of thought in a way unavailable to those to whom Jesus spoke and possibly avoid to some extent misunderstandings. With these "insider tips," these pregnant symbols, we can now turn to the narrative of the life, ministry, and testimony about the Word incarnate: all structured to defend and realize John's primary thesis about identity and believing.

---

53. Beasley-Murray, *John*, xxxiv.

## QUESTIONS FOR REFLECTION AND DISCUSSION

1. Why is the Prologue essential to the Gospel of John?

2. What are symbols? How do they function in John's presentation? What role do symbols play in your life?

3. Identify the symbols that John introduces in the Prologue. What is the significance of each?

4. Which of the symbols that John uses to identify Jesus do you find the most helpful for understanding who Jesus was (his identity) or his function or mission? Why?

5. If you were to add a new symbol to the Prologue for the identity or mission of Jesus that you think might make John's message to twenty-first-century people more relevant, what would that symbol be? What for you are the important features of that symbol? (Fans of C. S. Lewis, J. R. R. Tolkien, or John Bunyan might enjoy this question.)

6. How is "word" used in the Gospel of John? How is it ambiguous? Why is it so important for John's presentation of Jesus?

7. How does John use symbols to connect his Gospel to Genesis? Why is this important for understanding John's message?

8. What are John's various senses of the "world?" What do you think of when this term is used? Is "world" a useful term for believers today, or should they look for a substitute term?

9. How is "truth" understood in the Gospel? Do people have multiple understandings of truth today, or has the concept of truth changed?

CHAPTER THREE

# Book of Signs

THE AUTHOR OF THE Gospel of John clearly announces his intention for writing—
to bring about believing in Jesus as the Messiah, the Son of God. He thinks that if
we know who Jesus is, we will believe. The problem we have uncovered is that the
teaching of and about Jesus swims in words with multiple meanings. The resulting
ambiguity lies at the heart of his irony, riddles, sarcasm, penetrating questions, and
symbols. These features cannot function without multiplicity of meanings. Jesus and
the author believe that ambiguity and the presentational techniques that utilize it are
necessary to move the audience to see that obtaining eternal life requires adopting a
new perspective from an earthly or empirical to a heavenly or spiritual understanding,
and to allow time for Jesus to complete preparation for his mission. Yet ambiguity
creates misunderstanding, which though it delays his death, obfuscates his identity.

The Evangelist initiates a second approach to reveal Jesus's identity by reporting
signs or miracles that Jesus performs. "These [signs] are written that you may believe
that Jesus is the Messiah, the Son of God, and that by believing you may have life in his
name" (20:31). He assures us (2:23; 3:2; 6:2; 11:47; 20:30) that Jesus performed many
signs but presents in detail only seven.

Technically, the Evangelist terms only five of his miracles signs (σημεῖον)—the
two miracles at Cana (2:11; 4:54), the feeding of the multitude (6:14), the healing of
the blind man (9:16), and the raising of Lazarus (12:18). Since the healing of the paralytic in chapter 5 emulates the healing of the blind man in 9:6–7 and like the named
signs involves supernatural activity, there is good reason to include the healing of the
paralytic as a sign as well. This is strengthened by the subsequent discourse in which
Jesus claims to be doing the work of the Father. The most debated sign is Jesus walking
on the water in the storm to or passing by the boat carrying his disciples. However,
since Jesus's walking on water is a miraculous happening, "we should probably include
it among the signs,"[1] for it connects him and his power to what he created (1:3).

---

1. Morris, *Jesus*, 21.

Two other miraculous events are generally not treated as signs. The catch of fish (21:6) is usually excluded because, since it is presented in the Epilogue of the Gospel, it lies outside of Jesus's public ministry, as reported in the first twelve chapters.[2] Likewise, Jesus's resurrection, although a miracle, is not to be treated as a sign since it is done to Jesus and not through him.[3]

These signs are works of Jesus "that especially point to some spiritual truth."[4] They are *signi*ficant. Jesus tells the Jewish leaders that his works testify to who he is. "Why then do you accuse me of blasphemy because I said, 'I am God's Son?' Do not believe me unless I do what my Father does. However, if I do it, even though you do not believe me, believe the works (ἔργοις), that you may know and understand that the Father is in me, and I in the Father" (10:36–38). "This does not mean that for John the signs were the most important part of the Gospel. However, it does mean that when he wanted to make clear the purpose of it all, it was the signs to which he turned."[5] In what follows, we will look at these seven signs (works) to see what they tell us about who Jesus is and thus provide one piece of evidence in defense of John's thesis.

As we noted in the Introduction, although John's stated purpose is that the readers believe, it is not clear whether he writes to bring about believing in either diaspora Jews[6] or gentiles, to reinforce believing already held, or to settle internal disputes in the Christian community.[7] We discussed the audience in the Introduction, and for our purposes it will not matter which is the case. What is important is to follow John's desire to marshal the signs and to emphasize to what they point.

Except in John 9, which mentions the use of spit,[8] John spends little time describing exactly how Jesus performs the individual signs. Neither are they presented, as often done in the Synoptics, in terms of the power (δύναμις) that they manifest—although the divine power behind the miracles is not hidden, as the formerly blind man

---

2. The catch of fish also serves a very different function in the Gospel. Whereas the other signs point to the identity of Jesus, the catch of fish points to the identity of the person on the beach who is barely recognizable by someone out on the water. It is not "this is who Jesus is" but rather "that person standing there is Jesus."

3. For the counterargument that walking on the water is not a sign, since not only is it not termed a sign, but it is unclear whether there are one or two miraculous events, whereas the seventh sign is the death and resurrection of Jesus, see Crowe, "Chiastic Structure." Although he presents a very persuasive chiasm of the signs, he does not address the major objection that the death and resurrection are not acts of Jesus.

4. Morris, *Jesus*, 22.

5. Morris, *Jesus*, 2.

6. Robinson, *Priority*, 113.

7. Childs, *New Testament*, 123–24; quoted in Morris, *Jesus*, 1.

8. "The use of spittle was very common in the ancient world. . . . Spittle, and especially the spittle of some distinguished person, was believed to possess certain curative qualities. . . . The fact is that Jesus took the methods and customs of his time and used them . . . to gain the confidence of his patient" (Barclay, *John*, 2:41–42).

notes (9:33). Neither does John's emphasis rest on the miraculous component. "To the evangelist a σημεῖον (sign) is not, in essence, a miraculous act, but a significant act, one which, for the seeing eye and the understanding mind, symbolizes eternal realities."[9] They are events that stand for or point to something else, thereby conveying an important or *sign*ificant message. They show that "God was at work in Jesus, . . . accomplishing the decisive act for the salvation of sinners."[10] Thus, although they testify about Jesus, they also point decidedly to the Father, for Jesus performs signs to reveal God's glory (11:4, 40) and that "they might believe that you sent me" (11:42). Jesus can perform the deeds or signs only because he intimately connects to the Father.

The audiences to whom Jesus spoke believed that signs were meant to establish the authenticity and power of the performer. It is true that prophets could be believed even though they performed no signs (10:41–42), but the people demanded signs (6:30), expected signs (7:31), and were attracted by signs (11:45). Yet, understanding people and what motivated them (2:23–24), Jesus well knew that the persuasive and holding power of signs was brief and tenuous and refused to trust himself to those who believed based merely on signs. Signs are important, but as Morris points out, "we should not overlook the fact that in this Gospel Jesus mostly refers to his 'works' rather than to 'signs'"[11] to establish his identity.

As we shall note in chapter 10 when we address the Book of Completeness, by restricting himself to detailing only seven signs in the first half of the Gospel, John indicates that these seven are perfectly sufficient to establish Jesus's identity and to bring about believing (20:30).[12] The signs, coupled with Jesus's works, establish who he is (10:32, 37–38) and thus play a strategic role in the Gospel's account and in affirming its thesis.

## STRUCTURE OF THE SIGNS

John presents the signs not haphazardly but in a structured pattern. More specifically, he develops a chiastic parallel between the signs, beginning with Cana (chapter 2) and ending in Bethany (chapter 11), both proximate to his centers of ministry in Capernaum and Jerusalem respectively.[13]

9. Dodd, *Interpretation*, 90.

10. Morris, *Jesus*, 6, 8.

11. Morris, *Jesus*, 13.

12. John often alternates between nature and function when talking about Jesus. For example, in the Prologue John notes Jesus's nature—was the Word; Word was with God; Word was God; Word was with God (1–2)—and function—everything made through him (3). Again, his nature (in him was life, the light of men [3–4])—and function (he is the light shining in darkness, whose function is to make us children of God [12–13]).

13. Chiasm is "a literary form consisting of two or more parallel lines structured about a central theme whose detection and proper analysis open new and significant avenues toward understanding the author's message" (Breck, *Shape*, 1). The chiastic structure is "valuable as an aid to discerning the

Sign 1: at Cana: turning water into wine. 2:1–11

Sign 2: at Cana: healing the official's son. 4:43–54

Sign 3: at the pool called Bethesda: healing the paralytic. 5:1–15

Sign 4: by the Sea of Galilee: feeding the five thousand. 6:1–15

Sign 5: on the Sea of Galilee: walking on the water. 6:16–21

Sign 6: along the road near Jerusalem: healing the blind man. 9:1–41

Sign 7: at Bethany: raising Lazarus from the dead. 11:1–45

Various evidences point to John's use of a chiasm.[14] First, in both the *first* and *seventh* signs Jesus shows reluctance to act. In the Cana incident, it was not his hour (we will return to Jesus and time in chapter 9). Reluctant as he is, Jesus recognizes the social pressures on both the groom and family[15] and for some unstated reason on his mother and performs the sign. However, we are clearly informed that the point of the sign was not to satisfy the guests by turning the water for purification into the best wine[16] but to reveal Jesus's glory and bring about the disciples' believing (2:11). In raising Lazarus from the dead, Jesus also appears reluctant; he suggests that Lazarus's sickness is not to be fatal and so lingers for several more days. In both cases Jesus's reluctance is directed to the ultimate goal of bringing about believing (2:11; 11:14).

Second, the first sign is a kind of resurrection to new life. In Cana, Jesus changed purification water into something more powerful and potent. In Bethany, Jesus brings Lazarus back to life, transforming his dead body into a living body. Like the Cana sign, this seventh sign presages the upcoming death of Jesus at Passover and the new life to follow.

Third, the first sign is given at a wedding in Cana; the seventh sign at the death of a friend. "In ancient sources, weddings and funerals typified the most joyful and most sorrowful occasions, respectively."[17]

Fourth, both the wedding and the post-resurrection feasting were public, celebratory events of joy. Jesus changed the ritually used water into the best wine, a liquid of celebration and happiness, for the wedding. The family of the raised Lazarus threw

central message of the narrative or discourse. This is quite simply because in John's chiasms the central idea or message is almost always found in the central section of the chiastic pattern" (Ellis, "Inclusion," 274).

14. Robert Fortna, in concentrating on restructuring the signs in the sources, misses the beauty and significance of the chiastic structure (*Gospel of Signs*, 102–9).

15. Although it was traditional practice but perhaps not good etiquette (Koester, *Symbolism*, 83) to serve the best wine while the guests were sober and reserve the poorer quality of wine after the guests were inebriated and lacked discernment, wine was still the beverage to be served. Running out of it indicated either poor planning or an unexpected abundance of guests.

16. There is also the retrospective connection with Andrew's identification of Jesus as the Messiah (1:41), whose messianic coming was connected in the Old Testament to the vine and wine (Gen 49:10–11; Amos 9:13; Joel 3:18).

17. Keener, *John*, 112.

a party of gratefulness in Jesus's honor. The guests at both parties revel in abundance of life gained.[18]

Fifth, both the sign at Cana and at Bethany occur on the third day (2:1; 11:6—although Lazarus was apparently dead for four days, 11:39), presaging Jesus's own resurrection. Sixth, both signs raise the issue of Jesus's glorification. In the Cana incident, the sign reveals his glory (2:11); in Bethany, the sign is intended to bring about his glorification (11:4, 40). In sum, the connection between the two signs is essentially grounded in the foretaste of and Jesus's glorification through his death and resurrection, to which John devotes the end of his Gospel.[19]

The *second and sixth signs* also contribute to the chiasm, where John moves from describing a situation of crisis to a joyous new life of restoration. Both are instances of healing, the one of the official's dying son (4:43–54) and the other of the blind man sitting by the side of the road (9:1–7). First, of note are the respective contexts of the two sign stories, which exemplify believing that does not penetrate much beyond the surface. The sign of the healing of the boy occurs in the context of the Galileans who welcome him but who provide no authentic indication of believing, only recognition that Jesus could do signs (4:45).[20] Jesus acknowledges the lukewarm reception by the Galileans by his skeptical comment about the role of signs (4:48). The context of the sign in chapter 9 focuses also on Jews who had very shallow believing (8:31–53). In this case, those who listen to him and his claims, although originally believing, eventually pick up stones to kill Jesus for blasphemy (8:59).

Second, both signs are granted to persons who probably were outcasts in the community, so that true believing comes from the outsider. The royal official (βασιλικός) of chapter 4 probably was a gentile in the service of Caesar or of Herod Antipas.[21] If he was a gentile, he would be viewed from the Jewish point of view as unwelcome within the community. Even if he was a Jew, he would have been ostracized because he worked for the Galilean house of Herod, which was not Jewish. Likewise, the blind man of John 9 was an outcast, sitting along the road probably outside the village. In fact, he was such an outcast that after he received his sight, his own neighbors did not recognize the one they had walked past but not attended to these many years (9:8). Third, in both cases, although the healing was immediate upon the words or actions of Jesus, the discovery of the healing was delayed, both for the official until he met

18. The imagery of an abundance of wine may signal the restoration of Israel in the final days (e.g., Amos 9:11–13).

19. As an aside, one might even find a bit of humor in both signs. Jesus's response to his mother might well be seen as a bit of humor: "Well, Mother, that's not my problem. They should have hired a better wedding planner" (Lewis, *John*, 38). Similarly, Martha says she believes that he is the Messiah and by implication can do such amazing things, but hesitates at the last moment because Lazarus would emit an odor (11:39), although it does emphasize that Martha believed he was resurrected and not merely resuscitated.

20. Koester, *Symbolism*, 51.

21. Mead, "βασιλικός," 69–72; Lewis, *John*, 10.

his servants along the way and for the blind man until he washed the mud from his eyes. Finally, and most importantly, both signs led to believing, of the official and his household (4:53) and the blind man who became not only a follower but a worshiper (9:27, 35–38).

The *third sign*—the healing of the paralytic (5:1–9)—*and fifth sign*—Jesus's walking on the water by or to the boat (6:16–21)—initially appear to have less in common.[22] Yet both manifest important circumstantial commonalities. Water features centrally in both signs, as does a kind of despair. The paralytic lies by the waters at the Pool of Bethesda, waiting with his fellow disabled people for healing. His position is less one of fear than of hopeless resignation, for he has no control over either (the moving of)[23] the water in the pool or his access to it. The disciples rowing their boat likewise face a hopeless situation on the stormy lake. In their case, they also have no control over the raging storm and roiling waters that are stirred against their wishes, bringing fear of drowning in the night. In the one case, water is the source of hope but out of reach; in the other case, water is the source of danger and despair and much too close.

Looking more deeply, however, one can see a parallel between the third and fifth signs in that they both are directed to establishing the identity of Jesus. The sign of healing in chapter 5 testifies that Jesus's work is that of his Father, that he can only do what he sees his Father do (5:17–20). The sign in chapter 6 likewise reveals his connection with the Father, here with his possible self-identification as the "I am (ἐγώ εἰμί); do not fear."

If this chiastic analysis is correct, the central point of the signs is the *fourth sign*: feeding the multitude on the mountainside with the five barley loaves and two dried fish.[24] That this is the high point of the first part of John seems correct since by leading into the discussion of the bread it provides the key anticipation of what is to happen in the second half.[25] Jesus is the new Moses whom the Father gives as the life-giving bread from heaven. He does not come to distribute the bread; he is the bread of life.

22. Our chiastic analysis does not prevent the existence of other structural similarities. For example, there are features of the third sign that resonate with the second sign—and rightly so since it follows it and hence provides co-narrative connection. Since it is likely that the royal official in chapter 4 was an outsider, one might also find this to be the case of the invalid in chapter 5. We find him at a pool that, from modern excavation, bears resemblance to the healing shrines of the gods Asclepius and Serapis, which was outside the pale of traditional Jewish healing practices (Koester, *Symbolism*, 52–53).

23. The textual variant that speaks about a miraculous, sporadic moving of the waters for healing is not well attested.

24. It should be noted that once the two dried fish are mentioned, they no longer play a role in the discussion, which focuses on the bread (in obvious reference to Moses and manna and in anticipation of the Eucharist).

25. Peter Ellis places the central chiastic piece of all of John in John 6, but he places it in verses 16–21 ("Inclusion," 281). If my chiastic analysis of the signs is correct, the center of the chiasm of the first half of John is in 6:1–15 and the commentary on that sign in 25–71.

Let us investigate each of the signs individually, to see how the Evangelist uses them to achieve his goal of bringing about believing in Jesus. In reviewing them, we must keep in mind that although the miraculous is what attracts attention, to their function as signs we must attend.

## THE SIGN OF ABUNDANCE: WATER INTO WINE (2:1–11)

John tells us that the function of the signs is to point to Jesus as the Messiah, the Son of God, and to bring people to eternal life through believing in him. As we have seen, John understands eternal life both qualitatively and quantitatively. Given John's clues, the signs should point both to the identity of Jesus and to a life of wholeness (eternal life).

The first sign invokes transformation. Jesus's mother requests him to resolve a wine shortage at a wedding. To do this he identifies the water of purification contained in six stone jars. John uses this to symbolize the old system of purification under the law. Jesus's first official act is to transform this traditional water of purification into something new, something far better. The water of purification only affects external bodily parts that are washed with it; the wine enters the persons themselves in a refreshing way. Jesus transforms the inner person, on his own terms, in his own symbolic way.[26] We also get the puzzled (and perhaps messianic) question, "Why didn't we get this wine earlier?" From the story we get the important answer that it was not yet the right time. (We will return to the importance of time in chapter 9.)

John reinforces this transformation of the old religious system by following the sign with Jesus going to the Jerusalem temple where he expels the sacrificial animals and the money changers.[27] As he transformed the contents of the ceremonial water jars, Jesus transforms the temple, the place for daily religious ritual, from a sacrificial marketplace to his own body that will be given once for all (2:13–22). The days of animal sacrifice are numbered; their sacrifice will no longer be needed after his ultimate, once for all Passover sacrifice. The temple and its cultic worship will be destroyed, made irrelevant. However, when his temple (body) is destroyed, in three days[28] a new

26. Giblin ("Suggestion") notes that this is the first of four Johannine occasions that follow a distinctive pattern where Jesus is requested to act, rebuffs the requester, and then acts in his own way.

27. This probably alludes to the final words of Zechariah's vision of the kingdom of God: "No trader shall again be seen in the house of the LORD of Hosts" (Zech 14:21). Beasley-Murray suggests that Jesus's action should not be taken as a condemnation of the old temple worship. Jesus is not critical of those worshiping God but rather of those who were parasitical on and misused the worship. His "wrath was directed not against those engaged in or leading worship, but against those detracting from it" (Beasley-Murray, *John*, 39). At the same time, given what comes later in 4:20–24, the story emphasizes a radical transformation of sacrificial temple worship through Jesus's own death and resurrection.

28. "The expression 'within three days' points to a meaning of the words closely in harmony with the unique ministry of Jesus. 'After three days' or 'on the third day' and the like denotes in Jewish tradition the time when God may be counted on to deliver his people from their troubles. The Midrash

living, eternal temple will arise, which events the narrator tells us refer to his own death and resurrection.[29]

John further develops the picture of the wedding around Jesus, who will be the true bridegroom (3:29) who receives everything from the Father and knows his source (3:34–36), in contrast to the bridegroom of Cana who received the abundance without comment and without knowledge of its source (2:10).

In line with John's other subtle references to the stories in Genesis, the Cana sign also recalls the shortage and abundance that the ancestral Joseph addressed when he took control of the riches of Egypt.[30] Whereas in that story abundance preceded famine, here shortage precedes abundance. The link between these two passages is the statement of Jesus's mother to the steward, "Do whatever he tells you" (2:5), echoing Pharaoh's statement to the Egyptians regarding Joseph (Gen 41:55). As Joseph prepared the Egyptians to survive the approaching famine, Jesus gives life from emptiness. Abundant life it is, an extravagance of abundance. The stone jars held twenty to thirty gallons each, yielding between 120 and 180 gallons of the best new wine.[31] In him we have life to the full (10:10), grace upon grace (1:16).[32]

Finally, Jesus's act upends tradition. "To employ waterpots set aside for purification for non-ritual purposes violated custom; consistent with Jesus's values elsewhere in the Gospels, Jesus here values the host's honor above ritual purity customs."[33]

This sign, John notes, brings about the desired effect. It reveals Jesus's glory (which is the glory of the one he comes from (1:14)) and results in his disciples believing (2:11). The first sign thus has a narrow scope in affecting the believing of his disciples.


## THE SIGN OF LIFE: HEALING A SON (4:43–54)

John gives the second sign as a healing of the son of an official. Whereas in the first sign someone apparently extraneous to the immediate need made the request of Jesus, in this case it is the father who "begged Jesus to come and heal his son, who was close to death" (4:47). Although it is not mentioned, the context suggests that word of Jesus's

---

on Gen 42:17 contains the dictum, 'The Holy One, blessed be he, never leaves the righteous in distress more than three days,' and in its comment on Gen 22:4, it lengthily elaborates the principle from the OT" (Beasley-Murray, *John*, 40–41).

29. Coloe, *God*, ch. 4. "Understanding the jars as representative of Jewish rituals is also congruent with subsequent portions of the narrative, where Jesus uses images from Jewish festival practices to convey something about himself and his mission" (Koester, *Symbolism*, 11).

30. In many ways Joseph prefigures Jesus, including being stripped of his clothes, buried in a pit, subsequently raised, brought before a ruler, and forgiving of the perpetrators.

31. Gench, *Encounters*, 11.

32. Where Jesus is the creator of abundant new wine, John brackets the other end of Jesus's story with the soldiers giving Jesus only a soaked sponge of old wine vinegar (19:29).

33. Keener, *John*, 22.

performance of signs in Jerusalem had spread through Galilee, and very likely this official heard about what Jesus had done in Jerusalem and approaches Jesus with his request. As with the first sign, Jesus betrays a note of hesitancy. Here it is over the role of signs. Whereas those for whom signs are performed require them for believing, Jesus seems to perform them more reluctantly, for the faith they lead to can be shallow (2:23–25). Nevertheless, he performs the sign for the official. Like the first sign, this sign is also about transformation, changing the son from a trajectory of dying to one of life. Three times John uses the term "lives" ($\zeta\tilde{\eta}$) (4:50, 51, 53) in the present tense. For John, repetition shows the importance of an idea. The repetition of the present tense of "live" shows not only that Jesus makes the nobleman's son live, but that he is made alive at the very moment that Jesus speaks. The official cannot doubt that Jesus is the source of his son's renewed life.[34]

The outcome of the second sign, believing, is the same as the first. The first sign creates believers of the disciples. This time the royal official and his household come to believe in Jesus. Since it is possible that the royal official was a gentile,[35] the circle of believers is widened dramatically, perhaps even skipping over the Jews that elsewhere John portrays as gradually forming an opposition to Jesus's ministry (5:18). Believing is found outside the Jewish nation, a point John makes by preceding this sign with the story of the faith manifested by the Samaritan woman and her community. The ethnic diversity of this cadre of believers would not have been lost on the readers of the Gospel, for since they included gentiles, they could empathize with the widening of the gospel message beyond, and perhaps even over, Jews who spurned the testimony. Although the initial testimony was from a Jewish prophet, John the Baptizer, and the first believers were Jewish, it was not long before the roll of believers who responded to Jesus's message extended beyond Jews.

## THE SIGN OF HEALING: THE PARALYZED MADE WHOLE (5:1–15)

In the third sign, Jesus himself takes the initiative, asking the paralyzed man who is waiting for the moving of the water at the pool called Bethesda whether he wants to get well (5:6). It appears disconcerting to have Jesus start the conversation in this way, given that the paralytic is at the healing pool, surrounded by others needing healing. It is even stranger to find Jesus at a pagan, not a Jewish, place, and on the Sabbath. Archaeological excavations have revealed in Jerusalem a double pool, surrounded by colonnades, through which water flowed from one pool to the next. Very probably the pool was an asclepion, where people came to be cured of their illness.

---

34. This continues the theme from the earlier discussion with the Samaritan woman, where Jesus offers her the water of eternal life (4:14). Linking the previous dialogue with the succeeding sign emphasizes the connectedness that characterizes the Gospel.

35. The Herodian family, who were Idumean rather than of Jewish ancestry, employed many gentiles.

After bathing in the pools, they would give offerings or sacrifices to Asclepius, whom they worshiped as a savior god because of his healing powers, and then spend the night in the associated sanctuary. They would then report their dreams to a priest who would interpret them and prescribe the appropriate therapy. Evidence that it was an Asclepion is found in the narrative, which uses the Greek phrase "ὑγιὴς γενέσθαι" (become well (5:4, 6)). This phrase, which is unique to John, "appears frequently in ancient testimonies to the healing powers of Asclepius."[36] The popularity of the cult of Asclepius is attested by healing pools at various sites throughout the Roman empire. Yet, even though the Romans controlled Jerusalem, it would be unsettling to find this place of cultic worship of a pagan deity there. However, the brunt of the Jewish criticism of Jesus is not where he performed the sign or on whom, but the timing of it as being on the Sabbath and his command to the man to "pick up your mat and walk" (5:11), which the Jewish leaders saw as a type of work that was forbidden by the Law (5:16–17; Exod 20:8–11).[37] They overlook the overt paganism to focus on a minor, interpreted point of the Law.

The invalid finds it difficult to identify Jesus when Jews query him regarding why he is carrying his mat on the Sabbath, for Jesus disappeared into the crowd at the asclepion. It is not until Jesus returns and tells him to stop sinning that he can identify the healer.[38] With this second encounter the paralytic now knows the identity of the healer and informs the Jewish leaders who had healed him.[39] When accused of breaking the Law, Jesus defends his Sabbath healing by recalling contemporary literature about God's post-creation activity. God's resting on the seventh day from creating the earth is consistent with his subsequent activity.[40] He "raises from the dead and gives

36. Yeung, *Faith*, 79.

37. "It was part of the oral law that 'taking out from one domain into another' was one of the thirty-nine activities considered to be work forbidden on the Sabbath, and it is probably to some version of that law that 'the Jews' are referring" (Michaels, "Invalid," 430).

38. Whereas later Jesus rejects sin as being a reason for the blind man's blindness (9:2–3), here Jesus connects sin with a physical condition and warns of more serious, probably spiritual, consequences of sin (5:14). Barrett rejects this interpretation, noting that this sign too was for the glorification of God (*Gospel*, 213). But connecting sin and sickness is compatible with treating the sign as an event that glorifies God.

39. Some interpreters suggest that the paralytic's "going off" and reporting Jesus to the authorities shows that he is an informant rather than a believer (see 11:46). Informants are critical to the prosecution (11:46), betrayal (18:2–4), and death of Jesus. This would indicate that he has not changed his character but continues in sin, contrary to Jesus's warning (Koester, *Symbolism*, 90; Michaels, *Gospel of John*, 299). Others note that "we should not overlook the fact that there was a certain amount of danger for the man. He was still under the accusation of Sabbath breaking, an offense for which the death penalty was possible. His defense was that his healer had told him to carry his pallet. By producing the name he made his case" (Morris, *Gospel*, 273n37). "He might even have wanted to give credit, naively, to 'the one who made him well.' If so, he is naïve indeed, for his backhanded 'confession' identifies Jesus as a Sabbath breaker whom the Jewish authorities will from here on 'seek to kill' (v. 18)" (Michaels, "Invalid," 346). However, at this early stage of Jesus's ministry, there is no indication that the Jewish leaders are out to "get" him.

40. Philo writes, "Moses does not give the name of rest to mere inactivity. The cause of all things

them life" (5:21) and judges (5:22; Gen 18:25; Ps 67:4). Both activities, Jesus notes, the Father gave him to carry out, even on the Sabbath, since God does these on the Sabbath as well.

The point of the sign becomes clear in the following dialogue. Jesus reminds the Jewish leaders that the work he does continues the work of his Father and that he does only what his Father does. The sign makes clear the identity of Jesus as the Son of God (God is his, not their, Father) and that he is intimately connected to his Father in the work that he, the Son, does (5:19). Indeed, judging, including about how to use the Sabbath, is now given by the Father to Jesus, so that Jesus may be honored and thereby believed (5:23–24). Ultimately, he, not the religious authorities, will do the judging, and the judgment will be based not on keeping the finer points of the Law but on believing in the Son.

For John, this sign leads to the very important discussion of testimony about who Jesus is (5:16–47), which we will discuss in chapter 4. What John portrays is a total disconnect between the sign as a testimony and the interest of the Jewish leaders in his Sabbath-breaking. Jesus concedes their interest in his actions and states that they have seen his works and should have believed but failed to do so. His actions point to his relationship with his Father, for he does what the Father does (5:19). Since Jesus does the work of the Father, and since the Father continued to work after creation, the Sabbath belongs to Jesus to interpret, no longer to the Pharisees to circumscribe. As the Synoptics remind us, "The Sabbath was made for man, not man for the Sabbath. So the Son of Man is Lord even of the Sabbath" (Mark 2:27–28). Instead, the Jewish leaders see his deeds as a disconnect with God, for they see him breaking the very rules or laws established by God by healing someone who had been ill for thirty-eight years and whose life was not in danger; he could have been healed the next day rather than on the Sabbath without mortal consequences. The ultimate result of this disconnect between Jesus's view of his deeds and the view of the Jewish leaders is that they anticipate stoning him (10:31–33). The works failed to convince the Jewish leaders that he is the Son of God, so that he must repeat his identity claim openly, which in turn leads to the charge of blasphemy. (We turn to Jesus's self-testimony in the next chapter.)

This sign, then, in contrast to the first two signs, fails to bring about believing. We have no evidence that the healed man believed, for he makes no confession of faith but only identifies the healer. The warning Jesus gives him about not sinning may suggest he did not readily believe. The Jews make no profession of faith but turn to persecuting Jesus, trying to kill him, at first for breaking the Sabbath, then for "calling God his own father, making himself equal with God" (5:18). They completely miss the significance of the sign, and because of this, Jesus says, "you do not have the love of God in your

---

is by its nature active; it never ceases to work all that is best and most beautiful. God's rest is rather a working with absolute ease, without toil and without suffering" (*On the Cherubim* 87; quoted in Michaels, *Gospel of John*, 301n75).

hearts" (5:41) but cherish praise from others. Rather than accept God's true revelation, they turn to others who will praise rather than judge them. Ultimately, Jesus says, Moses, whose Law they claim to accept but wrongly interpret with their hyper-legalism, will accuse them, for Moses wrote about him (5:46–47; 1:45).[41] "Contrary to what 'the Jews' might think (see 9:28–29), trust in Moses and trust in Jesus stand or fall together. For the author, those who believe that 'the law was given through Moses' should be the first to acknowledge that 'grace and truth came into being through Jesus Christ' (1:17)."[42] In short, this time the sign fails to create believing, although it provides the context for Jesus's teaching about testimony.

## THE SIGN OF THE MULTIPLIED BREAD: CREATING THE NECESSITY FOR LIFE (6:1–15)

The theme of work plays a key role in the fourth sign and the accompanying dialogue. Jesus crosses the Sea of Galilee and ascends a mountain, pursued by a large crowd. The fourth sign occurs when Jesus feeds the crowd of five thousand persons who followed him because they witnessed the healings that Jesus performed on the sick. Jesus's unusual power to perform miracles rather than his teachings attracts them (6:1–2). Although John does not mention Jesus's emotions (in the way he does in the case of Lazarus), Jesus is apparently moved by the large crowd who followed him into a place without available food. Jesus heightens the tension by asking his disciples where he and they could purchase enough bread for such a large group.[43] Philip responds that even if bread were available, they lacked the resources to purchase it. The disciples apparently have little inkling about Jesus's powers or abilities but are realists, facing the impossibility of feeding a multitude with no money or provisions. This sets the contrast that Jesus himself has the resources to satisfy their need for bread, here through using the contribution or expropriation of a child's lunch of five barley loaves and two dried fish.

We are not told how Jesus performed the sign; only that he took the bread and fish and, giving thanks, gave it to the disciples to distribute (their distributing is specifically mentioned in the Synoptics but not in John). Giving thanks here, as with the resurrection of Lazarus (11:41–42), indicates that this sign is possible only because of

41. Jesus does not provide specific quotes. Suggested references are Gen 3:15 and Deut 18:15. "John's direct quotations are fewer [than other NT writers], and he comparatively rarely uses the 'proof-texts' by which the earliest Christians often sought to show that Jesus was the Messiah whose coming was prophesied in the Old Testament. . . . The Old Testament, therefore, so well-known and understood that John could use it not piecemeal but as a whole, may be taken as an essential element in the background of the gospel" (Barrett, *Gospel*, 22, 25).

42. Michaels, *Gospel of John*, 33.

43. This is the beginning of the significant Mosaic allusions and references in this story. Moses also ascended a mountain after crossing the Red Sea (Exod 19:20) and later asks where he is going to get food to feed a large group of people in a place where food is unavailable (Num 11:13).

Jesus's connection to the Father. Like the Cana sign, this was a miracle of abundance, for after everyone had as much as they wanted, the disciples collected the remains into twelve baskets "so that nothing is lost" (a theme picked up again with reference to the sheep in 10:28–29).[44]

The crowd, however, interprets the sign differently than Jesus intended. Those fed were not looking for Jesus as the truth-telling rabbi but for Jesus the provider for their stomachs (6:26). "Like a typical crowd in a Greco-Roman city, the multitude in John 6 had no interest in anything but bread."[45] What the crowd saw was that Jesus was a combination of a food-providing king[46] and a new Moses, the "Prophet who is to come into the world" (6:14), who would provide them with free, long-term food security.[47] Jesus rejects their move to make him the grocery king (6:15) but builds on the Mosaic theme. When Jesus indicates that obtaining bread will require some work, namely, the work of God, they want to know what work they can do to be doing the work of God and presumably thereby benefit from a new era of manna provision. They are unprepared for Jesus's answer (although we as readers are prepared); the work required is not manual labor but something even more challenging for them, namely, to believe in Jesus as sent from God. They could accept miraculous expansion of the food supply, but finding room in their religious worldview for the miracle of God come in the flesh was far beyond them. Thus, in response, the crowd continues to focus on the manna bread and not on Jesus the bread of life. They want a foretaste of this bread from this present prophet, the new or returning Moses.[48] That this event occurred near to Passover (6:4), which celebrated Israel's deliverance through Moses from slavery under foreign rule, might have further confirmed their expectations. Jesus disappoints them when he reveals that neither he nor Moses was the source of the wondrous bread in the first place; the bread came from God, a fact that puts the bread out of their immediate reach. Further, Jesus notes, he himself is the bread that the Father provides: "For the bread of God is he who comes down from heaven and gives

44. With the number "twelve," identifying with the twelve tribes led from Egypt and fed in the wilderness, John prepares for further Mosaic connections.

45. Koester, *Symbolism*, 56. "Roman rulers regularly placated the populace with distributions of bread or grain. Cicero recalled that the practice was agreeable to the masses, since it provided food in abundance without work" (56).

46. Elsewhere Jesus does accept the designation of King of Israel by Nathanael (1:49) and by the crowd in Jerusalem (12:13). It is less the kingship than the crowd's concept of an earthly, politically liberating, food-providing ruler that Jesus rejects and escapes from. His kingdom, Jesus later asserts, "is not of this world" (18:36). This concept of the kingdom of God being not of this world is another Johannine riddle (3:3, 5).

47. Perhaps they even recalled the story of the prophet Elisha, who fed a hundred men with twenty loaves of barley bread, with some left over (2 Kgs 4:42–44). "There was also a tradition that at the Messiah's coming, 'the treasury of manna will come down again from on high, and they will eat of it in those years because these are they who will have arrived at the consummation of time.' 2 Baruch 29:8" (quoted in Koester, *Symbolism*, 96).

48. Rabbinic tradition held that despite the reporting of Moses's death in Deut 34:5–8, Moses did not die but was taken by God into heaven (Hagner, *Matthew*, 493).

life to the world" (6:33). His bread of life is not only for them but also for the world; Jesus's salvific work is cosmic (κόσμον) (3:16). It does not perish, as did the wilderness manna and the barley bread he served them on the mountain (Exod 16:20–21; 6:12, 26–27). The double meaning of "bread" is lost on the crowd.

This sign sets in stark contrast the desire of the listeners for signs and Jesus's suspicions about the adequacy of signs. The crowd that was fed took the miracle as an indicator that he was the prophet, Moses himself (Deut 18:15), who in their tradition was promised to return. With this in mind, they wanted by force to make him the leader, with the eschatological hope that he would be like Moses of old who fed them manna, provided them with water to drink, and ultimately led them to the fertile land of promise. When Jesus tells them to work for the food that endured to eternal life, they notice the work dimension. They could handle the legal requirement to sign up for the master welfare program. They still think that it is a matter of gathering or doing (6:28; Exod 16:17–18), whereas Jesus wants them to see that it is a matter of active believing (6:29). The crowd focuses on the material sign but fails to see its spiritual significance; they concentrate on what they might be able to do but fail to comprehend that Jesus demanded a radical change of perspective and commitment.

The sign has diverse effects. The fed crowd responds by wanting to make Jesus their king to satisfy their ongoing physical needs. Jesus rejects their misguided effort. For the Jewish leaders, the sign, along with the accompanying discourse, becomes a grumbling block and a puzzlement (6:41–42; 52). Again, John makes connection with Moses, who faced the grumbling Israelites in the wilderness (Exod 15:24; 17:3). For those who either were hearers or had become his followers, Jesus's radical statement— "Whoever eats my flesh and drinks my blood remains in me, and I in him" (6:56)— proves too much. This statement, if taken literally, is so contrary to their religious beliefs that it alienates them. Cannibalism lies far beyond the pale, as was the drinking of blood (Gen 9:4; Lev 3:17; 17:14). Instead of the sign leading to believing, it becomes an impediment, not only to followers, but to subsequent interpreters who want to understand why Jesus would put the matter so bluntly and with a double meaning that facilitates significant misunderstanding. Offense appears to be part of Jesus's "modus operandi" (6:61), used to shock his audience into realizing that what matters are spiritual and not fleshly (earthly) matters (6:62). At the same time, even Jesus admits that this tactic is not very successful (6:64) and requires justification. He consciously winnows out his disciples, an interpretation confirmed by his claim that the Twelve had not chosen him, but he had chosen them (6:70).

Although the Twelve don't appear to have understood any of the double meanings found in this discourse, they stick with Jesus as their only hope. As Peter says, "Lord, to whom shall we go? You have the words of eternal life. We believe and know that you are the Holy One of God" (6:68–69). The outcome of the sign reinforces John's point about the purpose of the signs: to identify Jesus as God's Son and to bring about believing leading to eternal life. It happens for a few; it does not happen for others whom the Father does not enable. The latter see the sign and ask for more but fail to catch the *sign*ificance of the sign. For John, this is part of the divine mystery of calling. Discipleship rests both on our persistent believing and God's enabling.

## THE SIGN OF WALKING ON WATER: CALMING FEAR THROUGH IDENTIFICATION (6:16–21)

Closely associated with the sign of feeding the large crowd is the fifth sign of Jesus walking on the water of the Sea of Galilee. Jesus leaves behind the crowd he has just fed, that wants to make him king, and ascends farther up the mountain, a practice that apparently Jesus regularly engaged in for prayer and meditation.[49] By the time he descends to the lake, the disciples have already departed by boat to return to Capernaum. (Why they would leave without their teacher is an unaddressed puzzle.) With no boat transport left, John tells us that Jesus proceeded to Capernaum by foot over the big lake. Spotting Jesus walking by the boat, the disciples are rightly terrified, for it is night, dark and stormy. They take him to be an apparition.[50] Jesus assures them that it is he (we will address his use of "It is I" (ἐγώ εἰμί) in chapter 5). John writes that "they were willing to take him into the boat, and immediately the boat was at the land to which they were going." (6:21). Their willingness indicates that they recognized Jesus for the human that he was and not as an apparition. What happens next is quite unclear.[51] Were the boat and entire crew immediately transported to shore at Capernaum? Some think so. The result is that there are two miracles: Jesus walks on the water, and upon taking on another passenger, the boat carrying him and his disciples is immediately transported to the shore.[52] Michaels thinks rather that the boat was almost at the shore and that the miracle was not to be found in their quick arrival but in the fact that Jesus walked the entire distance across the lake, never entering the boat.[53] Others suggest that the wind died so that they could quickly finish the journey to shore (in accordance with Mark 6:51). Still others emphasize that the point of the miracle was Jesus's walking on the water, not the arrival on shore.[54] Rather than dividing up the incident and debating whether there were one or two miracles, it is best to take the entire account, both walking on the water and arriving at the shore, as a unified sign. The point simply is that John is not interested in how all of this happened,

---

49. Again, John alludes to the connection with Moses, who ascended the mountain to talk to God (Exod 19:20).

50. Matt 14:26. John lacks this part of the tradition, though it explains the disciples' fear.

51. For various interpretations, see Morris, *Gospel*, 310.

52. See Barrett, *Gospel*, 234.

53. Michaels, *Gospel of John*, 356. The first part of this explanation addressing their proximity to shore, however, seems unlikely, since John tells us that they were somewhere a little over three miles into the lake, which Josephus tells us was four-and-a-half by sixteen miles.

54. Bultmann, *Gospel of John*, 216.

which is the case with almost all his signs, but in the fact that Jesus uses this sign to convey his identity, the "I am" (ἐγώ εἰμί) to his disciples.

Why does John include this incident in the seven signs? One reason, already hinted at, is that it provides an opportunity for him to present an "I am" (ἐγώ εἰμί) affirmation. Since the point of the Gospel is to establish Jesus's identity, this provides a reasonable explanation. More likely, however, is the Evangelist's desire to link Jesus with Moses, which in this entire incident is unmistakable. Jesus provides bread for the hungry where there are no provisions, as did Moses in the wilderness. Jesus ascends the mountain by himself, as did Moses to talk with God. Jesus is the "I am" who controls the water, as Moses relied on God when he led the people of Israel through the Red Sea. Jesus demonstrates his control over the stormy water by walking on it, as Moses walked on dry ground through the walls of water blown aside by God (Exod 14:21–22). Jesus successfully arrives at the destination with his disciples; Moses died before he entered the promised land with his exodus people. He, the Son of God, is greater than Moses, the leader chosen by God, for Moses neither spread the waters, fed the people by himself, not entered the land.[55]

It also continues the theme of Jesus's dominance over and replacement of water, the source of life. In John 2, he "replaces the water of ceremonial purification; . . . he replaces the 'holy water' of a Samaritan holy site" in chapter 4.[56] In John 5, he replaces the healing waters of the asclepion; in chapter 6 he demonstrates his dominance over the waters of nature.

John does not immediately tell us the result of this sign, which is one reason some have suggested that it is not to be taken as a sign.[57] Yet there is reason to believe that it plays a role in cementing the faith of the Twelve who, at the very end of this incident, affirm their loyalty to Jesus.[58] Even though many others depart, the Twelve remain. They have seen Jesus's signs, and as Peter confesses, Jesus is their only hope (6:68–69). The incident plays a role in the larger picture of the entire chapter where it

55. "Moses, Joshua, Elijah, and Elisha all parted bodies of water, but only God trod upon the water (Job 9:8; cf. Ps 77:19)" (Keener, *John*, 57).

56. Keener, *John*, 46.

57. C. H. Dodd substitutes the sign of Jesus's resurrection for this event. William Barclay interprets the story as not being miraculous at all. At its northern end, the lake is four miles across, and John states that the disciples had rowed about three to three and a half miles, meaning that they were close to their destination. And since it was stormy, they would have hugged the shore. Barclay understands the phrase περιπατοῦντα ἐπὶ τῆς θαλάσσης as "walking on the seashore," (after 21:1), so that they saw Jesus walking along the shore, not on the water. Since John does not say that Jesus got into the boat, Barclay surmises that they reached shore before Jesus could get in (and why would he want to, since he had walked all the way there on the shore). Barclay, *John*, 1:208–9. However, being a half mile offshore on a dark, stormy night in a tossing boat would make viewing and identifying persons on the shore impossible.

58. "There can be little doubt that both Mark and John . . . intended to record a miracle" (Barrett, *Gospel*, 233).

is sandwiched between the sign of the multiplication of the bread and fish and Jesus's discourse on the bread of life.

## THE SIGN OF SIGHT: LIGHT REPLACES DARKNESS (9:1–41)

The sixth sign of healing brings together several themes that interest us. There is the sign of healing, the metaphor of identity that Jesus is the light of the world, and the narrative's dialogic structure. This evocative story can be approached from many thematic directions. In chapter 2 we dealt with Jesus as the light; here we will deal with the sign aspect, while in chapter 5 we consider the metaphor of identity, and in chapter 7 we address the dialogue itself.

Jesus encounters a blind man, and the disciples raise the question why he was born blind. They wonder whether it is because the man sinned or because his parents sinned. The question reflects the common Hebraic view that sickness results from sin (Jer 14:19–20).[59] Healing is needed because God directly or indirectly brings calamities on us. Yahweh does not cause or allow calamities randomly; they result from our sin, our failure to keep the covenant made with God (Exod 15:26; Deut 7:12, 15; 28:15, 27–28; Amos). This theme, so prevalent in the Old Testament, is found in the New Testament as well, although on a more personal basis. Jesus tells the leper whom he heals to offer the atonement offering upon being certified that he is clean (Matt 8:4). In John as well, Jesus tells the healed paralytic to "stop sinning or something worse may happen to you" (5:14). Indeed, for Jesus "you are healed" is synonymous with "your sins are forgiven" (Matt 9:1–8). One suggestion, then, is that it was the man's sin that caused his blindness. But when could this man have sinned? If he was born blind, he must have sinned in a former life. This was the doctrine of reincarnation prevalent in Greek but not in Jewish thought. The other option was a traditional Jewish notion: the sins of the fathers were visited on the children (Exod 20:5; 34:7; Num 14:18; Jer 32:18). The prophet Ezekiel rejected this view, contending that no more will the children be held accountable for the sins of their parents. Each will be held accountable for his own righteousness or his own sin (Ezek 18:14–20).

In this case, Jesus rejects all these options. The blindness was for revealing that God worked through Jesus. The intent of the sign was to show Jesus's identity, that he was related to his Father who sent him and whose work he was doing. Jesus emphasizes the urgency of the task, for soon he as the light of the world will be departing the world of darkness (12:35). He as the light touches individuals who are entrapped in darkness. Since we relate as disciples to Jesus, we too should be doing God's work (9:4–5). The readers are to follow up, spreading light where there is darkness and blindness to the truth.

59. See Brown, *Israel's Divine Healer*, and Reichenbach, "Healing," 119–23. For a philosophical discussion of the connection between sin and suffering, see Reichenbach, *Evil*, 88–96.

The result of the sign is both healing and continued blindness. The formerly blind man now sees (understands) who Jesus is, follows, and worships him. The Pharisees, on the other hand, willfully confirm their blindness by rejecting the blind man and his testimony and the one about whom he testifies.

## THE SIGN OF RESURRECTION: RESURRECTION BRINGS LIFE (11:1–45)

The seventh and final sign paves the way for the transition into the second part of the Gospel, which focuses on Jesus's death, resurrection, departure, and the coming of the Spirit. The raising of Lazarus, who was dead for four days, prefigures God's resurrection of Jesus, who will be dead for three days. The tomb, the removed stone, the linen wrappings, the resulting believing, even the presence of a Mary (different in both cases), all anticipate the later event (20:1, 6–8).[60] The story is both touching and puzzling. It is touching because it shows the human side of so many people: Jesus, Thomas, Martha, and Mary. John portrays Jesus as having love for the family of Lazarus.[61] Lazarus falls deathly ill, and his sisters, who obviously have a prior relationship with Jesus, tactfully send an urgent plea to him, "The one you love (your friend) is sick" (11:3). One can sense an expectation on their part that this message will bring Jesus to take some action. Again, later in the story, Jesus calls Lazarus "our friend" (ὁ φίλος ἡμῶν) (11:11), and John comments that Jesus weeps, which the Jews see as indicating how much Jesus loved (ἐφίλει) Lazarus (11:35–36).[62] One might legitimately ask why this is the only sign that is accompanied by love. Perhaps one reason love only occurs here is that in performing the other signs Jesus did not have to sacrifice anything of himself. In the case of Lazarus, the significance of the sign comes very close to Jesus anticipating his own impending death and his hope of resurrection to life thereafter.[63]

The story poses several recognized puzzles for the witnesses. First, Jesus says to the disciples that the illness will not lead to death, which is contrary to what transpires (11:4). This is a case of double meaning, for although the sickness did end in Lazarus's death (the earthly perspective), that was not the final scenario, which was

60. "Jesus's washing of the disciples' feet in a way that recalls the washing and anointing of his own [feet] by Mary . . . suggests that the description of the resurrection of Jesus is also consciously set over against the description of the raising of Lazarus" (Painter, Quest, 18).

61. In speaking of love, John uses both phileo (φιλέω (11:3, 36)) and agapao (ἀγάπαω (11:5)) to describe Jesus's love for Lazarus, suggesting that, "at least in this chapter, [the two words] are synonymous" (Barrett, Gospel, 324). Bultmann notes that "the verbs do not have a specific Johannine meaning here, but denote the human relationship" (Gospel of John, 397n2).

62. Beasley-Murray speculates that the Jews misunderstood Jesus's tears. They thought they were for Lazarus but in reality "they were brought about by the sight of the havoc wrought among people through sin and death in this world" (John, 193).

63. "The miracle is not an end in itself. It is a further summons to the people in the story and the audience of the story to reach beyond their own expectations, to accept Jesus as the unique sent-one of God, making known the glory of God, and thus coming to his own glorification" (Moloney, Studies, 18).

his resurrection that showed God's glory and that of Jesus (the heavenly perspective). Second, why go at all to Bethany since by going he was putting his life in danger (11:8)? He could just as well heal Lazarus at a distance, an ability he has already demonstrated (4:46–54). Jesus's response is to provide a proverb or riddle: "Are there not twelve hours in a day? Someone who walks by day will not stumble, for he sees by this world's light. It is when he walks by night that he stumbles, for he has no light" (11:9–10). In part, this riddle requires a commitment on the disciples' part to risk danger so that they can see God at work and glorify him. It reiterates Jesus's claim that they have nothing to fear until his hour has come.[64] In 12:35–36 he tells his disciples to walk in the light while they have it, to put their trust in him, so that they will be sons of light, a light to the world. In 9:4–5, Jesus tells his disciples to work for the night is coming. Then Jesus will not be with them, and they will have to feel their way in the enveloping darkness of his absence.

Third, as the Jews wondered, if Jesus really loved Lazarus, why did he wait two days to come and intentionally put Lazarus and the family through such sadness (11:37)? The answer must be found in the entire scope of the Gospel that addresses the death and resurrection of Jesus. The parallel with Lazarus does not work unless Lazarus dies. Thus, the sign is both immediate and anticipatory. As immediate, it shows the power of Jesus's Father, for after Jesus's prayer emphasizing that he has confidence that the Father always hears him, he calls Lazarus forth from the tomb. It is also doubly anticipatory. This calling fulfills the general resurrection invitation by the Son of God which "is coming and is now here" (5:25–29; 11:25–26). This resurrection also foretokens what Jesus will experience in the coming days. Jesus calls Lazarus to come forth; by parallel the Father calls Jesus to come forth. Lazarus emerges out of the tomb from which the stone had been rolled away and is released from the binding death clothes (11:43–44). As God could raise Lazarus from the bonds of death, signified by the strips of linen that wrapped him, he can raise Jesus as well, who likewise will have the entrapping stone rolled away and leave behind strips of linen (20:6). By being raised, he overcomes death and glorifies the Father who raises him.

Jesus gives us several reasons for this sign. First, it is for the disciples and others, that they might believe in him (11:15, 26) and that God sent him. It also reveals God's glory in that he has the power to raise people from the dead (11:4, 40–42). The main purpose of the signs—to demonstrate his identity in order to bring about believing—is consistently maintained.

It also had personal significance for each member of the family. It put Lazarus's life in jeopardy, for his resurrection brought people to believe (12:10), with the result that the Jewish rulers tried to kill him. It had personal significance for Martha, who resumes her ministry of service (11:2). And it had significance for Mary, who somehow senses a connection between what happened to her brother and what was about to happen to her friend, Jesus (12:3–8).

64. Michaels, *Gospel of John*, 619.

The results of this sign are, like many of the others, mixed. Nothing is said about whether this brought about the disciples' believing (although the Beloved Disciple's and Thomas's doubts later suggest that resurrection still was not part of their worldview (11:12–13; 20:9, 25)). Some Jews who witnessed the event believed, but others did what the paralytic did. They went to the Pharisees and reported on what Jesus had done. This, in turn, leads the Jewish rulers to seek to kill Jesus. As Caiaphas puts it in John's ironic fashion, Jesus should "not only die for that nation but also for the scattered children of God, to bring them together and make them one" (11:51–52). This, of course, is exactly what Jesus did (17:11, 22). In this dimension, this sign and what it prefigures achieves the highest goal of the Gospel.

## THE AMBIGUITY AND SUCCESS OF THE SIGNS

Having recounted the signs, we need to say something about their reception and interpretation. John's description of how observers received the signs makes clear that merely witnessing a sign or miracle is not enough in many cases to bring about believing. Observers might not believe their eyes but think that, like someone watching a magic show, they are being tricked. So it was that the neighbors of the blind man who had sight given to him wondered whether this sighted individual really was the same man who had been sitting year after year by the side of the road. Maybe he was a lookalike, or maybe the blind man had been fooling them all these years to live off their charity. Other observers might experience the sign and not care about the larger ramifications but simply focus on what this event has for them. The fed crowd falls into this category, focusing on getting additional sustenance from this Moses act-alike. Others overlook the wondrous event and instead focus on factors tangential to the miracle. The Pharisees attended to the question of when the miracle was performed rather than on the performance itself and its benefit for the sufferer. John tells us that where we come from—our perspectives and values—determines how we understand, interpret, and receive the signs. The success of the signs depends on the nature and preparation of the soil (Luke 8:1–15).

The signs create several problems. The first problem concerns miracle claims in general.

> A fundamental problem for the evangelist was that even in the first century miracles had no universally acknowledged meaning. The same action could be understood in diverse and often conflicting ways by people who viewed it from different perspectives. The problem was compounded by the evangelist's use of the signs to show that "Jesus is the Christ," since there is little evidence that Jewish people in the first century expected the Messiah to be a miracle-worker.[65]

65. Koester, *Symbolism*, 80.

Yet contrary to Koester, John thinks that miracle working is part of the messianic expectation. He quotes the crowd, "When the Messiah comes, will he do more signs than this man?" (7:31).

However, even apart from this,

> there was no consensus about the criteria that distinguished a divine man from a magician, and reports of wonders performed by these men fueled debates over their status. Miracles like those in John's Gospel were ascribed to a rabbi, the emperor, and a magician by other ancient sources. In themselves, the signs of Jesus were open to sharply differing interpretations.[66]

Philip, Peter, and John later encountered such in the person of Simon in Samaria, who used his powers to enrich himself rather than to point to God (Acts 8:9–25). In a context of miracle claims, one must ask how to identify legitimate, testimonial signs.

Furthermore, signs have meaning only in context. What was their context? What did the Jews expect? The messianic expectation "was centered on a figure who would liberate Israel from political oppression and rule the people with righteousness," an expectation the people demonstrated and Jesus rejected (6:15).[67] When looking intently for and expecting one thing, to realize that what is present is really something else is difficult. John attempts to resolve this by coupling the signs with dialogue and discussion, in which the crowd or Jewish leaders are given the meaning of the sign, but in which Jesus, sometimes in a hidden and obscure fashion, sometimes openly, reveals that *he* is the *sign*ificance of the signs. Even if the audiences hear the explanation, perspectives that provide or fail to provide interpretive understanding of events are difficult to change.

Third, who interprets the signs? We have the Prologue and the statement of the author's intent to guide his readers. What perspective did the people who witnessed the signs have? Sometimes Jesus himself interprets the signs, as in the discourse on the bread or coupling the healing of the blind man with comments about life and light (chs. 6 and 9). Sometimes the Evangelist interprets the signs and other events, especially from the post-resurrection perspective when he and the other disciples could look back and see how the sign or event fits into the overall pattern (2:17, 22–23; 12:16). Sometimes, as in the case of raising Lazarus from the dead or the wedding at Cana, the signs are left uninterpreted but evident to those who know the Prologue or the whole story. In short, both Jesus and the Evangelist (2:23–25) recognize the general inadequacy of signs but still present them for those who require them for believing (4:48) or for those like the blind man and the royal official whose lives they radically change.

66. Koester, *Symbolism*, 80.
67. Koester, *Symbolism*, 80.

## CONCLUSION

Jesus emphasizes that his deeds, which only the Father or those intimately related to the Father can do, proclaim that he is whom he claims to be. "Who are you?" the people and religious leaders ask. "Look at my works," Jesus replies, "and you will see that I and my Father are one. The Father uniquely works through me, and I do only what the Father does." John invokes the signs as one piece of the larger construction or argument he makes to affirm the purpose of his Gospel: that readers and hearers believe that Jesus is the Messiah, the Son of God, and through believing have eternal life. However, since signs are ambiguous, misunderstood, and misinterpreted, and often rejected, the Evangelist produces further evidence, providing diverse testimony from those who encounter Jesus and from Jesus himself about his identity and function.[68] To this we turn in the next chapter.

## QUESTIONS FOR REFLECTION AND DISCUSSION

1. What are the signs John appeals to? What is their purpose?

2. What is significant about each sign?

3. Do you think that the resurrection of Jesus is a sign? Why or why not?

4. How are the signs in John similar to or different from the miracles in the Synoptic Gospels?

5. Who were the recipients of the signs? Is John conveying something significant by informing us about who received Jesus's signs? What might that significance be?

6. Do these signs tell us about miracles today? Would a contemporary miracle function in the same way as Jesus's signs?

7. To what degree were the signs successful in achieving their purpose? If performed today, would they be successful in your contemporary society and culture? Why?

8. What question would you like to ask the author about the signs in his Gospel?

---

68. "Throughout the Gospel, faith that begins with the signs is challenged to press on to take account of Jesus's words (5:36; 10:37–39) which elucidate his relation to the Father" (Painter, *Quest*, 18n52).

CHAPTER FOUR

# Book of Testimony

IT MIGHT BE SUGGESTED that we are bundles of beliefs. We cannot live without believing. Some of our beliefs derive from our sense experiences. Other beliefs concern what lies beyond our experience, and for these we rely on the testimony of others. Often we lack the experience, location, resources, knowledge, expertise, relevant information, or wisdom to make reasonable, informed judgments on testimony presented to us. In these cases, we turn to other people or organizations whom we trust to have the relevant judgmental resources, abilities, information, or knowledge. We depend on our mechanic to identify the strange sounds coming from our car, our doctor to diagnose our pains or inform us about which inoculations are safe for our children, the FDA to tell us what drugs are safe, the labels on our food packages to apprise us about nutritional value, and our friends and neighbors to make recommendations on everything from hiring a good plumber to where to go for a vacation or which lake has the best fishing. Experts or experienced people help make sure we get it right. Similarly with spiritual matters. We are encouraged not to leave it to chance but to get the best advice on how to achieve eternal life.

The author of the Gospel of John leaves us in no doubt as to his purpose. He wants his readers to have eternal life and to discover the appropriate or best way to achieve it. For him, eternal life comes through believing that "Jesus is the Messiah, the Son of God" (20:31). For him, believing is not merely a matter of head knowledge but an activity in which, when we are filled with God's testimonial Spirit, we become an active disciple of the risen Lord. We are to believe, even if we have not seen or heard Jesus firsthand (20:29). We have seen the ambiguity that accompanies John's use of narrative techniques like irony, riddles, and symbols and Jesus's actions of performing signs. These often fail to achieve the results Jesus wants. Thus, to encourage us to believe, John garners what he considers is sufficiently worthy testimony that the reader will have good reason to listen to and accept. Based on the unique relationship that Jesus has with the Father, John gives us testimonial claims "that the Father has *functionally equipped* Jesus to serve as his unique Agent, who will reveal the presence of God."[1] The testimony he presents will not only be true (19:35; 21:24) but will be gathered from such a diversity of sources that readers of his Gospel cannot doubt that the testimony is authentic and reliably evidential. He presents testimony from rich and poor, women and men, Jews and gentiles, religious rulers and religious outcasts, prophets and laity, from people just like us and people very different from us. He is sure that the diversity and weight of it all, compiled in this magisterial Book of Testimony, presents a most compelling case to establish the identity and mission of Jesus.

At the same time, John knows that not everyone will accept the testimony. Some are willfully blind, caught up in their sin so that they cannot see the Lord of the Sabbath (9:40–41). Others lack the love of God and would rather accept the words of people who seek mutual affirmation (5:44; 12:43). Others study the Scriptures but fail to comprehend that in testifying to the Messiah the Scriptures testify about Jesus (5:39–40). Others place their confidence in and brag about their possession and understanding of the Law (the Torah) without realizing the source and purpose of the Law (7:48–49). Still others reject the testimony out of fear, lest they be thrown out of and lose their place in the religious community (9:22). From John's perspective, these people are ignorant, for they lack the background knowledge that provides the context for the testimony. In contrast to the Gospel readers, they do not have John's Prologue that, if they had it, would make clearer what the testimony is about. They would recognize the identity and function or mission of Jesus. Indeed, if we did not have access to the Prologue, we as twenty-first-century readers would be in a similar boat of confusion and reasonable doubt, with misplaced trust in our ancestry, position, education, peers, or knowledge, unsettled by strange riddles and metaphors, puzzled by symbols, dubious about the signs, and fooled by the apparently earthly origin and nature of this itinerant Galilean who claims a divine origin.

However, to those who accept the testimony John presents and who keep Jesus's words, it is a lifeline to an unsurpassed quality and quantity of life (3:16; 10:28): "the power of God unto salvation" (Rom 1:16). Their darkness is removed, and they enter into his light (12:35–36, 44–45). As in our ordinary experience, testimony can lead to believing.

In this chapter we will dive in and investigate some of the testimony that John adduces for identifying Jesus and understanding his function or mission. We will come to appreciate the extent and diversity of testimony, its power, and above all its ability to point to this unique person. Of all the Gospels, it is John who brings us more deeply into the lives of the people Jesus meets, who in turn testify about their personal encounter with him.[2]

---

1. Van der Watt, "Salvation," 110.

2. For an in-depth study of testimony, see Bauckham, *Eyewitnesses*, especially in relation to John chapters 1–2, 14–17.

## THE TESTIMONY OF THE PROPHET: JOHN THE BAPTIZER[3]

The place to begin is where the Evangelist himself begins, with an eccentric prophet who lived and preached somewhere around the Jordan River. His importance is clear, for the Evangelist mentions him twice in two testimonial contexts in the Prologue (1:6, 15), testifying for the initial appearance of Jesus (1:19–35), again testifying in a subsequent encounter (3:22–36), and then in two testimonial references (5:33–36; 10:40–41). In the first instance in the Prologue, this prophet is identified as specially selected and sent from God to bear witness (1:6). The same Greek verb, ἐγένετο, that begins verse 6 is used to describe Jesus's creating in 1:3. John the Baptizer was *made* for the purpose of testifying. As the Evangelist repeats frequently in the Gospel with respect to Jesus himself, our identity and reliability in measure depend on from where we come. Since John the Baptizer is sent by God, his identity and truthfulness, and thus his testimonial function, are divinely attested. In this, he is unique among the merely human testifiers John presents in the fourth Gospel. He continues the lineage of the great prophets of the Old Testament who were called, sent, and thus had their message authenticated by God: Moses (Exod 3:10); Samuel (1 Sam 3:10–18); Isaiah (Isa 6:8); Jeremiah (Jer 1:4–9); Ezekiel (Ezek 2:1–2); and all the Minor Prophets, who received and transmitted the word of the LORD.

The context of the Evangelist's presentation of the Baptizer's testimony in the Prologue is the manifestation of Jesus as the light. Although the Baptizer is *a* temporary light (5:35), he is not *the* light but points to the light shining through uncomprehending darkness (1:6–8). The Baptizer's testimony, as with all testimony, is to bring about believing (1:7), which is realized in the subsequent narrative account (1:35–37).[4]

The second context for John the Baptizer's testimony in the Prologue is the incarnation: the Word became human, connecting the heavenly and eternal with the earthly and historical.[5] The Evangelist sees more in Jesus than a mere human; the Word is the life-giving, divinely originated light not simply for Jews but for all people (1:4). The Baptizer testifies that Jesus is a cosmic figure. Jesus, whose origin identifies him as the Son of the Father, is the eternal one, who comes after but exists before the testifier, and is greater than the testifier. He is the bringer of grace and truth (1:15–16). The Evangelist's affirmation that started the Prologue is reiterated at the end of the Prologue, so that the truth about Jesus Christ bookends the Prologue: the Word is God, with God from the beginning, is God himself, come to make God the Father

---

3. Only one John appears in the Gospel of John. Although John is not named "the Baptizer" in the Gospel, to distinguish him from his namesake that tradition holds to be the author of the Gospel, I will reference him through his baptizing activity (1:26, 28, 31, 33; 3:23).

4. "There is one notable difference between 1:6–8 and 1:15. The former section represents John as a figure who appeared at a specific point of time in the past (1:6–8 is dominated by aorist verbal forms), but in 1:15 John speaks from the present (μαρτυρεῖ), offering a retrospective (οὗτος ἦν) assessment of Jesus's earthly mission" (Williams, "John," 49).

5. Painter, "Theology, Eschatology," 28.

known.[6] The Baptizer testifies about Jesus, God's chosen one, who himself testifies about God the Father and his relation to the Father.

Testimony is only as good as the testifier is knowledgeable and reliable. The Prologue already has asserted the basis for our knowing the Baptizer's reliability: God sent him. However, the listeners who come to hear the Baptizer know nothing about his origin and wonder about his identity. For diverse reasons, he attracted the curious attention of both ordinary people and the religious elite who puzzled over his identity and mission (1:19). Thus, John must establish for the Baptizer's audience, especially the priests and Levites deputized to find out about him, his credentials and purpose.

The Baptizer's initial response to questions about his identity is to distance himself from current messianic concepts: he tells those who query *who he is not*. The Baptizer says he is not the Messiah but only the announcing friend of the Messiah (1:20; 3:28). The Evangelist presumes that his readers and Jesus's audience will know the background of these ideas and so does not develop or elaborate on them (we will say more about this in chapter 11). Neither is he the Elijah of tradition, who had not died but whom the LORD took to heaven (2 Kgs 2:11) and who would return to prepare the way before the Lord and announce "the dreadful day of the LORD." His task was to set the community aright: "to turn the hearts of the fathers to their children and the hearts of the children to their fathers" (Mal 3:1; 4:5–6).[7] Neither is John the Baptizer the prophet spoken of in Deuteronomy (18:15–19), in whose mouth God's words would be put and who would "tell them everything I command him." The Baptizer is not the Word, but the testifier (a word) to the Word.

Finally, he is not the bridegroom but his friend. There is no competition between bridegroom and best man; rather, the Baptizer sees the fulfillment of his joy in the bridegroom's success (3:29–31). It would not have been lost on the listeners that in the Old Testament Israel was the bride of Yahweh (Isa 54:5; 62:4–5; Jer 2:2; 3:20; Ezek 16:8; 23:4; Hos 2:19–20) and that the concept of a bridegroom possessed messianic imagery. "This imagery made its appeal as a way of referring to the Messiah, and we find it applied to Christ, for example, in 2 Cor 11:2; Eph 5:32."[8] "The Baptist is made to indicate that not he but Christ is the head of the New Israel."[9] By these denials the Evangelist has the testifier dispel some of the confusion surrounding his identity

6. This provides an excellent example of an *inclusio*, which "refers to a technique in writing whereby whole works or sections of a work are 'packaged' by having a theme or structure at the end match a theme or structure at the beginning" (Brown, *Death*, 1:39). Here the same theme of Jesus's identity with God both opens and concludes the section.

7. "In the synoptic tradition, John himself becomes an Elijah figure, explicitly in Matthew (11:14; 17:12–13), implicitly in Mark (1:2; 9:13) and Luke (1:17) on the assumption that Elijah prepares the way not for God, or the 'great and dreadful day of the LORD,' but for Jesus the Messiah. But John's Gospel seems to reflect the older tradition, going back to Malachi and Sirach, in which Elijah is the forerunner not of 'the Christ,' but of the God of Israel, and therefore a messianic figure in his own right" (Michaels, *Gospel of John*, 98).

8. Morris, *Gospel*, 213–14.

9. Barrett, *Gospel*, 186.

and role,[10] which persisted after his and Jesus's death when the Baptizer's disciples continued to spread his message (Acts 19:3–4).

The Baptizer's *positive response* to persistent questioning about his identity highlights his role as the testifier.[11] In contrast to the Synoptic Gospels, the Evangelist tells nothing about the Baptizer's parentage (Luke 1:57–60), lifestyle (Matt 3:4–6), or repentance preaching (Mark 1:4–8); he is quintessentially the testifier. Quoting and invoking authority from Isa 40:3, he identifies himself as "the voice of one calling in the desert, 'Make straight the way for the Lord.'" He is authentically and reliably the messenger announcing the coming of the LORD, who now stands among them. Whether this is to be taken literally (Jesus was standing there incognito) or more broadly (living among the questioners) is debated, but that Jesus is present the next day suggests the former.[12] In the Gospel writer's representative system, the Baptizer represents all the Old Testament prophets who stood before the LORD and brought his message to kings, religious authorities, and the people. Thus, he connects the Old Testament tradition (the old word) with the older but new Word now present, who was before him, in the very beginning, now become flesh.

Through John the Baptizer, the Gospel raises its critical, all-consuming question: who are you, Jesus? In answering this question, the Baptizer says a lot, for he identifies both Jesus's nature and his mission or function. As to Jesus's *nature*, he affirms both his eternality and his connection with God; Jesus was before him both in time and in significance (1:15, 27, 30) and is the very Lord (1:23). The Baptizer also testifies to Jesus's *function or mission*. Jesus not only brings the gift of grace, he brings truth (1:16–17).[13] Some take this to mean that through Jesus we receive the Holy Spirit (1:33–34),[14] but this seems secondary. Jesus's function is to give himself, for he himself is truth (14:6), and through that gift we receive grace.[15] Jesus not only gives himself, he comes to reveal the hidden God, which revelation the Prologue anticipates (1:18). Through the Baptizer, the Evangelist sets the structure of testimony (it establishes both Jesus's identity and his mission) and its function (to bring about believing).

10. Barrett (*Gospel*, 142) suggests that part of the reason the Evangelist takes this tack is to show the superiority of Jesus and hence of Christianity to John the Baptist and his followers, for even after his horrible death, the Baptizer had an ongoing following (Acts 18:25; 19:3–4).

11. "The delegation was 'sent from the Pharisees.' 'Sent' ironically echoes the earlier notice that John himself was 'sent' from God (v. 6). Two 'missions' confront one another here" (Michaels, *Gospel of John*, 101).

12. Bultmann (*Gospel of John*, 91n2) thinks that Jesus is not present; Bernard (*Exegetical Commentary* 1:40) thinks he is.

13. Questions exist regarding whether 1:16–18 are part of the Baptizer testimony or that of the Gospel writer. This functional claim holds only if it is the voice of the Baptizer (Michaels, *Gospel of John*, 87–88).

14. Michaels, *Gospel of John*, 88–89.

15. Interestingly, after this, "grace" never appears in the Gospel, although clearly the Gospel is about grace.

The Baptizer's testimony becomes demonstrative the next day when he points out the man among them and discloses that his own mission is to identify and reveal Jesus's nature and function. He *is* the Lamb of God, whose *function* or mission is to remove the sin of the world (1:29). Although the designation "Lamb of God" does not occur as a title in the Old Testament, the Baptizer prophesies the future sacrificial death of Jesus by which he brings grace. In this, he might be recalling the reference to the lamb in Isa 53:7. The Gospel writer confirms this thought when he notes that Jesus is condemned at the very hour that the paschal lamb is sacrificed (19:14) (see chapter 11).

Jesus also *is* the chosen Son of God (1:34), whose *function* is to baptize with the Holy Spirit (1:33–34). The Baptizer testifies to Jesus's baptism, which the writer does not detail but only affirms. The testimony concerning Jesus's baptism is that Jesus is endowed not merely once but permanently with the Spirit, so that he can in turn baptize his believers with the Spirit. This echoes, or better, completes, the prophecy in Isa 42 from which the Baptizer drew the announcement of his mission; the LORD will put his spirit upon his chosen one (Isa 42:1–2). The attestation of this for the Baptist is that he witnessed the dove, signifying the Spirit, descending and remaining on Jesus. He reports that he had been told that seeing this happen would identify "the one who will baptize with the Spirit, . . . the Son of God" (1:33–34). Ultimately, the Baptizer's testimony is grounded on the internal witness of God, who is his sender, and on his external, personal experience of Jesus. "I have *seen* and I *testify* that this is the Son of God" (1:34).

In his final testimony, the Baptizer reaffirms the origin of Jesus as being sent by God and his mission to speak the words of God (3:31, 34). The Baptizer indicates Jesus's authority (the Father placed everything in his hands (3:35)) and his function (to give eternal life (3:36)). The Baptizer's testimony is definitive and important for the people who sought him out but not necessary for Jesus's own self-understanding (5:33–35), for it stems from a human being who has mortal existence: "John was a lamp that burned and gave light," but only for a time. Jesus rests confirmation of his identity and function on even greater testimony, namely, of the eternal Father himself (5:36–40) who "is light" (1 John 1:5) (we will return to this later).

John the Baptist's testimony produces mixed results. On the one hand, the Evangelist does not overtly inform us about the reaction of the initial, questioning religious leaders until later, when they attempt to kill Jesus for his Sabbath deeds and self-identification (5:18) and instruct the temple guards to arrest Jesus (7:32). However, there are unmistakable clues. The Pharisees do not know (οὐκ οἴδατε) the one who stands among them (1:26), and the Prologue tells us that not only did those to whom the Word came not know (οὐκ ἔγνω) him, they did not receive him (1:10–11). The die of Pharisaical unbelieving is already cast. On the other hand, we get a more positive response from those who become Jesus's first disciples. Two of the Baptizer's disciples leave him to follow Jesus, and they in turn become witnesses. Andrew witnesses to his brother Peter that we have found the Messiah. Philip witnesses to Nathanael that they have found the one about whom Moses in the Law and the prophets wrote (1:40–45). The Evangelist presents this not only as the commencement of believing in Jesus, but as the beginning of the testimony of others who encounter Jesus and subsequently give witness to Jesus's identity and mission. Jesus's disciple recruitment does not come easily; it creates a struggle between John the Baptizer's disciples and Jesus, who seems to be winning disciples away from John (3:26). Nonetheless, the Gospel writer wants to assure us that the Baptizer willingly gives up his position and his disciples so that Jesus's ministry increases (3:30).

Even after the Baptizer disappears from the scene, his testimony remains effective. In a parallel to an affirmation that the testimony of the Gospel narrator, the Beloved Disciple, is true ("We know that his testimony is true" (21:24)), the Evangelist tells us that the people affirmed the truth of the Baptizer's testimony. Even without him performing signs, they believed in Jesus because of that testimony (10:41–42). In effect, the Gospel writer affirms the truth of John's testimony by appeal both "from above" (God sent him) and "from below" (the people said).

John the Baptizer, in and perhaps representing the long line of prophetic witnesses sent by God, sets the standard for the testimonies in the rest of the book. He recognizes Jesus by signs (at baptism) and by revelation that the Spirit is on him, and in turn affirms his identity and mission. Thus, the Evangelist sees the Baptizer realizing his purpose as the friend of the bridegroom, not in gaining disciples, but in preparing the way for the Lord by his own witness.[16]

## THE TESTIMONY OF WOMEN: THE SAMARITAN WOMAN

In the contemporary Jewish culture, testimony from women was not accepted. Even the disciples stand dumbfounded when they see Jesus talking with a woman, let alone with a woman all by herself (4:27), although apparently they were leery of pursuing the matter with Jesus. Thus, we find it amazing that the Evangelist takes pains to include women among his testifiers.[17] Indeed, not only does he include them, it is to women that Jesus reveals that he is the Messiah (4:25–26; 11:27). Among them is the woman whom he encounters at the well in Samaria. Introducing this woman creates rich symbolism for John. First, she is a Samaritan, whose ancestry distinguished her

---

16. "After the 'telling' of the prologue, he emerges at a point of transition—both spatially (in the wilderness) and chronologically (on the first day)—embodying the Isaianic voice and announcing the appearance of the 'coming one.' Through his witnessing activity John is able [to] usher in and point to Jesus but, once Jesus's public ministry is underway and the in-between stage is passing, John's fate is to diminish and fade away. His legacy as a character is that he fulfils a bridge-like role. John's earthly mission belongs firmly to the past, but his testimony still speaks loudly in the present" (Williams, "John," 60).

17. Indeed, as Staley ("Structure") points out, women occur at the major turning points of John's Gospel.

from the Jews of Judea. In the Old Testament we are informed that the king of Assyria, Shalmaneser, after removing the native inhabitants, brought people from five[18] foreign places "and settled them in the towns of Samaria to replace the Israelites.[19] They took over Samaria and lived in its towns" (2 Kgs 17:24). These ethnic transplants did not "worship the LORD; so he sent lions among them and they killed some of the people" (2 Kgs 17:25). To address the problem, Shalmaneser sent one of the captive priests from Samaria back to Samaria "to teach the people what the god of the land requires." He was only partially successful, for though he taught them about Yahweh worship, "each national group made its own gods in the several towns where they settled, and set them up in the shrines the people of Samaria had made at the high places" (2 Kgs 17:29). The resulting religious syncretism continued to Jesus's time. Indeed, the woman herself realized the great religious chasm between Samaritan worship on Mt. Gerizim and Jewish worship at the Jerusalem temple. Thus, in John's eyes she stands outside the Jewish tradition and symbolizes those who have some knowledge of true worship but with mixed beliefs fail to fully recognize the exclusive sovereignty of the LORD. Their worship is misdirected to Gerizim.

Second, she is a woman and thus a second-class citizen. According to Rabbe Hiyya, "It is enough for us . . . that (women) rear up our children and deliver us from sin (by being sexual partners)"[20] Women were viewed as unclean, sexual temptresses. The Talmud describes a woman as "a pitcher full of filth with its mouth full of blood, yet all run after her."[21] Rabbi Eliezer said, "If any man teaches his daughter the Torah it is as though he taught her lechery,"[22] and "It is better that the words of the Law be burned, than that they should be given to a woman."[23] When it comes to the matter of testimony, Josephus, in his *Antiquities*, wrote, "The testimony of women is not accepted as valid because of the lightheadedness and brashness of the female sex."[24] Given this misogynist view of women, one can well understand the disciples' shock when they find Jesus alone talking with a woman. From their perspective, he was putting himself in a position, if not to be seduced, at least to have his reputation sullied. Since women could not even be trusted with the Torah, it is amazing that John included this testimonial event about the Messiah in his Gospel.

Third, from a Jewish perspective, she was ritually unclean. Some Jews believed that Samaritan women were menstrually impure from birth, and consequently any

18. Is it only a coincidence that the Samaritan woman had had five husbands (Gench, *Encounters*, 33)?

19. It is likely that it was particularly the elite and especially the men of military age who were deported, leaving at least some of the ordinary people in the land and creating the context for religious syncretism. Hobbs, *2 Kings*, 230.

20. Hurley, *Man*, 69.

21. Swidler, *Women*, 3.

22. Swidler, *Women*, 93.

23. Hurley, *Man*, 72.

24. Swidler, *Women*, 115.

Jew who came in contact with these permanently impure women, their husbands, or with objects touched by them was likewise impure. Thus, the woman expresses surprise that a Jew would ask for and accept water from her.[25]

Fourth, the Samaritan woman is not only a religious and gender outsider, she lives as an outcast in her own village. Village women went to the well to draw water early in the morning or evening but not in the heat of the day. Yet here we find this woman alone, drawing water by herself from the well at noon, which indicates that she is not accepted by the respectable women of her village.[26] Perhaps there was good reason, since John hints that she was sexually profligate. She had had five husbands and was living with a sixth who was not her husband.[27] Morally and socially, she found herself excluded from the mainstream of the community.

Yet it is this woman that John uses to garner testimony about the identity of Jesus. She wonders, perhaps sarcastically, whether Jesus is greater than "our father Jacob" (4:12), who dug the well.[28] "Who do you think you are?" The water Jacob could draw from the well gave temporary relief from thirst.[29] Jesus affirms that his living water provides eternal life, which John understands both qualitatively as fullness of life in knowing or experiencing God and quantitatively as eternal life.[30] Once Jesus reveals to her that he has knowledge that ordinary people in his situation would not have (4:17–19), she relaxes a bit and confesses that he is a prophet for, as he knew about Nathanael sitting under the fig tree, he knows about her marital situation even though he had never before encountered her. However, she continues to press him, this time about the proper place to worship. Jesus responds that worship will no longer be place

25. Bourgel, "Defining," 45–47.

26. At the same time, John is calling attention to the Old Testament precedence of the leading character meeting his future wife at a well (Isaac, Jacob, Moses), water being drawn, the woman rushing home, and a wedding prepared. But here there is no bride and no wedding, only a harvest. Culpepper, *Anatomy*, 136.

27. It is possible that she had had five legal marriages and the five husbands had died, or that she had five legal divorces, but the fact that she was living with a man who was not her husband and was not accepted by the women of the community argues against these possibilities. "To the Jew, who felt that three marriages were the most that could be allowed, the married life of the woman itself is a scandal, quite apart from the present illicit relationship, which is even more shocking" (Bultmann, *Gospel of John*, 188n4).

28. The Old Testament provides no record of Jacob digging a well, though Jacob did purchase land in Shechem (Gen 33:18) and gave it to Joseph (Gen 48:22). Sychar is about a mile north of Jacob's well, but close to and traditionally identified with Shechem.

29. Mary Coloe (*God*, 91) notes, "It is in the Targums and the rabbinic literature that well traditions linked to Jacob can be found. When Jacob arrives in Haran seeking a wife, he comes to the local well. According to the Targums, Jacob's presence brings a miraculous welling up of water that lasts twenty years," a length of time that contrasts with Jesus's promise of a well providing water eternally.

30. John's use of irony is evident in that Jesus, the giver of the water of eternal life (4:14), too thirsts (19:28). His thirst arises from the need to drink the Father's cup (fulfill the Father's mission, 18:11) and will be quenched not by wine vinegar but only when the Father gives him the water of eternal life through his resurrection (Culpepper, "Reading," 203). It echoes the psalmist's thirst for God in Pss 42:1–2; 63:1 (Michaels, *Gospel of John*, 961).

oriented; it will be neither Mt. Gerizim nor Jerusalem, but person and spirit, oriented. The earthly distinctions of "right place," the source of ethnic conflict, will be eliminated (4:21-24).

Most importantly, however, it is to this unlikely woman that Jesus reveals himself as the Messiah. Indeed, Jesus goes farther to affirm that he is the I am, the phrase used to refer to God (Exod 3:14) (we will say more about this in chapter 5). It seems unfathomable that Jesus would grant to a woman, let alone to a Samaritan woman of dubious character, the revelation and message of his messiahship. Yet, with this life-changing information that he provides eternal life and is a prophet and messiah, she leaves her water jar[31] and returns to the village that ostracizes her to testify about this man she met who knows everything she ever did.[32] Because of her testimony she effectively brings her community out to meet the man they in turn call the savior of the world (4:42). The citizens of Sychar get Jesus's identity right in a way that the Jewish leaders never do, for steeped in their religious traditions the leaders stand opposed to Jesus's messianic claims (2:20; 5:15; 7:1; 8:59; 10:31). That the villagers correctly understand, however, involves more than the testimony of the woman; her witness is followed up by their own encounter with Jesus, whose words they hear for themselves (4:42). Throughout the Gospel, testimony begins with someone's personal encounter and then leads others to experience Jesus. With this story, John tells us that it matters not whether the testifier is male or female, Jew or non-Jew, or even morally perfect. Any who have encountered the life-changing living water can testify truly and be the means of introducing others to Jesus.[33] However, real change occurs when the hearers encounter Jesus for themselves.

31. For various interpretations of the significance of her abandoning her water jar (4:28), e.g., that she becomes the vessel for carrying the good news of satisfying water, see Gench, *Encounters*, 36.

32. Mary Coloe sees this passage as a chiasm.

> A 4:1–6 Jesus leaves Judea for Galilee, travels through Samaria.
> B 7–15 Jesus asks a woman for a drink. Dialogue on two "waters."
> C 16–18 Woman told to go and bring her husband.
> D 19–26 Place and nature of true worship.
> C' 27–30 Woman goes and brings the villagers.
> B' 31–38 Disciples ask Jesus to eat. Dialogue on two "foods."
> A' 39–45 Jesus in the village then resumes his journey to Galilee. (*God*, 87)

From this she takes D as the core of and key to understanding the passage, teaching about God coming in Jesus as the new temple. But the passage serves, I believe, another purpose that ties up with the ultimate purpose of John, namely, testifying to the identity of Jesus and bringing people to believing in him.

33. The Samaritan woman "is much more than a woman with an interesting love life or a model of sin. She is the first character in John to engage Jesus in serious theological conversation. Moreover, she is the most effective evangelist in this whole Gospel, hence a model for Christian faith and witness" (Gench, *Encounters*, 38).

For John, in a broader sense, the testimony of the Samaritan woman was not only hers; she also speaks for non-Jews (foreigners) everywhere. Jesus says that the Samaritans worship what they do not know. Yet, because of testimony that will be included in the true worship, the time will come when people of every group (true worshipers everywhere) will "worship the Father in spirit and in truth" (4:22–23). The conversion of the Samaritans, which begins after Pentecost with Philip (Acts 8:4–8), receives its anticipation with the conversion and believing of the villagers who respond to the woman's testimony.

John indicates that the Samaritan woman of ill repute was more to be trusted than the religious elite, for although they witnessed his signs, most of them missed the fact that the signs connected Jesus to God. When Jesus returns to Jerusalem (chapter 5) the mood of the Jews differs greatly. The signs, performed on the Sabbath, lead to opposition and persecution. Even greater testimony, to which we will turn below, is needed to convert the doubters.

## THE TESTIMONY OF WOMEN: MARTHA AND MARY

The testimony of the sisters Martha and Mary brings us to an intimacy of relationship that is found elsewhere only in Jesus's relationship to Peter and possibly to Mary Magdalene. Jesus knew the family (11:3), staying with them when he came to Jerusalem since the village was less than two miles from Jerusalem (11:17; Matt 21:17; Luke 10:38). Before Jesus raises Lazarus from the dead, he weeps, and the Jews remark that this revealed his deep love for Lazarus. It also set the stage for the thrice-repeated, critical but prescient comment that Jesus could have kept Lazarus from dying in the first place had he come to Bethany earlier (11:24, 32, 37). The repetition reinforces the intentionality of Jesus's actions (11:14) and anticipates a similar contention that the Father could have prevented Jesus's crucifixion but chooses not to, for his own glory (11:40; 12:28; 17:1).

The context of Martha's testimony is the death of her brother, Lazarus. Jesus lingered elsewhere when he heard that her brother Lazarus was ill. Those who knew the case were puzzled (11:12, 37). The reasons Jesus gives have to do with his glorification (11:4) and the sign that eventually he performs to bring about believing (we addressed the sign in chapter 3). Lazarus was dead for four days when Jesus arrives and Martha comes to meet Jesus.

From John and the other Gospels, we obtain a striking picture of Martha. She likes to entertain; hosting dinners for Jesus, she apparently did much of the preparation herself (Luke 10:38; John 12:2). She is a person with strong opinions that she is willing to express. She goes to Jesus with a criticism of her sister who is listening to Jesus rather than helping her prepare food in the kitchen (Luke 10:40). Even before Jesus reaches her home, she boldly approaches him with the forthright accusation,

"If you had been here, my brother would not have died."[34] John also presents her as a person with great faith. Even after challenging Jesus, she reveals her trust in him: "God will give you whatever you ask" (11:22). At the same time, her faith is not without a human side, for she wavers when it comes to Jesus fulfilling his promise to raise her brother from the tomb. "But Lord, by this time there is a bad odor, for he has been there four days" (11:39). In short, John portrays her as a strong person with both faith and doubts that are both great and realistic.

Martha's testimony is a verbal, climatic confession of Jesus as "the Messiah, the Son of God, who was to come into the world" (11:27). It is precisely Jesus's *identity* that John expects those who hear the testimonies to affirm (20:31). Here, in the mouth of a woman John puts the confession anticipated by Nathanael (1:49) and given by Peter (Matt 16:16). Her verbal testimony demonstrates her faith and her belief about Jesus's identity.[35] Martha also testifies to Jesus's *function* as the resurrector. Although she anticipates this for the end times, she does not fully understand the Jesus standing in front of her. Jesus assures her that this resurrection power is even now present in him for those who believe, whether they are dead or alive.

The testimony given by her sister Mary is quite different. Whereas here Martha testifies by word, Mary testifies by action. Mary is the quiet sister, whom we find at Jesus's feet (11:32; Luke 10:39). Her position and actions signify her humility. She falls at his feet, a position of both worship and petition. At the subsequent banquet given by her sister, Mary took half a liter of expensive perfume, poured it on Jesus's feet, and wiped them with her hair.[36] The fragrance, we are told, filled the room, a stark contrast to the odor that Martha anticipated the dead Lazarus emitting (11:39.)[37] She says nothing by way of verbal testimony but instead acts. When Judas questions her actions, Jesus, not Mary, responds in her defense and explains the significance of her action. By portending what would be needed to mask the odor of Jesus's death, her pouring witnesses to what is about to happen, namely, Jesus's death and burial, which form part of his mission.

If one interprets the testifiers as representative of larger groups, Martha represents the apostolic community that pronounces the core confession of faith.[38] Martha's testimony is *verbal*, given in response to the promise made by Jesus that Lazarus

34. Michaels interprets this as "a tribute to Jesus's love and power to heal" (*Gospel of John*, 630). But it fits more with Martha's sharp character to interpret it as a criticism, in accordance with Luke's picture of her.

35. Morris (*Gospel*, 489) notes that use of the perfect tense here—"have believed"—"indicates a faith once given and permanently remaining. And she believes *that*—. Her faith is not a vague, formless credulity. It has content, and doctrinal content at that."

36. "Pouring the perfume on Jesus's head would not have had the same effect within the dramatic structure of the Gospel" (Michaels, *Gospel of John*, 666). In addition, Jesus's reclining position at the dinner would have made anointing his head difficult, if not inappropriate.

37. "A fragrant smell and grateful love now fill a house that had once been filled with mourning and the smell of death's decay" (Gench, *Encounters*, 95).

38. Brown, "Women," 693.

would rise from the dead, not simply at the last day, but now through him. Mary represents those Christians who testify by their *deeds* to who Jesus is and what he did. She says nothing in anointing Jesus yet publicly proclaims his future death and burial. The two thus present a complete testimonial package—words and deeds—that the early church professed and that we can and should emulate.

## THE TESTIMONY OF WOMEN: MARY MAGDALENE

The Evangelist's recruitment of women to testify continues after detailing Jesus's death. Whereas Mary of Bethany anticipates Jesus's death and burial, Mary Magdalene testifies to his resurrection. She is the first to arrive at the tomb on the first day of the week, the first to inform the disciples, and the first to see the risen Jesus (20:1–2, 11–18).

From the Gospel of John we know little about Mary from Magdala, a town on the shore of Lake Galilee. She stands with Jesus's mother and sister at Jesus's crucifixion but plays no role there (19:25). We must turn to the other gospels to find out that she helped support Jesus's ministry, sometimes traveled with Jesus and the Twelve, and that her attention to Jesus probably resulted from him curing her mental illness (Luke 8:2–3).

John carefully structures the discovery of the empty tomb in chiastic fashion.

A Mary Magdalene comes to the tomb and finds the stone removed (20:1).

  B She runs and announces to Peter and the other disciple the absence of Jesus (20:2).

    C Simon Peter and the other disciple run to the tomb (20:3–4a).

      D The other disciple outruns Simon Peter to the tomb and looks in but does not enter (20:4b–5).

        E Simon Peter arrives at the tomb, enters, and sees the burial cloths (20:6–7).

      D' The other disciple enters the tomb and confirms Simon Peter's observations and believes (20:8–9).[39]

    C' The two disciples return to where they were staying (20:10).

A' Mary encounters Jesus, whom she takes to be the gardener (20:11–17).

  B' Mary goes to tell the disciples the good news that she has seen Jesus (20:18).

John places Simon Peter, the leader of the disciples, at the center of this chiasm, authoritatively confirming the absence of the body from the tomb. However, Mary's

---

39. What it is that the Beloved Disciple believes is left open. Is it that he believes Mary Magdalene that the body is missing, that Jesus was resurrected, or that Jesus was divine (Michaels, *Gospel of John*, 991–93)?

bracketing position is critical, for she is the one who testifies to the disciples that something happened at the tomb, that her Lord (a term of discipleship) was missing, and, later and most importantly, that the Lord was alive. Simon Peter and the other disciple know that Jesus's body is missing; Mary knows that he is resurrected and alive, for she has seen him. Her testimony is no result of secondhand information; it is based on her own, firsthand experience. Western church tradition considered her to be "the apostle to the apostles."[40]

Given her cultural setting, it is difficult to think of someone who is a woman and had been mentally ill (demon possessed) being treated as a reliable witness. Yet John puts her front and center in his resurrection account. Indeed, to such a person Jesus entrusts his mission, specifically commissioning her, "Go and tell them" (20:17). People who once had mental issues can reliably proclaim the risen Lord, for they encounter Jesus and personally experience the life-changing healing that he brings. Thus, John conveys to his readers that they, no matter who they are, are to go and tell (4:35–38). No social stigmas, no gender roles, no denigrations should restrain them from being testifiers of the risen Lord.

## THE TESTIMONY OF SKEPTICS: NATHANAEL

One of John's more provocative *inclusiones* (a bracketing that places similar material at the beginning and at the end of a section to set it apart) concerns a pair of persons whom we will term skeptics. Their doubts and subsequent resolution, culminating in the doubters' testimony concerning Jesus, bracket Jesus's ministry: Nathanael at the beginning, Thomas at the end.

We encounter the first of these skeptics at the outset when Jesus recruits his disciples. He asks a man named Philip to follow him, and like his compatriot Andrew from Bethsaida, he goes to recruit another. Philip's recruit is Nathanael, to whom Philip testifies that "We have found the one Moses wrote about in the Law, and about whom the prophets also wrote—Jesus of Nazareth, the son of Joseph" (1:44). Philip's testimony connects with prior, respected, Old Testament testimony and reveals how important John believes Jesus's origin is. As we will argue in more detail in the next chapter when we consider John's portrait of Jesus's identity, John holds that who you are depends to a significant degree on where you come from. Obviously, Philip believes that Jesus's provenance is critical to Jesus's identity as a prophet.[41]

40. Brown, "Women," 693.

41. J. Neyrey (*Gospel*, 3–28) notes that identifying one's origin was an important part of an encomium or tribute in Greco-Roman society. He argues that the Evangelist creates an encomium for Jesus through his emphasis on Jesus's origin (comes from above), his patronage (he is the son of the Father), his nurture and training (Jesus does what the Father has shown him to do and teaches what he has seen and heard from his Father), his deeds (he does what pleases the Father, who loves him as his son), his favorable comparison with the Hebrews greats (greater than Jacob (4:12), Abraham (8:56–58), and Moses 6:32–33), and his noble death (courageously, voluntarily, on behalf of others).

Nathanael is quite unimpressed. For one thing, if Jesus were indeed the one about whom Moses and the prophets wrote, he should have a more significant pedigree. Nathanael knows nothing of Jesus's true pedigree, that he was in the beginning with and comes from the Father, for he does not have access to John's Prologue. Ignorance of the Prologue leaves those whom Jesus encounters at best perplexed and in Nathanael's case skeptical.

What Philip reveals about Jesus's pedigree does not further his cause with Nathanael. He notes that Jesus is from a small, rural town called Nazareth[42] and is the son of an ordinary man named Joseph. Nazareth is not mentioned in the Old Testament, and we know nothing more of the place except from the Gospels.[43] Nathanael apparently had heard about the town, since it was not too distant from his hometown Cana and was unimpressed with its reputation. In effect, Nathanael is skeptical about his friend Philip's new discovery. Yet Nathanael is an open skeptic, willing to look at the evidence, and hence responds to Philip's "Come and see for yourself." This is John's message of invitation throughout the Gospel: the witnesses announce, "Come and see" (4:28), for "I testify about what I have experienced."

On approaching Jesus, Nathanael is met with Jesus's welcoming recognition of him. Two items interest us in this reception. First, Jesus willingly entertains Nathanael's skepticism or doubt. Jesus recognizes that his doubt is sincere, for Nathanael is a person of integrity. "You are a true Israelite, in whom there is nothing false," says Jesus (1:47). Legitimate, open doubt or skepticism is not to be hidden, frowned upon, or denigrated. Rather, it is to be clearly addressed by testimony and evidence, the very thing that the Gospel of John presents. Second, Jesus reveals something that surprises the skeptic. Jesus shows Nathanael his extended knowledge: "I saw you while you were still under the fig tree before Philip called you" (1:48). This statement contains several clues. First, the evidence that Jesus confronts Nathanael with is that he was seen by someone with extensive knowledge, knowledge greater than accessible to Nathanael. This knowledge could only be had by someone special, someone divine, someone with a lineage that extended beyond the pedigree of a poor carpenter from a no-account

This encomium or tribute stands in opposition to the views of Jews who, viperously, see Jesus as from Nazareth and Galilee (1:46; 7:27–29), the son of a peasant Joseph, uneducated (7:35), demon-possessed and a sinner (8:48; 9:16); nothing in comparison with Abraham (8:57); dying an ignorable death at the hands of the Romans.

42. The New Testament uses two forms of the word of being from Nazareth. Mark and Luke use Ναζαρηνός, whereas Matthew, Mark, Luke, John, and Acts use Ναζωραῖος. Whereas the first clearly designates coming from Nazareth, commentators dispute the significance of the latter. Ultimately, the two are interchangeable, but whether something more is signified in the latter case is unclear. See Wallace, "Nazarene," 499–50.

43. "Nathanael's expostulation at the idea that the Messiah could come from Nazareth is comprehensible, for Nazareth was utterly insignificant; it has no mention in the OT, the Talmud or Midrash, or in any contemporary pagan writings. . . . The residence of Jesus in Nazareth is akin to his birth in a stable; it is part of the offense of the incarnation. Philip therefore can only reply, 'Come and see'; the answer to the offense of the incarnation is Jesus himself" (Beasley-Murray, *John*, 26).

town. It calls forth from Nathanael an admission to that very fact. Second, it connects Jesus's identity with the Old Testament prophecy of the coming Messiah. Jesus says that he saw Nathanael while "under a fig tree." "This alludes to Zech 3:10, . . . 'In that day, says the LORD of hosts, a man will call his neighbor under a vine and under a fig tree.' In that context, being called under a fig tree marked the arrival of the 'Branch' (Zech 3:8), who was understood to be the Davidic Messiah foretold in the Law (Gen 49:10) and the Prophets (Jer 23:6; 33:16; Zech 3:8; 6:12–13), just as Philip had said."[44] This connection elicits from Nathanael the recognition that this man from Nazareth was indeed more than a country rabbi; he was the Messiah, worthy of the messianic titles Son of God and King of Israel (1:49).[45] The skeptical, true Israelite[46] encounters the knowing King of Israel.[47]

The testimony John gives us through Nathanael concerns Jesus's pedigree. The theme of divinity that the Prologue announces begins to be confirmed in the subsequent text. He is the Son of God identified in the Prologue (1:18) and repeated by the voice in the desert, John the Baptizer (1:34). Jesus likewise comes from the royal Davidic line, an affirmation that prepares the way for the future messianic claims, though for John it is only alluded to (7:42), so that any earthly Davidic connection plays a secondary role to Jesus's heavenly connection with his Father. Jesus's kingship becomes a centerpiece at the end of his life when interviewed by Pilate and designated king on the cross.

The final, matching piece of testimony comes from Jesus himself, who announces with the affirmation, "Truly, truly," indicating the great significance of what follows. Indirectly invoking Jacob's experience with a ladder stretched between heaven (the royal throne) and earth, whereby the supreme Monarch receives and sends out his messengers to carry out his missions (Gen 28:12–13), Jesus prophesies, "You will see heaven open, and the angels of God ascending and descending on the Son of Man" (1:51).[48] The statement is a complex riddle whose meaning is variously interpreted. Jesus seems to suggest that through their experiences, the disciples ("you" is in the

44. Koester, *Symbolism*, 40.

45. This same movement, from human to prophet and from messiah to divine is found in chapters 7 to 9 (7:14–24, 25–52; 8:12–30; 9:11, 17, 35–38).

46. Culpepper sees Nathanael also as a representative figure, representing true Israel (*Anatomy*, 123).

47. "Jesus's reply that before Philip had called him he had seen Nathanael under the fig tree has led to considerable scholarly speculation. Perhaps the most plausible meaning relates to the parallels in Strack and Billerbeck concerning the Jewish custom of rabbis studying the law under a vine, fig tree, or olive tree. Such a custom was a picture of rabbinic seriousness in the study of Scripture and reflected the expectation of God's action in history. Jesus's reply thus served both to confirm Jesus's earlier evaluation concerning Nathanael as being an authentic Israelite and indicated that Nathanael was indeed speaking to the one who embodied Israel's hopes in Scripture" (Borchert, *John 1–11*, 148).

48. The order of ascending and descending here, replicating that of Genesis, suggests that in the vision the Son of Man will be in heaven, given power and worship, as depicted in Dan 7:13–14 (Loader, *Jesus*, 255–56).

plural, moving the discussion beyond Nathanael) will witness God's favor on Jesus, who comes from and will return to heaven.[49] Since the opening of heaven signifies revelation (Ezek 1:1), "[t]he expression [they will see the heavens opened] then is a figurative way of saying that Jesus will reveal heavenly things, a thought that is developed throughout this Gospel."[50] However, more might be in view, especially since it follows Nathanael's affirmation of kingship. Insofar as it anticipates the Father giving Jesus as the Son of God and Son of Man authority to judge (5:25–27), it echoes Daniel's vision (7:13–14), where one like the Son of Man enters into the presence of the Ancient of Days and is "given authority, glory, and sovereign power over all." Not only will "[t]he blessings of the saving sovereignty be poured out through him,"[51] but the theme of Jesus revealing the glory of the Father and his own glory courses throughout the Gospel. With this testimony from the skeptic and Jesus's enhancement, we get the whole panoply about Jesus, divine yet human, intimately connected to, serving and serviced by heaven, his origin.

Jesus's emphasis on Nathanael's integrity, situated in contrast to the duplicity that characterized his ancestor Jacob,[52] now serves John's purpose, to fully identify and reliably bear witness to this multidimensional Jesus. Jacob was untrustworthy, deceiving his father Isaac, cheating his brother Esau out of his inheritance, surreptitiously stealing his uncle's best flocks, even wrestling with God. Nathanael is otherwise. Even though Nathanael was a skeptic, because of his integrity we can trust his testimony about who Jesus is. This promise of revelation extends beyond Nathanael to all disciples, for the "you" of 1:51 is plural: all will be able to experience this heavenly revealed Son of Man and testify to the experience.

The other piece of the testimony to be noted is John's emphasis on seeing. Testimony does not develop out of thin air but arises from experience and encounter. Encounter runs through all the temporal modes. From Philip it is in the present, "Come and see." The experience is immediate, firsthand. The testimony is also from the past; Jesus affirms that he saw Nathanael before Nathanael ever encountered him. Being seen in the past assists in bringing about present faith. Seeing is also future. Nathanael's encounter with Jesus will lead to even greater events, where what Nathanael currently sees will be exceeded by further revelation to all about who Jesus is.[53] Jesus thus confirms to Nathanael the significance of his testimony.

49. Neyrey, *Gospel*, 101.

50. Michaels, *Gospel of John*, 150.

51. Beasley-Murray, *John*, 28.

52. Craig Keener (*John*, 19) suggests that Jesus, in referring to Nathanael as an Israelite without deceit, is making a contrast with Israel (Jacob), a man of deceit (Gen 27:35; 31:26), who was not at peace sitting under a fig tree (Mic 4:4) but worrying how to deal with the brother he deceived.

53. "The vision which is promised to the disciples is not conceived as the vision of heavenly beings, but as the vision in faith of his δόξα (glory) (1:14)" (Bultmann, *Gospel of John*, 106).

## THE TESTIMONY OF SKEPTICS: THOMAS

The skeptic that brackets the other end of Jesus's ministry is the apostle Thomas. John connects Thomas with three resurrection accounts, two actual and one by way of teaching. In the first, having to do with Lazarus, Jesus wants to return to Bethany near Jerusalem to visit Lazarus, whose death Jesus reports to the disciples (11:14). The disciples express skepticism about this travel venture. Since Lazarus is dead, they see little point in going to visit him, especially after they waited two days. (According to Jewish custom, the deceased were buried on the same day they died, if possible.) Further, the disciples expect more trouble, and their skepticism is well-grounded. The last time they were in Jerusalem Jews tried to seize Jesus (10:39) and stone him (11:8). However, in the end, Thomas expresses his willingness to take a chance on Jesus and encourages his fellow disciples ("let us") to accompany Jesus. Nevertheless, Thomas appears not to entertain great enthusiasm or optimism for the venture—"that we may die with him" (11:16).[54]

In the second encounter with Thomas, Jesus speaks about going away and that they know the way to where he is going. Perplexed, Thomas asks a perfectly natural question from an earthly point of view: "How can we know the way if we don't know where you are going?" (14:5). Thomas is skeptical about all this talk about places and the way to the places and would like something said clearer. Jesus's responding riddle—"I am the way, the truth, and the life" (14:6),where he has the heavenly viewpoint and his resurrection in view, is filled with double meaning and is no clearer than the initial statement. Jesus is going to the Father, and our way to the Father is through him. To know the way, you first must know the person who makes the way, and if you know the person who makes the way, you know the goal. "If you really knew me, you would know my Father as well" (14:7). Philip's response (14:8), "Show us the Father and that will be enough," correctly indicates that this teaching is very obscure and difficult. Neither of them has read the Prologue and hence cannot fully understand that "Jesus is in the Father, and the Father is in him" (14:10). Jesus is the Father's revealer, and only through knowing Jesus will they understand the way to the Father. Thomas displays a lack of understanding, although without the Preface and knowledge of the subsequent events we would be as ignorant, for we too would possess only the earthly viewpoint.

In our third encounter with Thomas, we find that for some unstated reason he missed Jesus's first resurrection appearance to the disciples. The other disciples reported what they experienced, but Thomas is dubious. Resurrection is not part of his

---

54. Michaels interprets "die with him" as dying not with Jesus (see Beasley-Murray, *John*, 189) but with Lazarus. "His is not a counsel of faith but of unbelief and despair" (Michaels, *Gospel of John*, 625). Nothing is subsequently said in the story either about the disciples or their believing. Yet, why would Thomas think that they would die with Lazarus? There is no hint of such in the text, whereas there is a reference to attempts to stone Jesus (11:8). Only after Lazarus's resurrection is Lazarus's life in danger (12:10). Perhaps Michaels means the sentence to say, "We will be dead like Lazarus."

framework, despite his experience of Jesus raising Lazarus and Jesus's prior intimations to Thomas and the others, veiled as they were, that he would be raised from the dead. Thus, Thomas reiterates the skeptic's point that he must see and touch for himself to believe. "Unless I see the nail marks in his hand and put my finger where the nails were and put my hand in his side, I will not believe it" (20:25). He relies on his personal experience to tailor his believing. When Jesus revisits[55] the disciples a week later he expresses no criticism of Thomas and his skepticism. Apparently, Jesus takes his doubt as legitimate, especially since Thomas leaves open the possibility of believing. Thomas does not say he will not believe, only that he has conditions. His skepticism is not dogmatic, refusing to see and assess the evidence. Although his friends testify to the risen Jesus, Thomas wants to see for himself the evidence for this radical claim about Jesus and his resurrection. Jesus willingly exposes the evidence—his wounds—to Thomas's sight and touch, without criticism, embarrassment, or hesitation. Thomas replies with his testimony of faith about the identity of Jesus: "My Lord and my God" (20:28). Thomas, once a skeptic, now testifies to the deity of the person he has accompanied, watched, and dialogued with. The appellation for which Jews wanted to stone Jesus, Thomas affirms with devoted conviction. The risen Jesus is not Lord and God in the abstract, but *his* Lord and *his* God in the most personal sense. We might think Thomas slow to incorporate resurrection into his worldview, but Thomas's skepticism is not unique. Many today, including people raised in the Christian faith and tradition, are Thomases: "I will not believe unless I see it for myself." We stand in the empiricists' lineage: believing requires seeing or touching. Incorporating resurrection into our worldview is difficult; we have not experienced or witnessed resurrections, let alone touched the resurrected.

John writes to a generation for whom touching and seeing Jesus are no longer possible. Thus, he has Jesus address readers and listeners who are not and will not be in Thomas's position to see and touch Jesus's physical wounds. These future skeptics or potential believers must rely on the testimony of others who have seen and whose witness John presented. John writes his Book of Testimony to assist them to come or hold on to their faith. Jesus says that in believing without their own sensory evidence but on the testimony of others, they too will be blessed (20:29).[56] Yet this is not all; believers who cannot see or touch will have within themselves the powerful witness of the Holy Spirit who will convict of the sin of unbelieving, assure righteousness because of Jesus's departure to the Father, and guarantee Satan's judgment (16:7–10). For Thomas and Nathanael, believing arose not merely from the testimony of others; their personal encounter with the Messiah and risen Lord, the all-knowing and

55. John reports that the disciples locked the doors because they were afraid (20:19, 26). Since Jesus is the door (10:7–9), he does not need doors to enter closed rooms occupied by shaking disciples.

56. [T]hose who have not "seen" . . . [have] a faith called forth by the word of the Gospel; but it is none the worse for that, for their trust in the Lord revealed through the Word is of special worth in his eyes. Their commendation is set forth in a beatitude, a declaration of happiness in the sight of God that conveys a revelation" (Beasley-Murray, *John*, 386).

wounded one, brought them to believing. God does not leave us without testimony when Jesus and the witnessing first generation pass off the scene; our encounter with Jesus through the witness of the Holy Spirit brings us to the position that we too may say, "My Lord and my God."

In sum, skeptics brackets John's testimonial account. These two disciples represent those who have doubts about Jesus. Skepticism is not denigrated, denied, or devalued. Indeed, John marshals the testimony of the skeptics for the skeptic.[57] He writes for the honest, open skeptic, the one who is willing to listen to the truthful testimony, the one who ultimately, when he or she comes to faith, will encounter the same Jesus as God's revelation that these initially skeptical witnesses Nathanael and Thomas experienced. Accepting testimony requires trust,[58] and John assures us that none are more trustworthy than his skeptical witnesses.

## OTHER TESTIMONY

As we will see in chapter 5, Jesus himself testifies about who he is and his function or mission. However, he also recognizes that according to the Law (Deut 19:15), self-testimony is insufficient; it requires confirmatory testimony (5:31).[59] Jesus appeals to confirmatory testimony given by the Baptizer and witnessed by his audience. However, although he realizes the significance and persuasive power of human testimonials to others, he believes that they do not seal the deal (5:36). Testimony such as given by the Baptizer and others is merely human. Thus, Jesus points to even more reliable, weightier, and authoritative testimony. Even if religious Jews reject Jesus's self-testimony and human testimony, given their religious beliefs about God they should not question this additional testimony.

For starters, Jews need only look at what Jesus does to see who he is. "The very works that the Father has given me to finish, the works I am doing, testify that the Father has sent me" (5:36). For Jesus, his signs are more than mere wonders. As

57. Matthew likewise presents skepticism among the followers (Matt 28:17).

58. "An irreducible feature of testimony as a form of human utterance is that it asks to be trusted. This need not mean that it asks to be trusted uncritically, but it does mean that testimony should not be treated as credible only to the extent that it can be independently verified. . . . Trusting testimony is not an irrational act of faith that leaves critical rationality aside; it is, on the contrary, the rationally appropriate way of responding to authentic testimony" (Bauckham, *Eyewitnesses*, 5).

59. Brown (*Gospel i–xii*, 223) writes that the issue in Deuteronomy is prosecutorial, specifically concerning witnesses needed to identify one accused of a crime, whereas Jesus is speaking from the perspective of the defense, confirming testimony to his identity. Bekken (*Lawsuit*, 137, 122) notes that the wider application is "common throughout the Hebrew Bible, the Second Temple literature, and the New Testament, and Philo may show that it is reasonable." A parallel, found in Philo, assists our understanding that the "two or three rule" applies broadly in judicial cases. "Philo's general and non-specific application of the prohibition of the single testimony, recalling the statement in Deut 19:15 LXX that '*any* matter' or '*any* word' should be established on the evidence of two or three witnesses, provides a cultural context for a corresponding application of Deut 19:15 that is reflected in John 5:31–39 and 8:12–17."

*sig*nificant, they point beyond the miraculous events themselves, testifying to both Jesus's identity and his mission. His identity is to be the Son of the Father, sent from him; his function or mission is to reveal the Father and to have or give life (5:26). As Nicodemus affirms, only someone connected with or coming from God could perform these deeds (3:2).

Since he is doing what his Father does and has given him to do (5:19, 36), he has a second testifier. "The Father who sent me has himself testified concerning me" (5:37). For Jesus, there could be no more reliable testifier, no more complementary testament, than that of the Father to the Son.[60] The Father authenticated his work by placing on him "his seal of approval" (6:27).[61] However, he notes, the Jewish leaders missed the Father's testimony, for they failed to hear his voice, did not see his form, and did not have his word dwell in them. They heard thunder but did not recognize the voice or the Light (12:28–29, 46). It is the Baptizer's unique *experience* of seeing the Spirit come upon Jesus, hearing God's voice, and listening to the words of identification (1:32–34; Luke 3:22) that brought him both to believe that Jesus is the Son of God and to testify about him.

However, even if the Jewish leaders missed the voice and did not see God, they at least had the Scriptures that testify about him (5:39). The scribes and Pharisees were professional Scripture students; the Scriptures contained the Law, and the Law, they believed, would give them eternal life. However, they missed the testimony of the Scriptures—the written word—to Jesus. The word simply was not a living part of them (5:38–40). The disciples, on the contrary, believed the Scriptures and tallied the teachings of Jesus with them (2:22). Jesus here does not state specifically to which Scriptures he refers. Elsewhere John gives us possible clues, but often these are little more than vague references.[62] Nonetheless, it is the Evangelist's opinion that if the Jewish leaders had read the Scriptures carefully, they would have seen the Messiah revealed in them and recognized the Messiah when they encountered him.

---

60. "Both Philo and the Johannine Jesus accept the legal rule of the prohibition of a single testimony and the criterion of multiple witnesses embedded in Deut 19:15 as a valid testimony. In a controversy with other Jews, however, Philo maintains that only God was capable of giving a self-authenticating testimony, without coming in conflict with the ruling about two or three witnesses. This argument supplies a Jewish context for the point made by John that Jesus could testify to himself because of his divine origin. Accordingly, both God and Jesus might present valid testimonies in compliance with the legal requirement of at least two witnesses to substantiate the claims made by Jesus in his own defense" (Bekken, *Lawsuit*, 121).

61. "Prominent individuals had distinctive marks on their signet rings, which they would press into hot-wax seals on the outside of document to attest that they were witnesses to the execution of the document.... Attestation could be figuratively conceived as a seal" (Keener, *John*, 33).

62. John 7:38 possibly correlates with Zech 14:8; John 13:18 with Ps 41:9; John 19:24 with Ps 22:18; John 19:36–37 with Exod 12:46 or Ps 34:20 and Zech 12:10 (See Michaels, *Gospel of John*, 465–67 and 975–78).

Even if they missed all this—the divine works, the divine sender, the divine word[63]—since they were experts on Moses and the Law, at least they should have recognized Moses's testimony. If they believed Moses, they would believe Jesus, "for he wrote about me" (5:46; 1:45). Again, unfortunately, no specific texts are cited. What one gets from John is that the Old Testament testimony is not so much to be found in specific passages as in the general tenor and witness of the sources that grounded their faith. Seeing that God is hidden, they should be receptive to the one who reveals him.

Finally, Jesus appeals to the Spirit, sent by the Father and by himself, who will testify about him (15:26). Again, John emphasizes the trustworthiness of the testimony to Jesus, for the Spirit's testimony has the character of truth, in contrast to the lying testimony of the devil (8:44).[64] The testimony of the Spirit, however, is somewhat limited since the world cannot accept the Spirit or his testimony (14:17). It will be a personal, private, internal testimony to his disciples, to those who had been with and had known (experienced) him. Yet this Spirit has a public mission, proving Jesus's case[65] by convicting the world about sin (they failed to believe in Jesus), righteousness (having completed his mission, Jesus goes to the Father), and judgment on the untruth (16:8–11). The Spirit's testimony will become public to the world through the testimony of the disciples (15:27), which reiterates the mission of the Fourth Gospel.

For John, readers should attend to Jesus's deeds and realize that the deeds are consonant with what they find in the Scriptures and would expect the Father to be doing. Readers should attend to the prophetic tradition and realize that the Baptizer fulfills that long tradition and in listening to him believe what he openly announced to them. The power of these additional testimonies is not in their individuality but in their coalescence. They unite and bring to bear the message of the Old Testament and the Spirit as preparing for the coming of God among them in word and deed. In this the hearers do the work of God: "to believe in the one he has sent" (6:29).

## THE TESTIMONY OF THE BELOVED DISCIPLE

The reliability of all the testimonies in the Evangelist's Gospel depends, ultimately, on the reliability of the Beloved Disciple who records them and whose book for the most part is his testimony ("This is the disciple who testifies to these things and who wrote them down" 21:24).[66] Hence, his reliability and that of his testimony also must

63. For a discussion of the possible relations holding between these three, see Bekken, *Lawsuit*, 125–26.

64. Although elsewhere in John the Spirit is referred to, only in these three passages (14:17; 15:26; 16:13), where testimony is in view, is he called the Spirit of Truth.

65. Bultmann, *Gospel of John*, 564.

66. The complementarity of the Epilogue (ch. 21) to the Prologue (1:1–18) is striking. "The Prologue goes back in time to creation, so the Epilogue previews the future mission of the disciples. . . . The time projected by the Epilogue runs to the parousia (future coming) of Jesus. Its last words, in v. 23, are Jesus's words 'until I come,' corresponding at the other end of time to the first words of the

be vouchsafed. Thus, at the very end of the Gospel we are provided an attestation to his reliability from a "we" whose identity is not given: "We know that his testimony is true" (21:24). This is the second time the testimony of the Beloved Disciple is affirmed. At the crucifixion we get the other attestation. "The man who saw it has given testimony, and his testimony is true. He knows that he tells the truth, and he testifies so that you also may believe" (19:35, presuming that "the man who saw it" is the Beloved Disciple). All the testimony noted in this chapter goes for naught if the testifier of the testimonies cannot be trusted.

Commentators debate the identity of the "we." To some it indicates the hand of an editor who put the finishing touches on the Gospel here and maybe elsewhere. This editor is sometimes identified with the so-called Johannine school, individuals who follow the narrator and assume his style and mission. Richard Bauckham suggests another option. He notes that referring to oneself in the third person was "in accordance with the best and regular historiographic practice," found in such notables as Thucydides, Xenophon, Polybius, Julius Caesar, and Josephus.[67] By means of this convention, the author can distinguish two ways in which he relates to the text, as the author or narrator and as a participant in the story he tells. "The use of the third person keeps the author *as author* hidden behind the narrative as he or she is in the rest of the narrative."

The Beloved Disciple's testimony is vouchsafed not only by the "we" but also by his position as an intimate of Jesus and companion of the lead disciple Simon Peter. Bauckham[68] suggests three criteria that the Beloved Disciple satisfies to be accredited as trustworthy. First, he is the intimate of Jesus, reclining on Jesus's breast (ἐν τῷ κόλπῳ τοῦ Ἰησοῦ, 13:23) at the final meal and trusted by the other disciples to obtain critical information (13:25). John's language, which parallels the intimacy of the Son, who is in the Father's breast (εἰς τὸν κόλπον τοῦ πατρός), with the Father (1:18), establishes the Beloved Disciple's authoritative credentials, endorses his revelatory testimony, and empowers him to make Jesus known (20:31). Second, he is present at key points in the salvific parts of Jesus's story: the supper when Jesus identifies Judas as the betrayer, the trial (if the mysterious person in 18:15–16 is the Beloved Disciple), the cross of crucifixion, the first disciple to the empty tomb, and the commissioning of Peter to serve the church. Third, if the Beloved Disciple is to be included among the larger group of disciples (more than the Twelve), he too does not fully comprehend the significance of the events immediately (13:28), but later recalls them and understands what they mean (2:17, 22; 12:16). They are brought to mind (14:26). In this he may be the most spiritually perceptive of the disciples, for in the role of narrator he adds asides that, coming from a post-resurrection perspective, display that he now recognizes the "from above" significance of what transpired. Like the promised Spirit,

---

prologue: 'In the beginning' (1:1)" (Bauckham, *Eyewitnesses*, 364).

67. Bauckham, *Eyewitnesses*, 393–94.

68. Bauckham, *Eyewitnesses*, 396–99; 556.

though clearly not the Spirit, he remains with the disciples, teaches and reminds them of what Jesus said, declares by testimony what he witnessed, and glorifies Jesus by his gospel word. We might add, fourth, that he notes being expressly trusted by Jesus and others, for to him Jesus entrusts his mother (19:26–27). He, along with Simon Peter, is the person Mary Magdalene entrusts with the important, enigmatic message that Jesus's body disappeared. He is the trusted companion of Simon Peter, confiding at the last meal and running together to Jesus's tomb. And he is the one Jesus entrusted with a final mission (21:24). The Evangelist uses all these instances to strengthen his case for the trustworthiness of the narrator and his Gospel testimony.

For those—the "we" (21:24b)—who testify to the reliability of the Gospel writer, their confidence must have grown out of their experience with the Beloved Disciple. In this way, it parallels the basis of the testimony of the Beloved Disciple himself, who claimed to have witnessed not only key events and received the testimonials but above all Jesus himself. But can we trust the "we"? The reliability of the testimonies goes back to and relies on the Spirit, for the Spirit "will guide you into all truth. He will not speak on his own; he will speak only what he hears, and he will tell you what is yet to come. He will bring glory to me by taking from what is mine and making it known to you" (16:13–14). Ultimately, the most critical testimony to Jesus's identity and his mission and function comes from the Spirit, and those who would believe need to attune themselves to the voice of the Spirit. In effect, the entire Book of Testimony rests on the promise of the coming of the Spirit and the Spirit's action to remind of what Jesus said.

## CONCLUSION

These testimonies have much in common. For the most part, the testifiers are named, not anonymous. Naming a testifier increases the credibility of the testimony. They testify from the experience they have with Jesus. They see the Spirit come upon him. They hear him tell them things about themselves that an ordinary person would not know. They see him demonstrate his power by raising the dead and healing the sick. They see and touch him, wounded but risen. They come from all walks of life: baptizing prophets, women, doubters, members of the inner circle, hesitant members of the council (Nicodemus). Some are people whose testimony would be suspect to the religious rulers but being ordinary folk might be more acceptable to ordinary people. Ultimately, however, the weightier testimony comes from God himself and his word. God, his Scriptures, and the prophet Moses would be more esoteric to the laity but should have been more familiar and acceptable to the religious leaders.

They testify that Jesus is worthier than we are, prior to us in time and significance, the Lamb of God who is the final sacrifice, the promised Messiah of hope, the Son of God who has come into the world, the King of Israel, the one who knows everything about us, and ultimately for believers, our Lord and God. He is the one foreseen and foretold in the Old Testament Scriptures, hidden yet known to those who searched them. He has come to take away our sin and the sin of the world, to baptize us with the Spirit, and to give us qualitative and quantitative (eternal) life.

In the end, the success of the testimonials is in doubt; the results are mixed. In some cases, testimony brings about believing, in others not. The Evangelist realizes this, for he has given us the option to believe or reject. He knows that Jesus's sayings are difficult and that many who once believed will fall away. However, those who come to believe or remain steadfast in their believing, although they have not seen or touched, will be blessed with the fruits of believing: eternal life. This is the message that John sends through his Book of Testimony to us modern readers as well, some of whom will believe and become disciples while others will remain dubious and skeptical. However, the evangelist does not leave the evidence for his thesis here; Jesus self-identifies. We turn to this in the next chapter.

## QUESTIONS FOR REFLECTION AND DISCUSSION

1. Whose testimony have you relied on in your experience? Is this similar to the way that the author relies on testimony in the Gospel?

2. Why does the Gospel begin with the testimony of John the Baptizer rather than with someone else?

3. What is the common testimonial theme of the first five testifiers?: (John the Baptizer, Andrew, Philip, Nathanael, and the Samaritan woman.) Why are these testimonies significant in the Jewish context and for John's thesis about Jesus's identity?

4. What does the fact that women were chosen as testifiers tell us about the author? Might that affect how the Gospel is understood, interpreted, and valued today? What is the role and acceptance of women as testifiers in your religious tradition?

5. Medieval Christians saw Mary and Martha as embodying two different lifestyles that Christians could pursue: the contemplative and the active, and that we should choose between the two. How do Mary and Martha embody these lifestyles, and are they incompatible? (If you are interested, you can find this discussion in Christine de Pizan, *The Treasure of the City of Ladies* I6).

6. Why are the testimonies of the Samaritan woman and Mary Magdalene so important and powerful?

7. Why does John introduce the testimony of the sceptics Nathanael and Thomas? How does Jesus react to their skepticism? What does being skeptical add to their testimony? How do you react to people who are skeptical about Jesus and the Christian faith?

8. Why is certifying the testimony of the Beloved Disciple, as John does at the end of the Gospel, so important to the Gospel of John?

9. How does John see the Old Testament Scriptures testifying about Jesus? Why would that be important in the time and culture of the author?

10. Which of the testimonies presented in this chapter do you find most convincing? Why?

11. If you were going to testify to someone about your encounter with Jesus or the gospel that Jesus taught, what might you say this encounter shows about Jesus's identity and mission? Does your testimony attract people to believing in Jesus? Explain.

12. What kind of testimony might the Pharisees have accepted? What kind of testimony might twenty-first-century hearers of the Jesus story accept as providing convincing evidence of who Jesus is and his mission? What might your friends say about the testimony stories in John?

CHAPTER FIVE

# Book of Identity

JOHN OPENS HIS GOSPEL with the theme of identity. Jesus's first words are, "What are you looking for?" (1:38). John likewise closes his Gospel with the same words, this time to Mary Magdalene (20:15). John presumes that we, like Jesus's listeners, are looking for something, something that has been a long time in coming and foreshadowed by the prophets. Philip identifies this "something": "Show us the Father" (14:8). To this Jesus quizzically responds, "I have been with you all this time and you still haven't seen the Father. Knowing me is knowing the Father" (14:8–10). We are, John intimates, looking for, desiring, God, who paradoxically searches for us (10:16), and the burden of the Gospel of John is to reveal him to us.[1]

Throughout the Fourth Gospel, the people and the Jewish leaders express deep puzzlement about this man from Galilee, whose parents and brothers they know but who seems different. Two questions repeatedly surface. The first is, "Who are you?" They ask the paralytic: who was this man who told you to pick up your mat and walk (5:11). The Jews query among themselves, "Is this not Jesus, the son of Joseph, whose father and mother we know?" (6:42). The people query, "Who is this fellow? Isn't this the man they are trying to kill?" (7:28). Or again, "Where is your father?" "Who are you?" (8:19, 25). "Tell us plainly if you really are the Messiah" (10:24). The second concerns his works: "What are you doing, healing on the Sabbath?" "How can a sinner do such signs?" (9:16). People come to see Jesus because of his signs, to which the Pharisees respond, "This is getting us nowhere. Look how the whole world has gone after him" (12:19). To not only understand the thrust of the Gospel but to also comprehend the context of bewilderment in which Jesus functioned, we must empathize with those who listened to Jesus, observed what he did, and wondered about his identity and mission. And we must hear the claims about himself and his mission that Jesus made in response.

---

1. Painter (*Quest*) portrays the Gospel, especially the first part, in terms of the motif of a quest for the Messiah.

The questions the contemporaries of Jesus and the Evangelist asked do not differ from those asked today. "Who was Jesus?" "What did Jesus really teach and do?" and "Why did Jesus teach and act this way?" still resound. The suggested answers are as diverse today as in the first century. They range from "We don't really know," "A strange self-promoter," to "Someone created by early Christians"; from a deluded rabbi and crazy peripatetic to a prophet figure and divine savior. For some, Jesus has a special aura or mystique; for others, he does not differ from a host of charismatic figures around whom people did and still do construct religious stories and religions. Hence, the question or puzzle of Jesus's identity is as relevant today as it ever was.

In chapter 3 we looked at the deeds or signs Jesus employed to direct the attention of those around him—disciples, bewildered onlookers, and antagonistic religious leaders alike—to understanding his identity. In chapter 4 we looked at how John reports that people testified about Jesus. In this chapter we will consider what Jesus says about himself. John tells us that his Gospel is written so that we might believe that Jesus is the Messiah, the Son of God, and have eternal life through that believing. The signs and works John presents help listeners and readers, but they are culturally ambiguous and need interpretation. To assist his audience, John reports Jesus's self-testimony regarding his identity and function. Jesus's self-witness has the last word.[2] However, Jesus's understanding and presentation of his identity and function are complex, couched in and enriched by metaphors. John brings out this unique identity and function in his Gospel by his use of the statement "I am" (ἐγώ εἰμί).

> In the Greek the personal subject of the verb is not normally expressed: the form of the verb makes clear what the subject is. But if it is desired to emphasize the subject, then the appropriate pronoun may be used. What makes this so important in John is that we find a similar usage in the Greek translation of the Old Testament. . . . It was a form of speech that was not much used in ordinary conversation or writing, but it seemed appropriate for the words of God. The point of all this is that when Jesus used the "I AM" construction he was speaking in the style of deity.[3]

John presents "I ams" in two ways. In one type, of which there are seven instances in the Gospel, the subject and verb are followed by a predicate that enriches the subject by presenting the nature and functions of Jesus. Jesus affirms, I am the bread of life; I am the light of the world; I am the door; I am the good shepherd; I am the way, the truth, and the life; I am the resurrection and the life; and I am the vine. In each case, the predicate expresses something about the "I," about Jesus. As we shall see, running through all these predicative uses of "I am" is an affirmation of Jesus's identity, enriched by a metaphor well known to his hearers, coupled with the claim

2. Painter, *Quest*, 20.

3. Morris, *Jesus*, 107.

that he is the source of life (1:3–4), the very points John tells us he intends to make in the entire Gospel (20:30–31). We refer to this as the predicative use of "I am."

In the second type of I am statements, the "I am" stands by itself, without a predicate. In this case, John apparently wants us to see Jesus as anticipated in the Prologue: He is with God and he is God (1:1–2). The usage derives from Exod 3:14, where Yahweh similarly identifies himself to Moses. Jesus repeats it, and as we have noted, when John engages in repetition, he emphasizes an important point that he wants his readers to notice and remember. The reaction of those who hear Jesus's assertion also shows us that John thinks that, to a significant enough extent, they get the point of the "I am" claim, although with varying degrees of understanding. For Jesus's contemporaries, Jesus's claim to be the "I am" was both ambiguously outrageous and unambiguously blasphemous. We will first consider the seven usages of the predicative sense of "I am" and then turn to reflect on the non-predicative usage.

## I AM THE BREAD OF LIFE (6:35, 41)

In the first of the seven "I ams" (ἐγώ εἰμί), Jesus identifies himself as the bread of life (chapter 6), the very staple of their existence. Passover is near, and knowing its symbolism, Jesus begins to anticipate his death. Having fed the large crowd that followed him on the mountainside where food was unavailable, Jesus disappears. When the fed crowd discovers that Jesus is gone, they return by boats to Capernaum, from where they started. There they discover that Jesus has returned from his respite on the mountain. They wonder how Jesus returned, but that is not the topic of their interest or discussion. Rather, the story focuses on Jesus's recognition that it is not Jesus they are looking for but his potential to supply more bread (6:26). The bread Jesus offers is not the temporal manna of ancient desert wandering but himself as the living bread. Employing his typical double meaning, Jesus contrasts the earthly physical bread that provides only temporary satisfaction with the heavenly eternal bread that gives eternal life (6:49–50). "Man does not live on bread alone but on every word that comes from the mouth of the LORD" (Deut 8:3).

Above, in chapter 3, we observed that John connects Jesus with Moses, the Lawgiver. "This imagery [of the bread referring to the Torah] seems to have been widespread and must be borne in mind through this chapter."[4] Through this metaphor, John reveals the superiority of Jesus, who gives eternal life, to the Torah, which by revealing sin binds us to death in that by our works we cannot keep the Law (Rom 7:7–11). Thus, the people search for how they can do the works of God and simultaneously keep the Law and be blessed with the manna of life. Jesus, the new Moses, replaces the multitudinous tasks prescribed by the Torah with the simple work (singular) of God, namely, to believe in Jesus as sent from God. The work of God is to accept him

---

4. Morris, *Jesus*, 30.

as their Messiah (6:27–29). The crowd cannot wrap their heads around Jesus's double meaning: it is not physical bread but the bread come from heaven, given to them by the Father, that gives real life. Jesus is the bread of life.

As the liberated Israelites murmured against Moses, so here Jews murmur against Jesus (6:42–43). John is not subtle, using the same word that the Septuagint employed, "murmur" or "grumble" (γογγύζω). As Moses had to endure the grumbling of the wilderness wanderers despite all he did for them, so does Jesus despite the signs he performs. The grumbling comes not only from the Jewish leaders but also from his disciples (6:61). John goes on to confirm that Jesus is the new Moses, giving life through bread. Whereas through Moses God provided manna for only forty years, the bread Jesus gives is eternal. The Torah, like the bread given in the wilderness, has a limited duration and is now replaced by Jesus, who will give his own flesh as bread to be eaten. The life given by the Torah had limited effectiveness, ultimately ending in death (6:58). All those who ate bread in the wilderness eventually perished; none except Joshua and Caleb entered the promised land. Indeed, the apostle Paul sees the Torah not only as bringing life but as bringing death, for through the Torah we know sin, whose wages are death (Rom 6 and 7). In contrast, the life Jesus brings is eternal.

To believe in Jesus the bread of life is not only to never hunger, it also is to never thirst (6:35). Here, too, Jesus is the new Moses, who brought water out of the rock (Exod 17:6; Num 20:8–11). However, the water Moses procured only temporarily slaked the wilderness wanderers' thirst; the water Jesus brings leads to eternal life, so that they never spiritually thirst again (4:13–14). Thus, Jesus provides the spiritual bread and spiritual water that are the basic elements that sustain life. These are not physical objects but his very life-giving words (6:68).

Jesus is not only the new Moses, he is also the new manna itself, for the bread that he gives is himself, his own flesh.[5] And how, the Jews wonder and argue among themselves, can Jesus give them his flesh (6:52–53)? Jesus continues his reply in provocative, perhaps eucharistic, metaphor,[6] which is rooted not only in the Exodus account, but in Isaiah who is both quoted in 6:45 and alluded to.

---

5. "John could well have preferred 'flesh' (over the word of eucharistic institution, 'body') because it belongs to the biblical language of sacrifice and because of the incarnational association that he had already given it in 1:14" (Bauckham, *Gospel of Glory*, 99).

6. Bauckham (*Gospel of Glory*, 96–97) suggests that the primary meaning of the text (though not its only meaning) is not an affirmation of the eucharistic rite, but the need to believe in (eat and drink) Jesus who will give his life for the world (6:51). Michaels (*Gospel of John*, 395) believes that the eucharistic dimension is later, part of the "reception history" (how the readers would have understood it), for those to whom Jesus was speaking, including the accompanying disciples, would not have recognized or known of a eucharistic meaning. "'The Jews' are confused by Jesus's reference to 'eating' him, and their confusion is hardly to be allayed by referring to a Christian ritual that did not yet exist. More likely, the sacramental or Eucharistic interpretation of the text belongs to the 'reception history' of the text rather than to the Gospel writer's intention (much less the intention of Jesus within the story!). The text should be read if possible from within the horizons of the dramatic confrontation being described at Capernaum . . . and to Christian readers after the fact" (*Gospel of John*, 396). However, Jesus frequently speaks about future events, like his being lifted up, that he foreknows or

There are a series of allusions to Isa 55:1–3 ('thirst . . . come . . . eat . . . bread . . . come to me . . . so that you may live') in verses 35, 37, 40, 44, 45, 47, 51, 54, 57, 58. The implied reading of this text from Isaiah is that, in contrast to the food and drink that cannot satisfy, God gives to those who come to him food and drink that truly sustain life. . . . Jesus here identifies himself not only with the bread of the Exodus text, but also as the divine speaker in v 55, who offers both food and drink to those who come to him.[7]

Without eating this new meal, "you have no life in you. . . . for my flesh is real food and my blood is real drink" (6:53). Eating his flesh and drinking his blood brings qualitative and quantitative eternal life. It is qualitative in that in *this* life the members will never "hunger" or be without what matters (6:35), for they will live in the Father and the Father in them. Because God dwells within them, they will live abundantly (6:57). It is quantitative in that God *will raise* them in the last day to live forever (6:39–40, 58). This first "I am," like the others to follow, addresses the *life-giving* function of Jesus. Believing in him moves those who partake from the old realm of death to the new covenant of life. Participating in him is fundamentally experiencing the gift of life.[8]

Jesus intends that Jews, along with us, be shocked by this saying.[9] For Jews of his day, as for unbelievers and even some believers in our day, the saying is troubling. His rhetorical question, "Does this offend you?" (6:61) shows the depth of dis-ease the Jews have with statements about drinking blood and cannibalism of the flesh (Lev 7:14; 7:26; Gen 9:4).[10] The latter was the extreme punishment, effected through their conquerors, for unfaithfulness (Lev 26:27–29; Deut 28:49–57), and as Jewish leaders, they could not see the need for any such punishment. Both the practice and the suggestion of the reason for it would be offensive. If we interpret the eating of his flesh and drinking of his blood as a metaphor for Jesus's death, that too is offensive, although in another way. As Paul puts it, it is the offense of the cross, where the innocent criminal is displayed to take on himself our sins (Gal 5:11).

Jesus's identity as the bread of life leads to the even more shocking claim that he is the Son of God—as if the monotheistic Yahweh could have children. Unless we listen to the radicalness of Jesus's claims, we cannot understand the depth and difficulty of choice that Jews faced when they encountered Jesus and his words in their

anticipates but of which his audience would have no comprehension.

7. Bauckham, *Gospel of Glory*, 96.

8. "Within the discourse, verse 51c makes the transition from the incarnation (Jesus as the bread that came down from heaven) to the cross (Jesus as the bread that he gives for the life of the world)" (Bauckham, *Gospel of Glory*, 97).

9. Bauckham (*Gospel of Glory*, 100) notes the parallel between Nicodemus's reaction to Jesus's suggestion of being reborn (3:4, 9) and that of the Jews (6:42, 52): "How can . . . ?" "It is notable that in both cases . . . the point at which Jesus apparently ceases to hope for comprehension from his auditors is the point at which he begins to speak of his death-and-exaltation" (100–101).

10. In ritual sacrifice, the flesh and blood were separated, used for different purposes (Lev 1:3–9).

own culture. We also cannot understand the depth and difficulty that many today in our scientific culture face with these very claims, that Jesus is divine, that he is one with God, and that he becomes incarnate as a human being. Yet for the Evangelist the choice remains: to reject Jesus means eternal death. It is to reject the life-giving food only to starve spiritually in the barren and waterless wilderness, where there are no other life-providing resources. To accept Jesus and his radical claims means eternal life, for only from him do we receive the life-giving bread and water.

The reaction to Jesus's self-identification is varied. On the one hand, the crowd fails to understand the double meanings of the terms Jesus uses and simply wants the bread.[11] They are willing to work for it, but the work of believing that Jesus is the Messiah proves much too difficult. The Jewish leaders are offended by the claim that Jesus is the bread from heaven, giving his flesh for us: "Who do you think you are?" (6:42). Many who became disciples likewise grumble over his claim to be the Son of Man who comes from heaven, sent by the Ancient of Days, with authority, glory, and sovereign power, to be worshiped (Dan 7:13). They abandon Jesus after this most difficult discourse; only a few remain because they see[12] that only this new Moses has the words of eternal life.

## I AM THE LIGHT OF THE WORLD (8:12; 9:5)

Jesus introduces the second "I am" statement in his discourse in the temple courts. At the Feast of the Tabernacles or Booths, he comes and announces that he is the light of the world. "Whoever follows me will not walk in darkness, but will have the light of life" (8:12). As in the first "I am" statement, Jesus's identity connects to life, a point anticipated in the Prologue where John identifies Jesus as the light of life. Jesus does not elaborate here on this theme of light, but his claim must have been striking since light played an important role in the ritual celebration of the Feast of Tabernacles.[13]

The rituals of the festival employed both water and light.

> Four huge Menorahs fitted out with wicks made from the worn-out garments
> of the priests illumined the entire temple area. Under them the celebrants
> danced a torch dance to the accompaniment of flute playing, and the Levites

---

11. "[T]he crowds come in response to the signs (6:2, 24, 26, 28, 30, 34). . . . John's treatment of the crowd lacks the hostility of his characterization of the Jews. The crowd represents that struggle of those who are open to believing, but neither the scriptures nor the signs lead them to authentic faith. They are the world God loves (3:16)" (Culpepper, *Anatomy*, 131–32).

12. For the importance of "seeing" in John, see Brown, *Gospel i–xii*, 501–3.

13. Morris notes that whereas "crowd" is mentioned eight times in chapter 7, it is not mentioned at all until 11:42. Thus, he suggests that the discussion was held not with the people at large but with his opponents, who are interested in the issue of testimony, and after the Feast itself, perhaps the next day (Morris, *Gospel*, 386).

chanted the Psalms of Ascent (120–34), one each on the fifteen steps that led down from the court of Israelites to the Court of the Women.[14]

> There is dispute as to the number of nights on which the illumination took place, but [no dispute] as to the fact that at the close of the festival [the illumination] did not [take place]. In the absence of the lights Jesus's claim to be the Light would stand out the more impressively. In favor of this view is also the fact that the candelabra were lit in the Court of the Women, the most frequented part of the Temple, and the very place in which Jesus delivered his address.[15]

In effect, Jesus's contrast between light and darkness would provide a stark, emphatic saying against the visual background of the ritual, where torches lighted the path while beyond lurked darkness. He boldly proclaims to be the two foci of the celebration, the source of eternal life-giving water (7:37) and the darkness-removing light of life (8:12).[16]

Chapter 8 continues John's connection of Jesus with Moses. In chapter 6 Jesus connects bread with manna in the wilderness. Here we might surmise that he connects light with the pillar of fire that guided the Israelites in the wilderness at night (Exod 13:21). Just as God provides Jesus as the manna bread, God gives Jesus as the light of the world. The Father not only furnishes the light but bears witness to the light (8:19). We are to follow the saving light as the Israelites did in the desert.

It is also significant that Jesus does not limit his light to Jews but is the light of the world. Here John ties together two themes from the Prologue, light and world (κόσμος), each with its double meaning. The light is both physical, highlighted by the immediate surroundings of the festival night, and spiritual, in that the light Jesus brings results in true life. Similarly, the world is both that which the Word created and the world of people, both Jews and gentiles, into which Jesus was born and to which he attends. John moves beyond the particularism of Jesus's immediate hearers in the courts of the temple to the larger world that later would be reading this Gospel and looking to it for the light of guidance in their lives.

Isaiah writes,

> We look for light, but all is darkness;
>> for brightness, but we walk in deep shadows.
> Like the blind we grope along the wall,
>> feeling our way like men without eyes.

---

14. Rylaarsdam, "Booths," 456. See Coloe, *God*, 120–21, 125.

15. Morris, *Gospel*, 388. "The strength of the illumination at Tabernacles is also significant: the Mishnah says that there was not a courtyard in Jerusalem that was not illuminated by the light from the great candlesticks (Sukk. 5:3)" (Morris, *Gospel*, 388n3).

16. Neyrey, *Gospel*, 195.

> At midday we stumble as if it were twilight;
>
> among the strong, we are like the dead (Isa 59:9b–10).

Jesus is not only the light, he is also the bringer of light to those who are blind (9:5). Although the blindness of the man by the roadside was not caused by sin, sin does cause blindness (9:41). Here Jesus again moves between double meanings, from literal blindness that afflicted the man born blind, to spiritual blindness. The Pharisees' spiritual blindness was willful; they rejected the very Light that enlightened the blind man and brought him to witness and worship.

As light incarnate, Jesus both reveals what is hidden in darkness and leads us to understand who he is and to the forgiveness, justice, and life that he provides. Jesus as the light can remove our blindness if we are willing to see him as he truly is. We must walk in that light of life, not in the darkness of fear (6:19) and death (8:12). He is the light of life, not the darkness of death.

## I AM THE DOOR (10:7, 9)

In his discourses on the shepherd and the sheep, Jesus develops two "I am" statements.[17] In the first, Jesus says "I am the door (for the sheep)." Jesus creates the image of a sheep pen out in the fields with high stone walls and one entry opening "by which the sheep came in and went out; but there was no door of any kind. What happened was that at night the shepherd himself lay down across the opening and no sheep could get out or in except over his body. In the most literal sense, the shepherd was the door."[18] The gate serves several purposes. It protects the sheep from intruders; those who attempt to enter by means other than the gate come to destroy or steal as thieves or robbers (10:1, 10).[19] The sheepfold is a sanctuary from harm; in protecting, the shepherd as the door saves the flock (3:16–17; 5:34; 12:47). The metaphor reinforces Jesus's critical protection function. "To be able to come and go unmolested was the Jewish way of describing a life that is absolutely secure and safe. When a man can go in and out without fear, it means that his country is at peace, that the forces of the law and order are supreme, and that he enjoys a perfect security."[20]

The salvation afforded by the gate leads to the second function of a gate. The door provides passage for the sheep to the fields of nourishment and hence opens not just to quantity or length of life but to abundant life for the sheep. The passage here stresses

17. Bultmann (*Gospel of John*, 358–60) believes that 10:1–26 has been mishandled and badly ordered and so attempts to reconstruct the passage to fit what he conceives to be a more logical progression. Since we are concerned with the narrative in its final composition, however this occurred, we will address the analogy as given to us.

18. Barclay, *John*, 2:58.

19. It is possible that the reference here is to the Pharisees and Sadducees who used their religious position to fleece the flock. Morris, *Gospel*, 451.

20. Barclay, *John*, 2:59.

the qualitative dimension of this life: "they will have life to the full." Thus, the third "I am," like the first two, connects Jesus with providing the full dimensions of eternal life.

Jesus stresses that not only is he *a* door to the sheepfold, by using the definite article he indicates that he is *the* door. Through him the sheep are saved, going in for protection and out into life-giving pastures. "If there is but one door for all the [human] race, then once more we are reminded of something very important about Jesus. Like the other I AM sayings, this one leads us to think of deity"[21] and of the exclusive role of Jesus in providing life and salvation for those who believe in him.

## I AM THE GOOD SHEPHERD (10:11, 14)

In presenting the fourth "I am," Jesus self-designates as the good (καλός) shepherd and goes on to tell us what he means by being a good shepherd.

> As Moses was once the shepherd of the sheep of God (Isa 63:11; cp. Ps. 77:21), so God has taken David from his flock "to be the shepherd of Jacob his people, of Israel his inheritance. With upright heart he tended them, and guided them with skillful hand" (Ps 78:70–72). . . . If faithless Israel repents, God will give her shepherds after his own heart, who will feed her with knowledge and understanding (Jer 3:15). Instead of the bad shepherds who neglect and scatter the sheep, God will provide better ones (Jer 23:1–4; cp. John 2:8; 12:10). . . . *The image of the shepherd in the NT* is very largely dependent on the OT.[22]

Jesus's metaphor of the shepherd again connects him to Moses, echoing Moses's request to the LORD to appoint a leader to replace him to lead the people of Israel into the promised land: "To go out and come in before them, one who will lead them out and bring them in, so the LORD's people will not be like sheep without a shepherd" (Num 27:17). Jesus, the good Shepherd, is Moses's successor, the new Joshua, as Jesus's very name indicates, whom the LORD appoints to finally lead his people into the promised land after years of wandering (10:4–5), into eternal life (10:28). On him the Spirit rests (Num 27:18; John 1:33).

The simile also reflects Ezekiel's discourse on the shepherd in Ezekiel 34. By declaring himself the shepherd, Jesus claimed to be the sovereign LORD who himself assumes the shepherding role, both saving and tending his sheep and also judging between one sheep and others who "trample the rest of the pasture with their feet; . . . who muddy the rest of the water with their feet," so that the rest of the sheep only have to feed on and drink from what is trampled and muddied (Ezek 34:11–24).

Ezekiel goes on to say that God "will place over them one shepherd, my servant David, and he will tend them; he will tend them and be their shepherd" (Ezek 34:23). The tribes of Israel identify David as the one to whom the LORD said, "You

21. Morris, *Jesus*, 114–15.
22. Bultmann, *Gospel of John*, 364–66. Italics are in the original.

will shepherd my people Israel, and you will become their ruler" (2 Sam 2:2; also 7:7). The concept of shepherd is employed for the promised Messiah. It may be that this messianic piece—Jesus as the new David anointed to shepherd Israel—is crucial for understanding Jesus's identity claim here. "I will set up one shepherd over them, and he shall feed them, even my servant David" (Ezek 34:23). Although "[i]t is surprising that there is no single instance in the OT of 'shepherd' ever being used in Israel as a title for the ruling king,"[23] Nathan the prophet tells David that kings have a shepherding function (2 Sam 7:7).

Jesus develops the analogy (παροιμίαν) of the shepherd in various directions. Some motifs—leading, protecting, caring for the sheep—follow consistently from the Old Testament portrayal of the shepherd. As we noted, David is the par excellence example of the actual shepherd (1 Sam 16:11; 17:34–35), caring for and protecting the sheep from wild animals that he slays single-handedly. That David was the ancestor of the Messiah was accepted by the people (7:42) and surely must have come to mind in Jesus's construction of this analogy of functional identity. As with David, the Shepherd protects the sheep: "no one can snatch them out of my hand" or of that of his Father (10:28–29). The LORD places woes on those shepherd-leaders who fail to care for the flock, who have "not strengthened the weak or healed the sick or bound up the injured . . . or have not brought back the strays or searched for the lost" (Ezek 34:2–4). In assuming the shepherd role to guard the sheep against the thieves, he presumably inveighs against the religious leaders who would lead them astray through mistaken interpretations of the Torah and a failure to recognize the Messiah when he appears. His role as saving and protecting/defending shepherd will require him to lay down his life on behalf of the sheep.

Other motifs—the contrast between the shepherd and the thief, and a reciprocal relation between calling shepherd and hearing sheep—are unique to John.[24] In this, Jesus takes a well-known motif and makes it his own in several ways that relate to his nature and function. *First*, by announcing himself as a good shepherd, he upends the shepherding roles. Normally, the decent shepherd cares for and defends his flock, but it remains the case that his own life is more important than that of any individual sheep. He would take risks to confront human or animal marauders to save his flock but would be unwilling to intentionally sacrifice his own life for the sheep. Not only is self-preservation an underlying value, but the shepherd also remains for the good of all the sheep. If the shepherd died, it would be accidental, not intentional.[25] Jesus, by contrast, as the good shepherd intentionally wills to lay down his own life for the sheep. In his case, however, he has complete command of his situation, for he has the unique ability to take up his life again (10:17–18), which means that there is less risk

---

23. Jeremias, *New Testament*, 487–88.

24. Bultmann, *Gospel of John*, 367.

25. Morris, *Gospel*, 453.

for the entire flock than any ordinary, risk-taking shepherd would assume.[26] Jesus refers to his future death and resurrection, but this double meaning is lost on his hearers who think he is demon-possessed or mad to assert that a shepherd would willingly die for his sheep. His suggestions of dying for his sheep and of taking up his life again seem part of his madness. Even those who defend him do not use what he has to say to establish his sanity but rather appeal to the signs he has done (10:21). Demon-possessed or mad men cannot drive out demons or heal epileptics, they note. However, they fail to understand the depth of love this Shepherd has for his flock.

*Second*, in this case the Shepherd owns the sheep; they are his, kept safely in the fold (10:3). Jesus is not a hireling. The sheep who receive him, accepting him as their shepherd, are his own, a theme introduced in the Prologue where the Logos will enable his own to be children of God (1:12).

*Third*, Jesus notes that he has other sheep outside his pen. He must seek them out, so that "they too will listen to my voice, and there shall be one flock and one shepherd" (10:16). This shepherd's function is not limited to protecting and feeding those already in the fold; his message is also evangelistic. Although not stated, the Johannine implication is that the members of the original flock are believing Jews, while other flocks awaiting his voice are gentiles. He wants them to hear his voice, join his flock, and have unity in the sheepfold (a need so great in the fledgling church (Rom 15:5; 1 Cor 1:10; 2 Cor 13:11; Eph 4: 3–6, 13; 1 John 3:14–15)). Although there is exclusiveness in being inside rather than outside the fold, the shepherd is inclusive in seeking and inviting others to join. The condition is that they listen to him, that they obey to the point of being followers (disciples), the point Jesus made earlier about those who "believed" but did not really listen and follow (8:31–32). The result of discipleship is not hatred born out of rejecting his word (8:37; 1 John 3:15) but loving that grows out of hearing and obeying his commands (14:21).

*Fourth*, the good shepherd knows his sheep in intimate detail (10:14). Between the shepherd and his sheep there is a deep reciprocity. Scripture connects knowledge with experience, so that when Jesus says he knows his sheep and his sheep know him, he points to the intimacy that holds between him and his followers. It is the same intimacy of knowledge he has with his Father: as the Father knows him, so he knows the Father and his sheep.[27] He knows and cares for each one, just as the Father in Matthew knows and cares for each sparrow (Matt 10:29). John emphasizes reciprocity in that the Shepherd's sheep know him and can believe in and follow him because they have experienced him. Part of their knowledge comes through the signs (10:24), but true knowledge goes beyond the indirect sign acquaintance to the experiential depth. His sheep recognize his voice and are willing to follow him day in and day out as they

---

26. Morris points out that the usual schema is that God raises Jesus from the dead, but that there are some passages that say that Jesus rose from the dead (Acts 10:42; 17:3; 1 Thess 4:14), and that "the present passage is part of this strand" (Morris, *Gospel*, 457n53).

27. The importance of this use of reciprocity in John we will discuss in chapter 8.

exit and enter the fold of safety. The intimacy of conversation between Jesus and his flock (disciples) imitates the intimacy of conversation that Jesus has with his Father. Discipleship arises from and thrives on the intimacy of experience (10:4–5).

This "I am," like the other "I ams," promises life. As the good shepherd, he willingly gives up his life so that his sheep will live. The good shepherd knows where the verdant, life-nurturing pastures are located and can lead his flock to them. He is the shepherd of abundant life. He also can create havens of safety from marauders. "My sheep listen to my voice; I know them, and they follow me. I give them eternal life, and they shall never perish; no one can snatch them out of my hand" (10:27–28). By this "I am," Jesus points to who he is, the person in deep reciprocity with the Father and with his disciples, and to his life-giving, life-protecting, and life-sustaining functions. As his name intimates, he is the new Joshua ordained by his Father to lead safely and securely to the promised pastureland of eternal life that he has already spied out (Num 14:7–8; Deut 31:7–8).

The reaction of the Jewish leaders to these two "I am" statements about being the door and the shepherd was mixed. Some thought Jesus mad when he claimed that he had control over his life. Others were more cautious in their assessment, not because of what he said but because of Jesus's sign of opening the blind man's eyes (10:21). For the Evangelist, the shepherd motif plays out at the end of the Gospel, where Jesus tells Simon Peter to love and emulate him as the shepherd. Discipleship is emulation. Peter is to tend and feed Jesus's sheep, even at great personal cost, just as Jesus the supreme shepherd does (21:15–17).

## I AM THE RESURRECTION AND THE LIFE (11:25-26)

John overtly connects Jesus's identity with life in his fifth "I am" saying: I am the life. The context is Jesus's delayed visit to Martha and Mary in the town of Bethany. Lazarus has been dead for four days when Martha approaches Jesus, who has just arrived after a fatal delay. Expressing a tacit criticism, she wonders why Jesus postponed coming, since if he had been there, he could have used his power to heal her brother Lazarus before he died. Jesus's reply is full of double meanings. As *the* resurrection and *the* life, he alone can give them: through him the dead will rise, and those who live will not die. Martha is comfortable with this hope-inspiring identity, although she takes it as a statement about the future. However, Jesus also means it for the present: hope has arrived in Bethany. The quantitative part is realized shortly thereafter in the raising of Lazarus from the dead. The second part—those who live will not die—can hardly be taken literally, since all present, including Jesus, would die. Thus, it must be taken either in the sense that ultimately all will achieve a state where death is a stranger, or else in a spiritual sense that Jesus is the giver of a unique quality of life, or in both senses. That is, the saying has both quantitative and qualitative dimensions: the fulfilled hope of life is both immediately present and a promised future. "The revelation to Martha thus is an assurance of resurrection to the kingdom of God in its consummation through him who is the Resurrection, and of life in the kingdom of God in the present time through him who is the Life. Both aspects of the 'life' are rooted in the understanding of Jesus as the Mediator of the divine sovereignty in the present and in the future."[28]

Again, the "I am" ties Jesus's identity with being the giver of life. Resurrection is moving from death into life. It is a second, new birth, following on the first (3:7). The first birth provides physical life here and now; the second birth gives eternal life here and now and in the dwellings Jesus prepares for us (14:1–4).

To this self-identification Jesus again receives mixed reviews (11:45–48). Some observers put their faith in him. Others seek to kill him, for he threatens their own identity and position. Believing in Jesus necessitates a radical reorientation of their lives, and without a willingness to change Jesus becomes for them a personal peril.

## I AM THE WAY AND THE TRUTH AND THE LIFE (14:6)

Jesus's sixth "I am" saying reiterates themes from the previous "I ams." In the fourth "I am," Jesus is the door to the sheepfold. He is the gate to both protection and to the life found in his good pasture. In the sixth self-identification, Jesus identifies himself as the way or path. Thomas is puzzled by Jesus's riddle and wants a simple answer to a simple question: "Where are you going? If we knew that, perhaps we could find the way." The destination helps determine the path for the journey. Jesus quickly moves from the ordinary meaning of the earthly destination response sought by Thomas to the deeper, double, spiritual meaning of "way." He himself is the way to the Father. On the one hand, Jesus rejects other approaches to the Father: the Law, circumcision, keeping the Sabbath, simply being good, all prove unsatisfactory. On the other hand, the Father is hidden and needs to be revealed. Jesus came to reveal the Father and here anticipates his return to the Father at the conclusion of his mission of revelation. To know who Jesus is, to discern his identity, is to glimpse the Father who sent him and to whom he will return. "John is not saying that Jesus shows the way, but that he *is* the way. This points us to the significance of his saving death. By dying for sinners, he brings them to God."[29] However, even more than this, by his death he reveals God's sacrificial and costly love (3:16).

Jesus also is the truth. He is not just a truth, but *the* truth itself. Again, as we noted in chapter 2, truth has multiple meanings. On the one hand, truth is propositional, characteristic of the statements or claims that we make. Jesus is the truth in this sense, for he is the revealer of the propositional truths found in God. What Jesus teaches about God, about himself, and about the way to live is true. On the other hand, truth is also personal, so that in his very person he accurately and reliably reveals the

28. Beasley-Murray, *John*, 191.

29. Morris, *Jesus*, 119. The Greek text has a definite article before each of the three nouns.

person who is God. To know Jesus is to know not only what God says (his Word) but also the very person God. Personal truth is rooted in God.

Finally, Jesus is *the* life itself, the very embodiment and source of eternal life. True life, both qualitative and quantitative, is found in Jesus and flows from him. Jesus's identity as connected with life is made unequivocal in the sixth "I am," which reiterates the theme of life found in all the predicative "I ams."

Some, such as Frances Gench, baulk at the exclusivity of Jesus's statement. "14:6 is addressed to insiders, offering comfort and assurance to fragile disciples in distress rather than a weapon to bludgeon others.... [T]he exclusionary ring of 14:6b reflects the pain of a small sect struggling for its existence after its exclusion from the synagogue.... But is that to say that Jesus is the only way by which humanity experiences the reality of God? Surely, some modesty is called for whenever we speak of the great mystery of God."[30] For religious *pluralists*, like Gench and John Hick, Jesus provides one way among others to God. Many paths lead successfully to salvation/liberation or personal transformation. Exclusivity is offensive and thus out of style in our diverse, religiously tolerant, cosmopolitan world. The problem here is that to get this meaning the text must be rewritten: the definite article that precedes all three nouns must be replaced with the indefinite article. What looks like a minor article change looms significant, for if Jesus is only *a* way, then his subsequent death and resurrection are gratuitous. Other, less gruesome means, like meditation or doing good works, suffice to liberate us and help us discover transformative meaning in life. The ending of the Fourth Gospel becomes one sideshow among many.

Religious *exclusivists* argue that not only is Jesus the only path to God and salvation/liberation, but these can be achieved only by personally believing in Jesus himself. Both the death of Jesus (the ontological factor—what really happened) and knowledgeable believing in him (the epistemic factor—what we know about what happened) are necessary and sufficient for salvation. The problem here is that while the ontological condition of Jesus's sacrificial and healing atonement can be met apart from our knowledge or believing, the epistemological condition cannot be met apart from us. The possibility of salvation is offered very narrowly. In limiting salvation to those who satisfy the epistemological or knowledge/believing condition, billions of people who lived before and after Jesus and who never had access to the Jesus story are excluded from salvation through no fault of their own. This knowledge-exclusivism is also not a feature of the text. Jesus makes the ontological claim that if you don't come through him, you cannot approach the Father. Jesus's atoning death is necessary for becoming children of God. Jesus also makes the epistemological claim that if you know (experience or believe in) him, you also will know the Father. However, a careful reading here shows that he does not make the claim that if you don't know him, you won't know (experience) the Father, that is, become one of his own. This is consistent with Jesus's statement in 11:25, where he says that if you believe in him, you will have

---

30. Gench, *Encounters*, 47.

life, but he does not say that if you don't believe in him you won't have eternal life. The passages provide grounds for ontological but not epistemic exclusivism.

This leaves the field to an *inclusivist* view of salvation that is consistent with the text. On the one hand, ontologically, we become children of God only through Jesus's death and resurrection. Jesus is the way God chose to reconcile the world to himself (3:16); there is no other. Hence, the passion account is essential to the gospel. On the other hand, the epistemological condition is not necessary for becoming God's children; God's saving work through Jesus can be accomplished even for those who, like those who preceded Jesus, did or do not know about him and hence are not in a position to believe in him. God takes the atoning work of Christ and applies it to people in life-giving grace, even when they do not know the basis in Christ of this grace. It is as if someone graciously pays my mortgage without my knowledge; my debt is paid regardless of my knowing participation in the payment.[31] At the same time, as the next "I am" affirms, full, enriched participation in the life-giving of Jesus is found in having and maintaining a knowing, discipling relationship with him.

## I AM THE TRUE VINE (15:1, 5)

In the seventh "I am" Jesus identifies himself as the true vine. This metaphor also has Old Testament roots. "In the Old Testament the vine is often a symbol of Israel, sometimes of degenerate Israel. For example, in Jeremiah we read, 'I planted you a choice vine, wholly of pure seed. How then have you turned degenerate and become a wild vine?' (Jer 2:21). However, where Israel failed and had become a false vine, we now see the true vine, the vine in which the purpose of God would be worked out."[32]

John makes two statements about the vine that differ slightly. The first identifies Jesus as the true vine and emphasizes the Father's role as the gardener who cuts off those branches that fail to produce fruit.[33] Even those that do produce fruit the Father prunes or cleanses (καθαίρει), so that they will become more fruitful.[34] Jesus thus explains the suffering that his followers will experience, tracing it to bearing fruit and

---

31. For a thorough treatment of religious diversity, see Peterson et al., *Reason*, ch. 14.

32. Morris, *Jesus*, 120.

33. Persecution thus has two roots, that occasioned by the world (15:20) and that which God uses to discipline us and improve our fruit-bearing (Heb 12:5–6).

34. Morris (*Jesus*, 121) writes, "This [καταρίζω] is often understood in the sense of 'prunes.' But the word does not mean 'prunes,' but 'cleanses,' and this is important in the context. Jesus proceeds to say, 'You are already clean on account of the word that I have spoken to you' (v. 3). . . . The word for 'clean' is used of those in the upper room" [13:10]. However, given John's penchant for double meanings, "prunes" is still appropriate in this vine metaphor, for καταρίζω has the sense of removing something in order to make an item clean or better, either in the sense of healing from a disease like leprosy (Matt 10:8; 2 Kgs 5:10, 14) that made one ritually unclean or in the sense of cleaning objects like tableware for ritual use (Matt 23:25–26) (Arndt and Gingrich, *Lexicon*, 388). In the vine metaphor, cleaning or pruning leaves branches better suited to be fruitful. See also ch. 8, n24 below.

ultimately to remaining in him. Without the connection to Jesus, the disciples will be fruitless. (We will return to this passage in chapter 8.)

In the second instance, the passage focuses on the branches that get their life, sustenance, and existence from the vine. Without abiding in the vine, the branches (disciples) will wither away and be good only for fiery consumption. Life will depart, and death will settle in ashes.

Thus, this metaphor likewise connects Jesus with life. Abiding in him means being alive, and this, we are told, will manifest itself externally in keeping the command to love each other in the same way that Jesus loves them. Indeed, Jesus here portrays a very radical love, one where the lover will sacrifice his life for the beloved. The sacrificing shepherd theme is present in the metaphor of the vine.

Emerging from these seven "I ams" is Jesus's rich use of double meanings. He takes common, everyday things from his listeners' experience and imbues them with new, spiritual meaning that helps the original audience and us to understand both his nature and his function. They become metaphors for displaying the truths of Jesus's identity and function of giving life. Only someone divine could make the exclusive claims that Jesus does about being the way, the door, and the provider of resurrection to eternal life. Ultimately, John assures us, believing in Jesus leads to eternal life.

## CHIASTIC STRUCTURE OF THE "I AMS"

Before we pass on to the non-predicative "I ams," we should note how John structures the predicative "I ams." For one thing, most of these "I ams" are explicitly repeated in the text (6:35, 48, 51; 8:12 and 9:5; 10:7, 9; 10:11, 14; 15:1, 5). As we saw in chapter 2, John uses repetition to emphasize his points to the readers, to inform them that something significant and memorable is being said. The repetitions of these "I am" statements show the emphasis John places on this identification of Jesus's nature and function or mission. For another, there is also a chiastic structure to the "I ams," with the highlight coming with the fourth "I am."

> I am the bread of life.
>> I am the light of the world.
>>> I am the door of the sheepfold.
>>>> I am the good shepherd.
>>> I am the resurrection and the life.
>> I am the way and the truth and the life.
> I am the true vine.

The author's likely eucharistic understanding connects the first (bread) and seventh (vine) through their emphasis on the bread and the fruit of the vine. The dialogue in chapter 6 summarizes this when Jesus affirms to the Jews his contention that to eat his body (the bread of life) and to drink his blood brings eternal life (6:53–56). It is true that the wine of the sacrament is not overtly present in John, but it is present in veiled form in Jesus's command to drink his blood, which is "real drink," shed on the cross, that leads to eternal life.[35] The second (light) and the sixth (way and truth) both address the close relation of the Son to the Father. In John 8 Jesus's response that the Father sends him and provides the testimony authenticating his identity follows the "I am" statement. In John 14, Jesus develops the "I am" statement with his affirmation that he is the revelation of the Father, with whom he is in closest intimacy—he is in the Father, the Father is in him, and he is doing the Father's works. Jesus appeals to his signs as evidence or testimony of this relationship (14:12). Also, one cannot overlook the necessity of having light on the way to avoid stumbling about in darkness (11:9–10). The connection between light and the way is both overt and emphasized: the light lights the way. The third (door) and fifth (resurrection) "I ams" are more loosely related, yet here again there is the hint that it is distinctively through Jesus that we have eternal life. As he is *the* door or gate of the sheepfold through which the sheep pass to life, he is *the* resurrection through whom we pass to life. That leaves the fourth "I am" at the center of the chiasm, and rightly so, since on the one hand it announces and incorporates the fullness of the shepherd motif found in the Old Testament, while on the other hand it points to the death that Jesus willingly undergoes for his followers, and still again, it points to our called mission to shepherd Jesus's people. It is through his death and resurrection that the I AM brings us eternal life. When laid out in this way, John's chiastic structure reveals the central motif of the "I ams": everything in the Gospel points to the defining moment when the one who identifies himself as the good shepherd voluntarily lays down his life for his own, to give them life.

## "I AM" WITHOUT A PREDICATE

John provides a second set of "I ams" that is just as striking. This time "I am" is not followed by a predicate but stands alone. Although some of the instances are disputed as simply instances of self-identification—"It's me"—(4:26; 6:20; 13:19), three passages stand out: 6:20; 8:24, 28, 58; and 18:5–8.[36] Here the I am (ἐγώ εἰμί) is firmly rooted in the Old Testament, where Yahweh reveals himself to Moses as the I Am (Exod 3:14). Again, John makes clear that Jesus is the new Moses, not merely repeating the prophet but transcending him as both revealer and revealed.

---

35. Brown, *Introduction to John*, 229–34; Bauckham, *Gospel of Glory*, ch. 5.

36. One possible interpretation of "It is I" in 4:26, 6:20, and 18:5–8 is that Jesus is simply identifying himself to others—the Samaritan woman, the disciples toiling fearfully in the boat, and the gang sent to arrest him, following the pattern in 9:9 of the self-identification of the formerly blind man. In reply, as we will note shortly, these provide further examples of Jesus's use of multiple meanings, where the obvious (identification of his earthly self) is supplanted by the heavenly.

In the first instance (6:20), Jesus comes to the disciples who are trying to control their boat in the stormy Sea of Galilee.[37] The disciples, in fear, apparently take Jesus as an apparition (although John does not say so directly, he implies what Matthew directly affirms (Matt 14:26)). Jesus attempts to calm their fears by saying, "I am (ἐγώ εἰμί); don't fear" (6:20). After inviting Jesus into the boat, they immediately arrive where they were heading. We are not told how this happens, whether Jesus actually got into the boat, what happened to the storm, and the reaction of the disciples to this announcement and miraculous arrival. John enigmatically leaves us to speculate about these intriguing details of the sign story. However, John gives us a clear revelation of Jesus's claim to divinity. "It is true that in the story, taken at its face value, these words might mean, as they do in the Synoptic parallels, no more than 'It is I'; but in view of the importance which the formula bears in other Johannine passages it seems more than probable that it is to be understood here as elsewhere as the equivalent of the divine name, I AM."[38]

Michaels is dubious about assigning this to a divinity-revealing saying. Rather, he argues, if it were truly a revelation of divinity, the disciples would have been even more afraid of Jesus than of the storm at night.[39] However, this fails to account for John's use of double meanings and the irony of Jesus's statement: a tension exists between the revelation of Jesus's identity and his comforting the disciples lest that revelation of identity create fear. If we look at this incident in terms of double meaning, we can see that, in an ordinary sense, Jesus's self-identification as "It is only me; don't worry" would calm their fears that it was a ghost. Yet, from John's perspective, the saying runs deeper than what the disciples do not discern at the time but could discern later, namely, that this is a truly divine moment, in which Jesus asserts his identity not only by what he says but also by what he has done, namely, the sign of walking on (controlling) the water. As I noted in chapter 3 and above, this is a Mosaic moment, in which Jesus reveals that he is greater than Moses (6:32) because of his relation to the Father. He is Lord not only of bread but also of water (Exod 14:21–22). Thus, John builds on his Prologue, where he affirms that whereas Moses brought the Law, grace and truth come through the Word become incarnate (1:17). Furthermore, Jesus's words not only self-identify but reflect Isaiah's formula that connects divine self-declaration with assurance: "Do not fear, for I am with you, do not be afraid, for I am your God" (Isa 41:10. Also Isa 41:4; 43:1–5; Gen 15:1). In this, the saying is rooted in the Old Testament, especially in connection with overcoming fear. The "I am" is thus multitextured and an implicit but unmistakable revelation of Jesus's claim to powerful, water-controlling divinity.[40]

---

37. We discussed the details of this story in chapter 3.
38. Dodd, *Interpretation*, 345.
39. Michaels, *Gospel of John*, 358.
40. Williams, "'I Am,'" 346–48.

In the second instance of I am (8:24, 28, 58), Jesus stresses the closeness of his relation to the Father.[41] He tells the Jews that he is from above, while they are of this world. "World" here carries the multiple meanings of being part of the created earth, humanity made from dust, and as standing opposed to God (1:9–10; 3:16–17). The Jews exhibit both latter traits. Jesus continues, "If they do not believe that I am, they will die in their sins" (Ezek 3:18). The response of the Jews, "Who do you think you are?" demonstrates that Jesus's claim to be the "I am" was so radical that they could not comprehend someone making it. Jesus then reiterates the point about his origin: from whom he comes and whom he reveals is the true one. The Jews still do not understand who this person is (8:27), and Jesus acknowledges their puzzlement. After all, he would not expect the Jewish religious leaders to fully understand or comprehend that they stand under judgment rather than stand in judgment of others (8:15). They were so comfortable with the latter role. However, he affirms, they will understand in the future, when they lift him up (again, a double meaning, referring literally to his crucifixion and metaphorically to his glorification (12:32–33)). Then they will know his identity as the "I am." "The one who sent me is with me; he has not left me alone, for I always do what pleases him" (8:29). "There is a revelatory aspect to the cross, and after the crucifixion those who reflect on it will be able to appreciate that Jesus was indeed more than man."[42]

At the heart of this passage is the Johannine contention that our identity is found in our heritage. This is not a novel claim for the Jews (1:45–46; 7:41–42), but John heightens it with respect to Jesus's relation to his Father. Whereas the Jews for their identity claim Abraham as their father, Jesus for his identity claims God himself as his father, and this is what they could not comprehend or, if they understood, acknowledge. Throughout this dialogue, Jesus says who he is but his conversers do not hear it with understanding. John notes that this self-revelation and radical claim led people to believe in him, but their believing was shallow, for they continue to rely on their heritage connection to Abraham and not to the Father. Further, they do not know Jesus in the sense of really experiencing or abiding connectedly to him and hence do not understand the full meaning of discipleship with Jesus. Instead of opting for the deep relationship of becoming Jesus's disciples and knowing and abiding in the truth (with its double meaning), they choose to reaffirm their connection with Abraham, whose descendants have "never been slaves of anyone" (8:33). Clearly, these "believers" have difficulty with both the personal and the propositional senses of truth! Heritage, not discipleship, is their comfort zone. Jesus attempts to set the record straight: he does not pursue their claim never to have been actual slaves, Egypt notwithstanding, but

41. Morris notes that 7:21 indicates a break from the previous discussion, which occurred at the Feast of Tabernacles. How long after this is unclear, but the issue is not important, for the train of thought of testimony to Jesus's identity and his connection with the Father forms a continuous fabric (*Gospel*, 395).

42. Morris, *Gospel*, 401.

spiritualizes their slavery by focusing on their slavery to sin and the freedom possible by knowing the Son, the truth. Thus, a tense dialogue ensues in which Jesus antagonistically reveals that the Jews, although seeming to claim to believe in him, are far from doing so.[43] Their heritage belongs more to the devil than to Abraham, for they purvey lies and seek to kill him. They deal treacherously with the Truth.[44]

This discussion comes down to the question of truth (8:52, 58). The truth leads to Jesus's clearest, most radical claim of identity and deity: "I tell you the truth, before Abraham was, I am (ἐγώ εἰμί)" (8:58). This time Jews get the point and try to kill him for blasphemy (Lev 24:16). They now understand and reject Jesus's claim to identity with God, using a formula harking back to God's revelation to Moses (Exod 3:14) and echoed in Isaiah (Isa 43:10–13; 45:18–19; 46:4; 48:12; 52:6). It was a point too extreme for them to accept but presaged for us in the Prologue opening: "The Word was with God and the Word was God." Jesus is the being of eternity, possessing a heritage far older than their progenitor Abraham. They hear about his identity claim but cannot understand or experience it, for their true heritage in the devil, the opponent of the divine, has darkened their minds. John states that Jesus was hidden from them, and so he was in a double sense: they could not understand the truth, and physically, Jesus was under his Father's protection until his time arrived (8:59).

The final revelation of Jesus's identity using this "I am" language occurs when a motley group comes to arrest Jesus (18:5–8). Guided by the traitor Judas, the group represents those who have been seeking or will participate in his death: Roman soldiers,[45] officials associated with the chief priests, and Pharisees. Unsuccessful in apprehending him in the past during daylight hours, Jesus's enemies band together to do their deed in the darkness of night, lit only by torches. What the religious rulers had sought all along is finally realized when they come to take Jesus by force. Here again, this "I am" might be simply an instance of self-identification when he responds to them: "It's I you are looking for." However, John quickly indicates that more than self-identification is involved. The arresting gang is stunned when Jesus comes to them out of the dark garden and asks, "Whom do you want?" This is the very phrase that

43. "The Gospel of John uses the term οἱ Ἰουδαῖοι (the Jews) 65 times, more than the Synoptic Gospels combined. While some of the uses of οἱ Ἰουδαῖοι are simply descriptive and essentially benign, most of the uses are hostile and represent the enemies of Jesus," in particular, the Jewish authorities (Cronin, *Raymond Brown*, 2; see Morris, *Gospel*, 115–16). This has raised the issue of whether the Gospel was polemical against Jews and could be so misused today. See Cronin, *Raymond Brown*, especially 154–86, for a survey of contemporary discussion in the context of Raymond Brown's pilgrimage on this issue.

44. It is worth noting the double meanings of "slavery," where slavery is both physical and spiritual, and "heritage," their physical heritage of which they were proud and their spiritual heritage manifest in their actions of attempting to kill him.

45. The size of the Roman contingent (σπεῖρα) is unclear. If the term is used as a technical, military term, it would have been of a substantial size, possibly in the hundreds. More than likely, the term is used informally referring to a detachment of soldiers sized appropriate to the mission. For discussion, see Hunt, "Roman Soldiers," 561.

Jesus uses to address Andrew who was following him and Mary Magdalene who was searching for him. However, the searchers in this instance are not looking to become disciples but apprehenders. Using his double meaning, John makes perfectly clear that beyond identifying himself as the one they were looking for and providing a context for the disciples to leave unharmed (fulfilling that he will not lose any of those given to him, 18:9), Jesus's utterance has a deeper meaning. He does this by noting the reaction of these adversaries, which in the context where they appear as an armed group of some size is quite abnormal. When Jesus says, "I am," they give the appropriate response to a theophany by "drawing back and falling to the ground." Although their subsequent action does not sustain this adoration (if it is adoration at all rather than surprise, an example of John's looking at an event from the two different perspectives of the heavenly and earthly) or reveal any long-term effects, John indicates that the taking of Jesus in the garden is a seizing of the I Am, the divine. They proceed to arrest the very liberator they expectantly anticipate.[46]

The point of these "I am" claims is clear: Jesus, the Word, is divine. He reveals his identity by using the very name used by Yahweh to identify himself. In Hebraic thought a name conveys the essence of something. Thus, Jesus renames Simon Peter or Cephas, thereby indicating his double character as the intransigent man who refuses to be washed by Jesus and who vehemently denies that he will repudiate his association with Jesus (13:6–8) but also is the firm rock/shepherd on which Jesus builds his church (21:17). Likewise, in the name "I am" Jesus reveals his divine essence. As John tells us, he is the Son of God, equal with God the Father, God himself.

To those who lack the Prologue these affirmations are cloaked in ambiguity, although they are clear enough to the audience to provoke responses of anger and awe. By the "I ams" John conveys his message of the dual nature of Jesus as Son of God and Son of Man and achieves his purpose of promoting Jesus as the giver of eternal life. John connects Jesus to the Old Testament; he is the new Moses and Joshua, the promised Messiah, the Lord who frees from fear. Once you understand the truth about who Jesus is and believe it as a true disciple, you have eternal life (8:51) and should fall down in awe. This is the point of John's Gospel: to bring readers and listeners to know, understand, believe, and worship, so that they will have both the quantitative and the qualitative eternal life that Jesus, who is life itself, promises.

---

46. Some suggest that this scene alludes to the Genesis garden scene, where Adam and Eve engage in "divine-taking" by assuming the prerogative of divinity for themselves, for they refuse to follow God's commands and instead seek divine knowledge of good and evil (Gen 3:1–5). Cyril of Alexandria wrote, "The place was a garden, typifying the paradise of old. For in this place as it were, all places were recapitulated and our return to humanity's ancient condition was consummated. For the troubles of humanity began in paradise, while Christ's sufferings, which brought us deliverance from all the evil that happened to us in times past, began in [this] garden" (quoted in Hunt, "Roman Soldiers," 565). It is noteworthy that God set cherubim guards at the entry to the paradisal garden to protect the tree of life (Gen 3:24). Here, the arresters of Jesus, who is life itself, do not enter the garden; rather, Jesus comes to them out of the garden (18:4).

## UNITY WITH THE FATHER (10:29-39)

We cannot leave the topic of the identity of Jesus without considering one more passage, this time without the "I am." John situates the event at the Feast of Hanukkah, the winter celebration of Jewish liberation from the Seleucids and the cleansing of the temple from its religious pollution (we will return to a discussion of this feast in chapter 9).[47] Jesus's dialogue with the skeptical Jews comes almost at the climax of his public ministry, where he begins to shift the discussion from where he has come from to where he is going and to the events that will precede his going to the Father. The Jews want a clear answer from Jesus about his identity: is he or is he not the Messiah? (10:24). John here brings the point of his writing the Gospel to the forefront: to establish that Jesus is the Messiah, the Son of God. The signs or works he has given them, Jesus replies, should have convinced them of who he is by connecting him to his Father, but even though they witnessed the signs, the signs failed to bring them to believing about his identity. They see without seeing and hear without hearing (8:47), so that whatever answer they get will not lead to the believing that Jesus desires. They are caught up in the façade of the miracles but miss the significance of the signs (7:31). Clearly, these Jews are not of his flock (10:25-27). Instead of replicating the revelatory signs, Jesus states clearly: No one can steal the sheep from his hand nor from the hand of his Father, for "I and the Father are one" (10:30).

Scholarly debate queries whether this oneness is metaphysical or functional. Barclay holds that the unity has nothing to do with metaphysics but rather affirms personal relationship. Just as Jesus prays for unity of believers in 17:20-22, and since the unity is based on love (13:34) and love is manifested in obedience (15:10), what Jesus refers to here is his perfect love for and obedience to the Father.[48] However, the radical reaction of the audience seems contrary to this understanding. A similar view likewise downplays the metaphysical, for "one" (ἕν) is in the neuter gender, meaning "one thing" or "one in action," not masculine "one in person."[49] Oneness is unity of purpose or action; as the subsequent discussion makes clear, Jesus does what the Father wants (10:31).[50] However, this grammatical point may not be so problematic;

47. Some see symbolism in John's note that it was winter: the relation between Jesus and his Jewish opponents has come to a head, to a cold climax, which begins the downward movement toward his death (Morris, *Gospel*, 460; Beasley-Murray, *John*, 173). Others see it simply as a time marker, especially helpful for non-Jewish readers to mark the progression of the feasts (Michaels, *Gospel of John*, 595n6).

48. Barclay, *John*, 1:74-75.

49. "The verse has played a not insignificant part in relation to the doctrine of the Trinity. It is upon the ἐκ τῆς χειρὸς [out of the hand], which is predicated jointly of the Father and the Son, that Ammonius of Alexandria bases his interpretation to the effect that the unity relates not to personhood (ὑπόστασις) but to nature (οὐσία); he draws attention to the activity, the δύναμις" (Schnackenburg, *John*, 2:511n121).

50. Beasley-Murray, *John*, 174. Yet, he goes on to suggest, "We have a glimpse of 'the metaphysical depths contained in the relationship between Jesus and the Father' (Schnackenburg, *John*, 2:308), so long as it is recognized that the Evangelist has not spelled out the nature of those 'metaphysical

reliance on the gender of ἕν may be insignificant, since Christian orthodoxy has long held that Jesus and the Father are not the same person; the Trinity consists of three persons but one being. For others, the identity is not merely that of function emphasizing his miraculous works but accords with 1:1.[51] It is a recasting of his earlier claim of being the I AM (8:58). Theological debate notwithstanding, the point of Jesus's claim is not lost on the dialoguing Jews, who understand his claim metaphysically in terms of his nature or deity and as they did in the prior scene (8:59), pick up projectiles to stone Jesus for blasphemy.[52]

Jesus attempts to divert the discussion by turning their attention to his works: "For which of these good works are you going to stone me?" he asks. In effect, if they won't believe his claim, at least they should recognize the signs and to what they point. However, the Jews are not about to be diverted this time; they focus on what Jesus said and charge him with blasphemy (10:33). Jesus, however, tries a second time to divert the discussion, this time with an appeal to a riddle from the Law, "Law" here understood as referring to the entire Old Testament (10:34–36). He introduces a quote from the Psalms: "I have said that you are gods" (Ps 82:6), and then proceeds to play with the double meaning of the term "gods." The Psalm speaks of God presiding over the heavenly court, designating certain of its members as judges to act as gods on his behalf. These judges are sons of the Most High when they act as his representatives, directed to render just judgment (which, as the Psalm notes, they fail miserably to do, knowing nothing and walking in darkness). If according to Scripture, Jesus continues, God called human judges gods and sons of the Most High, would it be inappropriate, let alone blasphemy, to call the one individual uniquely chosen as God's very own and sent into world to do the Father's work "god" or "God's son" (10:34–36)? Jesus again appeals to double meaning to make his case, for the godness of the human judges spoken of in the Psalm is very different from Jesus's godness. Jesus is much more than these judges and rulers, as shown by his works. "The Father is in me, and I in the Father" (10:38). Using this irony or riddle, Jesus toys with those who would be familiar with the language of this Psalm and affirm the authority of Scripture. They too would be judges accusing unjustly, ignorant and walking in darkness.

However, Jesus does not leave the matter of his oneness hanging; he exacerbates the situation by returning to the issue of his works to press his point. If the Jews cannot accept Jesus's own verbal testimony about who he is and his relation to the Father, "look," he says, "at my works." The opponents should observe his deeds and see that only if he and the Father stand in mutual reciprocity can he accomplish what he has

---

depths'" (174).

51. "Identity is not asserted, but essential unity is. These two belong together. The statement does not go beyond the opening words of this Gospel, but it can stand with them" (Morris, *Gospel*, 465).

52. "As for the neuter, it would not have to mean more than the two working together in harmony (see 1 Cor 3:8), but the force of the syllogism and the precedent of 5:17 will make it unmistakably clear to 'the Jews' that Jesus is in fact 'making himself God' (see v. 33)" (Michaels, *Gospel of John*, 601; see Bultmann, *Gospel of John*, 387).

done (10:37–38). No one can do these works unless intimately connected to the Father. Nature and function (works) go together to establish Jesus's identity. However, the Jews have had enough. To claim this reciprocal relationship, the evidence of which is found in his works or deeds, still leaves him committing blasphemy. They properly refuse to separate nature and function. Because he is divine, he claims that he can do what the Father does. The intimacy between them is vouchsafed. Thus, again the Jews attempt to seize him for blasphemy.

The point of this discussion with the Jews is clear. John wants us to see that Jesus's verbal claims—that he and his Father are one, that the Father is in him and he in the Father—are supported by his works or signs. He does not say one thing and do another. The doing is not mere doing, but points, as signs do, to something more significant than the event itself. It points to Jesus's oneness with the Father; he is the Son of God. All of this, of course, aims to bring about believing. And even if it failed to do so with Jesus's Jewish opponents, for the Gospel readers John wants it to bring about believing, for they have unique access to the claims John makes in the Prologue (1:1) and to the testimony of the Beloved Disciple who witnessed this.

## JESUS AND HUMILITY

We cannot leave the subject of Jesus's identity without facing the Jesus we encountered in chapter 1. The Jesus John portrays is a master of ambiguity, double meaning, irony, subtle questions, and riddles, a person very different from how people often imagine him. After reading the Gospels, many who write and speak about Jesus create a man who suits their own image. He is the baby in the manger, the one whose yoke is easy and burden light and who is gentle and humble of heart, the meek and unobtrusive servant to others, the lowly man without the vice of pride, who sweeps children into his arms. However, a careful reading of John reveals that the author complexly portrays Jesus as anything but a mere, traditional paragon of humility.

Jesus claims that he has been to and comes from heaven. "We speak of what we know, and we testify to what we have seen. . . . I have spoken to you of earthly things and you don't believe. How will you believe if I speak of heavenly things? No one has ever gone into heaven except the one who came from heaven—that is I, the Son of Man" (3:11–13). John presents Jesus's pronouncement of his identity in not very humble language: I have been to heaven and back! You must believe in me or else.

A little later, John notes: "On him (me, the Son of Man), God the Father has placed his seal of approval" (6:27). Those who hear Jesus wonder how he can claim such a unique status. Jesus continues on to make his radical "I am" claim: "Hear me! Unless you eat my flesh and drink my blood, you have no life in you. Whoever eats my flesh and drinks my blood has eternal life, and I will raise them up at the last day" (6:53–54). It is not the Father that will raise people up; Jesus asserts that it is I, the Son, the bread of life, who will accomplish this. Again, Jesus's language scarcely reflects modesty, as those disciples who turned back from following him reflected: "this is a hard teaching" (6:60) by an assertive and not very humble teacher.

Jesus's relations with his erstwhile followers were just as tense as those with his adversaries. When they claim to be children of Abraham, Jesus replies, "I think not. You are children of the devil" (8:44). Jesus does not beat around the bush: "By doing the works of the devil you demonstrate that you are sons of the devil." No truly meek person would speak so directly to another person, let alone a follower.

We have already focused on the way Jesus couches his identity. "I am the way, and the truth, and the life. No one comes to the Father except through me. If you really know me, you really know my Father as well" (14:6–7). Jesus claims that he is not merely *a* way, or *a* truth, or *a* giver of life; he is *the* way, *the* truth, and *the* giver of life. A humble person would not make such a radical claim about himself. It is not, "I am merely a resurrector," but "I am *the* resurrector and *the* life-giver" (11:25). Indeed, reading the Gospel of John, one cannot but be impressed how many times Jesus uses the first-person singular. His primary topics are himself and the Father; they flood his dialogues and discourses. Whereas humble people do not talk all the time about themselves, Jesus does. Indeed, in uttering the "I am," Jesus speaks in an uncharacteristically Greek fashion, for to the first-person pronoun subject indicated by the verb form Jesus unnecessarily adds the word for I: ἐγώ. The emphasis is on himself and his identity. The Gospel delivers no docile, self-effacing Jesus, but a person of strength and determination who understands in the deepest and most profound way who he is and announces it forthrightly, vigorously, even confrontationally.

Perhaps some would like their old Jesus back, the humble Jesus we have created or fixated on. However, John's Jesus is not a babe. Indeed, John skips the entire birth and baby business. The Word that was in the beginning is *God* come in the flesh. Jesus says, "Listen to me! Before Abraham was, I am" (8:58). Jesus uses the "I" again: "I (ἐγώ) know the Father" (8:55).

John's Jesus is not of easy yoke, but the Jesus who requires radical, costly discipleship. "Hear me! Unless a kernel of wheat falls to the ground and dies, it remains only a single seed. But if it dies, it produces many seeds. Those who love their life will lose it, while those who hate their life in this world, will keep it for eternal life. Whoever serves me must follow me" (12:23–26). The "following him" in this context is following him to his hour of glorification: to his death. Undue or misapplied humility will not garner disciples committed even to their death.

And the humble washer of the disciples' feet? Jesus is no unassuming wielder of the basin and towel. He sets an example of servanthood for us. But then he goes on to set matters straight. "Listen to me! The servants are not greater than their master; the messengers are not greater than the one who sent them" (John 13:14).

What then of the humble Jesus, especially of Phil 2, where the apostle Paul writes that Christ Jesus, although he was God himself, in his humility took human form and became an obedient servant? Paul avers that Jesus in his humanity demonstrated his humility by obeying God (Phil 2:8–9). Humility is a contextual virtue, and it is this humility that we find in the Gospel of John. It is not in respect to his contemporaries or to us that Jesus is humble. For us, Jesus is our Lord (20:18), and the servant is not greater than his lord. Rather, Jesus manifests his humility in relating to his Father. "I only do what I see the Father doing" (5:19). "My teaching is not my own. It comes from the one who sent me. . . . Whoever speaks on their own seeks personal glory, but the one who seeks the glory of the one who sent him is a man of truth. There is nothing false about him" (7:16–18). Jesus's humility derives from and is evident in doing the will of the Father; Jesus "only does what pleases the Father" (8:29). He has profound humility before the Father, assured assertiveness before his audience.

Unhealthy pride differs from proper pride. Improper and unhealthy pride is boastful, unwarranted pride about oneself. One fixates on the self as the center of meaning and life. Proper, healthy pride is grounded in relationship. "Let him who boasts boast in the Lord" (1 Cor 1:31). John tells us that through Jesus we are children of God; inheritors of eternal life; family members with brother Jesus, the Son of the Father. This relationship is wondrously proper about which to boast. Our humility, like that of Jesus, is founded on willing obedience to the Father.

## CONCLUSION

From the very beginning of the Gospel, John promotes the highest view of Jesus. Indeed, as he tells us, establishing Jesus's identity is why he writes the book. Everything is an argument for that identity. For John, Jesus's identity is complex. He is God himself, the Word who in the beginning was with God and was God. To this concept John adds other identities that convey the same idea but with the richness of diverse connotations. He is the Son of God (1:49) and the Son of Man, whose origin, authority, glory, and sovereign power is from heaven. He is the Lamb of God who through loving self-sacrifice removes the sins of the world. From the perspective of the people, he is the long-expected Prophet, but is more than one prophet among many; he is the unique Messiah (1:41) and the King of Israel (1:49; 12:13–15). Yet, he also is a human being, tenting in the flesh among us (1:14), raised in Nazareth of Galilee, whose father, mother, and brothers were known (1:45). He is the perplexing rabbi engaged in an itinerant, confrontational, public ministry in the synagogues, temple, towns, and mountainsides. "I have spoken openly to the world" (18:20).

Underlying all this is Jesus's claim of relationship to his Father. It is a oneness of *nature* in that Jesus claims to be divine. Jesus avers he is the "I am" (ἐγώ εἰμί), the LORD of the Old Testament and the Son of the Father in the New Testament. His identity is a oneness of *purpose* and *function*, for Jesus asserts that he can do and does only what he sees the Father doing, that he has come to do the Father's will. Jesus claims to be the giver of life, a point that runs emphatically through the predicative "I ams." He is not merely a shepherd, a door, a vine, a way, bread, light, and resurrection; he is exclusively these. "No one can come to the Father except through me" (14:6). He alone makes access to the Father possible.

We must face it: the claims Jesus makes about himself and affirmed by John are most radical and extreme. To put it succinctly with double meaning, they are out of this world. They can create believing but also lead to puzzlement and denunciation. For example, Jesus's repetitive discourses about himself as "I am" and the abstract, almost nonhuman nature of the predicates that follow "I am" alienate rather than attract his audiences.

> The more Jesus clarifies his identity [and] the more he makes himself the subject and the object of all action, the more those around him distance themselves from him. . . . Insistence that people believe in his name—society's mark of recognition—paradoxically disembodies or dehumanizes Jesus, rendering him alien to that society. . . . By describing himself with language that is highly egocentric and asocial, Jesus set himself apart from familiar and socially intimate relationships and defies identification with the familial and political structures of his society.[53]

What stimulates early curiosity (2:18, 23; 3:1–2; 5:28) becomes a matter of offense and rejection by chapter 6 and perceived blasphemy worthy of stoning by chapter 8. Jesus's humility of obedience to the Father by accepting crucifixion is emphatically, paradoxically countered by his strong, proud affirmations of identity. Being connected to God in the ways he and the Evangelist claim is not trivial, modest, or unassuming. Whereas Jesus identifies himself as the water of life, the bread of life, the light of the world, the resurrection and the life, and the way and the truth, "[o]ther than John the Baptist, who calls Jesus 'the lamb of God,' no one in the gospel uses language for Jesus that is so devoid of clear reference to human relationships."[54] Being sent from the Father and returning to the Father makes him otherworldly indeed.

If we could erase two thousand years of religious history, we too, as did the contemporary crowds and Jewish religious leaders, would find Jesus's identity claims difficult to understand, let alone to swallow. Son of Man and Son of God, indeed. Why should this person be unique rather than simply mad (9:48, 52)? One need only see how Christians and non-Christians have reacted to people over the ages who have claimed to be divine. We house them in our mental institutions, reject and ridicule them, and shake our heads and pens in disbelief for their false, unbelievable, or extravagant claims.

To read the Gospel of John is to experience the same conflicting ambiguities of wonder, awe, amazement, incredulity, and outrage as felt by Jesus's listeners and presumably some of John's audience. The Gospel is full of both rejection and believing

---

53. Brant, *Dialogue*, 170.
54. Brant, *Dialogue*, 170.

based on personal encounter. At the same time, it is an argument, a trial defense,[55] a carefully constructed plea for perhaps the most outrageous and important claim in history. John gives us signs, testimonies, and self-affirmations to support his case. However, what ultimately affects those whom Jesus encounters are the relationships they have with him. Their and our experiences of Jesus solidify their and our believing. John is a Book of Relationships, and to these we turn.

## QUESTIONS FOR REFLECTION AND DISCUSSION

1. When you meet persons for the first time and want to know about them, what might be the first questions you ask and want them to answer?

2. Jesus identifies himself with "I am" statements with predicates. What is an "I am" statement with a predicate? What "I am" statements with predicates does Jesus make?

3. What theme runs through all these I am-with-predicate statements? How does this theme connect with John's overall thesis about Jesus's identity and mission?

4. What is the significance of Jesus's "I am" statements without a predicate? What do you think that these statements show or mean? Do you think that Jesus's disciples or Jewish hearers understood these statements? Why? Would these statements meet with acceptance in today's culture?

5. What question would you like to ask the author or Jesus about the I am statements?

6. The Bible often speaks about humility. Do you think that there is a place for proper pride in the Christian life? How do humility and proper pride go together?

---

55. The Gospel writer's "forensic trials serve to highlight that his claims are truly defensible and that Jesus, the honorable man, knows how to defend his honor [worth, reputation, and status] and thus earn our continual esteem and praise" (Neyrey, *Gospel of John*, 226). Stibbe traces the forensic language in John to Isa 40–55, "where Yahweh is also shown defending who he is (ἐγώ εἰμί in LXX) in a quasi-courtroom setting" (*Storyteller*, 19). For development of the forensic motif, see Harvey, *Jesus*, and, more recently, Lincoln, *Truth on Trial*.

CHAPTER SIX

# Book of Relationships

OF ALL THE GOSPELS, John brings us more deeply into the lives of the people Jesus encounters. "Much of the power of the fourth Gospel comes from its vivid characterizations and their effects upon the reader."[1] Some of his characters have names or positions, relationships with others, real character traits, and emotions. We meet family, wedding hosts, a foreign woman, a divorcee, paralyzed and blind men, impetuous people and doubters, sisters with contrasting personalities, hyper-religious people and powerful politicians, people with class status and people without, true devotees and scoundrels. John treats each as a unique and distinct individual. Some we get to know by name, others by their occupation or situation in life, still others by their deeds and their disputes. Since "most of the characters appear on the literary stage only long enough to fulfill their role in the evangelist's representation of Jesus and the responses to him,"[2] much about them is not disclosed.[3] Yet even in a short, truncated conversation we learn significant information about them. Their character is individualized and developed in their conversations with Jesus, often in response to something he says or does, sometimes beginning with a statement or puzzle and leading ultimately either to some recognition of who Jesus is as the Messiah or Son of God or to doubt and active rejection. We find some of the characters, like the Samaritan woman, Peter, the blind man, and Thomas, in the process of change because they encounter Jesus, which gives John opportunity to develop their character more richly. Others, such as Pilate, the Pharisees, and Jewish leaders, are mired in their traits, which prevent their rethinking who they are and who Jesus is. With few exceptions (Peter, Nicodemus, Thomas, Mary of Bethany, Judas, the Beloved Disciple) we meet them only once. However, for each, what we learn about them is shaped by their encounter with Jesus.

1. Culpepper, *Anatomy*, 7.

2. Culpepper, *Anatomy*, 102.

3. "[Characters] speak and behave in such a way that our understanding of who Jesus really is is enhanced. Characters are therefore not generally introduced and developed for their own sakes" (Stibbe, *Storyteller*, 25).

In effect, John says that, for each of us, who we are is shaped by our encounter with the living Jesus. *We are who we are because Jesus is who he is.*

Our initial question is whether these are real individuals with distinct characters or mere archetypes, standing for types or groups of people. Perhaps the best answer is that for John sometimes they can serve as both.[4] This does not diminish either their historical or symbolic significance. "We may speak, for example, about the representative roles of Jesus and Peter without denying that they actually lived in first-century Palestine; and we may recognize that Jesus and Peter were actual persons without diminishing their importance as representative figures."[5] In developing the characters of the Gospel, their individuality is never lost; they are unique persons who engage Jesus and sometimes others in their community. "The intended readers of the fourth Gospel almost certainly would have assumed that the narrative depicted actual people and events from the past."[6] John paints them as people with whom we can identify.

At the same time, because many of persons are unnamed as well as named and revealed only with some of their characteristics, they may represent groups of individuals, either in their role as individuals (e.g., Nathanael and Thomas represent doubters) or as groups. Others, representing groups, speak with one voice (e.g., the grumbling disciples who leave Jesus (6:6–61, 66); the confused crowds (7:12, 20, 31); the antagonistic Jews (6:41; 7:15, 35; 8:48; 18:30–31; 19:6, 12); Pharisees (7:45–52, 8:13, 19; 9:40; 11:47–48); Greeks who want to see Jesus (12:20–21); Jews who demand conviction and crucifixion (18:28–32, 38–40)). The best evidence for this archetypal interpretation lies in John's grammar. "The introduction to an episode sometimes identifies a character with a particular group of people. The person in turn may act as the spokesperson for the group by using the plural, 'we,' and Jesus will often reply in the second person plural, *hymeis*, which we translate 'you people.'"[7] We will see this exemplified in the dialogue with Nicodemus shortly. Koester goes beyond this to suggest a wider representation; "a person or group (may) reveal something characteristic of human beings in relationship to God, so that they typify a faith stance."[8]

At the center of John's introduction and development of characters is Jesus. It is in terms of their relationship to him that all the characters in the Gospel achieve identity, personal features, and importance. These relationships are diverse. We have already pointed to the characterizations that arise from being testifiers to Jesus's identity. Not only are they individuals in their own right; for John they are persons who further the point of his Gospel by seeking to understand Jesus and become his disciples. They

---

4. "Only the barest outline of their past is ever related. . . . Instead, the characters are individualized by their position in society and their interaction with Jesus. This means that they may easily become types." Yet by being types they do not forfeit their individuality (Culpepper, *Anatomy*, 145).

5. Koester, *Symbolism*, 39.

6. Koester, *Symbolism*, 38.

7. Koester, *Symbolism*, 35.

8. Koester, *Symbolism*, 35.

also may be painted as contemporaries with whom John's readers can identify in their quest to understand the nature and function or mission of Jesus.

> The stories of the wedding at Cana (John 2:1–12), Nicodemus (3:11–15), the Samaritan woman at the well (4:4–42), and the trial before Pilate (18:28–19:15) are all self-contained and coherent in their own right, but John's larger story-act unites them by exploring the ways that different characters struggle to understand Jesus. John's plot achieves its rhetorical effect as the implied reader, who is informed of Jesus's true identity in the opening verses of the book (1:10, 18), observes and evaluates the adequacy of these various responses.[9]

Ultimately, the point of these relationships with Jesus is the inculcation of authentic faith in response to him. To know who Jesus is and to relate to him is to become his disciple in believing and deed. "The *existential response* to truth and its revelation within the human-divine discourse becomes the final interest of characterological analysis, but such cannot be ascertained effectively from a distance. It can only be embraced or rejected as a personal factor of authentic faith."[10] Thus, in these relationships we see how Jesus's contemporaries come and depart from him, and how their lives are or are not altered by this encounter. In this chapter we will focus on those who experienced a positive change.

We already have explored several changed persons in their role as testifiers. Here we will look closely at other individuals whose relationship with Jesus is particularly poignant and whose identity is developed and displayed in that relationship.

## NICODEMUS

Early in his ministry, following his expulsion of the animal sellers and money changers from the temple courts,[11] Jesus continued to perform signs, which for many became the basis of believing. Their believing apparently was shallow, for Jesus would not entrust himself to these new believers, "for he knew all people" (2:24).[12] One who saw the signs and was both impressed and puzzled was Nicodemus, a member of the Jewish ruling council. Nicodemus initiates a relationship with Jesus by coming to him

9. Thatcher, "Antinomies," 25.

10. Anderson, "Philip," 174.

11. Whether Jesus used the cords on the sellers is debated. Michaels says that he uses them on everyone because all (πάντας) is masculine (*Gospel of John*, 159n8; Barrett, *Gospel*, 165). Bultmann treats the phrase "both the sheep and the oxen" (τά τε πρόβατα καὶ τοὺς βόας) as a "poor modifier to πάντας" and hence a later editorial addition (*Gospel of John*, 123n8). But one might wonder why the modifier is there at all if it is an unnecessary addition. This additional phrase might qualify Jesus's action to indicate that Jesus used the whip of cords not on the people but on both the sheep and the oxen (2:15).

12. John plays on the Greek word for believe (πιστεύω) in 2:22–24. The disciples, on reflection after the resurrection, believed; many who witnessed his signs believed on the spot, but Jesus did not believe in (entrust himself to) them.

at night (3:2). The natural explanation for the night visit is that, as a person of position on the ruling council, he did not want to compromise his position by being seen by others meeting with Jesus.[13] The reference to night is also symbolic and sets up the image of the world and darkness coming to the light, a theme that is developed later in what is either part of the dialogue or the narrator's commentary (3:19–21, a second half of the *inclusio*).[14] The reference to night thus immediately sets the question whether Nicodemus will move from the darkness to the light.

We are never told why Nicodemus comes to inquire of Jesus, only that he makes an introductory assertion about who Jesus is (a rabbi) and that he performs signs. However, we can infer that what attracts him are the signs that Jesus performs while in Jerusalem (3:2). As a Pharisee, he can fathom that some sort of power lies behind the miracles. The power he is familiar with as "the teacher of Israel" (3:10) is divine power. Thus, he begins the conversation by noting that Jesus has some connection with God. In John's language, Jesus comes from God and God is with him, notably as the source of Jesus's power. Apparently, Nicodemus is curious to understand this relationship between Jesus and God.

Jesus does not ask Nicodemus why he came but moves quickly beyond Nicodemus's introductory statement. Whereas Nicodemus wants to know who Jesus is beyond being a teacher who speaks from God, Jesus broadens the scope of the discussion to participation in the kingdom of God and the prerequisites for such participation. As a Jewish ruler, Nicodemus should know something about and be immensely interested in the kingdom of God. Jesus informs Nicodemus that his coming has great universal significance for launching the kingdom. Jesus immediately turns to his riddling: to experience the kingdom of God one must be born again (3:3). Jesus takes the earthly experience of physical birth and turns it into a metaphor for a transcendent reality. Nicodemus fails to understand the wordplay on birth (physical vs. spiritual) and on ἄνωθεν, meaning either "again" or "from above."[15] "Being born anew" can be understood as referring either to being from below as physical rebirth or from above as spiritual birth. By this duality Jesus conveys to Nicodemus a point Jesus later

13. Beasley-Murray (*John*, 47) suggests that the visit at night was not done out of fear but for the desire for an uninterrupted conversation. But the fear interpretation fits better with the darkness/light motif of the pericope. Another suggestion for the visit at night is the "rabbinic custom of staying up at night to study the Law" (Brown, *Gospel i–xii*, 130; also Thatcher, *Riddles*, 266).

14. John has already prepared the reader for the significance of light and darkness (1:4–5, 9) and goes on to reinforce it (9:4; 11:10; 13:30; 21:3). For a nuanced treatment of Nicodemus, see Koester, "Theological Complexity," 163–79.

15. Michael Whitenton ("Dissembler") argues that Nicodemus does understand what Jesus says, but because he fails to grasp who Jesus is and thus believe, assumes the role of a dissembler, lavishing praise on Jesus and putting himself down. Jesus, he claims, recognizes this and instead of addressing Nicodemus's misunderstanding of the metaphor, turns to the matter of his unbelieving. To make this stick, Whitenton must claim that in the later portraits of Nicodemus, when his believing seems to emerge, he is no longer a dissembler. This interpretation of Nicodemus's misunderstanding does not comport well with the numerous other instances of misunderstanding in John.

reiterates (9:31–47): what is necessary for entering God's kingdom is not an earthly Jewish heritage and the keeping of the Law in which Pharisees prided themselves, but his heavenly, spiritual heritage claimed through believing in Jesus. Jesus sets before Nicodemus a radical choice of births or origins.

We must sympathize with Nicodemus's puzzlement at this riddle.[16] We understand that here the terms have a deeper spiritual application because we have read the entire dialogue, something not available to Nicodemus. For those who, unlike Nicodemus, have read the entire story and experienced birth from above, it is clear that water, wind, and being born again or from above have double meanings. We will say more about this in chapter 11.

It must be admitted that Jesus shows little sympathy for this puzzled Jewish teacher. He wonders why this Israelite leader has so little understanding of the significance of the events he has witnessed (3:10). Why does Nicodemus not grasp the riddle or comprehend this wordplay, and since he has witnessed the testimonial signs, why doesn't he accept what the signs signify or testify to (3:12)? Nicodemus is both attracted to (3:2) and limited by the possible (3:4, 9).

However, very quickly the perplexed Nicodemus as an individual drops out of the discussion and is replaced by being a representative of "you people" (3:7).[17] Nicodemus's initial "we" (3:2), suggesting he represents others, is answered by Jesus with a "you" (plural). Jesus's message is not only for Nicodemus. John never reports Jesus encountering Nicodemus again, so that we do not learn whether he ever understands "how this (rebirth) can be" (3:9). It is difficult, being given only a snippet of the conversation and having what is given move from the particular "Nicodemus" to the universal "world," to know how the conversation ultimately went. However, we meet him twice more.

Commentators on John's account of Nicodemus have debated what kind of faith he exhibited. Some see him as having only a sign-faith, as belonging to the group of people to whom "Jesus would not entrust himself" (2:24).[18] Those who adopt this view understand the positioning of this story following chapter 2 as indicating this. Nicodemus is like Jews who initially believe in Jesus but never maintain that faith, for they still rely on their origins, their Jewishness (8:31–41). He never really brings himself to believe. When later he challenges the rulers (7:50–52), it is not with an open affirmation of believing but with a query that Jesus just might be a prophet, though

16. Some commentators are less sympathetic. "Because Jewish teachers spoke of gentile converts to Judaism as starting life anew like 'newborn children,' Nicodemus should have understood that Jesus meant conversion. Yet it never occurs to him that someone Jewish would need to convert to the true faith of Israel" (Keener, *John*, 28).

17. The interjection of the plural "we" and "you" (3:11–12) has puzzled commentators. The plural "we" might mean that John broadens the testifiers and "you" those testified to. Alternatively, as a spokesperson, Nicodemus might have come with others to question Jesus, and now Jesus speaks to the entire group (Michaels, *Gospel of John*, 190–92).

18. De Jonge, *Jesus*, 33. See also Coloe, *God*, 79.

with no inkling that Jesus is more than a mortal prophet. In the end, he bestows on Jesus a fortune of spices for burial, thereby giving no indication that he hopes for anything beyond the grave for Jesus. Nicodemus "regards the burial as definitive" and is unable "to look further than the tomb in the garden." This perspective sharply differs from that of the Evangelist, who sees in Jesus's death the beginning of "a new era in God's dealings with mankind."[19] "Nicodemus's generosity does not exonerate him from John's generally low view of secret faith based on signs."[20] Nicodemus remains outside the kingdom of God.[21]

I suggest, more positively, that John portrays Nicodemus as moving gradually on the road to faith.[22] In his initial encounter he is at best in the beginning stage of faith, made curious by the witness of Jesus's signs. Jesus recognizes that Nicodemus has only sign-faith and needs to be instructed about the birth from above. As with others in the Gospel (the Samaritan woman, the blind man, Thomas), his faith grows throughout the narrative. Although we meet a puzzled teacher of Israel in chapter 3, we later find someone who, although he himself does not take a stand, is bold enough to challenge the Pharisees to carry out an objective investigation about Jesus's identity (7:50–51). That he is willing to challenge the religious powers indicates that although he still is concerned about his position, he is willing to risk suggesting that the truth be found. As a Pharisee, he knows that both sides of the case must be heard, with appropriate witnesses, to judge fairly (Deut 1:16; 17:4; 19:16–18). In doing so, he hints that another side, the side of Jesus whom he encountered, should be heard.

In John's third reference to Nicodemus, not only is night mentioned to identify Nicodemus, but also perhaps to note the contrast that now Nicodemus acts in daylight, stepping out to assume responsibility for Jesus's body (19:39–40). His faith is not fully informed; the amount of spices he uses to embalm the corpse indicates that he takes Jesus's death as permanent.[23] However, we may excuse him for this lack of total understanding. At least he acts. After all, even the disciples who traveled extensively with Jesus and had been told that the Messiah would rise did not understand about resurrection until after the event (2:22), and they are nowhere to be found at the cross. The direct relationship between Jesus and Nicodemus, then, may have been brief, or maybe not; John does not tell us everything. Nonetheless, Jesus has changed his life from a reluctant and fearful inquirer to someone willing to openly embrace a condemned and crucified man.[24]

19. De Jonge, *Jesus*, 33–34.

20. Thatcher, *Antinomies*, 17.

21. "Nicodemus is 'not far from the kingdom of God,' but he remains outside" (Culpepper, *Anatomy*, 136).

22. Schnackenburg, *John*, 1:365.

23. This may be another of John's double meanings, for the amount of costly spices Nicodemus uses is appropriate for the burial of a king, which Pilate proclaimed Jesus to be.

24. Raymond Brown (*Introduction*, 173–74) talks about crypto-Christians, who are unwilling to reveal themselves as Christians for fear of being social outcasts. However, because of his changed life

John gives clues that Nicodemus is to be taken not only as an individual but representative of a larger group, of the religious elite.

> Nicodemus plays an important supporting role in the text. Although he appears to be alone, he speaks in the plural: 'Rabbi, we know that you are a teacher come from God' (3:2). Jesus initially responds with singular forms of address but shifts to the Greek plural in the middle of the conversation, saying 'you people do not receive our testimony'; although 'we have told you people earthy things, you people do not believe' (3:11–12). Nicodemus's representative role is complex, like that of Jesus.[25]

From the plural form of address, "without pausing, Jesus broadens the scope of the conversation even further, to speak of the entire world's estrangement from God."[26]

If Nicodemus is such a representative, whom does he represent? Some see him representing the ruling religious elite. First, "[h]e is first 'a man of the Pharisees' and 'a ruler of the Jews' (3:1), thus representing the Jewish authorities who regularly refuse to believe in Jesus elsewhere in the Gospel"[27] In this interpretation Nicodemus represents the Jewish religious authorities who challenge (8:13, 19), reject (9:16, 34), and threaten to kill Jesus (11:46–53). "Second, he speaks for those who believed when they saw the signs Jesus did, but whose faith was untrustworthy (2:23–25; 3:2)."[28] As a representative of both groups, Koester sees Nicodemus as standing in contrast to true believers (3:11). He represents those who never really bring themselves to believe. Third, Koester also sees him as representing all humanity estranged from God, the universal man. "The reminder that Nicodemus had come to Jesus 'by night at first' (19:39) could suggest that he was 'still in the dark' and that the horizon of his thinking ended at the grave, for the piles of spices he heaped upon the corpse would be useless for one being 'lifted up.'"[29] On this view, those like Nicodemus are not on a journey from uncertain faith to bold witness but are trapped in doubt and uncertainty. Thus, he represents not people journeying in their faith but rather those who remain in the unbelieving world for whom God sent his son.

I have already suggested that if we take a more positive view of Nicodemus, we can see him as representing the Jewish leaders who are more sympathetic to Jesus and his message. Some of them are secret believers who "would not openly acknowledge their faith for fear they would be evicted from the synagogue, for they loved human glory more than the glory of God" (12:42). Nicodemus's statements in 7:50–52 hint that this was a stage of reluctancy, well justified by the expulsion the Pharisees carry

---

by coming into the light and by taking an active role, Nicodemus seems to be more than this.

25. Koester, *Symbolism*, 12.

26. Koester, *Symbolism*, 45.

27. Koester, *Symbolism*, 12.

28. Koester, *Symbolism*, 12.

29. Koester, *Symbolism*, 29.

out (9:22, 34). Others sincerely put their faith in Jesus (11:45) and act in ways that indicate their faith is sincere, as Nicodemus does later after Jesus's death by providing spices for his burial. Perhaps he stands for us as well, "Overly confident in our faith-based religious knowledge,"[30] but not really understanding or appreciating the meaning of it all. If we were honest, we would be as puzzled as Nicodemus was.

In sum, Jesus's dialogue with Nicodemus is fleeting and, as the discussion proceeds, becomes impersonal. Yet, the encounter must have been significant. The Gospel writer treats Nicodemus by name as a person, and the Gospel names few individuals who are not among the disciples. Second, he performs two other positive roles in the Gospel. In the one role, he recommends investigation of testimony, which is the theme of the Gospel. Nicodemus's boldness here to suggest investigation encourages readers to do likewise. We also see him acting in the role of a disciple. True, he lacks full knowledge of who Jesus is and of his function and mission. Nevertheless, his discipleship leads him to take a serious risk in associating with a condemned criminal. His very action of preparing the body demonstrates that something significant happened in his life when he encountered Jesus that night. Thus, we may see Nicodemus's encounter with Jesus as a first step on a pilgrimage to faith, and although we do not see the ultimate outcome in his life, it is encouraging for readers to understand the struggle of someone of significant position possibly coming to faith through that encounter.

## SIMON PETER

Although Mark is usually referred to as Peter's gospel, Peter really comes alive as a person in the Gospel of John. He appears seven distinct times, and from each we learn something more about his character. (We will say more about the significance of "seven" in chapter 10.) In six of those instances Simon Peter talks with Jesus; in the seventh Peter looks for him among the grave clothes without finding him. In effect, John develops Peter's character through his relationship with Jesus.

He first appears when recruited by his brother Andrew, who announces that (note the plural used frequently in John) "we have found the Messiah" (1:41). When Simon is brought to Jesus, Jesus renames him Cephas or Peter, which means "rock."[31] Although—unlike in Matthew 16:18—the meaning of the name is not given, the significance of the name change is evident. Jesus sees something in Peter that predicts his future, namely, that in him lies a steadiness and reliability strong enough on which to build his following. It is true that Simon Peter's steadiness stands in grave doubt

30. Gench, *Encounters*, 25.

31. Michaels notes that the name Cephas is treated as a surname, not as a nickname. "The name 'Cephas' is used only here in the Gospels, but eight times in Paul's letters (1 Cor 1:12; 3:22; 9:5; 15:5; Gal 1:18; 2:9, 11, 13). Paul uses the name 'Peter' in Galatians 2:7–8, where his language seems to have been dictated by that of a specific agreement drawn up by the Jerusalem church. Otherwise, Paul seems to have regarded Cephas as a real name, not a nickname, and consequently not to be translated, as the Gospel writer has done here" (*Gospel of John*, 124n28).

during Jesus's earthy ministry and does not really manifest itself until after Jesus's resurrection and departure, when Peter rallies the disciples to elect a replacement for Judas (Acts 1:15–22) and with his Pentecost sermon commences the establishment of the church (Acts 2:14–41). However, John's readers will now understand that Simon Peter's performance derives from Jesus's relationship to and confidence in him, manifest in both this first encounter and the last (ch. 21). Indeed, Jesus's confidence in Simon bookends the Gospel. In Simon's renaming we are given the promise of dependability; we need the entire history of the early church to discover whether Jesus's confidence is well placed.

We meet Simon Peter a second time after Jesus's ambiguous, tumultuous, and riddling presentation of himself as the bread of life. Seeing his followers leave in droves because of his eccentric claims, Jesus turns to the Twelve and pointedly asks them if they want to leave also (6:67). It is Simon Peter who responds, taking on his characteristic role of spokesperson for the Twelve. "We have no other option; we will stay." Peter is a betting person. The odds might not be all that great that Jesus is the Messiah announced by his brother Andrew; few of a kingdom army of followers are left after Jesus's discomforting and provocative statements about his flesh and bread. However, Peter is willing to place his money on this person, for he not only believes but knows both Jesus's nature (he is the Holy One of God) and his function (he gives the words of eternal life) (6:68). Simon Peter has an inkling that Jesus is special because of his relationship with Gód. Here we learn that Simon Peter really is a leader, willing to go against the departing crowd because of his insight. And we see that Peter manifests the "behavior of a model disciple" by showing that the true response to Jesus is to believe and know (6:69),[32] the very point the Evangelist wants his readers to understand.

Simon Peter falls out of the Gospel narrative until just before the Passover feast, when in our third encounter Jesus eats an evening meal with his disciples. After wrapping a towel around his waist and pouring water into a basin, Jesus demonstrates the servant attitude by washing and drying, one by one, the disciples' feet (13:4–17). When he comes to Simon Peter, the servant action of his Lord offends Peter. It breaks all the rules of order that hold between lord or master and servant. "Washing someone else's feet was an unpleasant task which no one except a servant or slave could be expected to do." In fact, where there were both slaves and servants in the household, "it would be a duty of the slaves, not of the servants, who performed the less demeaning tasks such as waiting at table."[33] Peter has already acknowledged Jesus's lordship (6:68) and should, he thinks, be washing his Master's feet. For the Master to wash his feet was an unthinkable, social outrage. Only after Jesus threatens to remove Peter from the core of disciples does Peter consent and then in his typically rash way goes all the way, asking Jesus to wash him all over: hands and head as well (13:9). Jesus's reply to Simon Peter is that if he had a bath before coming to eat, he only needed his feet washed.

32. Labahn, "Simon Peter," 155.
33. Bauckham, *Testimony*, 192.

"And you[34] are already clean" (here stated with an obvious double meaning of physical and spiritual cleanliness (καθαροί)).

The relationship here is full of irony. While Peter invokes the tradition of social hierarchy to refuse Jesus's offer to wash his feet, he breaks that very tradition by rebuking his Master for not behaving as he should (13:6), and then proceeds to refuse his Master all together: "You will not wash my feet!" (13:8). Jesus understands this volatile disciple and responds with gentle firmness.

In this relationship Jesus teaches Simon Peter the role and importance of being a servant to others, a skill he will develop and use later (Acts 10 and 11). Peter knows the common understanding of the proper relationship between master (lord, rabbi) and servant, and refuses to violate that tradition. We might say that he is a traditionalist who misunderstands Jesus. However, Jesus pushes him into a new understanding of his spiritual role. The servant is not greater than the master, but the master is not greater than the servant when it comes to service; leaders should be willing to do what they expect followers to do. Thus, Simon Peter is to follow the example of his master, even taking on the servant role. We learn that Peter can have a pendulum reaction to situations. On the one hand, he can be a traditionalist; on the other, when that position is threatened, he can run heedlessly to the opposite extreme and be "all in." Jesus instructs him (as does the Evangelist his readers) in servant leadership: to be both leader as servant to those he leads and as servant in service to the Master, he needs to hold to a steady course. (We will return to this dialogue in chapter 7.)

A short time later Jesus shares that someone will betray him, and although the other disciples are puzzled, Simon Peter, curious and wanting to know who it will be, requests the Beloved Disciple who is reclining on Jesus to ask Jesus for the identity of this person. When Jesus indirectly identifies Judas and Judas leaves, there is perhaps a sense of uncomprehending relief of tension. Yet the matter of betrayal is not settled. Peter, in his impetuosity, affirms his loyalty to Jesus: "Can't I follow you *now*; I will lay down my life for you" (13:37), a faint echo of his Master's statement (10:11). There is little doubt that Peter was sincere about this matter, as shown when he later valiantly draws his sword in defense of Jesus (18:10). However, Jesus knows that this impetuous and brave person has a fearful side as well. He is not yet a reliable shepherd, and Jesus predicts that he, like the man who left the meal, will also deny him, not once but three times. The rock is strong but not immune to the pressures others place on him. The contrast in the relationship between Jesus and Peter could not be clearer: Peter the rock, not Jesus, cracks. Again, it is not until Acts and Pentecost that we see Peter's fears take second place to his testimonial commitment, when he stands up to the pilgrim crowd who wonder about this seemingly intoxicated bunch (Acts 2:1–14) and to the Sanhedrin who imprisons him (Acts 5:17–32). In the end, according to Jesus's telling (21:18) and tradition, Peter will play the part of the Shepherd's self-sacrificing disciple.

34. In the Greek, "you" is plural, perhaps implying not just Peter.

In our fifth meeting with Peter, Jesus's prophecy of Simon Peter's denial comes to pass. Peter demonstrates his bravery by drawing his sword to defend Jesus before the arresting mob (18:10). Though facing a detachment of soldiers made the cause hopeless, it shows his love for Jesus (10:11) and fulfills his earlier promise to die for Jesus (13:37). However, Peter misunderstands that this is Jesus's time to "drink the cup that the Father has given him" and thus opposes Jesus's very mission (18:11). He continues to demonstrate his loyalty and concern as he follows Jesus to the courtyard of the high priest. However, here he loses his nerve, not in the face of powerful officials and the high priest who query and accuse Jesus, but in the face of servants, both a servant girl and a servant of the high priest (18:17, 25–27). "Jesus stands up to his questioners and denies nothing, while Peter cowers before his questioners and denies everything."[35] Peter warms himself by the dim light of the charcoal fire outside while the true light is being interrogated inside. John could not make the irony here sharper. Jesus tells his accusers to ask his hearers about his message, while his chief hearer repudiates any association with Jesus. By denying that he is one of Jesus's disciples—"I am not"—and denying that he had accompanied Jesus in the olive grove, he severs his relationship with Jesus at the most critical moment. The rock, we learn, is fragile, its crack ironically not caused by the rich and powerful but by comments from servants. We do not learn in John about Peter's reaction to his weakness of denial. For that we must go to the other gospels, where Matthew tells us that when he realized what he had done and recalled his impulsive response before his accusers, "he went outside and wept bitterly" (Matt 26:75). John indirectly confirms this, for the Beloved Disciple, not Simon Peter, was the only male disciple at the crucifixion. Peter is too much like us, at times brave in the abstract but fearful in the deed. However, Matthew assures, he is genuinely remorseful.

We have already recounted in chapter 3 Peter's sixth appearance. Given what had just happened, one can only imagine the mixture of joy and anguish, hope and despair, eagerness and confusion that Simon Peter had upon hearing that the situation at the tomb was not normal. Slower of foot than his friend, he arrives at the tomb behind the Beloved Disciple. Whereas the latter is hesitant to enter, Peter's impetuosity, curiosity, and perhaps hopefulness get the better of him, and he enters the rock tomb to confirm that indeed it is empty. However, we are told that this does not bring about believing; he returns to his home, seemingly unchanged, failing to understand that what Jesus had spoken about has happened. Despite witnessing the Lazarus event, resurrection from the dead is not part of his worldview.

Simon Peter's seventh and final appearance in the Gospel's final chapter provides the capstone to Peter's career of a relationship with the incarnate Lord. It is his definitive experience that brings about believing and commitment. We meet Simon Peter lake fishing with other disciples. This is his occupation, although we do not learn of it in John. The Evangelist's story in John is a post-resurrection account that mirrors

35. Brown, *Gospel xiii–xxi*, 842.

Jesus's first call of Simon Peter to discipleship as given in Luke 5:1–11. (Andrew, not Jesus, calls Peter in the Gospel of John.) Many of the same story elements are present in both—fishing on Lake Galilee (Gennesaret or Tiberias); a long night of futile fishing; Jesus is on or by the shore; Jesus instructs them to put their nets down in another location to obtain a good catch; the result is a net overly full of flopping fish; Peter impetuously comes to worship Jesus; Jesus commissions him to discipleship. In John's post-resurrection account, the disciples are not far from shore but weary after a night of vain fishing. Jesus greets them from shore in the morning fog and suggests that they fish on the right side of the boat. As soon as the Beloved Disciple recognizes Jesus and announces this to his fellows, Peter impetuously jumps overboard and heads for shore, followed by the other disciples towing their net full of fish. He had tried going overboard before (Matt 14:28–31), although apparently now Peter is not in over his head—but he still needs rescuing from his prior act of denial. After Simon Peter reclimbs aboard and drags the fish-laden net ashore, the fishermen breakfast with the Lord. Over a charcoal fire, Jesus prepares fish that he already, unaccountably has and gives to them with bread for their breakfast, as he had given to them bread and fish years ago to distribute to people stranded on the Galilean mountainside (6:8–12). Like those on the mountainside, these disciples by the lake also are stranded, not only in their unsuccessful resumption of the old way of life but in their misunderstanding and incomprehension of the apparently calamitous end of their adventure with Jesus and his startling reappearance in their old haunts. There is so much we would like to know about Jesus and the disciples in these brief post-resurrection days, but we are only provided a slim gap in the curtain.

As the Galilean appearance story unfolds, the Evangelist reminds his readers that without Jesus, fishing will prove unsuccessful. It is only when Jesus appears that the harvest is abundant, more than they can handle, yet not enough to break the net.[36] The abundance of the wine in Cana is matched by the abundance of fish in Galilee, all at the behest of Jesus. The narrative continues with a morning, not an evening, meal supplied by Jesus. The evangelistic task of fishing must continue in the day ahead, before night comes when "no one can work" (9:4). The church's outreach ministry is inaugurated. Jesus assures them through the bread and fish that the life of abundance has not come to an end, but he needs to be a part of it.

John's symbolism changes from fishing to shepherding (21:15–17), although food (eating and feeding) provides continuity between the two scenes. The Lukan metaphor of evangelistic fishing for persons (Luke 5:10) transmutes into the Johannine metaphor of shepherding the flock (the community of persons). The other disciples disappear from the conversation, and the focus turns to a semiprivate dialogue between Jesus and Simon Peter (apparently the Beloved Disciple is trailing along behind). After Simon Peter's denial of Jesus at the house of the high priest, his relationship with

---

36. The unity among believers that Jesus prays for (18:21) is here visualized in an unbroken (no schism, ἐσχίσθη) net, full of caught fish (Gench, *Encounters*, 145–46).

Jesus is on the line. Gently but firmly, Jesus helps Simon Peter through his threefold denial experience by asking Simon three times whether he loved him. Simon Peter is no longer the rock but Simon the initiate, again invited to come to the rediscovered Messiah, this time with a heart heavy from betrayal. Whereas Andrew his brother was the first inviter (1:41–42), here Jesus himself, his Lord and Shepherd, initiates the discourse.

The encounter begins with an invitation to a meal (21:12–13), and one might surmise Peter's trepidation at facing Jesus over another meal, after his bravado performance at the previous meal with Jesus (13:37–38). Jesus addresses Simon as the son of Jonas, linking this painful reinstatement with the story of Jonah, who flees his Lord and must be painfully restored to his mission.[37] The Shepherd is about to turn his precious lambs and sheep over to the care of a new shepherd (10:1–18), and the question in the air is what kind of shepherd Simon will make. Will he care for or abandon the sheep at the first sign of danger, or will he be the loving shepherd who willingly lays down his life for those in his care (10:13–15)?[38] Jesus's questioning is painful (21:17) but perhaps also therapeutic for Simon, for after each of Simon's responses Jesus gives Simon a mission of responsibility, affirming that Jesus still trusts him. Jesus has come to Galilee to search for and reinstate the strayed Simon. Initially called to the mission role of being a fisher of men, now he is summoned as the shepherd of the sheep. He must apply his once thrice denied but now thrice professed love for his Lord to the ministry of tending the flock. In this dialogue one can sense the painful forgiveness that Simon Peter received from his Lord and can appreciate in the end the love that Simon has and confesses for his all-knowing Lord (21:15–17). "There can be little doubt that the three questions, with Peter's three positive answers, are intended by the Gospel writer as a record of Peter's reinstatement, signaled in advance to the reader by a 'charcoal fire' (v. 9) recalling the setting of those three denials (see 18:18, 25)."[39] Pursuant to Jesus's three questions, Peter now knows that the Lord himself knows how many times he denied Jesus in the dark of the night and how many times he must reaffirm that love in the morning by the lake. New light must conquer darkness. His love is such that he will eventually fulfill his earlier promise to die for his Lord (13:37),

---

37. Jesus calls Simon "son of Jonas (Ἰωνᾶ)" in both (and only these) cases (1:43 and 21:15), thereby linking the two callings of Simon Peter. In the first case Simon is renamed as Cephas or, in Greek, Peter. Since John does not give the significance of this "calling" or name change, as does Matthew (16:18), one might presume that his readers were aware of the significance of the name change, that he is "the rock on which Jesus will build his church." In the second case, Simon Peter is called to discipleship and a mission. In both cases, Jonah, the missionary to Nineveh who initially denied but eventually fulfilled his calling, stands in the background, in the first instance anticipatory of the passion event, in the second retrospective.

38. "While Peter dies as the shepherd *of* Jesus's flock, Jesus is still the 'Good Shepherd' who gives his life *for* his flock" (Labahn, "Simon Peter," 165–66).

39. Michaels, *Gospel of John*, 1045. One-sidedly, Bultmann rejects this interpretation on the ground that there is no mention of the denial and Peter's repentance in this passage; instead, he focuses on Peter's commissioning (*Gospel of John*, 712).

despite the temporary deviation of denial. For that love, tradition tells us that he will die a martyr's death of crucifixion, although compelled rather than by choice.[40] Of course, Simon Peter is still Simon the curious about other people, such that he wants to know what is going to happen to his friend; Jesus replies tactfully: It is none of your business (21:21–22).[41]

Peter's restoration and renewed mission are matters of love. Indeed, love of Jesus is the prerequisite for anyone tending the flock. In Peter's case, Jesus's love comes through the forgiveness implied in dialogue through a trilogy of questions. Jesus demonstrated his love in his death while simultaneously Peter was denying him: "Greater love has no one than this: that one lay down one's life for others" (15:13). Now Simon Peter can move beyond the denial made in the past and respond to that love with his own love, which too will cost him his life.[42]

John uses two words for "love" in this dialogue, ἀγαπάω and φιλέω. Whether these two terms are used synonymously or with different meanings is much debated.[43] On the one hand, the current consensus is that John uses these two terms synonymously:[44] "In relation to the NT it is important to note that φιλέω often approximates to ἀγαπάω in meaning and use."[45] The evidence for this is that John often varies his terminology without changing the meaning.[46] To confirm this, defenders of this view appeal to the presence of other duplicated terms in this passage, such as "lamb" (ἀρνία) and "sheep" (πρόβατά) (21:15–17), "feed" (βόσκε) and "shepherd" (ποίμαινε) (21:15–17), "drawing" (ἑλκῦσαι) and "dragging" (σύροντες) the net (21:6, 8), and "boat" (πλοῖον) and "little boat" (πλοιαρίῳ) (21:3, 6, 8).

---

40. Tradition tells us that the choice came in the manner of death (upside down), not in the martyrdom. Michaels says that Jesus's prediction indicates but does not necessitate a martyr's death (*Gospel of John*, 1047–48).

41. "Following Jesus to martyrdom, however, is not the calling of every disciple. . . . There are different vocations in ministry, some less dramatic, and our task is to be faithful to the particular calling that God in Christ has given us" (Gench, *Encounters*, 151).

42. "Jesus's insistence that Peter follow his example of self-sacrificing ἀγάπη (chs. 13–17), and Peter's failure to do so, might impact our reading of their conversation in ch. 21. . . . The forceful threefold repetition of verbal forms in 13:34, ἀγαπᾶτε ('Love'), καθὼς ἠγάπησα ('as I loved'), ἀγαπᾶτε ('Love'), and the nominal form ἀγάπην in the verse that follows leave Jesus's hearers and John's readers in no doubt: ἀγάπη, as Jesus defines it at the outset of his Farewell Discourse, is a love that lays down its life and in so doing marks out those who call themselves Jesus's disciples. . . . In addition to this quantitative emphasis, Jesus's words in 15:13 emphasize this specific connotation of ἀγάπη qualitatively by means of his use of the superlative: 'greater love has no man than this, that he lay down his life for his friend'" (Shepherd, "Do You Love," 786–87, 781, 783).

43. For a discussion of positions see Shepherd, "'Do You Love Me?'" Also Morris, *Gospel*, 769–70n41, n42, and n43; and Brown, *Gospel i–xii*, 497–98.

44. Culpepper, "Peter," 174–76.

45. Stählin, "φιλέω," 116. Also Barrett, *Gospel*, 486; Bultmann, *Gospel of John*, 711n5.

46. Jesus has a "habit of introducing slight variations in all sorts of places without real difference in meaning" (Morris, *Gospel*, 770).

On the other hand, suppose that John is being selective and purposive about the words he chooses for love and uses them to trace Simon's pilgrimage to becoming a follower (21:19).[47] The word usage here alludes to the previous discussion with Simon in chapters 13 and 15.[48] This way of looking at the dialogue describes a distinctive progression as Jesus brings Simon back into relationship with him by reconnecting him with his original protestation that he loves Jesus so much that he would die for him (13:37). Jesus first asks Simon Peter, "Do you love me more than these?" (21:15). Jesus uses the term ἀγαπᾷς, which some believe stands for a higher love, one of devotion, "deep-seated, thorough-going, intelligent and purposeful, a love in which the entire personality (not only the emotions but also the mind and the will) plays a prominent part,"[49] a love willing to die for another (15:13). Jesus asks whether Peter has this higher, self-sacrificial love about which he spoke during his ministry (10:14–18). Simon Peter replies. "Yes Lord, you know that I love you." However, rather than using ἀγαπάω, Simon uses the word φιλέω, which in John (11:3, 36) and elsewhere in other Greek writings is used for the love of friends or of conjugal relations.[50] Perhaps embarrassed by his disowning Jesus at the house of the high priest, Peter hesitates to claim or reaffirm the higher love of sacrificial giving of oneself for Jesus and opts for the basic friendship that they had shared before that his denial.

The other interesting piece is that Jesus asks Simon whether he loves him "more than these." This ambiguous phrase is subject to various interpretations. One interpretation concerns whether Simon loves Jesus more than he loves his boat and nets, the instruments of his livelihood. For some, this seems unlikely, "for no such 'love' for material things has played any part in the story."[51] Yet Peter has abandoned Jerusalem, Jesus, and the quest for eternal life (6:68) and returned to his roots and previous trade in Galilee. A second possibility is whether Simon Peter loves Jesus more than he loves these, his fishing friends, for even though Peter saw the empty tomb and two appearances of Jesus (20:19, 26), we find him not looking for Jesus but fishing with his friends. A third possibility, adopted by most recent scholars, is that Simon loves Jesus more than any of the other disciples love Jesus. Here Jesus compares Simon's love with that of the others.

> Against this way of taking the words is the difficulty of thinking that Jesus would invite one of his followers to compare the strength of his love with that of other disciples. Yet we must remember that Peter had explicitly professed a devotion to Jesus that exceeded that of the others in the apostolic band (Matt. 26:33; Mark 14:29; cf. John 13:37; 15:12–13). It may be that Jesus is asking

47. Maynard, "Peter," 542.
48. Shepherd, "'Do You Love Me?,'" 787.
49. Morris, *Gospel*, 769n42. This is not Morris's view, however.
50. Stählin, "φιλέω," 115.
51. Michaels, *Gospel of John*, 1043.

Peter whether, in light of what has since happened, he still thinks that his love
for Christ exceeds that of all the others.[52]

Whatever the interpretation, we find Simon Peter shying away from any such
comparison by not making the comparison. He simply affirms that the Lord knows
that he loves him as a friend, and the hubris of *greater than* no longer plays a role in
his thinking. His denial has brought about a humbler Simon Peter.

We can imagine a long and uncomfortable pause, after which Jesus asks Simon
a second time whether he loves (ἀγαπᾷς) him, now dropping the troubling comparison. He need no longer remind Peter of his inappropriate feeling of superiority over
others. This point had already been made when Jesus washed Peter's feet (13:6–10),
but it took the denial to bring it home. Again, Peter replies in the affirmative, but also
not using the higher term of love (ἀγαπάω) but the love of friendship (φιλέω), for he
could hardly affirm a self-sacrificing love for the friend Jesus whom he had just thrice
denied in public. In effect, Jesus recognizes Peter's tacit affirmation of a new humility,
not comparing himself favorably with others.

After perhaps another long pause, Jesus asks for a third time whether Simon
loves him. This time Jesus uses Simon's own verb, φιλεῖς. Considering all that has
happened, does Simon wish to be his friend? Jesus has come down from the lofty,
self-sacrificial love (ἀγαπάω) about which he had instructed his disciples to the love
of friendship, to show humiliated Simon that he still loves and forgives him despite his
denial of self-sacrifice. Exasperated and hurt, perhaps because of Jesus's persistence or
perhaps in his recognition that Jesus has descended to his own humble level, which
reinforces his own human fallibility, Simon Peter repeats his affirmation of friendship
love (φιλέω), basing it on his believing that Jesus knows all things. With the posing of
the three questions, Simon Peter now knows that the Lord knows that Simon had denied him three times in the dimly lit courtyard. Simon Peter knows fully that he is an
open book to his dearest friend, who knows everything. Nothing of himself remains
hidden. "[T]he alternation [of terms] is best understood as a crucial part of Jesus's effort in chapter 21 to remind Peter of the kind of love (ἀγάπη) that Jesus had demanded
of him on the night he was betrayed (chs. 13–17) and that Peter subsequently failed to
grasp or express (ch. 18)."[53]

Regardless of what one decides about the meaning of these terms, that is, whether
the two words for love are synonyms or have distinct significance, Jesus's relationship
with Simon Peter here is not only backwards looking, emphasizing recognition of
denial and sin, but also forward looking, emphasizing forgiveness, healing, and calling. Simon denied his Lord in the depth of night before the rooster crowed,[54] but this

52. Morris, *Gospel*, 768.

53. Shepherd, "'Do You Love Me?,'" 792.

54. Dodson intriguingly suggest that the rooster crowing had nothing to do with chickens but with
the blowing of a horn between the second and third watch of the night. According to the Mishnah,
poultry were not allowed in Jerusalem for purity reasons (m. Baba Kama 7.7). Mark 13:35 presupposes

post-resurrection morning, centered around a meal, provides the possibility of a new beginning. Despite Simon Peter's denials and weaknesses in the night, Jesus trusts him enough to commission him to assume the role of shepherd in charge of his sheep, his most valuable treasure for which he died. With his immanent departure, Jesus needs someone sufficiently reliable to care for and nourish the flock not out of the power of position but out of love. He needs a servant shepherd who loves both him and his flock (10:1–5), a task for which Peter previously volunteered but for which he was woefully unprepared (13:36–38). Taking up Jesus's mission and shepherding the flock will prove to be costly for Peter, as Jesus predicts (21:18–19), but it complements Jesus's initial calling of him to be a fisher of men. Treating the distinctive language John uses helps the reader see the progress both of Jesus's expression of love for Peter, found in sympathetic forgiveness and reinstated calling (feed and follow), and of Peter's discovery of both humility and potential.

It is possible to see the qualities and characteristics of the church leaders to whom John writes in Peter. Their strengths of commitment, fortitude, affirmation, even impetuosity are sometimes coupled with fear, overconfidence, pride, swinging between extremes, and being hurt that can lead to painful denial. Peter's failings are their failings, and Peter's forgiveness is theirs as well. John, through Jesus, assures them that he has confidence in these imperfect rocks of the faith and commissions them to follow his lead. They are to be servant leaders, lovers of Jesus, selfless shepherds tending the flock, affirming the lordship of Jesus in the face of adversity within the flock and persecution without (2 John 6–9; 3 John 3–4), despite their own blatant weaknesses and subtle failings. However, their leadership is to be grounded ultimately in their experience of and love of Jesus through the reminding Spirit, who brings about believing and knowledge and asks the penetrating, definitive question: "Do you love me?" "Jesus doesn't *just* want his sheep to be fed; he wants his sheep to be fed by someone who loves him."[55]

## THE MOTHER OF JESUS

One of Jesus's more puzzling relationships is with his mother. She appears at the beginning of Jesus's ministry and then again at the end, but nowhere in between. She

---

the Roman tradition of four nightly watches and notes that the signal between the third and fourth watch is called the cock-crowing. "The signal the Roman divisions used to change the guard for each shift was a trumpet call. The Latin word for trumpet call is '*gullicinium*', which means, 'cock-crowing'. At the end of the 3 a.m. and 6 a.m. shifts, the guard change was announced by a Roman 'cock-crowing' or blowing of a trumpet." What Peter heard was the trumpet signal to change the guard. In a slightly different view, Turnage suggests that it refers to an early morning time (cockcrow, *m. Sukkah* 5.4), signaled by a trumpet call, when ashes were removed from the altar and the temple was prepared for a new day.

55. Powell, *Loving Jesus*, 178.

marks "the boundaries of the drama."[56] She is present before his hour has come (2:4) and when it is finished (19:30).[57] John sees her not as an independent character but in her relationship to Jesus. He never names her but only refers to her as the mother of Jesus (2:3). By contrast, Joseph his father is named but never appears on the scene (1:45). The non-naming of his mother may seem strange, but it is not limited to John's Gospel. In Mark, the Gospel writer and Jesus refer to "his mother and brothers." Mary is named, along with Jesus's brothers, only once, and that by someone offended by Jesus (Mark 6:3; Matt 13:55). Otherwise, it is only in the birth stories in Matthew and Luke and in the listing of those present at the first gathering (Acts 1:14) that we have his mother named.

She first appears at the wedding at Cana. We don't know why she is there, but she seems to be somewhat involved in overseeing the food preparation or service. Neither do we know why Jesus is there, especially with his brand-new disciples. Very possibly the invitation to Jesus to attend was issued because of Nathanael, who was from Cana (21:2). Jesus's mother observes that the wine is finished and conveys this message to Jesus. She clearly has some expectations of him, but what they are the Gospel narrator leaves unstated. Since Jesus has not yet performed any signs, it also is not clear what would be the basis for her confidence in Jesus. We—and probably she—do not know what to expect from him. But confidence she has, for she tells the servants to do whatever Jesus tells them to do (2:5).[58] Undoubtedly, the basis for his mother's confidence in Jesus is her long-standing relationship with him, whom she can implicitly trust to properly address the situation.[59]

Jesus's response to his mother is quite puzzling. When she informs him that the wedding party is out of wine, Jesus replies, "Woman, what is it to me; why involve me in this? My hour has not yet come" (2:4). Jesus seems to be asserting his independence from earthly human relations other than those found in believing discipleship. What he does will derive from his own concept of his own time.[60] The term Jesus uses to refer to his mother, "woman" (γύναι), is not a term of disrespect, but it also is not a term "that a son would use for his mother."[61] In fact, Jesus uses it elsewhere in addressing

56. Culpepper, "Symbolism," 52.

57. Lieu, "Messiah," 69.

58. Francis Moloney sees her as an example of authentic faith in that, despite her son's rebuke, she goes and instructs the servants to obey Jesus (*Johannine Studies*, 265).

59. "The Mother's apparently neutral comment, 'they have no wine,' can be understood as a linguistic strategy of indirectness where without making an explicit request, she presumes, because of her relationship with her son, that he will hear the implied request. Jesus's response indicates that her presumption is correct" (Coloe, "Mother," 205).

60. Thatcher, *Riddles of Jesus*, 232. Thatcher treats the setting as a riddle. "The riddle, 'My hour has not yet come,' explores the issue of Jesus's identity with a person who does not know who he really is" (233).

61. Koester, *Symbolism*, 82; Lieu, "Messiah," 66. Coloe notes that "among men and women of Jewish backgrounds 'a friendly argument is a means of being sociable' and that when a Jewish couple appear to be arguing, 'they are staging a kind of public sparring match, where both fighters are on the

the woman from Samaria whom he had never met, (4:21), a beloved woman follower named Mary Magdalene (20:15), and the woman accused of adultery (8:10). It lacks the warmth that one would expect in a filial relationship. Indeed, the emphasis is not on the relationship at all, but on the issue of the timing for his first sign and other signs, for the hour of his sacrificial deed had not arrived. "This peculiar interchange enables readers to see that Jesus's actions cannot be understood on the level of typical relations between mother and son, but must be interpreted retrospectively in light of his death and resurrection."[62] In the end, whereas for Jesus the interchange involves a matter of timing for his mission, his mother invokes the relationship as a matter of timing for the celebration.

The mother of Jesus appears again at the crucifixion, standing near the cross with other women (19:25). John does not state why she was in Jerusalem; for this we must turn to Mark: "In Galilee these women had followed him and cared for his needs. Many other women who had come up with him to Jerusalem were also there" (Mark 15:41). Jesus again uses the same generic term, woman (γύναι), he employed at Cana (19:26). While the language does not convey endearment, the concern for the welfare of his mother is manifested by entrusting her to the care of another whom he trusts. It is strange that Jesus would assign responsibility for his mother to one of his disciples when he had brothers who should and probably did take responsibility for her (Acts 1:14). It may be simply a matter of presence, the family being elsewhere and not followers of the itinerant. However, Jesus's relationship with his brothers appears strained (7:2–6) and not repaired until later when James becomes a leader of the church (Acts 12:17). Jesus's speech here must also be interpreted in light of his death, resurrection, and departure. He is, at this very last moment, taking care of the final earthly things that matter to him, for after this he utters "It is finished" (19:30).[63]

Some have proposed a more theological relationship here between Jesus, his mother, and the Beloved Disciple who stands beside her. These two significant, unnamed people, the mother of Jesus (whom John refers to as both "his mother" and "the mother") and the anonymous Beloved Disciple, are intertwined at the end because of their relation to the crucified one. Jesus speaks to his mother, "Woman, here is your son," and to the disciple, "Here is your mother," whereupon the disciple takes her into his home (19:26–27).[64] The unnamed woman becomes the mother of the unnamed son.

---

same team'" ("Mother," 206, quoting Tannen, *Gender and Discourse*, 44).

62. Koester, *Symbolism*, 83.

63. The parallel of Jesus's final statement here with Genesis, started in the Prologue, is striking. Although it appears that God finished creating and rested on the seventh day, Jesus claimed that God was still working (5:17), and that being sent to finish God's work (4:34; 5:36; 17:4), he brought it to completion on the cross (19:30). This "It is finished" has a double meaning: seen from above Jesus completes the Father's work; seen from below he finishes his earthly obligations as son. See Coloe, "Mother," 210.

64. The two relational terms used by Jesus and the Evangelist, "mother" and "woman," not only

Some see her now playing a theological role. John uses the phrase, "to his own" (εἰς τὰ ἴδια), in the Prologue (1:11), where Jesus comes to his own to make them children of God, and in 19:27 where, when Jesus gives his mother to the Beloved Disciple, he takes her "to his own (εἰς τὰ ἴδια)" (home). Coloe suggests that by having the same mother, Jesus indicates that we, represented by the Beloved Disciple, are adopted into his family as brothers and sisters and thus are children of God (Gal 4:6).

> The woman is now "mother" to the Beloved Disciple, and the disciple is now "son." But with this change, the disciple's relationship with Jesus also changes. If they now have the same "mother" then the disciple is now brother to Jesus and therefore participates in Jesus's relationship with God. This is the moment of divine filiation when disciples become brothers/sisters to Jesus and the children of God.[65]

The assignment of his mother to the Beloved Disciple forms an *inclusio* (literary bracketing) that "indicates that what was promised in the Prologue is brought to completion at the cross," namely, that we are "born anew as a child of God."[66] The creation of the church fulfills the intentional relationship between Jesus and his coming and the adoption into his family.

We might conclude that for the Evangelist, Jesus's relationship with his mother has less of an intimacy than a purpose. She is introduced at the outset when his time has not yet come and disappears from John's narrative when his time is finished. We find her at the two great pinnacles of life: at the wedding and at Jesus's death. Through the first we obtain an inkling of the purpose of Jesus's mission, to transform the old into the new; through the second we see its fulfillment in Jesus's transforming death that inaugurates the new age, inviting us to become children of God. One might rightly conclude that her primary role is to mark the boundaries of his ministry. In this, the heavenly perspective on which we focus transcends the earthly relationships. Seen from below, she is his earthly mother, and in the end, Jesus shows great care for her. The earthly is not forgotten. Seen from above, Jesus's relationship with her shows us that his time is not our time, and it is his time that demarks his significance. We fit into his time.

---

emphasize her relationship to Jesus, but echo relationships in Genesis, for at the creation of Eve the man states that "she shall be called 'woman'" (Gen 2:23) and then names her "Eve" because "she would become the mother of all the living" (Gen 3:20). "These two titles, when considered with other unique features of the Johannine Passion, suggest a deliberate evocation of the primordial Garden of Eden, and a theology of creation" (Coloe, "Mother," 210–11) and at the cross, of re-creation.

65. Coloe, "Mother," 208. Jesus also commands Mary to tell his brothers (20:17).

66. Coloe, "Mother," 209.

## MARY MAGDALENE

Mary Magdalene's relationship with Jesus has fostered diverse speculations, stories, and myths.[67] She is a significant woman follower and disciple, faithful to the end. We do not meet her in the Fourth Gospel until John says that she not only stands at the cross, witnessing Jesus's final hours (19:25), but is the first to arrive at his tomb (20:1). After she runs to Peter and the Beloved Disciple to notify them that the tomb is empty, she is so concerned and distressed about her absent and missing Lord that she returns, "standing outside the tomb crying" (20:11). From even this brief passage, we can discern a great deal about her close relationship to Jesus.

First, we find her persistently and passionately seeking to find "my Lord." Her devotion and concern are so deeply personal that even if she can find only his body, she will try to retrieve it (20:15). Her relationship to Jesus, her "rabboni" or teacher, dominates and gives meaning to her existence. The clue to explain this, not found in John, is that Jesus healed her from mental illness, an event that must have radically altered her life (Luke 8:2).

Second, when Jesus encounters her in the garden, he asks the same question that he initially posed to his first disciples: "What are you looking for?" (20:15; 1:38). This question is rich in possibilities of interpretation. On the one hand, it is the repeated question of identity: who is Jesus? The response for which Jesus seeks is discipleship and mission. Responding to Jesus's question, Andrew and Mary respectively become missionary testifiers to the Messiah and to the Lord. The question of identity and de- sired, responsive mission, given intentionally and radically to both men and women, bookends the Gospel. There is no space for misogyny in this Gospel. On the other hand, the "what" can be understood in terms of the mission of the gospel: to bring about eternal life. Seekers look for eternal life, and the what and the who merge, for Jesus is himself the eternal life. Unfortunately, the response to this question does not always lead to discipling. Jesus poses the same question to those who came to arrest him outside the garden (18:4). Their response is startling: they fall back. But nonethe- less they arrest him rather than become his disciples and testifiers. To them he is merely one they are sent to arrest; to Mary he is her teacher and lord.

Third, Jesus calls her by her name, "Mary." She is not anonymous to Jesus, not one of the crowd. The shepherd knows his sheep, calls them by their name, and they recognize and follow him (10:3–4).[68] Called and named by Jesus, Mary follows all the way to the foot of the cross and to the hewn tomb, bringing what she has to give him (Luke 24:1), and then becomes the apostle to the disciples, the future apostles.[69]

---

67. For example, she appears in the Gospel of Philip as Jesus's lover, in medieval legends as Jesus's wife and moving to southern France, and as Jesus's wife in the novel by Dan Brown (*The Da Vinci Code*. New York: Anchor, 2003).

68. Michaels, *Gospel of John*, 1001.

69. "The words, 'I have seen the Lord' are the very words Paul uses in basing his claim to apostleship on a vision of the risen Lord" (1 Cor 9:1) (Gench, *Encounters*, 133). Mary Magdalene satisfies the

Fourth, Mary's recognition of Jesus, as she hears him calling her name, and her turning to him, yields a moment of ecstasy, so much so that she responds to him verbally—crying out, "Teacher"—and physically, holding on to him so that he cannot disappear again (20:16). For her, great intimacy resides in his voice and her embracing touch. The physical, tactile relationship matters, for this is the embodied Jesus, the one she has known but even now has difficulty recognizing (20:25). He is alive, not a corpse to be embalmed. "Mary finds her sorrow dispelled, her vision transformed, and her life graced with new possibilities by the reality of the resurrection."[70] Finally, within this emotional event, Jesus both tells her not to delay his departure to the Father and simultaneously commissions her to take her experience—"I have seen"—and his message of mission and inclusion to his disciples (brothers). As we have already noted in chapter 4, Jesus places confidence in her as his first testifier to his resurrection. She has experienced Jesus by seeing, hearing, and touching, and from this has an important message to share with others. Mary sees, knows (experiences), and responds, the very Johannine characteristics of a disciple.

In this text Jesus's relationship to her is enigmatic. His post-resurrection response to Mary Magdalene—"Do not touch me"—is diversely interpreted. For some, it is cold, lacking feeling.[71] Others see warmth in Jesus's personally addressing Mary by name as one of his own sheep, followed by Jesus's desire that she not linger in worship of him or seek to detain him but to go and tell his disciples what he is about to do.[72] Others see Jesus's conversation as indicating a change in relationship rather than emotion. Jesus's mode of being moves from being an earthly rabbi to the Son returning to the Father, thereby altering the past human relationships.[73] "Magdalene is trying to hold on to the source of her joy, since she mistakes an appearance of the risen Jesus for his permanent presence with his disciples."[74] Mary thus must recognize that the old, human relationship she had with him must be transformed into a spiritual relationship with her departing lord. Jesus's response reflects his humanity; Jesus does in fact have an emotional bond with her as a devoted follower and does not want that to interfere with his mission to return to his (and her) Father. As human, he cannot help but be moved by her concern, persistence, and devotion, despite being from above.

---

Pauline criterion for apostleship.

70. Gench, *Encounters*, 131.

71. "He does not return the warmth and affection of Mary Magdalene, but rather is moved by a higher commitment" (Culpepper, *Anatomy*, 111).

72. Michaels, *Gospel of John*, 1000.

73. Jesus does "not return into an ordinary mode of life in this world, such as would permit familiar contact. The fellowship between the Risen Jesus and his followers in the future will be experienced only as fellowship with the Lord who has gone to the Father, and therefore it will not be in the forms of earthly associations. . . . [Mary] cannot yet enter into fellowship with him until she has recognized him as the Lord who is with the Father, and so removed from earthly conditions" (Bultmann, *Gospel of John*, 687). Also Barrett, *Gospel*, 470.

74. Brown, *Gospel xiii–xxi*, 1013.

The message Jesus commissions her to take to his disciples, whom he now calls brothers, is that he is going to his Father and their Father (20:17).[75] Through Jesus, we become Jesus's siblings and God's children.[76] Mary is part of "his own," God's family: a daughter of God and sister of Jesus, with access to his and her Father. The adoptive community includes women as well as men (19:26–27). Jesus's relationship to Mary remains intimate, full of compassion, trust, and commission.

Mary Magdalene is who she is because of Jesus, who is her healer, teacher, Lord, and commissioner. For John's readers as well, God does not choose them because of who they are, but they (we) are who they (we) are because God has chosen them (us) to be *his own* and commissioned them (us) to ministry.

## THE FATHER

So far, we have spoken about people's relationship with Jesus from their perspective. In these last two sections I want to explore the relationships Jesus had from his perspective. What do these relationships tell us about Jesus?

Jesus's most intimate relationship is reserved for his Father and his disciples. Since Jesus is the star of the show, John develops his character more than that of any other person. Yet, his character is very enigmatic. Jesus is not born, but "becomes flesh" (σὰρξ ἐγένετο). He appears (φαίνει), comes (ἦλθεν), and tents (ἐσκήνωσεν) among us (1:5, 11, 14). The divinity walks among us, human and yet more. His identity is defined by his relationship not to other humans but to his Father who has sent him and to whom he returns.

This accords with John's written desire that we believe Jesus is the Messiah, the Son of God. Moloney argues that if we understand "messiah" in the earthly way understood by Jews of Jesus's time, we miss the significance of this concept.[77] The people focus on the place of the Messiah's origin (7:26–27) or on his earthly lineage (7:40–43) but understand this origin and lineage from below, in earthly terms. Likewise, the people understand the signs Jesus performs in terms of quantity rather than qualitatively as *sig*nificant for establishing his origin (7:28–31). To see Jesus as the Messiah is to understand the concept in heavenly terms (from above), that he is from God. Indeed, he is the Son of God.

---

75. The point of announcing his going is not a point about time of departure, but about Jesus's identity in mission. As we noted previously, origin (and here, destiny) are keys to identity. Thus, Jesus again affirms his identity with the Father as his source and goal. "Instead of a statement concerning the fact of the resurrection and the sequence and locus of appearances, John has Jesus make a statement to Magdalene about the meaning of the resurrection. A willingness to neglect temporal implications for theological significance is not unusual in John" (Brown, *Gospel xiii–xxi*, 1015).

76. Brown, *Gospel xiii–xxi*, 1016.

77. Jesus's "messiahship is not to be determined by the messianic expectation of the people who interrogate him" (Moloney, *Johannine Studies*, 178).

His identity established by this relationship is illustrated or, better, defended, by Jesus's claims about what he does. His occupation is to glorify and reveal the Father by doing his will (4:34). Both he and his Father are working, and since only the Father could work on the Sabbath,[78] by working on the Sabbath he identifies with the Father, a conclusion the Jewish leaders immediately draw (5:17) but cannot accept. He does not what he wills but only what he sees the Father doing (5:19). As his Father brought life to the dead, so will the Son. Indeed, the Father hands over to the Son functions such as judgment that the Father does not (or no longer does) do (5:22). In a sense, Jesus claims to have no identity of his own; his identity is wrapped up with that of his Father, with whom he is one in being and purpose (10:30). The very purpose of his coming, of his existence, is to do the will of his Father (6:38). He has no message but that given to him by the Father (12:50). The word of the Word is the word of God (5:24; 8:31).

The relationship with his Father forms a unity or bond that determines everything that he does and says. Since he and his Father are one (1:1; 17:22), and since the Father sent and commissioned him (3:17; 6:29, 57; 7:29; 8:42; 11:42; 17:3, 8, 18, 21, 23; 20:21) and he will be returning to him (7:33–36; 14:12, 28; 16:5, 17, 28), nothing can break into this close bond. The basis of this unity of deed and purpose is the love that the Father has for his Son (5:20, 15:9–10, 35; 17:24), and the basis for the Son doing what the Father has commanded is his love for the Father (14:31).[79] Similarly, he speaks only what the Father wants him to speak; he is the Word of God (8:28; 1:1). Furthermore, the Father testifies of Jesus, affirming his identity as being sent on his mission (5:37; 8:18). Finally, they glorify each other (17:1–5, 22). Jesus's relationship to the Father shapes his character, and this in turn emphasizes his divinity (5:18). (We will return to this in chapter 8.)

At the same time, John's human characterization of Jesus is flat and at times uninviting. "While Jesus is not entirely lacking in human emotions, his emotional responses are noticeably different and therefore convey a sense of his being distant or aloof."[80] His response to the two disciples who follow him initially, repeated to the weeping Mary (20:15), may be seen as brusque: "What are you looking for?" (1:38). His response to his mother's request—"Woman, what is that problem to me?"—appears to lacks familial feeling (2:4), as does the use of the same term in 19:6 in setting up an "adopted family." To the royal official he talks about believing based on signs and wonders, rather than about the deep concern the official has for his terminally

---

78. "The contemporary Alexandrian Jewish philosopher Philo emphasized that though God rested on the seventh day, this means only that his activity requires no labor; he never ceases from his activity, because creation continues to depend on him. . . . Jesus reasons by analogy that what is right for God in sustaining his creation is also right for himself as the Father's Son and agent" (Keener, *John*, 49).

79. Contrary to expectations, however, John 14:31 is the only place that the Son's love for the Father is mentioned.

80. Culpepper, *Anatomy*, 109–10.

ill son (4:48). His question to the paralytic who waited for thirty-eight years—"Do you want to get well?—seems unnecessary and unfeeling. Jesus knows how to "push the buttons" of Jews with whom he converses, and when things become tense, he shrewdly but wisely withdraws (6:15; 8:59; 10:39–40; 11:53–54).

However, John does hint of another side to Jesus. Upon the death of Lazarus, John gives us the closest picture of Jesus's emotions. "When Jesus saw Mary and those accompanying her weeping, he became deeply moved (ἐνεβριμήσατο) in spirit and troubled himself" (11:33, 38). Jesus appears affected and sheds tears of his own, which the Jews take as signs of Jesus's love for this family. Commentators divide on the significance of Jesus's emotions here, giving various interpretations of them.[81] In any case, John's portrayal of Jesus's human character and his relationships is complex. He paints the clearest picture of Jesus's human relations in his concern for his disciples.

## JESUS'S DISCIPLES

Other than four passages that speak about God's love for the world and the Son (3:16, 35; 5:20; 10:17), love does not become a major theme until the second half of the Gospel, when Jesus no longer addresses the public but speaks to and prays for his disciples. The emphasis is on "the love of the Son for those whom the Father has given Him, for His 'friends.' Through the Son the love of God reaches the world of men (15:9)."[82] From the reciprocal love between Father and Son flows Jesus's reciprocal love for his disciples (17:6–26), and from there among the disciples (15:12–13, 17). By mutually loving each other they dwell in his love.

The Gospel reiterates the love that Jesus has for his disciples who are in the world (13:1). It is the basis for a new commandment, which is an old commandment refocused; because Jesus loved them and is about to demonstrate his love to the fullest, they are to love one another in this same sacrificial way (15:13). Mutual, reciprocal love will be the sign of discipleship (13:34–35). "This 'new' love . . . is 'new' in two ways. First, it focuses attention not on the 'neighbor' (defined in the Synoptics so broadly as to include the enemy), but rather on the fellow believer or disciple, thus accenting love's mutuality. Second, and perhaps more important, it bases the command very explicitly on Jesus's love for 'his own' disciples (13:1), based in turn on the Father's love for his Son (see 3:35; 5:20; 15:9)."[83] Even though Jesus knew one would

81. Michaels (*Gospel of John*, 636) translates ἐνεβριμήσατο as "was angered" and then, noting that the reason for Jesus's anger is unclear, suggests that it might be because the presence of Jews removes his privacy to intimately address Mary's deep concern. Culpepper (*Anatomy*, 111) interprets this scene very differently, moving Jesus even farther from human concern. "Jesus's emotion rises again when he approaches the tomb and when he considers his own death. The pattern of [Jesus's] emotions suggests that it is the approach of his own death rather than death in general or Mary's lack of understanding which moves him so deeply."

82. Stauffer, "ἀγαπάω," 53.

83. Michaels, *Gospel of John*, 759.

betray and the rest abandon him (13:18, 21, 38), the narrator assures us that Jesus's love was not temporary but enduring. Jesus would love them to the end (13:1), and even when he departed that too was a sign of love, for his departure made possible the coming of the Spirit who would dwell in them and "guide them into all truth" (16:13).

The love (ἀγάπη) of which Jesus speaks is a love not of mere emotion but of keeping Jesus's word (14:15, 21, 23). Four tests of this love are presented. First, "if you obey my commands, you will remain in my love" (15:10). Obedience shows love, for it mimics the very obedience that Jesus demonstrates in obeying his Father's commands out of love. The second test is that they love each other (13:34; 15:12). Again, this responds to the love that Jesus has shown them and will be manifested in mutual servanthood (13:14–17). Third, love will be demonstrated through fruit-bearing (15:16). Exactly what this is Jesus leaves ambiguous. Fourth, the ultimate sign of love is their willingness to give their life for another (10:11). "Greater love has no one than this, that he lay down his life for his friends" (15:13). "The reason my Father loves me is that I lay down my life . . . of my own accord" (10:17–18).

He informs them that he "will be with them only a little longer" (13:33), and that where he is going they cannot come at this time, although they will "follow later" (13:36). For the disciples, this is all a mystery, especially when he goes on to talk about his death and their denial. Even when they think he is speaking plainly and that they understand so that they believe, Jesus knowingly predicts that they will scatter when his "hour comes" and leave him to face death by himself (16:29–31). Only later will these friends understand. Yet out of his concern for the disciples, he seeks to comfort them to prepare them for these disquieting, forthcoming events (14:1). He assures them that after he departs, he will "ask the Father, and he will give you another Counselor to be with you forever—the Spirit of truth" (14:16–17). He does not intend to leave them as orphans. The language here attempts to realistically prepare the disciples for what will happen both immediately and later. In departing, Jesus reveals his love (ἀγάπη) and concern for the disciples, a love centered on remaining. They are to remain in him, and he will remain in them (15:9).

The disciples who remain with him are not only believers but followers. Although they have some idea of who Jesus is in the beginning, calling him Messiah, Son of God, and King of Israel, Jesus seeks to move them from intellectual recognition to believing, and then to being obedient disciples who put their faith into practice (1:41, 49; 2:11; 8:31; 13:35). John refers to them not simply as believers but as disciples.[84] They assist him in his ministry, purchasing food in town (4:8), collecting food distributed to the masses (6:11–12), and accompanying him on his journeys (11:7). Not all follow through on their faith commitment, though some do (6:66–71), and those that do become the core witnesses in fishing (21:6, with its double meaning), feeding the flock (21:15–17), and establishing the church (21:18–19).

---

84. "John uses the term 'disciples' (seventy-eight times) more frequently than 'the twelve' (four times) or 'the apostles' (never)" (Culpepper, *Anatomy*, 115).

The disciples are truly his friends, and for them he will lay down his life as the good shepherd does for his treasured sheep. However, for Jesus, friendship requires responses of love toward others, obedience, and continued fellowship. (We will see this more fully developed in the parable of the vine and the branches in chapter 8.) Even more deeply, as we have seen above, his disciples are his brothers (and sisters), for all have the same Father.

## CONCLUSION

Relationships are front and center in the Gospel. They are theologically rooted and practically manifested—the heart of John's defense. The love on which they are based is to be lived out by Jesus's followers in obedience to him, unity with other believers, and self-sacrifice for others. In a radical departure from tradition, the relationships are neither familial nor socially oriented. Rather, they are grounded in discipleship, where love is manifested in self-sacrifice and command keeping.

> Theological dimensions of human life emerge as the Word made flesh elicits responses of belief and unbelief, and the gospel makes clear that social position does not determine how one will respond. At the upper end of the social scale, the royal official believes in Jesus's word while the chief priests demand his crucifixion (4:46–54; 19:6). At the lower end of the scale, the once blind beggar exhibits a tenacious loyalty to Jesus (9:24–34), whereas the invalid at Bethzatha informs about Jesus to the authorities, who persecute him (5:15–16). Throughout these episodes, the evangelist discloses that no one can be understood in merely social terms; everyone relates to God in some way, and the question is whether that relationship will be faith or unfaith. From the perspective of John's Gospel, human identity can only be understood by asking who a person is in relation to God.[85]

The deepest relationship in John holds between the Father and the Son, and this in turns overflows between the Son and his disciples. As the Father is in the Son, so the Son will be in the believers (17:26). The love the Father has for the Son is passed on to the believers (17:23), so that as the Father and Son are one, so will be the believers (17:21). A dysfunctional, disobedient body of believers is incompatible with the ideal of believers who in love obey Jesus's commands. Those who become his disciples are given to him by the Father to be loved, protected, and sanctified, not to be taken out of the world but to be sent into the impure world that hates and threatens them, to make Jesus known. By their very nature as Jesus's disciples, their close, obedient relationship to him locates their identity. As he is in the Father, and the Father is in him, so he is in the disciples and the disciples are in him. That relationship ultimately defines them and us as believers. As Jesus's identity is bound up with his relationship with his

85. Koester, *Symbolism*, 76.

Father, so our identity as believers is bound up with our relationship with Jesus. We are who we are because we are "his own," children of God.

## QUESTIONS FOR REFLECTION AND DISCUSSION

1. Do your relationships with people tell something about who you are and what gives meaning to your life?

2. To whom does Jesus relate in the Gospel of John? Is there any pattern to these relationships, both in terms of whom Jesus relates to and the kind of reaction he gets?

3. Do you think that Nicodemus is on the way to becoming a believer, or does he remain outside the community of those who believe? Why? Do you know of any Nicodemuses in your relationships?

4. What did you learn about Simon Peter and Jesus from John's portrayal of their very complex relationship?

5. What did you learn about the relationship between Simon Peter and the Beloved Disciple, and what might be the implications of this for the early church?

6. Does Jesus's mother play a role in the Gospel? Is this role different from her role in the Synoptics, and if so, how do they differ?

7. Why did the medieval church include Mary Magdalene among the apostles? Do you think that this is an appropriate designation? What might be some implications for women in today's church of this early church affirmation? Is Mary a role model for us?

8. Is Jesus's relationship with his twelve disciples similar to or different from his relationships with non-disciples? Explain.

9. Which of the individuals in this chapter would you want to have a relationship with? What would you want to know about them, and what might they want to know about you?

CHAPTER SEVEN

# Book of Dialogues

OF ALL THE GOSPELS, John is the most dialogic. In the Fourth Gospel, while the narrator connects the dialogues with time frames, sets the initial stage, moves the dialogues along, and sometimes whispers comments in asides when clarity or interpretation is needed, the characters themselves often tell the story (for example, 1:32–34). John "allows the characters to lay out the plot through their speech. . . . [H]e frequently gives over the construction of action, setting, and character to dialogue, as though he were bound by the tight economy of a theatrical production."[1] Jesus always gets top billing, if not also the last word.[2] Yet, often those in dialogue engage in genuine exchange. It is not that the conversations end in conviviality, clarity, agreement, or acceptance. Indeed, quite the opposite. The exchanges, filled with irony, often leave confusion, and later in Jesus's ministry, disagreement, animosity, and rejection. These features make careful diving into the study of the dialogues interesting, challenging, informative, and worthwhile.

Paul Anderson notes that

> the dialogues basically function in two ways: comprehending and believing responses to Jesus are affirming and exemplary; misunderstanding and unbelieving responses to Jesus are disconfirming and corrective. Interestingly, these two rhetorical thrusts are characteristically signaled in the presentation by who takes the initiative. When Jesus or God's agent takes the initiative, the structure is nearly always revelational. As discussants respond in faith to the revelation, this is a positive example for others to follow; as they reject or respond incompletely to the divine initiative, this is presented as a negative example. However, when human actors come to Jesus asking a challenging question or make a self-assured statement, this presentation nearly always

---

1. Brant, *Dialogue*, 3–4.

2. "His presence pervades every scene; his authority dominates all interactions with others, even at his trial; his words govern every conversation in which he engages and the overall sense of his 'other-worldliness' is inescapable" (Domeris, "Johannine Drama," 31–32).

exposes their incomprehension and spiritual inadequacy.... It is as though the inadequacy of human initiative is mirrored in the actions of the discussants.[3]

Jesus's initial dialogues are affirming, although those with whom he speaks surely would have been puzzled by the exchange. In his first encounter with Simon, Jesus does not engage in welcoming or inviting banter but speaks perfunctorily in renaming: "Simon, you will be called Cephas" (1:42). Although Simon must have thought this a bizarre introduction to discoursing with Jesus, the author omits any response from him. Yet, the rest of the Gospel not only affirms that Simon sticks with the namer, but also that the name itself—Simon Peter—sticks (although strangely enough in John, after renaming Simon, Jesus never addresses Simon as Peter[4]). In the next dialogue, Nathanael also is caught up in this dialogic structure. Again, Jesus does not engage in introductory banter at his initial encounter, but immediately proceeds to identify Nathanael as a "true Israelite," affirming that Nathanael, whom he has never met, has integrity. John presents Nathanael's reaction of amazement at this characterization. When Jesus reveals his extraordinary knowledge, Nathanael becomes a testifier to this insightful rabbi.

The subsequent dialogue of Jesus with his mother is no less cryptic but exhibits the structure and characteristics of a one-act play. The narrator's opening, describing the setting of a wedding at Cana to which Jesus is invited, is brief but sets up the context of the dramatic dialogue. Only two people (or appropriate groups) are on stage and in dialogue at a time, intensifying the relationship between them. At the outset, Jesus and his mother are together on stage, perhaps somewhere near where the wedding servants were working. She does not hesitate to inform Jesus about the wine situation in a way that intimates that she is making a request. Jesus's response appears to quickly brush off the intimated suggestion. However, the dramatic dialogue does not terminate here. In the next scene his mother and the house servants are on stage, and the one-sided dialogue consists of her instructing the servants to do what Jesus requests, acting as if Jesus's retort is irrelevant to her expectations. In scene three the discussants are Jesus and the servants, where similarly Jesus gives instructions to the servants whose affirming response is to obediently carry them out (2:6–8). In scene four the dialoguers are the banquet master and the bridegroom, discussing the quality and timing of the distribution of the good wine. The narrator appears at the end of this little dialogue or play to provide the context, denouement, and meaning in terms of believing (2:11). (We have already spoken in greater detail about this event in chapter 6.)

It might be questioned whether this one-act play really represents a dialogue, since only in Scene One do the characters exhibit a verbal exchange. However, the author does not limit his dialogues strictly to verbal interchange. He also allows for a

3. Anderson, "Dialogue," 117.

4. In fact, only in Luke 22:34 does Jesus refer to Simon as Peter.

dialogue of statement and response as action. In the wedding dialogue, the response of the individual characters is as important as any verbal statements they might make. This is confirmed by the author's comment at the end, which identifies the meaning of the dialogue as action: bringing about faith.

Similar affirming responses come with Jesus's one-act dialogue with Nicodemus in chapter 3 and the Samaritan woman and the royal official in chapter 4. In all three instances there is affirming, though also puzzling, dialogue between the dialoguers.

When we turn to the dialogues in the middle part of Jesus's public ministry, beginning in chapter 5, where Jesus more fully takes his message of identity and believing to the Jews, the dialogues reveal more ambivalent, if not disconfirming or antagonistic, responses. The dialogue with the paralytic leads to threats by the Jewish leaders on Jesus's life for his healing on the Sabbath and his calling God his Father (5:18). In chapter 6 Jews grumble and argue among themselves about Jesus when he contends that he is the bread of life come down from heaven (6:41–43, 52). They are not sure what to make of him (7:25–27); some respond believing, others try to seize him (7:30–31).

The ambivalence gradually turns to hostility, confrontation, and opposition (7:32; 8:12–59; 11:48–57). Jesus's dialogue with the Pharisees about testimony (8:13–20) and with Jews who initially believed in him (8:31–59) about obedience and origin become especially testy, to the point where those in dialogue with Jesus want to stone him. These and other dialogues contain important dialogic elements that bring out the character of those in conversation and that point to Jesus's identification of himself as coming from the Father. What begins as open dialogue where those conversing with Jesus are genuinely inquisitive becomes closed, defensive argumentation. In a real sense, Jesus's ministry goes downhill in any attempt to convince and convert those with whom he is in conversation, gradually setting the stage for attempts to kill him in chapters 8, 10, and 11, and finally, for the impassioned response, "Take him away. Crucify him," at his trial (19:15). For the Evangelist, the rejection of Jesus at the end of the Gospel is not inexplicable or unexpected; its groundwork is laid in the dialogues Jesus has in the first part of the Gospel and the responses of and deteriorating relationships with Jews who later are responsible for his rejection and death (19:11).

One might wonder how these dialogues fit into John's overall argument. One response is that they demonstrate John's thesis, that recognition of Jesus's identity and function or mission, believing, and life go hand in hand. Acceptance of Jesus leads to renewed and deepened life; rejection of Jesus naturally leads to animosity, antagonism, blindness, and identification with the purveyor of death. Much depends on how we come to Jesus, on our attitudes, desires, presuppositions, and worldview.

## DIALOGUE AS DRAMA

Some twentieth-century commentators suggest that the author of the Fourth Gospel had significant familiarity with Greek drama and that this familiarity influenced the writing style of his Gospel.[5] Its dialogues, they note, are shaped, consciously or unconsciously, in the fashion of Greek drama. Those who espouse this view suggest that since the dialogues often have the structure of plays, readers should watch for theatrical elements. First, the dialogues commence with an introduction, provided by a narrator who delineates the setting in terms of place, time, and/or sequence. Although often brief, the setting delivers the context that instructively connects the dialogue with other dialogues or events. One finds such introductions, for example, in the initial dialogues with Simon and Nathanael (1:40–41, 44–45), the wedding at Cana (2:1), in the clearing of the temple (2:13–15), with Nicodemus (3:1–2), with the Samarian woman (4:1–7), the healing at the pool (5:1–6), the feeding of the five thousand (6:1–5), the Feast of the Tabernacles (7:1–13), with Pilate (18:28), with the disciples (21:1–4), and elsewhere.[6] Second, it is characteristic of Greek plays that only two people (or one as representing a group of people) are on stage at one time.[7] With the exception of the chorus—in John, often although not always the audience—the stage is not filled, as in modern plays, with diverse individuals engaging in multiple dialogues with each other.

Third, "[e]ntrances and exits are constitutive of drama. The arrival of a person to a setting begins a dialogue. . . . [The Evangelist] is attentive to the movement of people in and out of scenes, and that movement carries the action forward. When Nicodemus arrives, the dialogue begins. The Samaritan woman does not approach until the disciples have left to find food, and the disciples do not engage in dialogue until the woman departs."[8] Fourth, the dialogue emphasizes the characters, some of whom are named and developed, others unnamed and undeveloped. They may be understood as individuals and/or as representatives of groups of individuals. As noted above, Jesus is the central character, either having a direct role himself or as the topic of the dialogue (9:13–34). Thus, it is important to understand whom the dialogue is between when interpreting it. We looked at some of these dialogic characters in the previous chapters. Fifth, the dialogues contain conversations that resemble those found

5. See Brant, *Dialogue*, 4–5, 12 (especially n28).

6. "The narrator in the Fourth Gospel plays a more limited role than, or a qualitatively different role from, that in the Synoptic Gospels. In his capacity as the one who reports action that occurs largely through dialogues rather than narration, the narrator takes the position of a witness who relates the action from a position of hindsight—a role played by the messenger on the Athenian stage. Like the Euripidean messenger, the Johannine narrator violates the limits of his witness by claiming the ability to see into the minds of others. . . . He is a member in, rather than the architect of, a tradition of witnessing to Jesus's glory" (Brant, *Dialogue*, 202, 208).

7. Martyn, *History*, 37; Brant, *Dialogue*, 27.

8. Brant, *Dialogue*, 27.

in drama.[9] The dialogue might consist of a conversation containing words between the participants (2:3–4, 16–22; 3:2–10; and elsewhere). However, the dialogue might be such that only one character speaks while the other character responds in action (2:5–8; 9:1–7).[10] Sixth, John is adept at using speech as action, for example, as gesture indicating movement (19:14), deed (19:24), or as referring to the unseen (4:22–23).[11] Finally, "we see in these crowds the dramatic use of the chorus, sometimes confessing Jesus, sometimes raising questions devoid of real insight into his being."[12] "Numerous other features of Johannine language, including word plays, ambiguity and misunderstanding, dualism, irony and its interpersonal dimensions, are equally characteristic of (Greek) tragic language,"[13] as are ways of developing the plot.

In our treatment of four dialogues, we will first note the dramatic effects, identifying the setting and the movement of the participants in the scenes, and the careful organization, construction, and unity of the dialogue plots. However, it is not our intent to pursue in detail any thesis about the similarity of John's dialogues with Greek drama. There is no way we can do justice, either positively or critically, to the contention that the Gospel is itself a drama or contains mini dramas. This is not our concern in this book, although it is an interesting, provocative, and enlightening perspective. For those interested in a thorough presentation and analysis of this, James Martyn and Jo-Ann Brant provide excellent guides.[14] Second, we want to see what we can learn about the character of those involved in the dialogue. This will help us appreciate how the Evangelist uses the characters engaged in dialogue to enhance the identity and character of Jesus. Third, we will glean the main point of the dialogue. Sometimes the narrator/author will provide this; at other times he leaves us to figure this out on our own, an often difficult task. Ultimately, though, we want to see how John uses dialogue to further his overall mission of bringing people to believe that Jesus is the Son of God and thereby to have eternal life.

It is not feasible to consider all of Jesus's dialogues in this chapter. Consequently, I will focus on four significant dialogues that aid our understanding both of Jesus and of those with whom he dialogues and that help to further John's mission in writing the Gospel.

9. Domeris, "Johannine Drama," 30.

10. "The continuous use of direct speech, the naming of the speakers and the ease with which the Gospel can be reproduced in dramatic form suggests that John has deliberately fashioned his Gospel after the model of the Greek dramas and particularly the Tragedies. He does not abandon the form of a Gospel, but sets out to present the life of Jesus in such a way that someone familiar with the pattern of the Classical Tragedies would recognise the form" (Domeris, "Johannine Drama," 29–30).

11. Brant, *Dialogue*, ch. 2.

12. Domeris, "Johannine Drama," 33.

13. Brant, *Dialogue*, 3.

14. Martyn, *History*; Brant, *Dialogue*.

## THE BLIND MAN AND THE PHARISEES (9:1–41)

Perhaps none of the dialogues is as well-crafted and revealing as that developed in chapter 9.[15] The specific setting is not given, except that Jesus has attended the Feast of Tabernacles and avoided being stoned by the crowd of Jewish leaders on the temple grounds by slipping away from them (7:10; 8:59). How the story in chapter 9 connects in time to this temple visit John does not say. He simply notes that sometime later, on a Sabbath, as Jesus walks along, he sees a man blind from birth. This flowing narrative has features of an act in a play, with seven scenes.[16] In each scene only two people or groups of people converse simultaneously, so that the dialogue can focus on their conversation. As the scenes progress, we get to meet each of the actors or participants and understand and discover their character and character development, both as individuals and as representative of groups of people Jesus encountered and with whom he dialogued.

In Scene One (9:1–7), Jesus converses with his disciples, who query him about a blind man.[17] We noted in chapter 5 the significance of the false dilemma the disciples pose regarding the man's blindness. It is of interest that the disciples are fully concerned with the origin of his blindness and not with his beggarly condition or the possibility of his cure and future life. They have been with Jesus, witnessed his numerous signs of healing, but make no request to have this blind man healed. To them, the man has no significance except as providing the ready opportunity for raising a difficult theological question about the problem of evil or suffering. They appear as theologians, not as humanitarians. Having posed the question as to why he was born blind, the disciples disappear until chapter 11 and the story of Lazarus, where again their concern is for their own safety and not for Lazarus (11:8, 16). John does not portray the disciples as reaching out in concern for others; their own interests always take priority.[18] Jesus responds to the disciples' theological concerns for the man's blindness in terms of his own identity: the mediator of God's work and the light of the world (see our discussion in chapter 5). The blind man is not part of the initial exchange but the occasion for and subject of the discussion; he dialogically enters as the person who responds to Jesus's command and sets the stage for the remainder of the scenes.

John uses this scene to connect the work of Jesus with that of those who carry on his mission after he departs from the scene. Not only must Jesus do the work of God, but by using the plural form "we," John indicates that we too have the obligation to

---

15. "In the case of *the lame man* and *the blind beggar*, John's Gospel shows the miracle story of being the first of a sequence of scenes. . . . [By] constructing a sequence of scenes based on the miracle stories, someone created *literary genre* quite without counterpart in the body of the Gospels. We may call it a drama" (Martyn, *History*, 32).

16. Martyn, *History*, 37.

17. For the dramatic presentation of this story, see Martyn, *History*, ch. 1.

18. See 6:5, where it is Jesus and not the disciples who initiates the concern about feeding the audience.

do the works of God (9:4). For "anyone who has faith in me will do what I have been doing. He will do even greater things than these, because I am going to the Father" (14:12). Tension exists between these two passages. On the one hand, when Jesus is present doing God's works the light is among them; when he departs the light is gone and, according to 9:4, no one can work. On the other hand, his departure will enable his followers to do even greater things.

One way to resolve this tension is to suggest that we live in the in-between stage, between the earthly presence of Jesus who is both the remover of blindness and the light of the world and eschatological darkness when he is absent and God pours out his wrath on humanity (Rev 16:10). After Jesus's departure, remnants of the Light remain, for Jesus does not leave us without any light. The glimmer of light lit by the sent Spirit reminds us of the Truth (16:5–16). Indeed, perhaps John also understands the light being present through Jesus's followers, who when they put their trust in the Light "become sons of light" (12:36) and thus lights themselves.[19] Darkness, in any case, cannot completely overcome the Light (1:5), so that John's immediate readers and we are implored to do God's work in the harvest (4:35–38).

In Scene Two (9:6–12) the members on stage are the neighbors/others and the blind man. We quickly learn about the neighbors/others; they had so little concern about the less fortunate that they could not agree whether this man who now had his sight was the same or a different person than the blind man daily begging by the roadside. "Who is this man who can see? Isn't this the blind beggar?" Some say, yes; others, no. Clearly, they had paid little attention to him when he sat begging, for other than now being sighted, he had changed little physically. Like the disciples, the neighbors express no concern for the blind man nor rejoice in his restoration. Rather, they are more curious about how this happened than celebratory about the man's new prospects.

We also learn about the blind man, who is quite puzzled by all that happened to him. He did as the stranger commanded and washed in the Pool of Siloam.[20] However, being unable to see before the washing, he could not identify his benefactor; he had to rely on others' testimony that his healer was called Jesus. This dialogue accomplishes two things. First, John portrays the formerly blind man as a surrogate of Jesus, giving a version of Jesus's identity statement—"that I am" (ὅτι ἐγώ εἰμί, 9:9)—in testifying

---

19. Michaels (*Gospel of John,* 542–44) resolves the tension differently, suggesting that "[M]ore likely, by 'we' Jesus means himself and the blind man, as if to say '*He and I* must work the works of the One who sent me as long as it is day.'" Jesus does the works of his Father by healing the blind man. The blind man does the works of God by believing in Jesus (6:29). Michaels notes that since the disciples play no subsequent role in the dialogue, the "we" cannot refer to them. However, if this statement has relevance to John's readers, their continuing to be lights doing God's work would be important.

20. John creates a double meaning around the name of the pool, Siloam, which means "sent." "As Jesus in John describes himself repeatedly as one 'sent' from God, we are meant to identify the pool somehow with Jesus and given to understand that the blind man, by washing in water, is plunged into Jesus's own life—that his cure resides not in the waters but in his contact with the Sent One" (Gench, *Encounters,* 66).

about his own identity. Second, this leads to the purpose of the entire dialogue as a testimonial to Jesus. Jesus has anointed (ἐπέχρισέν, 9:11) the blind man's eyes, so that he becomes Jesus's called-by-grace witness. The blind man begins his whirlwind journey from ignorance to discipleship, not knowing who or where Jesus is.

After a brief interlude where they (his neighbors?) bring the formerly blind man to the Pharisees (for what reason we are not told, although some see malice in it[21]), we begin to get a glimpse of the character of the Pharisees in the third scene (9:13–17). The Pharisees likewise are unconcerned with the man as a healed person with new vision (note the double meaning), but like the neighbors want to know how it happened and when it happened. That it happened on the Sabbath is what catches their attention, for Jesus's claim to origin is now in question. How, they ask, can someone sent from God work on the Sabbath? Kneading (mud) into a ball is a form of work prohibited on the Sabbath.[22] For the Pharisees, Jesus's identity is that of a Sabbath breaker, which is inconsistent with any claim of being sent by God. Yet some wonder how a sinning lawbreaker could perform such a healing act. The sign intrigues, although it does not convert, them.

This third scene, with the two discussants, the Pharisees and the formerly blind man, on stage, helps us to further penetrate the character of the formerly blind man. The Pharisees now ask him to testify about the sight-restorer, and this time the formerly blind man testifies based not on what others say but on his own limited encounter. Forced to choose, he identifies his unrecognized healer as a prophet. In his understanding he moves past hearsay to the beginnings of an understanding of who Jesus is as connected with the religious tradition he knows. The man who healed him, whom he has not seen, is not a Sabbath-breaking sinner but a prophet, a person with unusual powers and foresight (9:17).

The Pharisees are left in a quandary both about Jesus and about the formerly blind man. They skeptically wonder about the truth of identity: is the formerly blind man whom he claims to be, and is the healer what the man claims he is? To answer these questions, in Scene Four they summon the man's parents, looking for testimony about the formerly blind man and about Jesus ("how it happened"; 9:18–23). Again, the Pharisees are interested not in the welfare of the formerly blind man but in whether he was really blind and how the change came about. The parents are willing to claim him as their son but assert nothing more than his birth condition for fear of being excommunicated from the synagogue, a realistic fear given what the Pharisees eventually do to the formerly blind man (9:34). John affirms the spiritual hold of fear that the Pharisees have over the people through their control over the context for religious practice that centers their lives.

---

21. The man's neighbors "are not just curiosity seekers but are in some way in league with the religious authorities" (Michaels, *Gospel of John*, 550).

22. "Jesus had kneaded the mud into a ball in performing the miracle, [and] the Mishnah lists kneading among 39 activities forbidden on the Sabbath" (Michaels, *Gospel of John*, 550).

Scene Five gets us to the heart of the dialogue, to the matter of believing and unbelieving. The Pharisees again summon the formerly blind man, and again we have two discussants on stage. They want him to accept that he has had his sight restored by God but to condemn the restorer as a sinner (9:24). They are unaware of—blind to—the paradox of praising for the healing and condemning the healer, as well as of the paradox of the divine identity of the healer. The Pharisees remain unwilling to fully accept the healing and question for the third time how it happened (9:26). At this point the formerly blind man develops great backbone, refusing to castigate the healer as a sinner and to simply accept what happened. Out of frustration the formerly blind man turns to irony: "Do you want to hear about the healing again?" And even more forcefully, "Do you want to become his disciples, too?" (9:27). The blind man reveals his pilgrimage: he is on the way to becoming a disciple of the healer he has never seen.

The Pharisees operate from their own ignorance, which they impose on the formerly blind man, and from their religious certainty that they are disciples of Moses, not of this rabbi who makes claims they cannot authenticate and whose origin is unknown. They move from insulting the formerly blind man to overt unbelieving. They know that God spoke to Moses; it is essential to their tradition. However, they don't know where Jesus came from, of whom he speaks, or for whom he acts. They trust their Law and not their senses, since the very authentication of origin they seek stands as a sign of healing before them. Again, John ties origin to identity and identity to signs. However, the formerly blind man is no longer threatened. He puts the Pharisees in their place: "You are Pharisees, followers of Moses, and don't know where he came from. Yet I know, for only if he came from God could he open my eyes." He even indirectly accuses them of being sinners whom God does not hear. There is nothing to fear, for he can see that the Pharisees are blind to the reality that Jesus the healer is really from God, otherwise he would be powerless to do what he did for the blind man. God can speak through Jesus as well as through Moses since he performed this sign (9:30–33). Ultimately, the Pharisees respond to the disciples' initial question about the relation of blindness to sin. The man, they claim, was sinful at birth, but they cannot say why. It is simply that since he was blind, he must have been a sinner. The Pharisees explicitly reject the significance of this sign. Their deepening spiritual blindness, in contrast with the increasing in*sight* of the formerly blind man, prevents discipleship. The Pharisees put their faith in Moses and the Law, not in Jesus. In the end they only deal with the result of their accusation and throw the man out (9:34). His parents' fear was justified.

John, however, continues tracing the journey of the blind man from ignorance to faithful discipleship and worship in the climax found in Scene Six. For a second time Jesus takes the initiative of coming to the man who now has become a disciple and is excluded from the synagogue.[23] These two now occupy center stage. This

23. Whereas in the Synoptics it is common for people to approach Jesus (Mark 3:10; 5:1, 22, 27, 35; 6:55–56; 7:25, 32; 8:22; 9:12, 20; 10:1, 13, 17, 46; 12:28), in John frequently Jesus takes the initiative

time Jesus completes the healing of the man by addressing his spiritual being. Jesus reveals his identity to him, that he is the messianic Son of Man, the divine one with the authoritative (here, healing) power promised in Dan 7:13–14. The man might have been blind, but he was not ignorant; he knew what this self-identification meant and became a worshiping believer. "The blind," Jesus says, "will see." The blind man's pilgrimage from blindness and ignorance, through hesitancy and then boldness in affirming discipleship, culminates in his worship and believing. He is the ideal role model for the person John seeks to produce through the testimonial message of his book. He is the one who, encountered by Jesus even in blindness, says, "Lord, I believe," and worships.

We are finally brought to the ironic denouement in Scene Seven. Again, only two persons or groups are on stage, Jesus and the Pharisees. This scene gives Jesus the opportunity to develop his irony. The Pharisees sarcastically and rhetorically step into the trap: "What? Are we blind too?" (9:40). John's use of double meaning reappears, this time with an emphasis on blindness. John wants us to recall that the Pharisees connected blindness with sin, so for someone to question whether the Pharisees were blind would be to accuse them of being sinners, something they as the religious elite could not abide (hence their rhetorical question expecting a negative response). Jesus responds with ironic double meaning as well. If they were truly blind, they would not be guilty. They would have an excuse rooted in their ignorance, for blindness has nothing necessarily to do with sin; indeed, blindness can be a reasonable justification for one's actions. In morality, blinded ignorance can be an excuse. If the Pharisees were blind in this sense, they have hope of seeing. As Jesus restored sight to the blind man, he could restore their sight also if they only believe. However—and here is the irony—their rhetorical question about being blind indicates that they are not blind (9:40). They really do see; yet are blind. They will not see and believe who Jesus is. They have no excuse; their blindness—their dwelling in darkness and refusing to see the Light—is willful. They put themselves in a position of blindness of denial, and since they do so willingly, they are guilty of rejecting Jesus.[24] Their spiritual blindness connects to sin in a way that the physical blindness of the man by the road did not.

The dialogue manifests much of John's style. It has the Greek dramatic form of two persons on stage at a time, engaging in dialogue. It has dialogic progression, here a definite pilgrimage from blindness and ignorance to believing and worship. The blind man's testimony evolves from being based on a sign (9:16) to the claim that Jesus might be a prophet (9:17), to Jesus's being sent from God (9:33), to worshiping. Its plot develops with twists and reversals. Through insult, revelation, irony, and humor it makes its points. The discussants have real character traits. The blind man is obedient, uninterested in theories about Jesus's identity (9:25) but in his own experience, has spunk and develops fearlessness (9:27), and knows the connection between miracles

---

(2:14–16; 4:7; 5:5; 6:5; 11:11).

24. Aristotle, *Nicomachean Ethics*, III, 1.

and God (9:30). His neighbors show real lack of care and concern; they don't really know the blind man since they cannot recognize him (9:8–9). We get to meet his wary parents, who have legitimate fear of being evicted from the synagogue. We encounter the Pharisees who have more interest in their interpretation of the Law than in persons who are healed (9:16). They have no time for sinners, for Sabbath-breakers like Jesus, or for the blind man. What we hear is, "Throw him out!" Finally, we meet Jesus, who, taking the gracious initiative, seeks out the blind and heals them, both physically and spiritually. He intentionally approaches the blind man a second time and reveals himself to this nascent disciple. At the same time, Jesus has no qualms about confronting the spiritual elite about their own blindness, directly and with irony. That they dwell in spiritual darkness and cannot see him results not from their birth but from their choices. They willfully put themselves in ignorance.

The high point of the dialogue addresses discipleship (9:27–28). The formerly blind man sets the options: discipleship to Jesus or to Moses. One leads to worship; the other to blindness, unless one sees the person Moses anticipated (5:46). The man's journey to faith becomes complete, for in confronting the Pharisees about discipleship he shows his willingness to become a testifying disciple, even under threat of excommunication. The author hints at what is taken as a messianic passage: "those who walk in darkness have seen a great light" (Isa 9:2). Believing leads to worship.[25] However, believing also may result in exclusion from the community.

## JESUS AND SIMON PETER (13:1–17)

The second dialogue we will consider, which we briefly noted in chapter 6, is between Jesus and Simon Peter. The narrator places the setting just prior to Passover, when Jesus eats an evening meal with his disciples. Since contrary to the Synoptics this is the night before Passover, this does not appear to be the Passover meal. The all-knowing narrator sets the dramatic stage by telling us Jesus's mind. Jesus knows that his time for bringing his mission to finality has arrived (we will say more about his time in chapter 9). He is to accomplish the work given to him by his Father and return to his Father (13:1). The narrator also reiterates the theme of the previous chapters about love; Jesus continues to love his disciples, although now he intends to leave them. Departure is not a sign of abandonment but of love. This love will be fully demonstrated, first in the little, intimate action of servanthood and then in the great, public event of his crucifixion. Jesus's departure is necessary for the Spirit to come and be with them (16:7). They are the new "his own," chosen by him (6:70) to replace "his own" who rejected him (1:11). As the first "his own" had been selected by God to form the covenant people by obeying God (Deut 4:37; 7:6–8; 1 Chr 16:13), so these

25. Προσκυνέω (worship), which John uses here, is used elsewhere in the Gospel as directed only to God (4:20–24; 12:20).

too are selected to become children of God by believing in and obeying him. (We will say more about becoming children of God in chapter 11.)

After the meal, Jesus takes off his outer garment, wraps a towel around his waist, and stooping down proceeds to wash the feet of the disciples.[26] The action is what a gracious host would have his slave perform for a visitor prior to the meal; it shows humility (partially disrobing and bending down) and respect for the other. Here Jesus as the host washes their feet after the meal. Ironically, the washing does not prepare for a meal but for a final journey to his servant death on a cross.[27] After performing the ritual for some of the disciples, Jesus comes to Simon Peter, but Simon Peter is not about to let Jesus wash his feet. After all, Jesus is his master, indeed the Holy One of God,[28] and the roles should be reversed. So far, Jesus has said nothing, and Simon Peter initiates the dialogue. He asks the rhetorical question, "You aren't going to wash *my* feet, are you?" (13:5). The format of only two people on stage simultaneously continues, with the other disciples sitting as a chorus in the background. Jesus replies with irony: "You can see what I am doing, but you won't understand it until later" (13:7).

Simon Peter shows that he misses the point of Jesus's reply. This is not hard to imagine, since in his ambiguous way Jesus does not give the reason for his action and only hints as to when he will explain it. Peter thus indignantly retorts, "Well. You are never going to wash my feet at all." (13:8). Peter is his old, assertive self; Jesus simply adopts the wrong role for a rabbi, and it is up to Simon Peter to set matters straight. Jesus has reversed the pecking order.[29]

Jesus's reply to Peter is no longer ironic or ambiguous but straight to the point: "If you want to be my disciple, one of my sheep, then you have to do it my way" (13:8). This part of the footwashing scene emphasizes the salvific portent of Jesus's act. With typical double meaning, on the earthly level Jesus tells Peter that with this attitude he cannot be part of Jesus's fellowship. From the "from above" perspective, Jesus affirms that unless Peter goes Jesus's way, he can have "no part with me," no role in his kingdom.

26. Blaine (*Peter*, 62) suggests a notable parallel between Jesus the shepherd laying down his life and taking it up again in 10:17 and Jesus the servant laying down his outer garment and taking it up again (13:4,12). The same words, lay down (τίθημι) and take up (λαμβάνω) are used in both instances.

27. "It symbolizes the true cleansing the disciples are to receive through the sacrificial death of Christ on the cross. . . . The fact that the ritual does not occur until the hour when Jesus is to depart from this world and go to the Father (13:1) . . . strongly suggests that the sacrifice prefigured in the ceremony is Jesus's death and not some lesser offering" (Blaine, *Peter*, 60). It anticipates Jesus the living water pouring out himself (19:34) (Beasley-Murray, *John*, 436).

28. We have not heard from Simon Peter since he uttered this identification (6:68–69).

29. Bultmann (*Gospel of John*, 468) interprets Peter's refusal theologically. "We are not . . . to interpret this psychologically, but as a matter of fact: the natural man simply does not want this kind of service. Why not? The service in question is not just any personal act of kindness—for why should this not be acceptable to the natural man?—but it is service performed by the incarnate Son of God. And even if man can reject it out of pride, Peter's words do not just express this kind of pride, but rather the basic way men think, the refusal to see the act of salvation in what is lowly, or God in the form of a slave."

Simon Peter responds to Jesus, but in typical Peter fashion overreacts: "Then wash all of me." "If I am made good by you washing my feet, I will be even better off if you wash all of me." However, his overreaction, his hyperbole, demonstrates that he still misses the point of the symbolic washing. Jesus's saying and performance are not about cleanliness, as if one is cleaner if more than feet are washed, but about participation in Christ, specifically in his upcoming death. "Without the cleansing to be effected by Jesus's death, Peter cannot participate in the eternal life to be had in union with Jesus's life."[30] As with Nicodemus, Peter operates on the earthly level of normal host practice in entertaining guests and makes what appears to be a silly reply because he fails to see the deeper, spiritual application of Jesus's demonstrative parable.

Jesus replies with another piece of irony based on ambiguity: "You (ὑμεῖς) are all (ὅλος) clean (καθαροί), but not all (πάντες)" (13:10). Whom does he refer to by "you" (in the plural), and what does he mean by "all"? The narrator takes the position that by "you" and "not all," Jesus means that one of the group is not clean, for as we discover later, Judas engages in treachery (13:11). However, given Jesus's use of double meanings, the exception of being not all clean could also apply individually to each disciple so that none are wholly clean, i.e., totally committed to Jesus, given their absence at the crucifixion.[31]

Finally, after dealing with side issues that arose with Peter's reluctance, and having finished washing the disciples' feet, Jesus gets to the point of his action. He asks the rhetorical question whether they understand what he just did and assuming a negative answer, explains to them the significance of his washing their feet.[32] However, his lesson is ambiguous. On the one hand, he says that if the teacher is willing to serve by washing his disciples' feet, they should be willing to serve each other as well. He set the example for them (13:14–15). The success of the enterprise depends upon working together in mutual service. On the other hand, after demonstrating to them the servitude that they should show to each other, one would expect him to say that leaders are not greater than the followers. Yet this is not what Jesus says. Rather, he makes two parallel statements: "the servant is not greater than his master, nor is the messenger greater than the one who sends." Taken literally, this seems to be the very point Simon Peter made to justify his refusal to have his feet washed. However, Peter's response was one-sided. Jesus advocates both mutual service and the value judgment

30. Bauckham, *Testimony*, 195.

31. "Jesus introduces a different word for 'all,' [πάντες for ὅλος] moving the thought in a different direction by considering the disciples individually, not just as a group . . . . Now they must look at themselves . . . with the question of individual purity in mind" (Michaels, *Gospel of John*, 733).

32. Some suggest that this command to wash each other's feet is to be taken literally, so that Jesus is creating or sanctioning such a ritual (Michaels, *Gospel of John*, 724–26). Others see footwashing as "what the crucifixion is, at once a divine deed by which men are released from sin and an example which men must imitate" (Barrett, *Gospel*, 364). It seems more probable, in light of John's use of symbol, that Jesus is taking a common, earthly practice that is performed with visitors to make a heavenly point (Bultmann, *Gospel of John*, 475).

that the master's and sender's serving does not imply that the servant and those sent are now superior. We serve each other and are blessed in doing so (13:17), but being served does not make those served more important than the master or sender or too important to serve others.[33] They remain Jesus's pupils or servants in their kingdom roles, just as Jesus remains the Father's messenger in his kingdom role (13:13, 16). Servanthood does not eliminate the respective roles and responsibilities of leader or teacher and follower or disciple. What it establishes is the model of servant leadership and servant follower, a point Jesus will again make with Peter after his resurrection (21:15–19). Thus, in this fashion Jesus "lays aside his garment" (a double meaning indicating his death; 19:23) to serve but takes it up again and "returns to his place" (a double meaning for resurrection and return to his place with the Father) (13:4, 12).[34] Peter will emulate the Shepherd's service by loving Jesus and becoming a sacrificed shepherd.

The dialogue follows the pattern noted earlier, where it occurs between two principals, and if others are present, they stay uninvolved in the background. It also reveals something about the character of the discussants. Simon Peter sees himself in the role of disciple to his master and by refusing to have his feet washed shows it is difficult to comprehend Jesus's concept of servant leadership. When Jesus later dialogues with Peter, he makes the point that leadership has its cost. In the book of Acts we learn that Peter took on a servant leadership role as the believers organized and witnessed, and for him it began to have a cost (Acts 4:3, 21; 5:33; 12:3–5).

We also learn about Jesus. He continues his ambiguous teaching style, but here, as in a drama, he both acts out and speaks the point he wishes to make. The humility he is about to show in obeying his Father and voluntarily giving himself to die for the world is intimated in his giving himself to his disciples as the servant leader to wash their feet. A bit later Jesus goes even further; you are no longer servants but friends (15:15). Love changes relationships and the status of people, for in love one seeks the good and benefit of the other. Servanthood is not abandoned but powerfully transformed by self-sacrificing love. As we noted in the previous chapter, Jesus has a special relationship with his disciples, and it is nowhere better exemplified in practice than in this preparatory event for the passion to follow.

## JESUS AND PILATE (18:28–19:15)

Our third dialogue also embodies features of a dramatic dialogue we noted above. The introduction gives the place, time, and connection to previous events; throughout the

---

33. Barrett, *Gospel*, 370.

34. "By means of the footwashing, in which Jesus 'lays aside' his garment and then 'takes it up again' (see the occurrences of τίθημι (lay aside) in 10:11, 15, 17, 18 and 13:4, and λαμβάνω (take up) in 10:17 and 18, and 13:12), Jesus acts out a love for his disciples that presages his death for them" (Culpepper, "Peter," 169).

scenes two persons or groups are on stage; there are clear entrances and exits to subsequent scenes; characters are developed, with real dialogue and conversations between them; the plot is complex with surprises; and there are wordplays, ambiguities, double meanings, irony, riddles, uses of words as action that point to time, place, and action; and movement and gesture.[35]

In detail not found in the Synoptic Gospels, John takes us through Jesus's trial before Pilate. The initially speedy narrative of the Gospel slows to a measured crawl. In chapter 10 we will look at the trial through the lens of John's concern for completeness, noting the chiastic structure of seven scenes in which Pilate appears alternately outside the palace with the Jewish leaders and then inside the palace dialoguing with Jesus. John carefully constructs a setting of outside and inside to demonstrate Pilate's alternating weakness and strength. "Pilate's constant passing from one setting to the other gives external expression to the struggle taking place within his soul, for his certainty of Jesus's innocence increases at the same rate as does the political pressure forcing him to condemn Jesus."[36] Here, however, I focus on the dialogues Pilate has with Jews outside the governor's palace in setting the stage for Jesus's crucifixion and with Jesus inside the palace. In particular, I focus on the real reason John gives for Pilate crucifying Jesus and how Jews and Jesus manipulate Pilate to achieve their respective purposes.

Before proceeding to the dialogues, we should note that the accusations, arrest, trial, and punishment of Jesus given in the Gospel follow the provincial procedures of the Greco-Roman administration.[37]

> The course of these legal procedures, which can be gleaned from the legal protocols attested in the Greco-Roman papyri, distinguishes between the policing on the part of the municipal magistrates and judicial proceedings before a more competent judge. The course of the Greco-Roman proceedings might thus include elements such as the following: (i) The issues of crime and policing were introduced by an accusation or a petition directed to the local police authority. (ii) The accused person was immediately summoned, or if he was a fugitive, he was searched for, in order to bring him for further inquiry into the case. In the Roman empire, this task was performed by police attendants or specialized liturgical policemen.[38] (iii) If the fugitive still did not show up, other means like public "wanted" posters or some kind of denunciation might be the outcome in order to get hold of the fugitive.[39] (iv) If the "outlaw" then

---

35. Brant, *Dialogue*, 81, 86–87.

36. Brown, *Gospel xiii–xxi*, 858.

37. "The Egyptian papyrus *P.Oslo* ii 17 is unique in displaying most of the main features of the Greco-Roman proceedings outlined [below], and thus can serve to shed fresh light on the course of the official legal actions against Jesus, as these appear in John's narrative" (Bekken, *Lawsuit*, 71).

38. See John 11:53–54.

39. See John 11:57. See also Bekken, *Lawsuit*, 94–96.

either appeared of his own will or by means of the police attendants,[40] (v) the leading municipal police magistrates . . . made an examination (διάγνωσις) of the case by interrogating the various parties involved, such as the offender, the plaintiff, and the witnesses.[41] (vi) If the matter could not be settled by the local magistrates, a referral of the case was made to more competent judges (*epistratêgoi* or the provincial Roman prefects), (vii) who carried out another examination (διάληψις; lat. *cognitio*).[42] (viii) Eventually, if the accused was found guilty in an open court (lat. *pro tribunali*),[43] (ix) the punishment followed.[44]

Thus, it is reasonable to conclude that the Evangelist accurately situated the passion drama in the judicial structures of the time.

The dialogues in this dramatical act follow patterns we noted at the outset of this chapter. First, John sets the stage for the dialogue at Pilate's palace. The detachment of soldiers and associates first bring Jesus before Annas, the father-in-law of Caiaphas and according to John, serving as the high priest that year.[45] Since legal proceedings, including the questioning witnesses, signing documents, and judgments of capital punishment were prohibited at night,[46] Annas can only conduct a preliminary hearing. The prohibition of witnesses accounts for Jesus's comments about the absence of witnesses against him (18:20–21). From this hearing, Annas sends Jesus to Caiaphas and the Sanhedrin for more formal proceedings that result, in the early morning, in condemnation (Matt 26:57–66). From there, still in the early morning, the Jewish leaders, whether with or without Caiaphas John does not tell us, bring Jesus to Pilate, who is staying at the governor's praetorium in Jerusalem. At this point the "trial," based on escalating charges, occurs. The narrator provides the background fact that Jews lacked the authority to execute Jesus as the reason they involved Pilate in the affair. (18:31). It also may be that they were reluctant to take Jesus's life, given the royal acclamation by the Jerusalem crowd less than a week before (12:12–19).

---

40. See John 18:3–13. "The terminology of the 'officers', 'attendants', 'servants' in the narrative of John seems to reflect a distinct policing function under the command of "the chief priests and the Pharisees", who represented the superior municipal security authority in Jerusalem. It is interesting that the Greek term for 'officer' in John 7:32, 45; 18:3, 12, ὑπηρέτης, which in the New Testament is used most frequently in policing situations, is the same word that is used for the police officers under the command of the *stratêgos* in the papyri" (Bekken, *Lawsuit*, 97).

41. See John 18:19–24.

42. See John 18:28–19:12.

43. See John 19:13–16a.

44. See John 19:16b–18. Bekken, *Lawsuit*, 71.

45. Annas was appointed high priest by Quirinius in AD 6 but was removed from office by the Roman procurator Gratus in AD 15. However, he continued to rule indirectly through his five sons and son-in-law Caiaphas. John treats Annas as holding the office directly, whereas Matthew says that Caiaphas held the position. John's tradition is consistent with Acts 4:6, when Peter and John are brought before Annas as high priest, who was head of the Sanhedrin, and his family.

46. Bacher and Landsberg, "Night," 304.

Second, the trial before Pilate fits the structural pattern where in each of the seven scenes two people or groups of people appear dialogically active on stage simultaneously. Outside the praetorium we find Pilate and the Jewish leaders (the one time the Evangelist notes Jesus's presence outside as a passive bystander, a visual presentation of the subject discussed). Inside the palace, Pilate and Jesus dialogue on stage. (The one exception is when those active are Pilate who gives the order to flog Jesus and the soldiers who carry out the torture, with Jesus present as part of the setting as the object of the torture but not participating in any dialogue (19:1–3)).

The third feature of the dialogues is that we learn about the characters of those in dialogue through their interaction. John clusters together the Jewish leaders who emerge as a group character with one voice. Through both dialogue and narrator's comments, we learn about Jesus's character, who although not always on stage is the central character, that of the Jewish accusers, and that of Pilate. As the scenes in the act progress, we get clearer and more detailed pictures of each.

Early in the morning before Passover the Jewish leaders bring Jesus to Pilate. One can imagine Pilate impatient and disgruntled by being disturbed at this early hour, particularly since, contrary to the customs dictated by the power differential, he is forced to come out to them (rather than they coming in to him). They claim that their religious sensibilities related to the upcoming Passover do not permit them to enter his praetorium. John exhibits his irony here, for while they are scrupulous about maintaining their pre-Passover purity by not entering a gentile habitation, they are willing to pursue the execution of one of their own against whom no charges substantiated by the requisite witnesses could be found (18:23).[47] To Pilate's query, "What charge do you bring against this man?" the Jewish leaders present the *first* charge: Jesus is a criminal, doing evil (18:30).[48] Pilate replies that they do not need his permission to try petty criminals; they have made no accusation of broken Roman laws. This is not the response the Jewish leaders desire, for they want the official death penalty that only Pilate can sanction (18:31–32). Their rejoinder clearly indicates that they have already made up their mind not only about Jesus's guilt but also about the severity of his crime, its appropriate punishment, and who should take the fall for enacting the punishment.[49] To this end they hand their evildoer over to Pilate, the representative of the gentile king.

When Pilate returns inside the praetorium we discover the *second* charge, apparently brought by the leaders (intimated in John and affirmed in Luke 23:2) since the general charge of being a criminal was insufficient to motivate Pilate to undertake

47. Michaels, *Gospel of John*, 915.

48. Luke's account is much more specific in the charges the Jewish leaders bring, stating that Jesus "subverts our nation, opposes payment of taxes to Caesar, and claims to be the Messiah, a king" (Luke 23:2).

49. Here, as elsewhere in the Gospel, John uses a more general term, kill or deprive of life, (ἀποκτείνω) to describe the Jews' request, rather than the term for capital punishment (θανατόω).

Roman judicial proceedings. Pilate inquires of Jesus whether this second, political charge—being a king of the Jews—is true. Jesus's kingship dominates the entire trial. Fifteen times "king" or "kingdom" appears.[50] Jesus first asks whether the accusation is his own idea or that of the Jewish leaders. If it is Pilate's own query, perhaps he would have a genuine interest in the topic. However, Pilate quickly assures Jesus that he is not a Jew and thus has no interest in these inconsequential, internal religiopolitical affairs (18:35). He knows who truly is king and whose interests he faithfully and fearfully serves. But Jesus does not abandon the issue of kingship, which bookends the Gospel from Nathanael to Pilate. Without directly asserting kingship, Jesus implies that he is a king because he has a kingdom, but from "another place." Around the double meaning of "kingdom/king," Jesus poses a riddle for Pilate to solve. Since his kingdom is from elsewhere, the theme of origin or source establishing identity again arises. Pilate, of course, would not be privy to this ironical play on the source of Jesus's kingdom.

Jesus recognizes ("you say"; λέγεις[51]) that Pilate perceives the logic that being a king follows from having a kingdom but changes the subject from kingship to truth (18:37), from identity to mission. Titles do not matter; what is important is testimony to the truth. Indeed, to testify to the truth is Jesus's mission; truth is the criterion by which one decides where one stands: on the side of truth or on the side of falsehood. "Truth" here has a double meaning. Jesus has in mind not merely truth in a propositional sense but truth understood as a person. Jesus is the Truth (18:37; 14:6). In this Jesus offers Pilate a second opportunity to think about the identity and function of the person standing before him: first about being a king from somewhere else; now about testifying to and believing in the Truth. In effect, Jesus asks Pilate, "Will you be on the side of truth? Will you be on my side and follow me?" The issue ultimately is about who Jesus is and the proper response of discipleship upon recognition of his identity.

Pilate could have chosen the side of truth, an opportunity for discipleship, but dismisses the suggestion with his comment, "What is truth?" What he means by this enigmatic question is unclear. Is he rejecting Jesus's offer of becoming a disciple? Probably not, since there is no indication that he catches Jesus's double meaning and his discipleship to a Jew or pretender to the Jewish throne is undoubtedly inconceivable for Pilate. Is he a classic epistemological relativist: truth lies in the eye of the beholder? This might be too sophisticated a position to ascribe to the Roman governor. Pilate's question might also reflect his frustration at his inability to get a straight accusation other than "he is a criminal" from the Jews or a straight answer (truth) from Jesus.[52] Bultmann seems closer to John's meaning when he notes that by this statement Pilate

50. "John has with keen insight picked out the key of the passion narrative in the kingship of Jesus, and has made its meaning clearer, perhaps, than any other New Testament writer" (Barrett, *Essays*, 443).

51. In sales technique, it is more effective and persuasive to have the customer assert the critical features.

52. Stibbe, *Storyteller*, 107. Barclay says that "he asked the question wistfully and wearily" (*John*, 2:242).

shows that the state, including Pilate as its representative, is not interested in the truth about the reality of God but in pragmatism.[53] Whatever is the case, the narrator does not interpret for us. Pilate leaves the Truth behind and returns to the Jews outside the praetorium who, having already rejected and handed the Truth to the gentile, stand in untruth. Pilate comes to them with an answer they are unprepared to accept: "I don't find any basis for your charge against this man." Jesus is crazy, deluded into thinking that he is royalty, maybe, but hardly a king of any dominion recognizable to Pilate. The Evangelist cleverly portrays Pilate's movement between untruth outside the praetorium and the truth inside. Vacillating back and forth, from outside to inside, from Jesus's guilt to innocence, Pilate can never settle on truth because he is interested in self-preservation rather than truth. He can find no fault in Jesus yet cannot bring himself to support Truth with any finality. He is unwilling to offend the Jews, given the political skirmishes he has had with them during his tenure as governor. Pilate does not want to take sides about truth, and in this he is like "many well-disposed men who would try to adopt a middle position in a struggle that is total."[54] Instead of deciding the matter himself, he offers the provoking Jews a choice between two criminals: their alleged criminal-king and a robber.

John paints the irony of the choice offered in bold colors. In the Old Testament the leaders of Israel were shepherds (2 Sam 5:2; Ezek 34; Zech 13:7), responsible for their flock. Jesus self-identifies as the good Shepherd (10:14) who leads his flock and protects against thieves and robbers who could come from outside to attack the sheep (10:1–2).[55] Pilate offers the Jews a choice between the Shepherd and Barabbas, whose name means "robber." The question that Pilate poses, although he does not realize it, is whether the Jewish leaders will side with their authentic shepherd-king who guards and nourishes the flocks, or whether they will side with the thieves and robbers who are bent on destroying the flock. The antagonistic relationship between the good shepherd and the robber who is out to steal the sheep is subtly and dramatically repeated here. In this instance, the robber gains temporary victory. Subtly, John uses Jesus's shepherd discourse about his identity to prepare for the crucial encounter with Pilate and the Jewish leaders.

John fills the trial narrative with irony. For one, Jews sought to arrest Jesus out of fear that he would stir up problems with the Romans (11:50). Yet, responding to Pilate's offer, they choose the robber or insurrectionist who operated secretly instead of the caring shepherd who taught publicly in the synagogue or temple (18:20). For another, "in their zeal to eat the Passover lamb (28) they unwittingly help to fulfill its

---

53. Bultmann, *Gospel of John*, 656.

54. Brown, *Gospel xiii–xxi*, 864.

55. The Greek word for Barabbas, robber (λῃστής), is used elsewhere in John only in 10:1, 8. For a discussion of John's use of the shepherd teaching in 10:1–20 in the passion account, particularly in regard to the structure of the sheepfold, the garden, and the courtyard outside Annas's house, see Stibbe, *Storyteller*, 101–4.

significance through their demanding the death of the Lamb of God, at the same time shutting themselves out from its saving efficacy."[56] They maintain their alleged ritual purity to eat the Passover lamb while simultaneously calling for the death of the real Passover lamb. Forbidden by the Torah to murder, they accomplish it through a third party. Third, John uses this to fulfill the ironical prophecy of Caiaphas regarding the death of Jesus, which in turn affected all the "scattered children of God" (11:49–52). Fourth, it is the judge, Jesus, who is judged, but whereas Jesus judges truly (8:16), here we get mob justice. Truth itself stands in the dock.

Remaining reluctant, Pilate wants no part of this Jewish affair (19:4). After all, he had nasty encounters with the Jewish leaders previously and is temporarily in Jerusalem simply to keep order during the Passover Feast. Josephus states that while Pilate's predecessors had respected Jewish customs by removing all images and effigies on their standards when entering Jerusalem, Pilate allowed his soldiers to bring military standards bearing the likeness of Caesar, who claimed to be a god, into Jerusalem. Jews protested that this was contrary to their religious law and requested Pilate to remove the banners from Jerusalem. After days of confrontations during which Pilate threatened to kill the Jewish demonstrators, Pilate relented and removed the image-bearing banners.[57] This loss of face might lie behind Pilate's reluctance to go openly against the Jewish leaders and the crowd they amassed.

After an unsuccessful attempt to placate the Jews by offering them a choice between the Shepherd-King and Barabbas, Pilate returns inside the praetorium to have Jesus flogged. He acts perhaps partly from his own cruelty, perhaps partly from his desire to assuage the crowd, perhaps to visibly show the Jews Rome's power over them by demonstrating what happens to rebellious king-claimants,[58] perhaps to extract a confession.[59]

After the flogging, Pilate returns to the Jewish leaders to present to them their bloodied king. Here too is irony; the hated Romans mock the Jews by torturing and debasing their real king with a crown of thorns and royal, purple robe, while the Jews chant "Crucify, crucify" (19:6). Seeing that they are not making progress in getting a favorable verdict for capital punishment, the Jewish leaders bring a *third* charge: Jesus blasphemes, making himself to be the Son of God (19:7). This charge is both true and false. It is true that he is the Son of God, although the Jewish leaders only recognize it as a claim, not as a true claim, and fail to comprehend what the claim would really mean for them if it were true. However, it is also false: Jesus did not *make* (ἐποίησεν)

56. Beasley-Murray, *John*, 327–28.

57. Josephus, *J.W.* 2.9.2–4. Josephus also recounts another incident where Pilate took money designated for the temple to construct an aqueduct. When the Jews protested, Pilate signaled to his disguised soldiers hidden in the crowd to attack the protestors, some of whom were killed (Josephus, *Ant.* 18.3.2).

58. Carter, *Pontius Pilate*, 145.

59. Dodd, *Historical*, 102–3.

himself the Son of God. "On the contrary his claim has always been that he says and does nothing on his own and that his identity and function as the Son have been granted him by the Father."[60] This charge hits home to Pilate, for in his world there is only one son of a god, the Caesar. Pilate becomes afraid, concerned that the ante has been raised: Jesus is no longer a common criminal or crazy pretender to the Jewish throne but a pretender to divinity. If word got back to Rome that he was protecting a rival who claimed to be another semidivine son of God, Pilate could be viewed as disloyal to his semidivine Caesar (19:8). And if this seemingly helpless individual really is divine, he might have some extraordinary, threatening powers (18:36).[61]

Pilate needs to know more about this man, and so turns to Jesus and asks the question frequently posed in the Gospel: From where do you come? Clearly, he missed the import of Jesus's earlier claim that his kingship comes from another place. However, the origin that interests Pilate is the earthly one. As elsewhere in John, one's identity is tied to one's origin (9:17). When Jesus refuses to answer, Pilate threatens him with a power move. Pilate is ever careful and fearful about his own power and authority. Jesus does not identify his own origin but rather the origin of Pilate's power (19:11). Jesus ironically asserts his own authority and informs Pilate that he is not able to do as he wishes but only as his wishes accord with another's power, a power from above. "Power" takes on a double meaning of political and spiritual; in Pilate's understanding power and authority flowed from Rome; for Jesus, it came from his Father. Jesus here (19:11) uses the same word, "from above" (ἄνωθεν) that he used when talking to Nicodemus about being reborn from above (3:3). Pilate's power, like our rebirth, derives ultimately not from himself, and as a dependent Roman governor he is mindful of what happens to the power of those who fall out of favor. Jesus's power, that of the Son of Man (Dan 7:14), comes from his Father, and to him Jesus gives up his life not fearfully or out of egoistic concern for self but willingly and sacrificially (10:18; 18:11). His death will be his glorification in which he will draw all to himself (12:23, 32). What would normally prove to be a power struggle turns out not to be, for the power and intent of God here lie conjoined with and realized through Pilate's political power.

John gives his readers several reasons why the Jewish leaders want Jesus dead. Some want Jesus stoned because he claims to be God (8:59). John thinks that Caiaphas wants Jesus dead because he is afraid that Jesus will somehow stimulate Roman retaliation against the Jews so that the nation will perish (11:50).[62] The chief priests and some Pharisees want Jesus and Lazarus dead because many people are becoming followers of Jesus (12:10, 19, 42).

60. Lincoln, *Truth on Trial*, 131.

61. Carter, *Pontius Pilate*, 148.

62. John sees this as ironic, because Caiaphas is in fact prophesying what would really happen to Jesus, that he would die for the nation and indeed, for the "scattered children of God" (11:51–52).

However, even their new accusation that Jesus claims divinity fails to bring the deadly result the Jewish leaders want. They persist in their desire to permanently rid themselves of this troublesome person who asserts a special relationship to God. Thus, the Jewish leaders play their final trump card with a *fourth* accusation, now not against Jesus but against Pilate: "If you let him go, you are no friend of Caesar. Anyone who claims to be a king opposes Caesar" (19:12). The term "friend of Caesar" was a title of privilege given to Roman senators and others for faithful service, something to which Pilate would aspire.[63]

This time their challenge to Pilate is *ad hominem* and not about Jesus at all. Up to this point, Pilate has functioned more like an arbitrator conducting an examination (ἀνάκρισις) than a judge, unsuccessfully seeking to resolve the conflict between the parties somewhat amicably.[64] At the same time, he has shown his power, taunting the Jews with references to *their* king (18:39; 19:5, 14, 15, 19): he is still in charge.[65] With this last Jewish thrust, Pilate relents, for what is the skin of this insignificant, deluded king worth against his own? With all the sarcasm he can muster, Pilate sits on his judgment seat and pronounces, "Here is your king." The Jewish leaders, caught up in their anger, hatred, and heat of the moment, take the bait and respond to Pilate's almost unbelieving question, "*Your king* you want me to crucify?" "We have no king but Caesar, they reply."[66] They, as others before them, turn their back on their true king, God, the one who delivered them from the oppressors (1 Sam 8:4–9). They win but choose the oppressor and false claimant to divinity over the liberator and truly divine and in turn fail to understand the real meaning of Pilate's action until it is too late. In crucifying Jesus, they relinquish their political sovereignty to Caesar (19:15) and ironically affirm the very servitude that they denied (8:33). Only later do they realize that Pilate has the last laugh when he places the sign "The King of the Jews" in multiple languages over the crucified Jesus. They demanded the death of their own king, for which the Romans were all too ready to oblige.

One of the ironies of the trial is that, from an earthly perspective, Jesus is crucified, not because of charges brought against him and not because he is found guilty of any misdeed. Indeed, in John's ironical way, the charges laid against Jesus are in some sense true. From the Pharisees' point of view, Jesus is a law breaker when it comes to keeping the Sabbath (5:16), the people have rebelliously proclaimed him a king (12:13), and Jesus claims that he is the Son of God (10:36). Rather, Pilate had Jesus executed because of a personal threat, because Jewish hatred aroused his fear of being socially excluded from the high ranks of Roman society. Some think that John wants to accuse the Jewish leaders, particularly Caiaphas, who brought the charges (19:11)

---

63. Beasley-Murray, *John*, 340.

64. Bekken, *Lawsuit*, 108–10. See the use of the term in Luke 23:14.

65. Lincoln, *Truth on Trial*, 131.

66. "They misquote the Passover Nismat in 19:15, changing the words 'We have no King but Thee' (Yahweh) to 'We have no King but Caesar!'" (Stibbe, *Storyteller*, 111).

while excusing Pilate, since unknowingly he is not acting on his own authority.[67] Yet ultimately, Pilate's ego, vanity, and fear lead to his capitulation to the Jewish demands.

If one of the features of dialogues is to reveal the character of the members, what do we learn about each of the dialoguing members? The Jewish leaders are presented as a unified group. We learn that the opposition to Jesus was persistent and focused on their task of eliminating this perceived threat to the status quo, where supposedly the Law in all its subtle colors was respected and rigorously obeyed, and teachers of the Law and the Pharisees were recognized as the proper interpreters and ultimate arbiters of the Law. They single-mindedly pursued Jesus's death, cunningly using their legal powerlessness to bring about their desired result as they gradually upped the charge against Jesus. To accomplish their end, they willingly sacrificed in an ironic way their own allegiance to their nation and their own God. As ancient Israel demanded a king like the other nations in place of ruling Yahweh, so the Jewish leaders recognized and hailed a Roman king in place of their messianic king (19:15). They performed a national betrayal. It was only after the heat of the moment and the fulfillment of their desires that they realized, in part and in retrospect, the gravity of their misplaced avowal (19:21).

Pilate's character is the most developed. We get a very intimate portrait of him. He is unhappy with being roused early in the morning to deal with a trivial matter of a common criminal (18:31, 33). Responding to petty complaints is not what he had come up from Caesarea at Passover to do. He is testy and brash in confronting those socially and politically inferior to him, both the Jewish leaders (18:31) and Jesus (18:33, 35). He is logical (18:37) and calculating, sizing up those who appeared before him. He is sarcastic, not about to play into the hands of others (18:38). Yet, ironically, he is indecisive (18:39; 19:6), not wanting to get involved in the internal battles of the Jews. These conquered but religiously obstinate people had once too often burned him. He is cruel (19:1), willing to unleash his considerable Roman power against another human being. Yet he is fearful, both of complaining Jews whom he is supposed to be holding in check and of those in Syria and Rome who have authority over him (19:8, 13). He recognizes and relies on power, both his own and that of those over him, knowing that what he wields can be wielded against him. He is self-concerned, lest when he returns to Rome, he is denied the social privilege of being a "friend of Caesar." Finally, he is vengeful. In the end he gets his reprisal on the Jews who frustrated and threatened him, embarrassing them by placing the sign, "King of the Jews" over the crucified Jesus and refusing to replace it with a more nuanced sign about Jesus's claim to kingship.

Finally, the dialogue tells us about Jesus. Ironically, whereas in chapters 13–17 John has Jesus doing all the speaking, in the trial with Pilate Jesus says very little.

---

67. Sherwin-White, "Pilate," 869. Tradition held that Pilate became a Christian ("a Christian by conscience"; Tertullian, *Apology*, 21.24). In a piece of supreme irony, the Coptic Church ultimately canonized Pilate, based on later, probably apocryphal stories about his conversion.

He shows no reluctance to confront those in political power (18:34, 36; 19:11). He is self-assured, knowing where he is from, what his support system is, and the reason for this entire event—to testify to truth, that is, to himself, who he is, and where he is from (18:36–37). He also knows that this trial and its results are purposive events, for they bring to culmination one reason for his coming, namely, to save the world, and extends his kingdom rule from heaven to earth (18:36).

The end of the dialogue continues John's use of irony. The Jewish leaders think that they are victors (19:16) but discover that Pilate has turned the tables on them, claiming that they killed their own king (19:21). Pilate also thinks that he has succeeded in gaining victory over both the Jewish leaders and the man who would be king, but the kingdom movement the crucified man begins lasts longer than the empire in which Pilate is a political cog. Appearing powerless, Jesus ultimately is victorious, both ascending to his Father and sending his disciples on their mission (20:17, 21). Caiaphas was unknowingly correct after all; the Shepherd, not Barabbas, ultimately wins, while Pilate dies in ignominy.

## JESUS AND THE ACCUSED WOMAN (7:53—8:11)

We have good reasons to think that this story about the accused woman originally was not part of the Gospel of John. Not only do the earliest and best manuscripts omit it, but other manuscripts place it elsewhere in the Gospel. Some manuscripts even have it after Luke 21:38 and not in John at all. It is not quoted by earlier church fathers, and "[i]ts text contains a disproportionately large number of variants, which is generally a sure sign that it has received less than average care in transmission."[68] Yet, although its theme word "forgive" is found only one other time in the Gospel (20:23), and no direct forgiveness is given in this passage, the emphasis on the absence of judgment and condemnation is very Johannine. Jerome and Augustine speak of the story, and many have noted that the point of the story, the way the account unfolds, and how Jesus acts are what one would expect from a Johannine Jesus.

This one-act play follows the same pattern we noted above. At any given time two persons (or in this case, the group treated as a person) are in dialogue. First, the scribes and Pharisees dialogue with Jesus. After they depart, Jesus converses with the woman who is left alone with him. One might ask, are there not three persons involved initially: the religious elite, Jesus, and the woman? However, the woman initially is nothing more than a stage prop for the first conversation; she plays no active role in the dialogue. The accusers simply place her in the middle as a distressed spectacle functioning as a conversation starter.

In this dialogue we again find Jesus teaching in the temple courts, for him a familiar place where he witnesses worshiping, buying and selling, and socializing.

---

68. Tenney, *John*, 137.

When in Jerusalem, Jesus comes there with some frequency to teach because that is where crowds of people hang out. "I always taught in synagogues or at the temple, where all the Jews come together" (18:20; see 7:14, 28; Matt 26:55). As people gather around to listen to him, the teachers of the Law (scribes or legal experts) and the Pharisees approach him, dragging with them, probably most reluctantly, a hapless woman. The scribes are the legal technocrats who, because of their knowledge of the minutiae of the Law, frequently were called upon to render judgments in the community. The Pharisees, especially in this instance, are the holier-than-thou bunch. The embarrassed woman is the victim, the show-and-tell object whom they stand unceremoniously before Jesus and the crowd of public witnesses.

The scribes and Pharisees initiate the conversation, a move almost always antagonistic. "Teacher, this woman was caught in the very act of adultery" (8:4). Why, one might ask them, have they brought her to Jesus, of all people, rather than handling the matter themselves? Clearly, their tactics have changed. The previous day the chief priests and Pharisees sent temple guards to arrest Jesus, a venture that proved unsuccessful (7:32–52). At that time Jesus presented two riddles that confounded the people and befuddled the prospective arrestors, who returned to their handlers empty-handed. Now the Pharisees enlist the teachers of the Law and approach him in person, so that they might develop a case against him, or if not that, set him at odds with the crowd that seems to support him, though not without division. The legal scholars here have a specific role to play. "In the Law, Moses commanded us to stone such women. Teacher, what do you say? How do you judge?"

The expert lawyers and super-righteous manufacture an apparent dilemma for Jesus in order, the narrator informs us, to trap him and exploit divisions in the crowd. On the one hand, if he adheres to the Law about adultery and condemns the woman, he will lose favor with society's outcasts who attentively listen to their champion in the temple market. The Gospel of Luke tells us, "Tax collectors and sinners gathered around to hear Jesus. However, Pharisees and teachers of the law muttered, 'This man welcomes and eats with sinners'" (Luke 15:1–2). The down and out are his lost sheep for whom he will lay down his life (Luke 15:3; John 10:14–18). To condemn her would damage his countercultural reputation of siding with pariahs. On the other hand, if he turns against what Moses commanded in the Law, he violates his claim that he has not come to break the Law but to fulfill it. "Anyone who sets aside one of the least of these commands and teaches others accordingly will be called least in the kingdom of heaven" (Matt 5:19). He will have elevated his personal opinion above the Law, as he was accused of doing when healing on the Sabbath. Hence the dilemma: how can he both show compassion (forgiveness) and fulfill the Law?

The accusation contains several enigmas. First, who caught this unfortunate woman in the act? There had to be more than one witness (Deut 17:7; John 8:17). If it were the super-righteous, it puts them in a dilemma, for one would wonder what the teachers of the Law or the Pharisees were doing to catch this woman in the adulterous act, especially if she was reputedly known to lead a loose lifestyle (8:11). Their know-ing where she was to be found compromised their accusing presence in the temple courts. Second, did the accusers *really* catch her in the *very* act of adultery (8:4); how did they gain access to that place and event? Or is this a setup? Catching her in the act would be problematic, for the crowd would wonder, as before, why the super-religious were snooping around unsavory places in the middle of the night. Third, where is her sexual partner? According to the Law, he is as guilty as she is and should suffer similar punishment (Deut 22:22). Their misogyny is manifest. Finally, did the teachers of the law get the penalty completely right? Capital punishment was demanded for adultery, but the Law did not prescribe stoning, which was reserved for the urban rape of a virgin (Deut 22:23–24).

In this short play or encounter, Jesus pursues none of these questioning ap-proaches. Instead, he stoops down and writes in the dust with his finger. Despite the extreme gravity of the situation, despite the persistent questioning[69] ("What about her, teacher?" 8:7), Jesus shows no haste to judge. Rather, he pauses to think about this test case. His deliberation models the need to be careful before we engage in judgment, lest we be accused of hasty judgment and fall into its errors. Judging is, Jesus's action indicates, serious business ("Do not judge, or you too will be judged. For in the same way that you judge others, you will be judged, and with the same standard that you use, it will be applied to you," Matt 7:1). It may also be the case that in bending down, he visibly demonstrates his unwillingness to stand with the obnoxious accusers. He "offers a visible sign of disengagement" from that crowd.[70]

It is intriguing that the author's account mentions that Jesus writes "with his fin-ger." The scribes' test derives from the Law, which originally was written by God with his finger on stone tablets (Exod 31:18). As we have seen in chapter 5, since John's Jesus identifies with God elsewhere, it is appropriate to see him here also identifying indirectly with God with this act. The Johannine-style irony is that the religious lead-ers are testing the very Lawgiver. They have no clue about the identity of the one they query and seek to trap. Who can ensnare God?

Jesus could have raised the question whether the teachers of the Law and the righteous Pharisees were actual witnesses of the event, because if not, they were not entitled to be the first to throw stones. Under the Law, the witnesses were required to be the first to enact the penalty (Deut 17:7), thus preventing the (in)justice of mob violence. However, Jesus does not directly argue potentially embarrassing questions of witnessing. Instead, he focuses on the heart of the issue: the Law's requirement of righteous judging. His first response is to the accusers, not to the woman: "Let the person who has never sinned be the first of you to cast the stone." It surely caught these puzzle-makers off guard. Whereas they focused on the first part of the Law's command dealing with capital punishment for adultery, Jesus invokes the second part

69. The Greek imperfect ἐπέμενον ἐρωτῶντες is employed, indicating repeated pestering.

70. Gench, *Encounters*, 53.

of the Law's command dealing with righteousness: "You must purge the evil from among you." Jesus asserts that evil could not be purged from the community if those who judged and did the stoning were themselves evil or unrighteous. Although in judgment one evil would be recompensed, other evils would remain, if not increase. In short, Jesus affirms the very Law they want to wield over him. The Law demanded the complete innocence of the witnesses, judges, and the executioners. Anything less and the Law was broken.

This condition of righteous judging is impossible to keep, and the accusers know it. They now are the ones caught in a dilemma. They could affirm their own innocence and righteousness by casting the first stone, but not only would that raise the question of the circumstances of their witnessing the alleged adultery, it would be a questionable self-affirmation of their sinlessness that the witnessing crowd would undoubtedly contest. After all, the Pharisees' daily, public attempts to demonstrably convince others of their own righteousness would not have been necessary if the people were already convinced of it. Or they could abandon their mission to trap Jesus as a project gone awry. Jesus cleverly turns the tables by upholding and using the Law itself. The accusers focus on punishment of the guilty; Jesus counters with the righteousness required of the witnesses, judges, and executioners.

One by one, the accusers depart. The eldest leave first. Not only are they the first in importance among the group, they also are undoubtedly the wiser, realizing that they could not satisfy the stringent righteousness the Law required. They could not escape the dilemma but could only retreat as sinners more embarrassed than the woman they hauled into the temple court.

Only Jesus, the worried woman, and the attentive crowd remain. The Johannine theme of Jesus alone with a woman is repeated. Jesus now becomes the judge. Indeed, only he is qualified to judge, for only Jesus could meet the Law's standard as both perfectly righteous and all-knowing (8:16). As he knew Nathanael, he knew the woman and her lifestyle, though he had never met her. Yet despite this knowledge, his judgment spoken to the woman was not to condemn her but to forgive. Brought as an accused captive, she is free to go, no strings attached. Jesus does not pronounce judgment of guilt or innocence: only non-condemnation. Being forgiven does not make one innocent, only not condemned. Jesus's forgiveness saves and frees (Luke 7:48–50).

Jesus's forgiveness does not require her to admit guilt or repent. He attaches no prerequisites to his forgiveness. It is truly an act of grace on the part of one who knows the truth. Confession of sins is not necessary for forgiveness, only sufficient (1 John 1:9). If we confess our sins, we are forgiven; it is *not* that unless we confess our sins we are not forgiven. These two claims are not equivalent.

One might wonder whether Jesus conveys cheap grace. The woman and we can obtain God's merciful forgiveness without being sorry (repenting). However, to the contrary, Jesus's grace is not cheap. For *one* thing, as the remainder of the Gospel shows us, it requires that Jesus fulfill God's will through his experience of death.

Grace comes at an exorbitant price. For *another* thing, repentance is recommended elsewhere. What repentance does is restore the relationship broken by sin. Confession signifies that the person wants to be restored. Thus, it provides the first step in the reintegration of the person into the community (Luke 15:21). *Third*, confession as part of repentance is necessary to bring about personal healing. Without confession, the wounds of sin remain festering. Confession, acknowledging one's guilt, is the medicine for being healed. It is I, not another, who has sinned and take responsibility. *Fourth*, after confession it becomes possible to move on to change one's life. Jesus does not leave the woman with mere forgiveness. He commands her to change her lifestyle: "to leave her life of sin." Jesus has not rescued her so that she can be more vigilant and not get caught the next time she engages in illicit sex. He commands her to demonstrate a changed heart.

In this dialogue each member enters with a calling: Jesus to teach, the religious elite to defend their Law, and the woman to be judged. Each departs with a mission: Jesus foregoes condemnation to bring salvation through forgiveness, the religious elite to fight another day, and the woman free to go yet commanded to change. The witnessing crowd will continue to listen and puzzle over Jesus's radical, nonjudgmental forgiveness. In the subsequent stories we discover more about the forgiving Jesus and the defiant Pharisees. We hear nothing more about the forgiven woman. Yet the message to the readers is clear: although we lack the innocence to be qualified, perfect judges, we are forgiven people, called to be forgiving.[71]

## CONCLUSION

The author of the Gospel of John effectively weaves dramatic dialogue throughout the book. One event leads almost seamlessly to the next, despite the often temporal ambiguities of the events. One encounter heightens the tension in preparation for the next, until we reach the passion account, and even then the narration moves powerfully onward. The dialogues are key movers of John's larger story. In themselves, the individual dialogues can be seen as little dramas with introductions, diversity of scenes, entrances and exits, characters interacting in dialogue, skilled manipulation of language to serve diverse functions, and a plot of their own that contributes to the overall plot and purpose of the Gospel. When this dramatic dialogic structure is revealed, we see more clearly how the Evangelist clearly and cleverly brings to the fore the mission of Jesus as the revealer of God and how he constructs the dialogues to reveal the origin, nature, and mission of Jesus. Jesus brings people into worship and discipleship through his healing. He acts out the servant leadership he expects of those who will take up his mission in demonstrating his love to his own. He demonstrates that he is the truth and, in consort with his Father, controls his destiny and

71. It is Matthew who reminds us that only if we forgive others are we ourselves forgiven (Matt 6:14). This is the only NT condition imposed on receiving God's forgiveness.

mission, despite the assertions and demonstrations of power by religious and secular authorities. He frees through gracious forgiveness, yet challenges those he encounters to change their lifestyle. The stories are not merely told. Jesus's dialogues themselves bring out these critical features that show Jesus as the revealing Son of God, creating believers as loving disciples, through their words and actions.

That Jesus engages in dialogues does not rule out that he is a teacher. Indeed, as the book of John progresses, Jesus moves more and more to discourse about himself and his mission. He has something to say, first to the public and then in private to his disciples. To Jesus's discourses and monologues we turn next.

## QUESTIONS FOR REFLECTION AND DISCUSSION

1. Group exercise: Could you perform one of John's dramas about Jesus with one of your friends? Write out a script that brings one of Jesus's dialogues to life.

2. What is it about the structure of Jesus's dialogues that gives the dialogue its power and relevancy?

3. Each of the dialogues involves either internal or external struggle. How is John able to capture that struggle in each of the dialogues?

4. Each of the dialogues is about redemption. How do the characters find or fail to find redemption in their conversation with Jesus? What makes the difference in each case?

5. Trace the blind man's journey to faith. Do any of his stages or responses echo in your own experience? Which of the characters–the blind man, the disciples, the neighbors, the parents, the righteous Pharisees–do you identify with?

6. Do you feel any sympathy for Pilate, or do you think that he was the master of his own fate? How much does external people-pressure affect the way you act?

7. Why did the Pharisees take the accused woman to Jesus rather than a priest (Deut 19:17–18)? Do you think that the accused woman was guilty? Do you think that the encounter with the Pharisees and Jesus changed her life, and if so, how?

# CHAPTER EIGHT

# Book of Discourses

As the Gospel of John moves to its passion climax, the Evangelist increasingly presents Jesus through discourse rather than dialogue, until Jesus's monologues totally dominate chapters 14 to 17. Many of these discourses are either responses to brief, often antagonistic queries or to skeptical comments or function as contextually connected standalones. To understand them properly we must adopt a different approach from that taken toward the author's dialogues. In the previous chapter we noted that the dialogues follow a classic drama pattern where two people at a time converse on stage and the focus is on the individuals' dialogic interaction. Each is given his or her own voice, such that we learn about them, their character, and their interests through what they say. The discourses, on the other hand, employ a triadic structure that sets them apart from John's dialogues. The dialogues feature three members, resulting in a triadic as over against a dyadic structure. Although the only voice is that of the speaker, other persons or groups function centrally in the discourse. Since members of the triad are not directly heard, we are forced to understand them through their described positions, actions, or functions, and interrelationships given from Jesus's perspective.[1] To elicit the triadic structure, I will first identify the discourse members. I term them "members" because even though John provides a monologic presentational structure for Jesus's discourses that we examine, in each case he portrays three group participants, agents, or agent groups of varying importance acting and/or being positioned inter-relationally.

By visually displaying the triadic structure of the discourses, we can see more clearly how John structurally presents, develops, and integrates actions, positions, roles, and relationships and reveals their importance. The members of the triad and their roles vary from discourse to discourse.[2] In some cases, one or two members

---

1. "The ancient historical writers' *relative* freedom to compose discourses appropriate to the speaker and the context is probably the feature of ancient historiography that diverges most from the practice of serious modern history" (Bauckham, *Testimony*, 20–21).

2. Neyrey notes that roles are relational. "A role implies a set of expectations for interaction between a person who holds one position in a group and another person who holds a reciprocal

dominate, while in others all three play relatively equal roles. As one would expect, Jesus is the central member in every discourse, for he is the speaker and the discourses are his. In addition, Jesus is central because John wrote the Gospel as a witness to Jesus to bring readers or hearers to believe in Jesus (20:31). Often the second member of the triad is the Father, who by sending Jesus and calling disciples enables believing. Furthermore, even the degree of member involvement can vary significantly. When one or the other member dominates, the seemingly less important members may appear to have relatively minor roles, as indicated by the fewer agency verbs assigned to them.[3] In these instances they may function less as agents than as objects of other agents' actions. Yet, even where these members appear to play a more minor role, closer inspection of the literary structure shows that all three members are necessary for the discourse to succeed in conveying the author's intended theological message. Sometimes even the very presence of apparently minor members alters the dynamic of the relationships, turning a seemingly minor role into something textually significant and theologically crucial. Thus, even in their "passivity," apparently minor members contribute to the message conveyed; they provide a stance, position, or point of conflict in relation to the principal member(s) in the dialogue. For example, the very presence of Pharisees (John 8) or thieves (John 10) creates the tension (validating testimony or needing a leading shepherd) that requires resolution.

We will construct a tabular analysis of the triadic structure that reveals how the roles of the members change as the discourse develops. I especially focus on the verbs, both of action and position, John employs to highlight the roles of the respective members. The author carefully chooses the verbs to identify the respective roles; roles assigned to one member generally are not assigned to another. The exceptional cases, where "Jesus does what he sees his Father doing" and so emulates his Father's actions (for example, John 15 and 17 below), show how the relationship between Father and Son develops as the Gospel moves towards its climax. The discourses that in the first half of John are directed toward general listeners (Jews, temple worshipers, or their leaders) and emphasize Jesus's coming or being sent, are more personally directed in the second half toward the disciples for the purpose of encouraging reciprocal action that either mirrors that of the Father and of Jesus or indicates the response, for example, of obedience or remaining, that Jesus desires from them as he anticipates returning to the Father and leaving them behind as effective witnesses. Many discourse verbs are active (*give, send, pray, raise, sanctify, prune, love, come, know, believe*), indicating *agency*. In such cases we will concentrate on who is acting, what they are doing, and

---

position" (*Gospel*, 31).

3. Since discourse differs structurally from dialogue, my treatment of major and minor roles differs somewhat from Stephen Levinsohn's narrative features. Whereas he notes that "one difference is that [in narrative] minor members just appear and disappear, without any formal introduction," in the discourses, as one would expect, the members do not come and go. He also notes that in narratives major members "are involved in a series of events," which accords with my focus on the complexity of the roles revealed in agency verbs ("Member Reference," 32).

who the action affects. Other verbs are linking or passive verbs, indicating the *status* or *position* of a member. This status provides a basis for the kind of relationships that can be established. For example, the Father prunes the "fruitful branches to make them more fruitful" (15:2). They have the status of being fruitful.

Since almost without exception the agency verbs take objects, we need to focus not only on the verbs and their subjects but on their objects as well, showing whom the members' actions affect. Affecting and being affected establish the relational dynamics featured in these discourses. They may reflect authority lines (the Son expecting obedience; the Father giving authority to the Son); they may establish the identity of the persons who are expected to respond to actions (the sheep listen and follow); they may invite relational motifs (they are prayed for, drawn, called, sanctified, hated, not of this world, or objects of Jesus's provision of eternal life).

As we proceed, our tabular analysis will reveal a subtle shift in the relationships between the members. In the earlier discourses the members manifest an *action-response* of one member to another such as manifested in obedience; in the later discourses the interactions deepen to an action-response of *emulation* and eventually to *reciprocity*. In emulation the action taken by one member calls for the same action to be directed to another party (Jesus's love of friends is in turn to be directed to one's friends). In reciprocity the response is manifested in mutual interaction (remain in each other).

Repetition, constantly present in John's Gospel, is central to these triadically structured discourses.[4] What are termed "repetitions" in the literature come in diverse varieties. Van Belle notes such structures as repetitions of words, phrases, or ideas; variations; and amplifications that occur in diverse contexts such as parallelisms, antitheses, chiasms, and inclusions.[5] These repetitions in turn occur at the word, sentence, rhetorical-narrative, and socio-rhetorical levels.[6] For example, in 6:35–40 *come, believe,* and *raise* are repeated to take center stage. In 8:14–18 the repeated words are *judge* and *testify/testimony*. In 15:1–8 the monologue focuses on the repetition of *remaining* and *bearing fruit*. In fact, in the passages we will look at, the author uses a limited number and variety of verbs; five or six agency verbs suffice to do the work in the discourse. Even in the longer monologue of John 17 the number of verbs used is quite restricted. Where verbs are repeated directly or with synonyms, they frequently form part of the structures of parallelisms, contrasts, or even chiasms so common in Hebrew literature. John employs these literary devices, along with others noted in chapter 1, like irony, analogy, riddles, and double meaning, to emphasize member roles and relationships, and ultimately to contrast the unknowing with the knowing, even if the knowing that arises from recollection occurs much later (2:22; 12:16; 20:9).

---

4. Van Belle, "Theory of Repetitions," 13–32.

5. For an extraordinarily comprehensive treatment of repetition, see Van Belle, "Repetitions and Variations," 33–85.

6. Van Belle, "Theory of Repetitions," 21, 25, 27, 29.

These repeated verbs also tie into the larger framework of key Johannine themes. Verbs like *come, send, see, raise up, believe, remain, testify, teach,* and *choose* play significant roles in other parts of John's Gospel. These discourses are only one set of stops on the tramlines of thematic development.

Jo-Ann Brant writes that "the author of the Fourth Gospel gives the narrator a limited task and allows the characters to lay out the plot through their speech."[7] The Gospel contains a "language of actions." Her analysis illumines the text where dialogue is present, but in the *discourses*, where true dialogue is absent, the members of the triad are individually silent; they comment and interact only through the one, Jesus, who presents the discourse or monologue. Thus, the Gospel centers on the "action of discourse," revealed through verbs of position, action, and relationship. Through these verbs and the ways they structure the presentation, we will approach the literary form and theological and practical content of the discourses.[8]

In this chapter I present seven examples of triadic discourses (or parts thereof) and comment on each. John has other examples, but these should suffice to show the structure, diversity, and the possibilities for understanding and insight that arise from using this tabular approach, as over against mere sentential analysis. I present the analyses tabularly in terms of three members, with a column pertaining to each.[9] The columns contain *agency* verbs (italicized to make their progression easier to trace), *positional* status verbs (underlined), and *direct and indirect objects* (indented). Sometimes I will place the grammatical object in brackets (indicating duplication) if it is given elsewhere laterally in the table under a different member-heading or if it is needed to make the meaning or referent of the action clear.

I use tables to elicit attention to and visualize this triadic structure to help readers better understand and appreciate the discourses. This tabular analysis makes the triadic members' positions, relationships, and roles visible.[10] The tables present verbal pictures, and a picture, they say, is worth a thousand words. I intend that through this structural analysis the careful and attentive reader will gain additional insights from and a deeper understanding of the text.

---

7. Brant, *Dialogue*, 3.

8. For an overview of discourse analysis, see Reed, "Discourse Analysis."

9. Van Der Watt terms John's style pictorially argumentative. A "pictorial or relational argumentative structure could explain certain of the features of the way the arguments are developed" ("Repetition," 107). Our analysis elicits this argumentative structure in a tabularly pictorial way.

10. "The essential thing is that the verse structure should be represented to the eye by proper printing of the text. Where this is done, further explanation is superfluous; where structural arrangement is wanting, no amount of explanation is likely to be of much avail" (Moulton, *Literary Study*, viii).

## JESUS AS THE BREAD OF LIFE (6:35–51)

We already discussed in chapter 3 the two miracle signs that provide the context of this discourse on the bread of life. The second is the unexpected appearance of Jesus walking on the water to meet his disciples in the darkness of night and speaking to them the enigmatic "I am" (ἐγώ εἰμί). The first is the feeding of five thousand hungry listeners with a complete meal (seven—symbolizing completeness—items consisting of five loaves and two fish), with enough left over to fill the full complement of twelve apostolic baskets. None—served and servers—is denied sufficiency, to receive or to give. However, the true bread that provides sustained life is found in the provider, not in a boy's lunch box. This discourse has two complementary parts.

### PARALLEL ANALYSIS OF 6:35–40

| | The Father | Jesus | Believers (as responders) |
|---|---|---|---|
| 35 | | I am the bread of life. | |
| | | to me | Whoever *comes* . . . will never hunger. |
| | | in me | Whoever *believes* . . . will never thirst. |
| 36 | | me, | But you have *seen* . . . |
| | | | but still don't *believe*. |
| 37 | the Father *gives* . . . | to me; | Everyone . . . will *come* |
| | | to me | He who *comes* . . . |
| | | I will never *drive away*. | |
| 38 | | I *came down* from heaven; | |
| | | I do not *do* my will, | |
| | | but [I *do*] the will of . . . | |
| | [the Father] who *sent* | me. | |
| 39 | [the Father] *wills* that | I shall *lose* . . . | none [will be lost] |
| | that the Father *gave* | me. | |
| | | I will *raise* . . . up at the last day. | them [are raised up] |
| 40 | My Father *wills* that | to the Son, | everyone who *looks* . . . |
| | | in the Son, | and everyone who *believes* . . . will *possess* eternal life. |
| | | I will *raise* . . . up at the last day. | them [will be raised up] |

Identifying the types of verbs in the first section of Jesus's discourse helps us to see that Jesus's self-understanding and mission are rooted in his identity. Jesus begins with a complex claim regarding his identity: he *is* the bread of life, come down from heaven. His origin is his identity. John then describes Jesus's mission of doing the Father's will by using task verbs: the negative task of not driving away parallels the not losing, and not losing leads to raising up. These are expressed in two chiasms that emerge from this tabular analysis.

| Chiasm 1 | Chiasm 2 |
|---|---|
| 37 All the Father gives me | 39 I raise up in the last day |
| 37 I never drive away | 40 everyone who looks |
| 38 I came down | 40 everyone who believes |
| 38 not to do my will | 40 I raise up in the last day |
| 38 to do the Father's will | |
| 38 I was sent by the Father | |
| 39 I shall not lose. | |
| 39 those he gave me | |

Another way of looking at this passage focuses on the respective tasks of the Father and the Son, evidenced by verbs that form a divine dance. "The Father *gives,* the Son will *not drive* them *away.*" "Father *sends*; Son *comes down.*" "Those the Father *gives,* the Son will *not lose.*" "The Father *wills,* the Son *will raise.*" The parallel structure emphasizing the Son's response to the Father's initiatives can be put:

37 The Son will *not drive away* those the Father *gives.*

38 The Son *does* what the Father who *sent wills.*

39 The Son will *not lose* those the Father *gives.*

40 The Son will *raise* according to what the Father *wills.*

The structure shows the responsive interaction between the Father and the Son around the centrality of the Father's will, which in turn connects with and leads to the double emphasis on raising up (6:39–40). It also reveals the time dimension of the Son's acts: came down (past); am not doing what I will but the Father's will (continuing present); raise up (future).

If one of the Father's tasks is to give to the Son those who believe, the corresponding task of the potential responders is to come, see (look), and believe. The verbs are formed in two identical triads in 6:35–36 and 37–40, with John characteristically using two different verbs for seeing (ὁράω and θεωρέω). (The *see and not believe* in the first set presupposes that the seeing occurred before believing but for some did not lead to believing.)

These actions of the disciples lead to never hungering or thirsting, which are tied to bread and water that are essential for life. Jesus uses these metaphorically for the eternal life that, according to the Father's will, Jesus will provide for those the Father gives.

The balance between the three members and eight functional agency verbs (treating *not drive away* and *not lose* as synonyms) in this monologue helps us understand the actions of the Father (*give, send*) and the Son's response (*come down, not lose, raise up*) and of the sequence of salvation for believers (*come, see, believe*).

The raising up that ends this part of the discourse inaugurates the second part of the discourse, which likewise stems from Jesus's concept of self-identity as the bread of life descended from heaven.

### PARALLEL ANALYSIS OF 6:44–51

|  | | The Father | Jesus | Believers (as responders) |
|---|---|---|---|---|
| 44 | | | to me | They cannot *come* . . . |
| | | unless the Father who *sent* draws . . . | me | them. |
| | | | I will *raise* . . . | them up at the last day. |
| 45 | | Isa 54:13 God teaches them all. | | |
| | | from the Father, from [the Father], | | Everyone who has *heard* . . . , and everyone who has *learned* . . . [they] *come* . . . |
| | | | to me. | |
| 46 | | the Father. | | No one has *seen* . . . |
| | | the Father. | Only I, who <u>am</u> from God, *have seen* . . . | |
| 47 | | | on me | Whoever *believes* . . . <u>has</u> eternal life. |
| 48 | | | I <u>am</u> the bread of life. | |
| 49 | | | | [Your fathers *ate* the manna in the wilderness and *died*.] |
| 50 | | | I <u>am</u> the bread that *comes down* from heaven; | whoever *eats* will not die. |
| 51 | | | I <u>am</u> the living bread that *came down* from heaven; | whoever *eats* will *live* forever. |
| | | | I *give* this bread, my flesh, | so the world will *live*. |

This discourse connects with the previous one through several key concepts: the Father sending, the Son coming down and raising up; the believers responding by coming, hearing, and believing; and the resulting bestowal of eternal life.

The above table reveals that in Jesus's second discourse, the Father's role is fundamentally the same as in the first discourse, circumscribed to sending Jesus and drawing (vs. giving) believers.[11] However, his role is not unimportant, for without sending or drawing neither the central position of being the bread to be eaten nor the action of raising up those drawn would occur. Nonetheless, the Father's role is not the central focus; it is primarily indicated by "the Father" functioning grammatically as a direct or indirect object (6:45–46). Likewise, Jesus's active role of coming down and raising up (giving eternal life now and later) is carried over from the previous section, but with a greater emphasis on who he is as the source of this life (the living bread).

What emerges from our tabular analysis of this second discourse is the relationship between Jesus and the progressively developing believers, who are drawn to Jesus and receive from him eternal life. As repeated frequently in John's Gospel, Jesus's origin is essential to and indicative of his identity (7:16–18, 25–42, 52; 8:14; 9:29; 18:36). Jesus comes from the Father with whom he has been and whom only he has seen (1:18).[12] Thus, he is the manna (bread) God sent down from heaven. This affirmation connects him to the exodus tradition, which symbolically anticipates him, but here also directs us to the present (6:50) and the future (6:51) as the completely filling and nourishing bread of life. The being-identity of Jesus provides the gift-basis for the sacramental provision for eternal life.

The structure of this discourse specifies a sequence for the disciples' response.

| 45 | come | 47 | believe |
| 45 | hear | 50, 51 | eat |
| 45 | learn[13] | 51 | live |

Some suggest that these two discourses on the bread of life might have been separate presentations, one to the crowd (6:24) by the lake, the other to Jews (6:31) in the Capernaum synagogue (6:59).[14] Whether part of the same discourse or separate, the two convey similar themes. Both address Jesus's identity in relation to the Father who sent him and his mission of feeding, preserving, and giving life to those whom the Father gives him. The multiple repetition of *bread, eating,* and *eternal life* is very evident from our structural analysis. The Father's giving the responders to Jesus is emulated in Jesus giving eternal life to the responding and believing bread eaters.

---

11. Although one might see selectivity in the Father's drawing, it is balanced by the Son's universal drawing in 12:32. Although drawing (ἕλκω) can imply compulsion, as with drawing an inanimate object like a sword, boat, or net (18:10; 21:6, 11), here as referring to drawing persons it is better understood as attraction.

12. Seeing might seem tangential to the key ideas here. However, placing of seeing here parallels seeing the Father's will, for both doing God's will and being with and seeing God lead into Jesus giving eternal life.

13. Since "come" is repeated before and after "hear" and "learn," the order is unclear. Perhaps both coming then hearing and hearing (as being called) then coming are intended.

14. Morris, *Gospel,* 326. Michaels (*Gospel of John,* 383) suggests that "[t]he point is not that the Galilean 'crowd' has disappeared, to be replaced by a different set of interlocutors, 'the Jews,' but that the 'crowd' is 'the Jews,'" who stand in tension with Jesus.

This eternal life, as we learn in John's commentary in 17:3, connects back to the Father through knowing him. The passages are unified in the expected response of the audience: they are to come, see or hear (eat, experience), and believe, which is the unequivocal message of the Fourth Gospel.

## JESUS AND TESTIMONY (8:14–18)

The debate among those whom Jesus taught regarding his identity provides the context of this discourse. As we noted previously, in the minds of Jesus, of his puzzled hearers in the temple courts, and of his antagonists the priests and Pharisees, his identity is linked to knowing where he came from and, for Jesus, where he is going. One is from where one originates, a point reiterated later in the chapter in discussion with tentative believers about their assertion of their origin from Abraham and Jesus's accusation that their identity connects with their source in the murderous and deceitful devil (8:39–44). Uncertainty about Jesus's origin and destiny leads to intriguing uncertainty about his identity. The dispute can only be settled by knowing the truth about his origin and destiny, and this can only be determined by reliable, validated testimony. Thus, after identifying himself as the light of the world (light is needed to reveal the truth; 3:19–21), Jesus discourses about the testimony that sheds light on the truth.

### PARALLEL ANALYSIS OF 8:14–18

| | | Father | Jesus | Pharisees |
|---|---|---|---|---|
| 14 | A | | If I *testify* on my own behalf, | |
| | B | | my testimony is true, because | |
| | C | | I *know* where I came from, and I *know* where I am going. | [don't *know* where I come from.] [don't *know* where I am going.] |
| 15 | D | | I *judge* no one | since they *judge* by (inadequate) human (fleshly) standards, |
| 16 | D1 | | If I *judge*, my judgments are true, because | [implied: their judgments are not true] |
| | C1 | | I am not alone. | |
| | | the Father who *sent* me. | I [*judge*] with . . . | |
| 17 | B1 | | | [Since your Law requires two witnesses for truth,] |
| 18 | A1 | the Father who *sent* me *testifies* for me. | I *testify* for myself; and | |

We saw in chapter 4 that testimony is a major theme supporting the identity claims of John's Gospel. Our structural analysis reveals how the members of the triad, through their roles and interaction, assist in understanding and appreciating the nature and function of Jesus's testimonial. The structure of this passage exemplifies a chiasm. Jesus testifies to himself (A), and this testimony is supported by that of another (A1). Testimony to be true must be properly grounded (B), and truth is established by two witnesses (B1). The basis of Jesus's testimony connects to where he is from and where he is going (better, from whom and to whom he is going) and his knowledge of that (C). That is, it is based on his connection with the Father (C1). The Pharisees are ignorant of this basis and hence judge him only by human standards (D). Thus, Jesus's judgment, whether rendered or not, is true because, contrastingly, it has a proper basis (D1) and satisfies the criteria required by the very Law to which the Pharisees appeal.

The chiasm amplifies as it proceeds.

A Jesus testifies.

  B His testimony is true, because

    C Jesus knows where he is from and going, while the Pharisees do not.

      D Jesus does not judge, or if he does uses adequate standards.

      D1 The Pharisees judge [him] by inadequate, earthly standards.

    C1 Jesus is not alone but [judges] with the Father who sent him.

  B1 The law requires two witnesses to be true.

A1 Both Jesus and his Father testify (truly).

The verbal structure is very simple. Three repeated action verbs are applied to Jesus: *testify, know,* and *judge*. Two action verbs are applied to the Father, *send* and *testify*; the missing prerogative of judging, we are told in 5:22, is given by the Father to the Son. The Pharisees actually *judge*; Jesus does so hypothetically. The Pharisees do not know enough to *testify* truly about him. They are only left with judging based on their human (fleshly) standards—the external appearance of a human Galilean who seems not to keep the Sabbath law in the way they envision—that stand in stark contrast to the judging possible to Jesus who knows the divine essence of what lies behind appearances. Jesus's origin and destiny and his knowledge of that validates his testimony; it is impeccable. The Pharisees' ignorance and their use of inadequate criteria invalidates their judgment. The unified, reliable, ongoing,[15] testimonial action of Jesus and the Father compensates for the imbalance between Jesus and the Pharisees.

One might wonder whether 8:14—"Even if I testify on my own behalf, my testimony is true"—is consistent with 5:31—"Even if I testify about myself, my testimony is not true."[16] In chapter 5, Jesus accepts the prohibition that one cannot serve solely as one's own witness (Deut 19:15). One's testimony must be confirmed by

---

15. "The two verbs [in 8:18] expressing witness are both in continuous tenses," as also in 8:14, showing that Jesus and the Father bear continuous witness to Jesus (Morris, *Gospel*, 393).

16. Barrett, *Gospel*, 264; Brown, *Gospel i–xii*, 224.

the testimony of others. Jesus then advances additional witnesses in his defense—the Baptizer, Jesus's works, his Father, the Scriptures, and Moses. However, in chapter 8 he claims that his own testimony is sufficient. To resolve the apparent discrepancy, Ramsey Michaels contends that we should note that in 8:14 Jesus adds the qualification that "although he is testifying *about* [περί] himself, he is not testifying *by* himself, 'on his own,'"[17] for he has a special relation with his Father. In chapter 5, Jesus emphasizes coming in the Father's name (5:42), whereas in chapter 8 Jesus has come as the very revelation of the Father who sent him. That is, whereas in chapter 5 Jesus is willing to play the legal game of witnesses independent of him, in chapter 8 he puts his own twist on the requirement for two witnesses, including himself as the authenticating witness because of his identity with the Father who sent him.[18] As Philo writes in response to those who would want God to swear by something other than himself, doing so would require that God's word be authenticated by someone greater than and independent of God, but no being that is greater than and independent of God exists.[19] Jesus's move, then, from chapter 5 to chapter 8 further solidifies his claim of deity, which becomes full-blown in 8:58–59.

Returning to our thesis, our analytical structure brings out both the striking simplicity of the carefully constructed discourse and the interrelatedness of the members of the triad, both in terms of congruence and contrast. We will see how this interrelatedness deepens into action and response in John 10 and further into reciprocity and emulation in John 15.

## JESUS AS THE LEADING SHEPHERD (10:1–5)

When we turn to John 10, the monologic character of Jesus's discourses becomes more apparent (although not uniformly). Chapter 9, which provides the context of chapter 10, places the Pharisees as Jesus's antagonists. In claiming not to be blind, they manifest both their intentional animosity and their refusal to accept Jesus's healing of their blindness.[20] If they were (spiritually) blind, which they are, they would be guiltless, but though they are blind they claim not to be blind, and on that claim ironically rides their accountability. Jesus hides the symbolic and metaphorical in the guise of literal blindness, a ploy for which his immediate hearers inevitably fall (See chapter 1 above).

---

17. Michaels, *Gospel of John*, 480.

18. "On the one hand, in 5:31–32, Jesus as a human being is totally dependent on his Father and in need of the Father's validating testimony. On the other hand, here in 8:14, he is so at one with God that his witness is self-authenticating, for by definition God needs no one to validate God's testimony" (Lincoln, *Truth on Trial*, 84–85).

19. Philo, *Legum Allegoriae* III, 2:205–08; see Bekken, *Lawsuit*, 128.

20. Du Rand, "Syntactical," 98.

PARALLEL ANALYSIS OF 10:1–5

|  | Shepherd | Sheep | Thieves and Robbers |
|---|---|---|---|
| 1–3a | *Enters* by the gate. | | *Do not enter* the sheep pen by the gate. |
| | Let in by the gatekeeper. | | *Climb* up by some other way. |
| 3b | *Calls* his own sheep by name; | *hear* his voice. | |
| | *Leads* them out. | | |
| 4 | *Brings out* all his own. | | |
| | *Goes ahead* of them. | *Follow* him | |
| | | because *know* his voice. | |
| 5 | | *Do not follow* strangers; | [are not followed] |
| | | *Run away* from strangers, | |
| | | because *do not know* the voice of strangers. | [voice unrecognized] |

As our tabular analysis shows, in this parable John uses sets of contrasts to create interaction between the triadic members in this discourse. Calls/hear; leads out/follow differentiate the roles of the shepherd and the sheep. "Enters/don't enter," "let in/climb up" differentiate the roles and actions of the shepherd and the thieves. This contrast also introduces the central question regarding the status of the sheep—are they safe or in jeopardy?—and the role or function of the shepherd.

Consequently, although the active role of the thieves in this monologue seems limited in that their only action is negatively portrayed by the amplified parallels—they don't enter by the gate/they climb up some other way, both actions contrast with action of the true shepherd and continually lurk in the background as representing the threat of strangers to the sheep. Consequently, although their role might appear minor, they provide the essential tension in the triad by giving a reason for the need for continuous, active shepherding and, more broadly, the need for Jesus to give the discourse to both the Pharisees and disciples. One might say that the Pharisees themselves, perhaps by luring or threatening a return to prescriptive, synagogal legalism, create the continued tension, requiring that Jesus reassure his disciples (flock) of his leadership and protection, a message to his contemporaries and from John to his readers.

The sheep respond to the shepherd's actions, indicated by a set of parallels (*calls/leads; brings/goes ahead*).

Shepherd action: calls by name; leads out; brings out; goes ahead.

Sheep respond: hear his voice; know his voice; follow him.

Sheep do not respond: (may hear); do not know their voice; do not follow but run away.

The shepherd does not send them out on their own; he not only is with them the entire time they face their enemies but takes the lead. In persecution and trial, they can be assured of his empathetic presence, for he has experienced the enemies before the followers are attacked and presumably has triumphed over them.

Our analytic presentation shows the *action* of one member and a *response* from another. The shepherd calls and the sheep respond by listening. The shepherd brings out and goes ahead, and the sheep respond by following. The actions of the sheep mirror the disciples' actions in 6:35–40: come, listen, follow (believe). Following requires recognition, a Johannine theme emphasizing that Jesus wants his responders to recognize him—who he is, where he comes from, what he will do, and where he is going—for them to become true believers. Jesus refers to the sheep in the third person, in contrast to the use of the second person in the later vine discourse. Yet intimacy is indicated in that he calls them "by name" and they are "his own," a theme introduced in 1:10–13 and repeated later in 13:1 and 15:19. Because of familiarity they recognize his voice.

Our structural analysis, making full use of contrasting actions and responses, reveals the carefully constructed interaction between the three members.[21] Although the one group stands in the background, the shepherd responds to their threat as if they were continually present. The sheep respond to the shepherd and not to the strangers because of their ability to recognize the voice, the calling of the one who cares, later identified as the good shepherd who is willing to die (an act identified as love in John 15:13) for the sheep. Calling is emphasized by the use of "hear" and of "voice" three times. *Action-response* becomes audible and, when demonstrated in leading, visual.

## THE PRUNER, VINE, AND BRANCHES (15:1–17)

Whereas the discussion of the shepherd and the sheep illustrates action and response, the discourse on the vine and the branches brings us into relationships of *emulation* and *reciprocity*. Invoking Jesus's predicate use of "I am" (ἐγώ εἰμί, see chapter 5), this discussion focuses on Jesus's identity as the vine. We are now well into Jesus's monologic discourses, one following the other, often connected by important words or ideas.[22] The literary approach serves the reader well in that several precedent ideas or threads lead naturally into this passage. One originates from the reciprocal relation

---

21. It might be objected that this monologue fails to follow the triadic form, since we have not accounted for the gatekeeper. However, the gatekeeper plays no role in relating the members or in furthering the point of the analogy, but rather is antithetically parallel in function to what keeps out the thieves who climb up.

22. "Asking the Father in my name" (14:13) leads to Jesus asking the Father to send the Spirit (14:17). The command to love each other (15:12) leads to reflection on the hatred of the world (15:17–18). The testimony of Jesus's works (15:24) leads to the testimony of the coming Spirit and the future testimony of the disciples (15:26–27).

between Father and the Son. "Now is the Son of Man glorified and God is glorified in him. If God is glorified in him, God will glorify the Son in himself" (13:31–32); "I am in the Father, and the Father is in me" (14:10); and between the Father, Son, and disciples: "I am in my Father, and you are in me, and I am in you" (14:20). These direct the listener/reader naturally to the analogical lesson that the vine and branches require continual attention to remain reciprocally in each other. Remaining is not an option but a command. The second lesson, which tells how one remains in the other, derives from the command to love one another, emulating the love demonstrated by Jesus for his disciples (13:34–35; 14:21).

### PARALLEL ANALYSIS OF 15:1–17

| | Father | Jesus (I) | Disciples (You) |
|---|---|---|---|
| 1 | Father is the gardener. | I am the true vine; | |
| | PART ONE | | |
| 2 | Cuts off . . . | | fruitless branches; |
| | Prunes/cleans . . . | | fruitful branches to make them more fruitful. |
| 3 | | the word I have spoken to you. | You are already pruned/cleaned by . . . |
| 4 | Charge: | as I [remain] in you, | Remain in me . . . to bear fruit. |
| | Reason: | | A branch cannot bear fruit if it does not remain in the vine. |
| 5 | | I am the vine; | You are the branches. |
| | | I remain in you | You bear fruit if and only if you remain in me and . . . |
| 6 | | | If you don't remain in me, you are thrown away, dried up, gathered, tossed into the fire, and burned. |
| 7 | Consequences: | my words remain in you, | If you remain in me and . . . then what you want and ask for gets done to you. |
| 8 | [is glorified] | | to bear fruit shows you are my disciples and glorifies the Father. |

| PART TWO | | |
|---|---|---|
| | Father | Jesus (I) | Disciples (You) |
| 9 | As Father *loved* (ἠγάπησέν) me | [loved by the Father] *I loved* you. | *Remain* in my love (ἀγάπη). |
| 10 | | as I *have kept* my Father's commands ... and I *remain* in his love. | If you *keep* my commands, ... you *remain* in my love, ... |
| 12 | | I *command* that ... as I *loved* you. | you *love* each other ... |
| 13 | Love defined: | willing to *sacrifice* one's life for one's friends (φίλων). | |
| 14 | Evidence of being my friend: | what I *command*. | *Do* ... |

| PART THREE | | |
|---|---|---|
| | Father | Jesus (I) | Disciples (You) |
| 15 | What the Father *spoke* ... | to me, I *made known* ... | to you. So you <u>are</u> my friends, not servants. |
| | | | Friends *know* their master's business. |
| 16a | | I *chose* and *appointed* you to bear lasting fruit; ... | you did *not choose* me. |
| 16b | Consequence: the Father *gives* you. | | If you *bear* lasting fruit, whatever you *ask* in my name ... |
| 17 | Command: | | *Love* (ἀγαπᾶτε) one another. |

Our tabular analysis reveals the flow of the roles and reciprocity of relationships. The apparent, new literary feature is the addition of editorial comments within the discourse. I have incorporated these into the table as titled comments. It is difficult to place these literary pieces, but one might note that these differ from the rest of the text in not being straightforward assertions but as asides, hypothetical conditionals, or commands.

At first glance our tabular analysis of this passage suggests that both Jesus and the disciples function as the main members in the triadic relationship. However, whereas the Father's role initially seems minor, our structural analysis reveals that it is critically important in that his actions provide discourse turning points that set the stage for each of the three parts.[23] The Father takes on three roles, each of which initiates a section. In Part One he cuts and prunes or trims clean (cleanses).[24] Because

23. This stands in contrast to Beasley-Murray's claim that "the Father as the Vinedresser stands in the background throughout" (*John*, 271).

24. The Evangelist, a master of language manipulation, plays on the similarity of Greek verbs here: αἴρει (takes away) and καθαίρει (trims clean). Michaels, *Gospel of John*, 802; Brown, *Gospel xiii–xxi*,

of his position as the horticulturalist or surgeon gardener, he is responsible for the current status of the disciples—pruned or cleansed.[25] John here picks up the theme from 13:10, that the disciples are already clean, here emphasizing how it is done: through the word (τὸν λόγον, with its double meaning). Part Two, abandoning the vine analogy, commences with the Father's love, setting the model for the love found in Jesus and in the disciples. In Part Three, the Father again models the standard, speaking so that Jesus hears from him and the disciples in turn hear and learn from Jesus. Whereas the Father's role of pruning is directed toward the branches (disciples), his acts of loving and teaching are directed toward Jesus, who in turn transmits them to the disciples. The emulation is obvious: What the Father says, Jesus hears and learns from, and in turn Jesus makes known to the disciples. In short, in terms of agency verbs, it might seem that the Father's role is less central to the discourse, yet when the relationships emerge from our tabular analysis, this initial characterization is shown to be inaccurate. In all three sections, the Father initiates the action.

The Father's role is critical in more subtle ways, for in what Jesus does he emulates the Father. Jesus prunes or cleanses through the word he has spoken (15:3), loves the branches (15:9), and teaches the disciples in an intimate way (5:15). Jesus does not take the lead. The Father does these works; the Son emulates. This notable motif of Jesus doing the same works as the Father echoes 5:16, 19 and thus firmly establishes the emulation relationship, indeed, the unity, with the Father (10:30–32).

The branches (disciples) constitute a main partner in this triad. They manifest both action and position. As actors, they have the basic function, repeated several times both positively and negatively, to remain in the vine and in Jesus's love. If they do this, they bear fruit. They also are to emulate the Son as the Son emulates the Father: to love, keep his commands, and know.[26] In contrast to the sheep members in John 10, where those referred to are sheep (although they are still "my sheep"), here the disciple-branches are addressed and treated more intimately in the second person. It is "I the vine" and "you the branches." You, not branches in general, will bear the fruit if you remain in me.[27]

Our structural analysis helps us see more clearly the construction of the discourse. In Part One, the Father prunes fruitful branches so that they bear more fruit, which in the end will result in more pruning. The pruning and the bearing fruit, both of which have already occurred in the case of those who hear the discourse (whether from Jesus or from the Gospel), are an ongoing *action-response* relationship of the

---

660. See chapter 5 above, note 34.

25. Since pruning is a painful process, this may allude to the current persecution the readers are undergoing or are promised (connecting this to 16:1–4). Suffering is part of God's discipline.

26. Segovia ("Theology," 120) takes the conditional as indicating a problem in the church community for which the Gospel was written; it already is being fulfilled by the lapses of the hearers. But there is no reason not to take this (also) as an anticipatory warning.

27. Bultmann notes that chapter 10 is the last of the impersonal discourses. "They no longer talk *about* this relationship but rather talk *from the stand-point of* the relationship" (*Gospel of John*, 363).

Father and the branches. Between the vine (Jesus) and the branches (disciples) *reciprocity* is very evident. Each is to remain in the other if fruit is to result. The vine remains connected to the branches; otherwise, the vine itself is unproductive, for it cannot produce without branches. At the same time, the branches are to remain in the vine, for without its nourishment and support they wither away, die, are cut off and burned rather than pruned and bear fruit. Each must remain in the other for successful fruit production. The repetition of *remain* sets the challenge to produce.

Part Two, connected with the first through *remain*, expands on the reciprocity featured in that concept. The metaphors of cutting and pruning the branches are left behind for a straight-out discussion of the Father's love for the Son, the emulative love of the Son for the disciples, and the reciprocal love of the disciples for each other (their friends). The love between the Son and those loved is intimately expressed in remaining. The Son has shown his love to the Father by keeping his commands and in turn instructs the disciples ("you") to reciprocally keep his commands to demonstrate their love for him. Through responsive obedience love is confirmed, for by keeping his commands you remain in his love and bear fruit.[28] When the obedience of love is defined in terms of self-sacrifice, reciprocity to others is manifested. The Son will sacrifice himself willingly for his friends (his passion is in view), and in the same way, reciprocally, he expects that the disciples will do the same for their friends and for him. Persecution lies just around the corner, if not is already present (16:1–4; 21:18–19).

Part Three concentrates on emulation. What the Father tells the Son (what the Son heard from the Father), the Son in turn makes known to the disciples. The result is that the Son knows the business of the Father, and the disciples know the business of the Son. They are "business partners," not as strangers but as friends, if not family. Neither the Son nor the disciples are mere servants (though the servanthood of 12:26 and 13:12–16 is not abandoned but deepened), but they are moved into the more intimate relationship of friendship, for which the sacrifice out of love is most appropriate.[29] However, the relationship is ordered. The Son ("I") chose and appointed the disciples, not vice versa (6:65). The vine comes first and then the branches develop. This order is meant to be liberating, freeing the branches not to worry about whether they are included in the mission of the vine, but to concentrate on the task for which they were chosen. They are to bear fruit through remaining, nurtured through love manifest in obedience.

This discourse is most intimate. It invokes suffering (pruning probably through persecution, 15:20–21), the closeness of mutual remaining, love deepened to self-sacrifice for the other, and friendship arising from missional choice. Disciples are selected not because of who they are but because Jesus commissions them to bear fruit,

28. As verses 9–14 and 17 show, bearing fruit goes beyond "growth in life and growth in union with Jesus" (Brown, *Gospel xiii–xxi*, 676). It specifically connects with obedience and demonstrating love.

29. For more on friendship, see Talbert, *Reading John*, 214.

whose outward sign is unity manifested in love (15:16–17). However, bearing fruit requires painful pruning. Love, like grace, does not come cheap. Yet, as the grain of wheat, to become fruitful, must die, through dying one attains eternal life (12:24–26). The love to be demonstrated is not one-sided but modeled by the relation between the Father and the dying Son. The summary command is succinct: "Love each other."

## JESUS AND THE WORLD (15:18–25)

The previous discourse leads into another monologue through the medium of love and its contrary hate and through being chosen by Jesus. Our tabular analysis shows the Father is absent (John unites him with the Son grammatically via a direct object); the agency of the world members now takes premier place.

### PARALLEL ANALYSIS OF 15:18–25

|  | Jesus (I) | Disciples (You) | World (They) |
|---|---|---|---|
| 18 | [is hated] | [are hated] | *Hated* Jesus first; now *hates* you disciples. |
| 19 |  | If you <u>belonged</u> to the world, . . . | they would *love* (make friends with) you as its own. |
|  | Jesus *chose* you out of the world; | You do not <u>belong</u> to the world, because . . . | therefore, the world *hates* you. |
| 20 | Principle: Servants are not greater than their master. |  |  |
|  | [persecuted] | [will <u>be persecuted</u>] | *Persecuted* Jesus; will *persecute* disciples also. |
|  |  | [could <u>be obeyed</u>] | If they *obeyed* Jesus's word; they would *obey* the disciples. |
| 21 |  | [will <u>be persecuted</u>] | They will [*hate* and *persecute*] disciples because of my name, |
|  | [<u>Sent</u> by the Father] |  | for they *do not know* the one who sent me. |
| 22 | Jesus *came* and *spoke* to them | | Since <u>spoken to</u>, they <u>are guilty</u> of sin; <u>are</u> without excuse. |
| 23 | [hated] |  | They *hate* both the Father and the Son. |
| 24a | Jesus *did* unique *works* among them. |  | *Having seen* the works, they <u>are guilty</u> of sin. |
| 24b | [hated] |  | They *hate* both the Father and the Son. |
| 25 | Conclusion: [hated without reason] |  | *They hate* the Son without reason. |

This short discourse contrasts with the previous one. Here two primary members appear in the triadic relationship: Jesus, to whom four actions are ascribed (choosing, coming, speaking, doing works) and the world, which is both an agent (it hates and persecutes Jesus and will do the same to the disciples, and witnesses of Jesus's works) and is positioned or has a status (is spoken to and is guilty).

Jesus is understood in terms of his relation to the Father, from whom he is sent, his disciples, and to the world, although in contrast to the previous discourses there is no action-response, emulation, or reciprocity. Jesus calls or chooses his disciples out of the world. He acts on their behalf, but no response is called for from them. Jesus interacts with the world by coming to them through a ministry of words (9:22) and unique works (9:24). The combination of these two leaves the world sinning without excuse, expressing no positive response, only antipathy.

The disciples as members of the triad are understood in terms of Jesus and the world—chosen by Jesus out of it and hated by it. Here the intimacy of the relation between Jesus ("I") and the disciples ("you") contrasts with the impersonal world, indicated by the third-person "they," that hates and persecutes. The tabular analysis shows that the world's attitude toward the disciples is not directed at them *per se* but because of their relationship to Jesus.

John introduces a dual role for the world to create the tensions he wants us to feel in this passage. Tension holds for the disciples between being chosen out of the world and being hated by the world and between being persecuted by and the (unlikely) possibility of being listened to (obeyed) and loved (made friends, ἐφίλει) by the world.[30] Likewise, tension holds for the world between being spoken to and witnessing (seeing) (6:36, 45) and being without excuse and guilty of sin. *Guilt* and *seeing* (15:24) pick up from 9:41 and help identify the world.

In the end, taking the world as agent, John draws the conclusion: they hate Jesus and derivatively the Father and those whom Jesus chose. The repetition of the words "hate" and "persecute" calls to mind the contrast with the world being loved by God, who sends his Son into it (3:16–17). The editorial quote from the Psalms (35:19; 69:4) ends with "for no reason." Its inclusion here leads one to ask why it is included and consequently what it means. An answer to this indicates the important role of perspective. From the perspective of Jesus and the disciples there may seem to be no reason, but if we could hear the voice of the world (which we do not) it may suggest the reason, namely, that some are chosen out of the world by Jesus and, apparently, some are not (see the first active verb for Jesus). It is possible that being neglected, ignored, discriminated against, or not chosen provides the basis for antipathy. No one likes to be unselected, left out. If Jesus did not choose the disciples to be taken out of the world, the world would not care what they were like or doing. Discrimination and separation create the basis of hatred for both those choosing and those chosen. Yet, the offer is made to the world in that Jesus comes and speaks to them and performs signs so that they might see, know, and believe. Here, again, we have an example of

---

30. Note the difference between the love (ἀγαπάω) the Father shows in 15:9 and the friendship (φιλέω) offered by the world in 15:19.

John's compatibilism: God selects, yet those not selected have his offer to recognize him and be his disciples.[31]

## JESUS PRAYS FOR HIS DISCIPLES (17:1–19)

We come to Jesus's final monologue. His death, which will complete his mission, is near. Jesus prays to his Father that his Father glorify him as he was before his incarnation so that he can reciprocally glorify his Father who sent him. This prayer provides the capstone for the other discourses. Examination of the italicized, active verbs—*reveal, give, obey, know, accept, believe, remain,* and *come*—and the important nouns—*world, word, name,* and *joy*—provides evidence that here Jesus takes up these recurrent and central Johannine themes and presents them as a gift to the Father in a glorification and petitionary prayer for himself and his disciples.

We can fruitfully apply the same structural analysis of the triadic relationship we have been using to the prologue to Jesus's prayer for his disciples.

### PARALLEL ANALYSIS OF 17:1–5

|   | Father | Son | Those Given |
|---|--------|-----|-------------|
| 1 | *Glorify* your Son, so that . . . | the Son may *glorify* the Father. | |
| 2 | *Gave* the Son authority over all people, so that . . .<br><br>the Father *gave.* | the Son may *give* eternal life to . . . | those . . . |
| 3 | you, the only true God, you *sent,* . . . | and Jesus Christ, whom . . . | To *know* . . .<br>is <u>to have</u> eternal life. |
| 4 | you *gave* (the Son) to do. | The Son *glorified* you on earth by *finishing* the work . . . | |
| 5 | *Glorify* (the Son) in your presence with . . . | the glory the Son <u>had</u> with you before the world began. | |

The first thing this table reveals is the chiasm with respect to the Father, with a parallel chiasm with the Son.

| Father | Son |
|--------|-----|
| 1 glorify me | may glorify the Father |
| 2 gave me | gives eternal life |
| 3 sent me | |
| 4 gave me | glorified the Father |
| 5 glorify me | |

31. Compatibilists hold that being free is compatible with being causally determined. Although God selects or foreordains (6:37, 65), we are at the same time free to act and choose and thereby are morally responsible for the choices we make and acts we perform, so long as we are not externally compelled to act against our will. See Reichenbach, *Divine Providence,* 37–50.

Clearly, glorification, made possible through sending, brackets this part of Jesus's prayer.

Second, the limited number of verbs in this prayer prologue is striking. The message of the entire prologue rests, with the exception of one use each of *know* and *send*, on two agency verbs, *glorify* and *give*. *Send* here functions as a synonym of *give*, in that the Father gave his Son, while *know* occurs in the author's comment defining *eternal life* and hence is not an intrinsic part of the prayer's petition. Forms of "glory" (δόξα and "glorify" (δοξάξω) are used five times, while forms of give (δίδωμι) are found four times. Furthermore, these two words are connected, for glorifying is giving honor. In effect, the prologue is entirely about giving: giving the Son, giving eternal life, and giving glory.

The inter-relational intimacy developing through the Gospel discourses here comes to full flowering. 17:1 demonstrates the richly realized reciprocity between the Father and Son in that the Son requests glorification on the grounds that he has completed the task the Father gave him, the completion of which glorifies the Father. The Son accomplished the task under the auspices of the authority the Father gave him to grant eternal life to those the Father has given him. The passage develops a combined or completed chiasm, which by highlighting its structure reveals the nature of this relationship between the Father and the Son.

> 1 Father is to glorify the Son
>> 1 so that the Son will glorify (give honor to) the Father.
>>> 2 Father gave authority to the Son.
>>>> 2 Father gave disciples to the Son
>>>> 2 so that Son can give them eternal life.
>>> 4 Father gave a task to the Son.
>> 4 Son glorifies (gives honor to) the Father by having completed the task.
> 5 Father is to glorify (give honor to) the Son in the Father's presence.[32]

The table also reveals that the Son does what he sees the Father doing, a point we have made often. The Son glorifies the Father after the Father glorifies the Son. The Son gives eternal life after the Father gives people to the Son to be given eternal life.

The editorial comment in verse 3, which refers to Jesus the Messiah in the third person, portrays this eternal life not as a temporal extension of life but as coming to know the Father and the Son. Since knowing is often understood biblically as experiencing, intimacy is furthered. How communicated words realize this knowing state is further clarified in verses 7–8. The absence of the words *eternal life* in the remainder of this discourse and the concentrated attention on the realized eschatology of

---

32. The second to last line might be parsed differently, so that the second part—having completed the task—is made parallel to the Father giving a task. Our chiastic analysis differs from that of Ellis ("Inclusion, Chiasm," 278–79) not only in detail but in treating 17:3 as an editorial comment.

sanctification in the disciples' present time is a significant Johannine contribution. John clothed eternal life with, or transmuted eternal life into, the sanctification that should result from intimately knowing the Father and the Son he sent (vv. 23–26). Here John takes a qualitative rather than a quantitative approach to eternal life (as in 6:54).

The discourse proceeds with Jesus's prayer for his disciples.

### PARALLEL ANALYSIS OF 17:6–19

|  | Father (You) | Jesus (I) | Disciples (They) |
|---|---|---|---|
| 6 | your name you *gave* . . . | I *revealed* . . . (to) me | to those whom out of the world. |
|  |  |  | They <u>were</u> yours; |
|  | You *gave* | to me. | them . . . |
|  |  |  | They *obeyed* your word. |
| 7 | you *gave* . . . comes from you. | to me | Now they *know* that every- thing . . . |
| 8 | you *gave* me | I *gave* the words (that) . . . | to them, and they *accepted* the words. |
|  | from you. | (that) I *came* . . . | They *knew* with certainty . . . |
|  | you *sent* | me. | They *believed* that . . . |
| 9 |  | I do not *pray* for the world; |  |
|  | you *gave* me. | I *pray* for . . . | those . . . |
|  | yours. |  | They <u>are</u> . . . |
| 10 | all your things are mine. | All my things are yours; |  |
|  |  | I will <u>be glorified</u> | through them. |
| 11 |  | I will *remain* in the world no longer; | they <u>are</u> still in the world. |
|  | to you. | I am *coming* |  |
|  | *Protect* . . . by the power in your name, |  | them; |
|  | the name you *gave* . . . | (to) me, |  |
|  | as we <u>are</u> <u>one</u>. |  | that they <u>may</u> <u>be</u> <u>one</u> . . . |
| 12 |  | I was *protecting* . . . while I <u>was</u> in the world with . . . | them them. |
|  | you *gave* me. | I *kept* . . . safe by the name . . . | them |
|  |  |  | None <u>were lost</u>, except the <u>doomed</u> one. |

|    | Father (You) | Jesus (I) | Disciples (They) |
|----|--------------|-----------|------------------|
| 13 | to you. | I am *coming* now . . . | |
|    | | I *say* these things now in the world (so that) . . . | they <u>may</u> fully <u>have</u> my joy. |
| 14 | | I *gave* them your word, | they <u>were hated</u> by the world, for |
|    | | as I <u>am</u> not of this world, | they <u>are</u> not of the world. |
| 15 | Do not *take* . . . out of the world | | them |
|    | *Protect* . . . from the evil one. | | them. |
| 16 | | as I <u>am</u> not of this world. | They <u>are</u> not of the world, . . . |
| 17 | *Sanctify* . . . by the truth; your word is truth. | | them |
| 18 | You *sent* . . . into the world. | me | |
|    | | I *sent* . . . into the world. | them |
| 19 | | I *sanctify* (consecrate) myself | so they <u>may be sanctified</u> in truth. |

Several interesting observations emerge from this structural analysis. First, the passage manifests an imbalance in agency. In this final discourse Jesus is the major participating triadic member; more agency is ascribed to him than to either the Father or the disciples. Most of Jesus's actions are directed to the disciples—*reveal*, *give*, *pray for*, *protect*, *keep*, and *send*,[33] whereas only one action is directed to the Father: Jesus is coming to him. John highlights these actions by his broad use of parallels (*reveal/ give*; *not remain/come*; *protect/keep*), contrasts (*pray for* or *don't pray for*), or diverse but related words (*send/sanctify*).

Second, the actions ascribed to the Father are either past—giving, sending—or else the subject of Jesus's request—protect, sanctify. Since the requests made of the Father are in the aorist or past tense, there is reason to think that the Father has already done this. It may be the case that it is not so much that the Father is already acting as that the Son requests that he do it again. As we noticed in the tables of chapter 15, here what the Father has done—give, send, protect, and sanctify—Jesus did or is doing. In three of the four cases in this discourse Jesus is reported as doing in the subsequent verse or two what the Father did or is asked to do. As we noted in our discussion of chapter 15 and again in the introduction to this chapter, this motif of Jesus doing the same works that the Father has done recalls 5:17, 19, and this recollection suggests that the Son has seen the Father already do what he requests of him. If the Father has done it in the past, the request is for him to do it again. The unity or oneness of the

---

33. He sanctifies himself, such that the action is directed to himself, but the purpose of the action is directed to the disciples.

Father and the Son is manifested in Jesus's works (10:30–32), although the reaction of Jews who picked up stones to kill him for blasphemy shows they conceived the one-ness to extend beyond Jesus's works to the very nature of Jesus.

Third, this table makes clear that the disciples find themselves both in the role of agents and as being positioned (acted upon) by Jesus and the Father. Their agency is highlighted by a chiasm in verses 6b–8.

> 6 obey
> > 7 know
> > > 8 accept
> > 8 know
> 8 believe[34]

It reinforces the purpose or intent of John's gospel to bring about believing (20:31).

After ascribing believing to the disciples, Jesus goes on to describe their position or setting. They are in the world but not of the world, hated by the world but protected and not lost, experiencing joy (15:11) and sanctification. In these roles they are the recipients or intended recipients of the agency of the Son and the Father: revealed to, prayed for, kept, protected, sent, and sanctified. Here again our triadic structure reveals the chiasm in 17:14b–16.

> 14 They are not of the world
>
> > 14 as I am not of this world.
> >
> > > 15 Do not take them out of the world,
> > >
> > > 15 but protect them from the evil one.
> >
> > 16 As I am not of this world,
>
> 16 they are not of the world.

Jesus also completes the reciprocity motif begun in the prologue to this chapter. In the prologue he asks the Father to glorify him as he glorified the Father. Here the glorification comes through the disciples the Father gave him. Jesus takes up the as-signed task, completes it, and in doing so is given glory both by the disciples and by the Father. The theme of giving and givenness introduced in the prologue to the prayer comes to completion in the prayer.

That this prayer summarizes much of the Gospel of John is evident both from its structures and from the verbs and nouns that recur here. They evoke earlier discus-sions about sending and coming, giving and keeping, word and truth, knowing and believing, and reciprocal glorification, all central Johannine themes.

---

34. John connects believing with obedience through the mediation of love (14:15, 23; 15:10; 16:27).

## CONCLUSION

This type of triadic structure is unique to John's Gospel. For example, perusal of Jesus's Sermon on the Mount or eschatological discourses in Matt 23 and 24 yields a series of injunctions and woes, but nothing resembling John's presentational structure. It also differs from the dyadic structure found in Jesus's dialogues in John. From this visual analysis we can see both the simplicity of John's presentation of Jesus's discourses as well as their complexity and artistry. However, above all, we can see the central focus of the Gospel. The discourses help us to see more clearly Jesus's identity and function. They also reveal the important relationships that are central to John's case for authentic believing in Jesus. Abiding in these relationships grounds our eternal life. Thus, finally, they show that Jesus's discourses encourage response to his actions and foster emulation and reciprocity between the Father, Jesus, and us, his disciples. The Father initiates the actions, Jesus takes them up and in turn acts toward us, expecting us in turn to respond in love shown in obedience. All of this, in the end, leads to the glorification of God. Our tabular analysis of John's account of Jesus's discourses should lead not only to increased understanding of Jesus's identity but to eternal life as the author understands it in John 17.

## QUESTIONS FOR REFLECTION AND DISCUSSION

1. How do Jesus's discourses differ in structure from his dialogues? What does this structure reveal about Jesus's identity and function?

2. Discuss how the triadic structure reveals the relationships that hold between Jesus and his Father? Between Jesus and his disciples? Between Jesus and the world?

3. The chapter distinguished between an active response, reciprocity, and emulation in the relationships. Give examples of these from Jesus's discourses. Describe how you see these playing out in your own discipleship to Jesus.

4. Jesus tells the parable of the good shepherd. Stories about shepherds and sheep made sense in Jesus's environment, but not in today's urban setting. Can you construct a different, culturally relevant parable or story that would tell someone about who Jesus is and what he does?

5. How does Jesus's prayer in John 17 show his view of and concern for his disciples? Do you find John 17 informative, comforting, and/or challenging?

# CHAPTER NINE

# Book of Time

CLEMENT OF ALEXANDRIA REFERRED to the Gospel of John as a "spiritual gospel."[1] And so it is, since it is filled with the spirit of Jesus, the promise of the endowment of the Holy Spirit, and the heavenly contrasting with the earthly. Some have taken Clement's saying as confirmation that John is less to be relied on than the other gospels if we are to understand Jesus's ministry as an historical event; the Synoptics allegedly provide a more reliable account of Jesus's ministry.[2] Yet, others note that John appears to give a stronger temporal framework on which to hinge Jesus's ministry. Since time provides a multidimensional framework for the Gospel, we need to explore how it functions.

## TIME MARKERS

One thing that stands out from a reading of the Gospel of John is John's use of time words or markers for Jesus's ministry. Every chapter has at least one temporal marker, and most chapters contain several. Here is a partial accounting.

> Chapter 1: in the beginning (1); was before me (15); then (21, 39);[3] the next day (29, 35, 43); about the tenth hour (39).
>
> Chapter 2: third day (1); my hour (4); after this . . . not many days (12); the Passover was near (13); three days (19–20); forty-six years (20).
>
> Chapter 3: came at night (2); second time (4); after these things (22); hour is coming and now is (23); stayed with them (22).

---

1. Clement of Alexandria, *Hypotyposes*, cited in Eusebius, *Historia Ecclesiastica*, 6.14.7.

2. According to James Martyn, since the Gospel was written for the Johannine community, it reflects the interests and needs of the community at the time it was written. "The literary history behind the fourth Gospel reflects to a large degree the history of a single community which maintained over a period of some durations its past and rather peculiar identity" (*Gospel*, 91).

3. I omit further references to "then" (οὖν), since it is found in every chapter except 14, 15, and 17.

Chapter 4: about the sixth hour (6); stayed two days (40); after the two days he left (43); seventh hour (52).

Chapter 5: after these things (1); thirty-eight years (5); a long time (6); day was the Sabbath (9, 10, 16, 18).

Chapter 6: after these things (1); Passover feast was near (4); when it became evening (16); immediately (21); the next day (22).

Chapter 7: after these things (1); Feast of the Tabernacles was near (2); my time . . . your time (6, 8); after his brothers left for the Feast (10); halfway through the Feast (14); Sabbath (22–23); little time (33).

Chapter 8: his hour had not yet come (20); not yet fifty years old (57).

Chapter 9: blind from birth (1); Sabbath (13, 16); second time (24).

Chapter 10: Feast of Dedication (22); winter (22).

Chapter 11: stayed two days (6); twelve hours in the day (9); when he came (17); four days (39); that year (51); from that day (53); feast (56).

Chapter 12: six days before the Passover (1); next day (12); (Passover) Feast (12, 20).

Chapter 13: before the Passover Feast (1); his hour had come (1); after this (7); after (taking) the morsel (27); immediately . . . it was night (30).

Chapter 14: a long time (9).

Chapter 15: when the Paraclete comes (26).

Chapter 16: an hour is coming (2, 25, 32); hour comes (4); in a little while (16–19); hour (21–22); day (23, 26).

Chapter 17: the hour has come (2).

Chapter 18: that year (13); immediately (27); Passover (28, 39).

Chapter 19: after this (28); after these things (38); day of Preparation (31, 42); next day was a special Sabbath (31).

Chapter 20: early on the first (day) of the week (1); still dark (1); on the evening of the first day of the week (19); after eight days (26).

Chapter 21: after these things (1); during that night (3); early in the morning (4); third time (14).

What are we to make of John's frequent use of these time markers? For the narrator they serve several purposes.[4] First, they put order into the Johannine narrated world, enhancing the overall sense of temporality, connectedness, movement, and progression of opposition that leads to the climax of the book.[5] A good example of this is John's use of οὖν (then), which appears about 195 times in the text. Rarely, οὖν

4. For a discussion of various types of narrative time, see Culpepper, *Anatomy*, ch. 3.
5. Rowe and Neyrey, "'Telling Time,'" 5.

functions logically, indicating a conclusion that follows from premises (e.g., 12:50; 13:14). Most frequently, it is used temporally to establish connection and continuation within a scene or dialogue.[6] It may indicate an action that follows from previous conditions (e.g., 4:6, 40; 6:10), internally connected dialogue (e.g., 1:22, 25; 2:18, 20), or express contrast (9:18).

Second, temporal markers are used by narrators "to signal a thematic shift and to segment narratives."[7] In the Gospel of John, they construct narratives by organizing "the Gospel into thematic clusters of episodes each introduced by a temporal marker." For example, "after this" (μετὰ ταῦτα) and its lexical variations are used to establish a "nonquantitative temporal shift from one narrative dimension to another (2:12; 4:43; 5:1; 6:1; 7:1; 11:7, 11; 19:28, 38; 21:1)."[8]

However, references to time are meant to do more than provide continuity in narrative or dialogue, chronological detail, or segment narratives. Although questions of historicity of the Johannine account, discussion of whether the time frames in the Gospel are absolutely linear, and comparison with time frames in the Synoptic Gospels are important, the following discussion will concentrate on John's diverse literary-theological-symbolic uses of time concepts and markers, considered both directly and indirectly, to make his testimonial case for Jesus's identity and mission.[9] Put another way, we will attend both to his symbolic use and to his narrative use of time markers and concepts, realizing that since John typically employs multiple meanings, they cannot be isolated from the above-mentioned usages.

## NUMBERED AND SEQUENTIAL DAYS AND HOURS

At times, John presents the reader with specificity and sequence. John numbers the days and years: the third day (2:1); in three days (2:19–21); after two days (4:43); forty-six years (2:20); not yet fifty years (8:57). He even gives us the time of day: the tenth hour (1:40); about the seventh hour (4:52); at night (3:2); the sixth hour (19:14); early morning (21:4). John also links the narratives through temporal markers. "After this," "the next day" (1:29, 35, 43; 6:22), and most frequently "then" (οὖν), characterize his transitions. John also talks about time in terms of length: a long time (5:6); a short time (7:33); immediately (6:21; 18:27); not many days (2:12). This frequent use of temporal language suggests that John means the text to be a temporally linked narrative moving in a definitive direction, not a disparate collage of events and teachings. The author deliberatively chooses the narrative pace, not only to maintain interest but to proceed

---

6. Martha Reimer, "The Functions of οὖν in the Gospel of John," START 13 (1985) 29, in Brant, *Dialogue*, 38; Bauer, "οὖν," 597.

7. Estes, *Temporal Mechanics*, 151.

8. Estes, *Temporal Mechanics*, 152, 154.

9. Bruns, "Use of Time," 287.

inexorably yet purposively to its prescribed climax. These temporal references are not the subject matter of the Gospel but its background.

Yet these quantitative particularities are only part of the story of John's use of time. The specificity of his time markers conveys additional significance beyond establishing time frames, narrative sequences, and literary movement. When John the Baptizer points out Jesus to his disciples, two of them, one of which was Andrew, follow Jesus and spend the day with him. Although the exact quantitative time frame is ambiguous, by using a time marker John conveys the qualitative importance of this encounter, for they stay with him until the tenth hour (1:39), which is four in the afternoon. Apparently, Andrew spent significant time determining who this person really was, time enough to convince him that Jesus is the expected Messiah and worthy not only of personally pursuing but also of inviting his brother to join him. The time marker here indicates investigative carefulness and depth, which characterizes this Gospel itself as it conducts a careful testimonial investigation of Jesus's identity and mission.

John states that Nicodemus comes to Jesus "at night" (3:1). Although the time marker indicates a general temporal setting, its significance is qualitative, conveying the idea that Nicodemus, as a respected member of the Jewish ruling council, does not want to be seen in the presence of the suspect and mysterious Jesus.[10] This secretive investigative motif is further heightened in 7:51, when Nicodemus (the text recalling the first visit at night) suggests to gathered Pharisees, openly but still privately to a select group, that further investigation would be appropriate before they take drastic action.

John states that Jesus encounters the Samaritan woman at Jacob's well about noon (sixth hour) (4:6). The time marker signifies more than a time of day, for respectable women, who were responsible for drawing the daily water for the family, did so early in the morning or in the evening but not in the midday heat. By this time reference, John indicates that the woman is a social outcast in her community, without having to say so directly. The time marker here indicates value, worth, and social status.

Later in this same chapter (4:52–53), John mentions the "seventh hour" and "that (same) hour" to especially connect the healing with Jesus's statement that the royal official's son would be healed. By temporally coordinating Jesus's statement and the healing, he affirms that the boy's healing is no mere coincidence, strengthening John's message that Jesus's signs are carefully enacted to bring about believing.

In the crucifixion account John gives the time of the crucifixion at "about the sixth hour," which was the traditional time when the Passover lambs were sacrificed (19:14). John's precision (sixth hour) and vagueness (about, ὡσεί) comport with the vagueness in the time stated in Exod 12:6, "between the two evenings."

10. We have already noted in ch. 6 that night and its darkness also function here symbolically in contrast to the light that Jesus brings into the dark world (3:19–21).

At the time of Jesus, the [sixth hour] was the hour when the priests in the Temple would begin the slaughter of the lambs to be used in the Passover meal later that evening. Exodus 12:6 required that the lambs had to be killed "in the evening" of the preparation day. In the first century, the large number of pilgrims meant that tens of thousands of lambs needed to be slaughtered; rabbinic law, therefore, interpreted "evening" to begin at noon so that the necessary work could be completed before the Passover festival began at sundown.[11]

Regardless of whether this time conflicts with Mark's account of the timing (Mark 15:25), the point for John is that it ties the beginning of Jesus's story, where the Baptist announces Jesus as the Lamb of God (1:29), with its salvific fulfillment at Passover. For John, the entire salvific history, from Exodus on, reaches its culmination in Jesus's voluntary (echoing 10:18), new, once-for-all Passover sacrifice. John captures all of this by framing the time of the crucifixion; the time takes on qualitative significance. (We will return to this in chapter 11.)

Mary Magdalene comes early in the morning to check on the tomb. "Early on the first day of the week, while it was still dark," (20:1) sets up the comparison with Nicodemus, who also came at night but with no hint of morning. Although with Mary we do not get the sense that she comes with much hope, the reference to morning indicates that there is hope. Night (death) is overcome; Mary and the disciples will experience a new beginning. Indeed, this new beginning is realized sometime later in the new day of forgiveness and recommissioning that Jesus presents to Peter in the morning in Galilee (21:4). The night of fishing brings emptiness; the disciples catch no fish. However, the risen Jesus now appears on the shore in the early morning, and their fishing changes from futility to fruitfulness, to more fish than they can haul into the boat.[12] The abundance of the new day replaces the emptiness of the old night. The difference between fruitless fishing and the catch is not merely a temporal difference; it is a qualitative difference when they again encounter the risen Jesus. Bread and fish, which Jesus used to provide food for the crowd, Jesus now provides for a beginning-of-the-day breakfast for his disciples. Jesus then commissions them to carry on his mission by feeding his sheep. Hope is fulfilled, and Jesus's mission can proceed through the fed and commissioned disciples. Time markers signal that life, hope, and abundance triumph over death, darkness, and emptiness.

Time thus frames, connects, and signifies meaning and value in John's story. Time is not an accidental or extrinsic feature of the narratives but central to conveying

---

11. Senior, *Passion*, 96.

12. That John gives an exact number of fish, 153, has long puzzled commentators. One suggestion, found in Augustine, is that 153 is the sum of the number of dots in an equilateral triangle, the base of which is seventeen, symbolically significant in that seven and ten are perfect numbers. Emerton ("Hundred,") speculates that it might be based on the values of the consonants in Gedi (17) and Eglaim (153) present in the fish-catching prophecy about the New Age in Ezek 47:10.

the deeper meaning of the events and the value of the persons or events involved, structured to bring about believing.

## SPECIAL DAYS

John becomes more specific and open to symbolic interpretation when he couches his narratives in reference to special days, each of which bears a unique religious significance. John references the Sabbath in four passages. In chapters 5, 7, and 9, the Sabbath achieves significance because it not only frames the time of some of Jesus's signs, it establishes their importance as events for which Jesus's arrest was sought (9:16). Their theological point is that proper judgment is to be rendered about the function of the Law and about whose Law it is (7:24). If a boy's bodily part can be ritually circumcised on the Sabbath because it fell on the eighth day after birth, addressing another bodily part to bring about wholeness is also justified. As stated in Mark 2:27–28, "The Sabbath was made for man, not man for the Sabbath. So the Son of Man is Lord even of the Sabbath." Jesus not only does works that emulate those of his Father (5:19–21), he also performs works of doing good for which God instituted the Sabbath. The Sabbath is not to be a day or time of oppression but a time of bringing forth God's good work. This is precisely what the Pharisees miss in the healing of the paralytic and the blind man. They are so absorbed with the specific time Jesus performed the healing sign that they completely miss both that this is a work of God and that it is God's work for good. Indeed, they come to the opposite conclusion: since Jesus heals on the Sabbath, he is not from God (9:16) but is a sinner like the blind man who deserved his blindness. From their perspective, Jesus is blind to the Law. Jesus replies that their own blindness to the reality expressed in and through the Sabbath leads them to misjudge by appearances (echoing Isa 11:3). John's use of the Sabbath, then, highlights Jesus's relation to creation and to the Law. Jesus is the creator (1:3) and continues the creative, good-bestowing work of God after creation.[13] He also is lord of the Sabbath and of the Law, which word God gave to Moses and now is revealed in the new Word come in flesh. In each instance when the Sabbath is mentioned, the discussion moves quickly to the key issue of Jesus's identity.

John also connects Jesus's ministry with the special feast or festival days, mentioned seventeen times: the Festival of Tabernacles or Booths, Hanukkah, and Passover. The references to these celebrations evoke a double significance. On the one hand, they create a historical framework for the ministry of Jesus. From them we learn something about possibly how long Jesus ministered, provided the Gospel gives

13. "Jesus is picking up the thread of a rather familiar discussion in Judaism about the Sabbath. The notion that God 'rested' after creating the world in six days (Gen 2:2–3) could not be interpreted to mean that God is now inactive in the world. On the contrary, God is at work constantly, giving and sustaining life, rewarding the righteous and punishing the wicked. In short, God, and God alone, lawfully breaks the Sabbath" (Michaels, *Gospel of John*, 301).

us a linear account. We also learn about the diverse loci of Jesus's ministry. Whereas the Synoptics frequently have Jesus on a secluded mountain or in the Galilean countryside teaching his disciples and those who come to him, John tells of Jesus teaching in public, in the temple and courtyard, at the busiest times of the year. Jesus is not secluded but openly testifies to his identity to any who will hear him: curious, puzzled, sceptic, tentative believers, and foe alike. On the other hand, in the final year of Jesus's ministry, he moves from the Feast of Tabernacles, which is a joyous, autumnal celebration, though Hanukkah, which is a winter celebration, to his final Passover (in the spring). More importantly for our qualitative treatment of time indicators, each festival presents a symbolic meaning for the ministry of Jesus. "The importance of the Gospel's festivals lies . . . in their fulfillment through Jesus who enters into their divinely ordained practices in order that he might bring the festivals to the fulness of their eschatological purpose. Each of Israel's festivals existed for the purpose of furthering Israel's hope in the promise of its restoration."[14]

The seven-day *Feast of Tabernacles* (*Booths*), which began on the fifteenth day of the Jewish seventh month, Tishri, served a double purpose. Lev 23:33–43 (Exod 23:16; Deut 16:13–15) mandates the festival as both a celebration showing gratitude for a prosperous harvest and as a recollection of the difficult and hazardous wilderness journey. During this pilgrimage festival, celebrants built temporary shelters from the branches of palms, willows, and other trees, remembering the rough shelters the Israelites constructed during their desert wanderings and imitating the temporary shelters constructed in the fields at harvest where the farmers stayed to protect their grape and olive crops. The reference to the festival gives the setting of Jesus as he moves from Galilee to Jerusalem, here amid his unbelieving brothers (7:1–13) and the wariness of Jewish leaders looking for him.

Initially, Jesus shows reluctance to go to the festival, understandable because his life had been threatened (previously, 7:1, and then frequently during the festival, 7:19–20, 25; 8:22, 37, 40) and because it was "not his hour" (more on this later). There is also an implied curse for failure to celebrate the festival. The attackers of Jerusalem who survive the plague but fail to go up for the festival will be punished by drought and plague (Zech 14:16–19).[15] Although strictly speaking, Jesus does not fall into this category, there is an implied mandate to celebrate with thanksgiving, although his brothers seem to encourage him to attend for other, more dubious reasons.

Jesus's teaching at the festival raises the question of who Jesus is, and many responses are given, including being the Messiah (7:26, 41) and the Prophet (7:40; Deut 18:15). Both the festival's origin, the water libation ritual (water was brought from the Pool of Siloam and poured on the temple altar[16]), and the prophecy about the Prophet are Mosaic, reinforcing that Jesus is the "new" Moses, who brings forth living water

14. Schuchard, "Temple," 387.

15. Coloe (*God*, 121) notes that Zech 14 was read on the first day of the festival.

16. Schuchard, "Temple," 386.

(7:38; Exod 17:6).[17] He brings his teaching of liberation and life in a way parallel to the way Moses brought the law, coming directly from God. Unfortunately, his listeners treat his teaching in the same way some treat the Law: by seeking to take his life they ignore the divinely given commandment not to murder.

The festival setting thus provides the opportunity for John to introduce, discuss, and answer in a timely setting the question of Jesus's identity and mission. Invoking the symbols of light (8:12) and water, which were important features of the festival celebration, it contextualizes Jesus's claim to be the "light of the world; whoever follows me will never walk in darkness, but will have the light of life" (8:12), and emphasizes his mission of bringing living, refreshing hope.[18]

Hanukkah (*Festival of Dedication*) (10:24) was the eight-day celebration of the temple cleansing by the victorious Judah Maccabeus in December 165 BC. The Maccabees expelled the hated Seleucids, whose king Antiochus IV assumed the title of Epiphanes ("God manifest") and erected a pagan altar in the temple to offer sacrifices to Zeus. To cleanse the polluted temple, holy oil was needed, but only one cruse of ritually pure olive oil was found to light the menorah. Miraculously, this cruse lasted for eight days until other oil could be rendered holy. At this festival of lights, Jesus appears in the temple area and is questioned as to whether he is the Messiah.

Although in this passage John does not make an overt connection between this festival of lights and Jesus as the light of the world, the theme is recurrent in John (1:4–9; 3:19–21; 12:35–36), including Jesus's self-identification as the light of the world (8:12; 9:5). At Jesus's final Passover, John connects being the Messiah and the light (12:34–36); as the light, the Messiah will be with them only briefly until he is "lifted up." Like the cruse of oil, but extending far beyond it, he gives inexhaustible light, but his earthly presence is limited before he returns to the Father.

The Festival of Dedication more importantly provides the context for Jesus's identification of himself. When Jesus claims identity with the Father (10:30), Jews prepare to stone him for blasphemy, for he claims to be God, one of the very claims for which the Maccabees rebelled against Antiochus IV. The importance of this festival for John becomes clear. How is Jesus going to explain his claim that he and the Father are one, a true claim in contrast to that of Antiochus? Jesus responds initially with a play on the word "god." In Ps 82:6, the psalmist refers to humans as gods, sons of the Most High, yet for all that still mortal. So, Jesus argues, if humans as sons of the Most

---

17. That Jesus is the source of living, life-giving water, besides connecting back to 4:10, may allude to several Old Testament passages. In Isa 55:1–5, thirsty people are urged to "come to the waters," the Lord, to be satisfied and in turn to become a witness who "summons nations." Looking at the spiritually thirsty celebrating the festival, Jesus invites them to come and drink from (believe in) him, implying that the festival is insufficient to satisfy their deepest needs. When they do so, the water will flow from them as summoning witnesses. John, in his aside, indicates that this witness-water will be the truth-speaking Spirit who lives in and will flow out of them (14:17; 16:13). The appeal to living water may also allude to Ezek 47:1–12, where out of the temple flows a stream that rapidly swells and eventually waters the desert and freshens the Dead Sea, bringing it and what is around it to life.

18. See the discussion in chapter 5 of the presence of light and water at the Feast of Tabernacles.

High can be called gods, he too, as the Son of his Father, can claim to be divine.[19] Why should they take him to be the Son of His Father? They should judge him by his works, which distinctly set him apart from Antiochus. Jesus has this relationship to the Father because he does the works of his Father, not that of pagan rulers who like Antiochus desecrated the temple by sacrificing a befouling pig on the altar. Jesus drove the animals out of the temple to cleanse it; he did not bring them in to pollute it. Neither is he like the Jewish rulers who want to stone him and who are not of his flock but belong to the class of thieves and robbers, out to steal, kill, and destroy (10:10, 26). Jesus invites his hearers to compare his work with those who once and who now occupy the temple precincts. God's restoration has begun.

He will attend one more feast, the third time not as a celebrant but as a sacrifice. The *Feast of the Passover* dominates Jesus's festival observances. John's first presentation of Jesus celebrating the Passover occurs early in his ministry (2:13), when he symbolically, powerfully, and authoritatively cleanses the temple and prefigures his death. The second reference to the Passover (6:4) sets the stage for his sign of the feeding of the large crowd and, most importantly, his proto-eucharistic discourse on being the bread of life. In giving his flesh and blood to be consumed to preserve life Jesus embodies the Passover feast.

The third reference to the Passover begins John's passion account in the second part of the Gospel (11:55; 12:1). As we noted earlier, the symbolism of this festival becomes clear when Jesus himself is the lamb sacrificed at the very hour—sixth—when the sacrificial lambs were slain (19:14).[20] For John, the time of his crucifixion, both in terms of the hour and the festival, fulfill John the Baptizer's identification and prophecy: "Look, the Lamb of God who takes away the sin of the world" (1:29). Jesus is the paschal lamb without blemish (Exod 12:5); no bones are broken (19:36; Exod 12:46). As with the Passover lamb, Jesus is bound (18:12, 24).[21] Whereas sacrificial performance at the first Passover brought protection from the plague of death and ultimately liberty from oppressive Egyptian slavery, sacrificial performance at this Passover also brings both protection from eternal death and liberty from the oppression of sin (8:34–36). Whereas the original Passover lambs had no choice in the matter, Jesus voluntarily lays down his life for his sheep (10:11, 15). Each of the three Passovers emphasizes a different aspect or role of Jesus: his power and authority,

19. "If the word of God came to men, that they might be called gods, how can the very Word of God, who is with God, be otherwise than God? If by the word of God men become gods, if by fellowship they become gods, can He by whom they have fellowship not be God?" (Augustine, "Homilies," 48–49).

20. Brown, *Death* 1, 847; Barrett, *Gospel*, 454.

21. Coloe (*God*, 191) notes the parallel between the binding of Isaac and of Jesus and that both carried the wood to be used in their sacrifice. "Support for the Isaac typology is strengthened by the book of Jubilees (ca. 160 B.C.E.), which portrays the sacrifice of Isaac as the origin of Passover observance (Jub 18:17–19)."

his presaged death and resurrection whereby he is the eternal life-giving bread from heaven, and his sacrifice for sins.

Thus, John connects the identity of Jesus, both in terms of nature and function, with the appropriate and central Jewish festival times. Time sets the framework of the Gospel, but with events conveying theological and salvific significance. The times are religious, characterized by memory, piety, worship, and religious festivals. The story of Jesus is not political but deeply set into the religious events, motifs, and culture of his day. The believing John seeks is not believing that Jesus lived or that he was a significant cultural figure, but rather that the Son of Man truly is the Son of God. "The God of Israel's festivals has become incarnate in their midst, no longer in symbols or rituals but in the σάρξ [flesh] of Jesus."[22] Three (festivals and Passovers) symbolically denotes completion. The liberation the festivals prefigured has come in time.

## TIME BRACKETS JESUS'S MINISTRY

John uses time markers in narration not only to bracket important events, but to indirectly show their relationships and thereby convey his purpose. Richard Bauckham suggests that the author creates a parallel structure between the week that begins Jesus's ministry in chapters 1 and 2 and the week that terminates Jesus's ministry in 18–20.[23] Both weeks, he notes, begin in a Bethany. The last week begins at Bethany in Judea, a short distance outside Jerusalem; the first week begins in Bethany on the other side of the Jordan, probably somewhere south of the Sea of Galilee. That Jesus's activity in both weeks commences from a Bethany suggests that John purposively pairs these weeks of seven days. At the beginning of Jesus's ministry, day one finds John the Baptizer testifying to the priests and Levites, the delegates from the Jewish leaders of Jerusalem, that he is not the Messiah but that the Messiah is present (1:19–28). "The next day," day two, the Baptizer identifies Jesus to the crowd as the Lamb of God and alludes to Jesus's baptism as a Spirit-descending event (1:29–34). "The next day," day three, two of the Baptizer's disciples leave him and follow Jesus, spending the day with him until four in the afternoon. On day four, Andrew finds his brother Simon Peter and brings him to Jesus (1:40–42).[24] On "the next day," day five, Jesus starts out for Galilee and finds Philip, who in turn recruits Nathanael (1:43–51). Bauckham suggests that since Bethany beyond the Jordan was a considerable distance from Cana, day six is not mentioned but is a travel day. The seventh day, which John refers to as the "third day,"[25] is the day of the wedding (2:1–11), which according to

22. Coloe, *God*, 155.

23. Bauckham, *Gospel*, ch. 7.

24. Bauckham suggests that "John does not have to specify 'the next day' in this case because he has already made clear . . . that the previous day has ended" (*Gospel*, 133).

25. Bauckham, *Gospel*, 140. "Presumably [the third day] simply means (as it normally did) 'the third day after the event just narrated'" (Keener, *John*, 20). That is, day one is the calling of Nathanael,

Jewish custom for marriage of a virgin, would have been the actual fourth day of the Jewish week. On this day Jesus turns water into wine; the abundance of the kingdom of God begins.[26]

When we turn to John's presentation of the end of Jesus's ministry, we find a similar reference to a week (seven days). It begins "six days before the Passover," with Jesus coming to a dinner at Bethany, although this time to Bethany in Judea, Lazarus's home, outside Jerusalem (12:1). "The next day," day two, presents Jesus's triumphal entry into Jerusalem. The Baptizer's identification of Jesus as the Lamb of God in the second day of the first week is paralleled with the palm-waving crowd announcing the prophesied coming of the king. During days three and four Jesus hides himself (12:36). Day five is the preparation of the Passover, during which Jesus partakes of the evening meal (13:1–38) and is handed over to the Jewish leaders and crucified (18:1–19:42). Day six is Passover. Jesus is resurrected on the seventh day (20:1–18). The life brought about through the resurrection and transformation of Jesus mirrors the "resurrection" and transformation of the water into wine at Cana. As the water of purification becomes the new, refreshing wine, Jesus's death and resurrection provide life for all who believe.

That John brackets Jesus's ministry by two weeks does not require that all the days have parallel events or have parallel significance. Yet both parallels and contrasts align with John's overall purpose of identifying Jesus, narrating about his mission, and bringing about believing. We have already noted that both weeks begin at a Bethany, one across the Jordan and the other outside Jerusalem. By this John indicates the connectedness of the weeks. Second, both weeks contain events and persons that identify Jesus. In the opening week, John the Baptizer identifies Jesus as the Lamb of God, one endowed with the Spirit, God's chosen one. Andrew identifies Jesus as the Messiah, and Nathanael calls him the Son of God, the king of Israel. The crowd on day two hails him as the king of Israel who comes in the Lord's name, while Pilate on day five orders the placard that names him as the king of Israel. In both weeks, day six is not spoken of, though this might not have any significance; in the first week, it is a day of travel; in the last week Jesus is entombed. Both weeks end with a demonstration of abundant life. In Cana, Jesus transforms the water for purification encased in jars into life-giving wine. In Jerusalem God transforms the corpse of crucified Jesus, anointed with myrrh and aloes, to life.

Finally, a significant personal encounter follows both weeks, the first week with Nicodemus in chapter 3 and the last week with Thomas in chapter 20. Both have the same focus: to create life-change by bringing about believing. Nicodemus must go beyond what he heard about Jesus and beyond his physical understanding of

---

day two is not mentioned; day three is the wedding.

26. For a different understanding of these days and especially the "third day," see Moloney, *Johannine Studies*, 15–16. "The setting of four days of preparation, culminating with the revelation of the δόξα [glory] 'on the third day' matches exactly the celebration of the Jewish Feast of Pentecost."

the processes of biological life to enter a new worldview that incorporates personal, heavenly rebirth. Thomas must transcend what he heard about Jesus from the other disciples and his worldview that doubts bodily resurrection to engage Jesus in the intimate encounter of wound touching, leading to believing.

These weeks frame Jesus's ministry. After the first he heads to Jerusalem and its temple to subtly announce his future death and resurrection; after the second he heads to Galilee to commission his followers to continue his ministry and care for his flock. For the first week, his time had not yet come. Much remains to be accomplished to testify to who he is and to die for the world. For the last week, his time has come and deeds are finished. He heads back to the Father while entrusting his mission to chosen human hands. By this narrative structure, John shows the unity of Jesus ministry; how it begins intrinsically links to how it ends. Time both quantitatively and qualitatively delimits and structures his mission.

## COMING, GOING, AND JESUS'S TIME

Deep within John's usage of time markers and concepts lies the fundamental motif of timely coming (origins or parentage) and going (destiny).[27] These motifs critically capture John's central theme: the identity of Jesus. Who we are depends in part upon where we come from and to where we are going. Can anything good, Nathanael wonders, arise out of Nazareth (1:46)? At the Feast of the Tabernacles the people continue the quest to identify this strange man, a person whom some seek to kill. Jesus cannot be the Messiah because they know where Jesus is from, but no one will know the origin of the Messiah (7:27). However, it is not long before the people assert that the origin of the Davidic Messiah is Bethlehem in Judea, whereas Jesus is a Galilean (7:41–42). Jesus is comfortable with, indeed, encourages, this connection of identity with origin. He asserts with irony, "Yes, they know where I came from, but not really" (7:28). He comes from, is sent by, the Father. Jesus is who he is because of his (divine) origin. For this assertion the authorities try to seize him but cannot, for his time had not yet come (7:30).

The themes of coming/being sent and going permeate the Gospel. The first part of the book emphasizes Jesus's *coming/being sent*. Jesus uses this to establish his identity and relationship with his Father. He came into the world (1:9; 3:19; 9:39); he became flesh (1:14); he came to his own (1:11) from God (3:2; 7:28–29; 8:14, 42; 9:16, 29), from heaven (3:13; 6:38, 41, 46, 51; 8:23). He came into the world (11:27) in his Father's name, sent by the Father (5:43; 7:28–29; 8:18, 29, 38, 42, 59; 10:35; 11:42). It is important to note that with only two exceptions (12:44–45; 18:37) Jesus does not speak about coming or being sent in the second part of the Gospel. Indeed, we

27. "[T]he narrator views Jesus and his ministry from the twin perspectives of his 'whence' and 'whither,' his origin as the pre-existent *logos* and his destiny as the exalted Son of God. Only when these perspectives are combined can Jesus be understood" (Culpepper, *Anatomy*, 33).

might divide the Gospel at this point between coming in chapters 1 to 11 and going in chapters 12 to 21. Jesus's public message is that he is sent from God. His audience will recognize him by the works he can and does perform in virtue of being sent.

The second part of the Gospel emphasizes *going*. This establishes Jesus accomplishing his redemptive purpose and makes possible the coming of the Spirit. Where he is going is somewhat ambiguous in John. At times, it is left open (8:14, 21–22). Elsewhere he goes to his death, being lifted up (3:14; 12:8, 32, 34) and glorified (13:31–36). He goes to the Father who sent him (7:33–36; 14:2–5, 12, 28; 16:5, 17). He comes home to the Father (17:11, 13). Here again the book divides; except for 3:14; 7:33–36; and 8:14, 21–22, "going" does not occur in the first eleven chapters. John develops the theme of going in the second part of the Gospel when Jesus speaks privately to his disciples. Not the past but the future now is most relevant to them, for where he goes foreshadows their destiny. "I go to prepare a place for you. And if I go and prepare a place for you, I will come back and take you to be with me that you also may be where I am" (14:2–3).

What can we say about the in-between time? For a while Jesus is reluctant to make himself known, and when he does reveal his identity, he often disappears, a feature that adds to the "excitement and suspense of the story."[28] Knowing that the crowd that received a free meal wants to make him a political king, Jesus withdraws to a mountain by himself (8:59). When Jews pick up stones to kill him for blasphemy, Jesus hides himself and leaves the temple, going through the midst of them (8:59). Later as well, after confronting the crowd with his claim of being light to counter their darkness, Jesus leaves and hides himself from them (12:36). He is not only the ambiguous revealer, he also is the elusive and mysterious hider.[29]

The reason for this early reluctance has to do with Jesus's idea of salvific time. It is not his hour; the hour or time is not right for his glorification. In the first four instances where "his hour" is introduced, his hour (ὥρα) or his time (χρόνος) has not yet come (2:4; 7:6–8; 7:30; 8:20).[30] In the transitional chapter 12 (vv. 23, 27), the hour is about to come.[31] In the final two instances, Jesus knows that the hour to depart from the world has come (13:1; 17:1). The time for which he became incarnate has arrived; Jesus grasps it and does not avoid it. He reveals that he has control over "his" hour. It

---

28. Stibbe, *Storyteller*, 21.

29. Bekken (*Lawsuit*, 74, 94) suggests that the authorities had already put out an arrest warrant for Jesus, such that anyone with information about his whereabouts was obligated to report him.

30. Culpepper notes that the narrator knows that Jesus knows his hour is not yet come, indicating the unity of viewpoint between Jesus and the narrator/author (*Anatomy*, 40).

31. "When Jesus finally heralds the arrival of the hour, the steady linear stream of time overflows its boundaries. Past, present, and future are mingled together inscrutably in the Farewell Discourses" (Parsenios, "Transformation," 4). Jesus announces to the disciples (13:3) but later says he has already left them behind (17:12). He refers to his conflict with Satan as both future (14:30) and past (16:33). It is as if there is a double timeframe of Jesus on earth and of his already-happened resurrection and glorification (Parsenios, "Transformation," 5, 7).

is not the time determined by his mother (2:4), by his brothers who presumably are close to him but suspicious (7:6), or his enemies (7:30; 8:20). Rather, his death and glorification are perfectly fulfilled in the hour of his own and his Father's choosing. Although this time is the disciples' hour of grief (16:22), it is Jesus's time of glorification. He even refuses to request that his Father save him from this hour of destiny (18:11), identifying and willingly affirming his proper hour. Indeed, as the dialogue with Pilate reveals, the time and the power to determine it lie in his hands and those of his Father; the implementation he grants to his accusers. "Hour" is thus less a quantitative time marker than an ideological construct, emphasizing the qualitative.[32]

Jesus's coming and going are part of a divine, timely plan of redemption. No one, not even the powerful Pontius Pilate, has the power to determine the proper time of Jesus's being lifted up (19:11). Jesus, doing the will and works of his Father, has control over his time and by extension over all time, for he is the maker of everything. He was in the beginning, and "without him nothing was made that has been made" (1:3), including time. To him alone belongs the time of his coming and the time of his going (returning to the Father).[33] We will return to the concept of "his hour" in the next chapter.

The Gospel's significant emphasis on coming and going raises the provocative question why specific events associated with Jesus's coming and going found in Matthew and Luke have no place in John. John gives no birth story, only the statement in the Prologue that the Word became flesh (1:14). Jesus just appears in the context of the Baptizer's ministry. The Epilogue likewise contains no account of Jesus's departure or ascension but rather features an inclusio or bracketing of the entire Gospel around the theme of testimony (1:7, 19; 21:24–25). Whereas Luke creates a completed account, neatly wrapping everything up with a beginning (including a genealogy) and an end, John seems incomplete, unconcerned with details of Jesus's fleshly arrival and timely departure. How then does he demonstrate completion? The absence of a birth story accords with John's concern to establish, not the humanity of Jesus, which for him or his readers is not in doubt, but his divinity. Hence, his emphasis is on the eternal origin of Jesus the Word, who in the beginning was with God and was God. Completion does not require a beginning in time. The coming was from all eternity, and his genealogy is not merely a human lineage but from the Father. The going likewise fits into the Johannine scheme, for Jesus frequently simply disappears, at first benignly between appearance events (5:13; 6:15, 25), then for somewhat longer hiatuses (between chapters 4 and 5, and chapters 5 and 6), and later facing death threats (8:59; 10:39–40; 11:54; 12:36).[34] Jesus's final disappearance is not in the face of death threats, for his

32. Rowe and Neyrey, "'Telling Time,'" 4.

33. John's narrative has two time frames, that of the Jewish festival cycles and that belonging to Jesus (Moloney, *Glory*, 12).

34. Stibbe notes that elusiveness also characterizes the Father (5:37; 14:8) and the Spirit (3:8) (*Storyteller*, 90).

death has occurred, but as a promised conclusion to his earthly ministry (14:4; 15:26; 16:7; 17:13). It is a transition return to the eternality from which he came and thus, like the coming, is not temporally delimited. His coming was tenting in the flesh, but his departure is not described, not only because it is not his end but because it is indescribable. Taking off flesh and still being a person is such a mystery that even the apostle Paul can only resort to ambiguous agricultural and celestial metaphors (1 Cor 15:35–56). Whereas for humans completion is found in birth and death, for Jesus it is found in his eternity from which he came and to which he goes.

## ETERNITY

Finally, the Fourth Gospel is a book about eternity. The Word is in the beginning before creating all living things, in the now providing abundant life (6:57), and in the unending future with the Father raising his own to live forever (6:39–40, 58). His identity is the eternal Word, whose mission is to provide eternal life (20:31). As we have noted, the eternal life that Jesus gives us is both quantitative (6:40) and qualitative (17:3). As quantitative, eternal life is future in time, connected to our resurrection or re-creation (3:16; 6:54). It is a life rising from the grave (5:24–25, 28–29), anticipated by Lazarus's bodily resurrection from the cave in which he was buried (11:25–26). As qualitative, the eternal life Jesus provides is abundant life that begins here and now (10:10), anticipated in the living water Jesus offers (4:14) and fulfilled in knowing the Father (17:3). His time ushers our present time into the time of eternity.

## CONCLUSION

Time defines Jesus's ministry, not only in a quantitative sense, but most significantly in a qualitative, deeply spiritual sense. John uses time to construct his narrative, beginning with the eternal Logos coming from outside time, so that he who was before all things chooses to operate within the boundaries of time. The incarnation was a temporal and timely event. Jesus's death and resurrection were temporal and timely events: both come with qualitative significance. John's time is a spiritual time, as shown by locating Jesus's ministry and death in the religious festivals and by the amount of narrative connected to the festivals. But most important, time belongs to Jesus, not only because the Word is the creator of time, but because he possesses time with the power to determine the progression of his mission: "I lay down my life—only to take it up again. No one takes it from me, but I lay it down of my own accord" (10:17–18). In his own time, he determines how and when his ministry will be complete. Jesus's time is not only for his own glorification (17:1) but for that of those given to him, that they may be protected, sanctified, unified, and sent (17:15–19). In this, our time also is his time, for he takes us into the eternity of his life with the Father.

Ultimately, time is an intrinsic feature of John's case for Jesus's identity. The Son of God, eternal in origin, becomes temporal in incarnation. He takes the time that began with the world and frames it for his own purpose. In the end, the maker of time returns to the eternal Father, having voluntarily accomplished in his time the mission for which he was sent. His time merges qualitatively and quantitatively into eternity.

## QUESTIONS FOR REFLECTION AND DISCUSSION

1. What are the different ways that John treats time in his Gospel?

2. How is the way John treats time similar to or different from the way you treat time?

3. What are the three feasts or festivals that play a role in Jesus's ministry? How does John use the feasts and Jesus's presence at them to convey his message about the identity and function or mission of Jesus?

4. John divides the Gospel into Jesus's coming and Jesus's going. Why do you think he did this, and what is the significance of this division and emphasis?

5. How does Jesus make time his own? What does this reveal about how John saw Jesus, from the beginning of the Gospel to its end?

6. How is your concept of time similar to or different from that of Jesus? What can you learn from his view of time?

CHAPTER TEN

# Book of Completeness

THE GOSPEL OF JOHN is the book of completeness. The Gospel begins with "in the beginning," a time long past any memory. In this past time, John sees the Word assuming the task of creating: "Through him all things were made (γίνομαι); without him nothing was made that has been made" (1:3). However, after the incarnation, the incarnate Word has a new task, to create (γίνομαι) children "not of natural descent" but "children of God" (1:12). He "is to do the will of the Father and to finish his work" (4:34; 5:36). Indeed, the work that Jesus does is not just his own; it is the work of his Father. He does only what he sees his Father doing; he can do nothing by himself (5:19). This task begins with revealing the Father "to his own." Since in knowing Jesus one knows the Father (14:6), John uses the ironies, signs, testimony, identity claims, dialogues, and discourses to point to who Jesus truly is. Thus, when Jesus comes to the end of his earthly ministry, he claims to have finished the work his Father gave him to do (17:5). He has revealed the Father to those the Father gave him, and he has brought them into obedience, knowledge, and acceptance (17:6–8). Having completed the task of glorifying the Father, one task remains: to willingly go to the cross in a sacrificial death. This death-event terminates when the hyssop branch doused with vinegar is put to Jesus's lips. It echoes the hyssop, dipped in the blood of the slain lamb, the Israelites used to paint the lamb's blood on the doorframe of their houses (Exod 12:22). For the Children of Israel, the recognition of this blood by the angel of death allowed the "passing over," accomplishing salvation from death and then liberation from slavery. Analogously, this Lamb brought salvation from death and liberation from slavery to sin. "Knowing that everything had now been finished, . . . Jesus said, 'It is finished'" (19:28, 30). He accomplished what at the behest of his Father he came to do. "God so loved the world that he gave his one and only Son, so that whoever believes in him shall not perish but have eternal life" (3:16–17). Jesus saves the world through his voluntary death. What remained for Jesus was to "wait" on the promise of the Father that his "temple" would be raised (2:21).

Although the Gospel author states the completeness of his treatment of Jesus's identity and mission in overt ways, he also is a master of subtilty, providing multiple clues within the text about Jesus's true identity and his full, accomplished divine work the Father sent him to do. This chapter explores one of those subtle ways that bears on the author's theological purpose.

The number seven has important symbolic significance in many cultures,[1] including the ancient Judaic culture, where it symbolized wholeness or completeness.[2]

> The use of numbers in ancient religious texts was often *numerological* rather than *numerical*; that is, their symbolic value was the basis and purpose for their use, not their secular value as counters. . . . Seven has the numerological meaning of wholeness, plenitude, and completeness. This symbolism is derived, in part, from the combination of the three major zones of the cosmos as seen *vertically* (heaven, earth, underworld) and the four quarters and directions of the cosmos as seen *horizontally*. Both the numbers three and four in themselves often function as symbols of totality, but a greater totality results from the combination of vertical and horizontal. Thus the number seven (adding three and four) and the number twelve (multiplying them) are recurrent biblical symbols of fulness and perfection.[3]

References to "seven" are embedded in the Old Testament Scriptures from Genesis, where after completing creation God rests on and blesses the seventh day (Gen 2:2–3), to the seven thousand loyal Yahweh followers who refused obeisance to Baal (1 Kgs 19:18), to Zechariah, where "seven" appears in his symbolic account of seven facets in a stone (Zech 3:9), seven lamps on a candlestick (Zech 4:2), and the Lord's all-seeing eyes (Zech 4:10). The number is prevalent in the New Testament as well, from forgiving seventy times seven (Matt 18:22) and Paul's seven-day stays with groups of believers in Acts (20:6; 21:4), to the book of Revelation, with its seven churches, seven golden candlesticks, seven stars, seven seals, seven angels, seven plagues, and seven kings. "Seven" and its cognates occur well over five hundred times in the Bible. "Although in some instances the number seven may be meant literally, its symbolic significance is not far beneath the surface."[4]

In the fourth century, Augustine debated the significance of various numbers in the Gospel of John, including the number seven.[5] Mikeal Parsons pushes the issue even earlier, documenting how the numerology of seven plays a role in the construction of the New Testament texts, in the organization of the NT writings, and

---

1. Chevalier and Gheerbrant, *Dictionary*, 859–66.

2. "Many instances are found in the divine authorities, in which the number seven is . . . commonly used to express the whole, or the completeness of anything" (Augustine, *City*, XI, 31).

3. Hyers, *Meaning*, 74, 76–77.

4. Birch, "Number," 559.

5. Augustine, "Homilies," VII, 10; XV, 21; XVII, 2; XVII, 4–6; XXIV, 5–6; XXV, 6.

in the interpretation of texts.[6] Mark Stibbe suggests that number patterns such as units of seven are part of John's "narrative strategy."[7]

What follows traces familiar and lesser-known ways the Gospel of John employs sevens, comments on their import for the theme of completeness, and responds to those who would downplay their significance. I will commence with the more widely recognized instances and then move to more obscure but nonetheless important, supportive ones.

Readers need to go beyond looking for the word "seven" in John, for except for one reference to "seventh" (4:52), it is not there.[8] John's approach is indirect, challenging the reader not only to interpret the text in its obvious meaning but to find the symbolic meaning,[9] just as the Gospel of John challenges the reader to identify and then respond to its riddles, double meanings, and irony. Focusing on presenting the author's unstated but underlying invocation of sevens as highly symbolic does not exclude other significations of the passages considered. The Gospel's presentation is extraordinarily rich and multilayered. Richard Bauckham aptly puts it, "[T]he literal meaning—the meaning on the level of the events narrated in their chronological placement within a developing narrative—has its own integrity that is not manipulated or disrupted by other levels of meaning. Interpretation of this Gospel sometimes misses that. However, equally important is to recognize that further meaning is generated in a variety of different ways."[10] The warning is instructive; while we focus on the significance of the Gospel's numerical symbolism, we do not intend this as providing an exhaustive interpretation of any given text but rather indicative of an additional strain of the meaning the Evangelist assigns to the texts.

## SEVEN SIGNS

The Evangelist presents exactly seven signs (miracles) that Jesus performs to encourage his readers to believe and thereby have eternal life (20:30–31). Identifying the signs as seven advances and deepens our understanding of the signs.[11] We noted in

6. Parsons, "Exegesis," 27–30. For comparison, see Verman's treatment of "threes" in Jewish thought ("Power").

7. Stibbe, *Storyteller*, 17.

8. Jesus gives life to the official's son at the seventh hour. When the family hears that their son was healed at the time of Jesus's pronouncement, they believe. The timing of the complete healing leads to believing.

9. "In a symbol, there is both a literal meaning and a second level of meaning—what Paul Ricoeur calls 'an excess of signification.' . . . The literal meaning gives access to the non-literal," showing that the literal meaning allows or contains "still more meaning" (Coloe, *God,* 80).

10. Bauckham, *Gospel,* 132.

11. Koester cautions that "Numbers may acquire significance through association with the central images, persons, and action in an episode, but the primary meaning of an episode never depends on a number. As a way of testing the significance of a number, it is useful to ask whether the meaning would change if the text cited a different number or made a more general statement about quantity"

chapter 4 that the seven signs have a chiastic structure. At the heart of the sevenfold chiasm lies the discourse about the bread of life, the eating of it, and the promise of eternal life. This chiastic structure draws attention to John's central thesis that Jesus is the incarnate bread of life come from heaven and reinforces the function of the signs to bring about believing that Jesus brings eternal life. By its proto-eucharistic motif, the central sign of bread multiplication points to the climax of John's narrative in Jesus's death and resurrection (6:54–57). Thus, for the reader John paints the Eucharist as standing at the completed center of Christian celebration.[12] It is not that these seven signs exhaust what Jesus did openly. But through the completeness of seven, John indicates that more are unnecessary to bring about believing that "Jesus is the Christ, the son of God."[13]

## SEVEN EPISODES, DIALOGUES, AND DISCOURSES

C. H. Dodd identifies seven episodes in the Gospel. "The Book of Signs, chs. ii–xii . . . seems naturally to divide itself into seven episodes, each consisting of one or more narratives of significant acts of Jesus, accompanied by one or more discourses designed to bring out the significance of the narratives."[14] The first section is the new beginnings (2:1–4:42), where the old (ceremonial water, temple structure, cultic worship) is replaced by the new (wine, temple of Christ's body, birth, and worship). In the second section (4:43—5:47), the narratives of healings connect to the following discourse on the life-giving Word. The third episode (ch. 6) focuses on Jesus as the bread of life, whereas the fourth episode emphasizes light and life (chs. 7 and 8). Jesus is the light of the world yet suffers rejection and threat to his existence. Dodd calls the fifth episode judgment by the light (9:1—10:39). In the sixth episode, Jesus raises Lazarus from the dead: life is victorious over death (ch. 11). The seventh and final episode contains the anointing at Bethany and Jesus triumphal entry into Jerusalem (12:1–36). Here the discourse focuses on Jesus's death and the life made possible by it.

Raymond Brown expresses doubt about this structure, going on to critique Dodd's division of Book One into seven episodes. "There is a certain unity in chapters 2–4, but is this 'unit' to be put on equal footing with a single chapter like chap. 11?

---

(Koester, *Symbolism*, 313). However, as Bovon ("Names," 288) points out, "If we fail to recognize the significance of names and numbers, we . . . are vulnerable to losing a depth to our understanding of Scripture and deeper insights into its message."

12. Brown, "Creation's Renewal," 287–88.

13. The reader of the Gospel is reminded of the request of the rich man in Luke to "'send Lazarus to my father's house, for I have five brothers. Let him warn them, so that they will not also come to this place of torment.' Abraham replied, 'They have Moses and the Prophets; let them listen to them.'" When the rich man protests it is not enough, Abraham replies, "'If they do not listen to Moses and the Prophets, they will not be convinced even if someone rises from the dead'" (16:27–31). There is a point of sufficiency beyond which all is excess.

14. Dodd, *Interpretation,* 290. Dodd details the episodes in 277–379.

Chapters 2–4 are composed of at least five different stories set in different locales; chapter 11 consists substantially of one well-knit narrative." Rhetorically he asks, "Has not Dodd too been hypnotized by a desire to find a pattern of seven in the Gospel?"[15] The Evangelist's penchant for ambiguity plays a conspicuous role in this disagreement.

Dodd also sees seven dialogues in what he terms "the central block of the Book of Signs: chapters seven and eight." The introduction (7:1–13) sets the scene for the seven dialogues: 7:14–24; 7:25–36; 7:37–44; 7:45–52; 8:12–20; 8:21–30, and 8:31–59. "The tone of the whole is markedly polemical."[16] The debate concerns the identity of Jesus as the Messiah and ultimately as one with the Father. Throughout, opponents threaten Jesus's life because of his radical claims, but these seven dialogues are sufficient to settle the matter.

Another classification of the seven episodes associates them with changing locales. The first occurs across the Jordan (1:18—2:11), where John the Baptizer identifies Jesus and Jesus begins to recruit his disciples. In the second section (2:12—3:36), Jesus attends the Passover in Jerusalem and reveals himself as the "temple" who will be destroyed but raised again. In the third section (4:1–54) Jesus works in Galilee, whereas in the fourth section (5:1–47) he is again in Jerusalem for an unnamed Jewish festival, healing the paralytic on the Sabbath and talking about life and testimony. This same pattern repeats in the fifth section (6:1–71), where Jesus discourses in Capernaum on being the bread of life, and in the sixth section, where Jesus returns to Jerusalem (7:1—10:39) to more openly campaign for believing based on his works, if not on his self-affirmation. There is a brief interlude in 10:40, where Jesus retreats across the Jordan to the place where John was baptizing, before his final foray into Jerusalem and the seventh section (11:1—12:50) which anticipates his forthcoming death.

Leon Morris also lists seven discourses: the new birth (3:1–21); the water of life (4:1–42); the divine Son (5:19–47); the bread of life (6:22–59); the life-giving Spirit (7:1–52); the light of the world (8:12–59); and the good shepherd (10:1–42).[17] He, like others, debates whether the discourses can be aligned with the signs, especially since some precede and others follow the presented signs. Morris sees a clear connection between the first sign at the wedding at Cana and the first discourse. The transformation of water into wine anticipates the new birth discussed with Nicodemus in chapter 3. Between these John discusses the cleansing of the temple, where the old of the temple, with its sacrificial animals and coin exchange, is thrown out and the promise made that it would be replaced with a newness found in himself by his own death and resurrection.

In the second discourse, Jesus promises the Samaritan woman the water of eternal life. Worship in the spirit and in truth will replace the old worship, whether at Gerizim or Jerusalem. "Jesus brings people life, life in the Spirit," a point reinforced in

---

15. Brown, *Introduction to John,* 304.

16. Dodd, *Interpretation,* 345, 346.

17. Morris, *Jesus,* 23.

the subsequent sign when Jesus gave life to the royal official's son. Morris connects the third discourse with the third sign, the healing of the paralytic on the Sabbath. Jesus, he notes, affirms that he can do things on the Sabbath not permitted to the Pharisees because he relates to the Father as his Son.

The connection between the fourth sign of the feeding of the five thousand and the following discourse on the bread of life is obvious. Jesus uses the sign and the reaction of the crowd that pursues him to communicate his identity as the one through whom God gives eternal life. The fifth pair—the sign of walking on the water and the subsequent discourse in the temple about the life-giving Spirit (7:1–52)—is much less obvious, whereas the relation between the sixth sign of healing the blind man and the discourse of Jesus as the light of the world flows freely. Problems also attend linking the seventh sign of raising Lazarus (11:1–57) and the good shepherd discourse (10:1–42).[18]

Given the uncertainty and the many ways to interpret the *relation* between episodes, signs, dialogues, and discourses, it would be unwise to be dogmatic about the significance of seven. As Morris writes, "Thus it may be preferable to see all the parts as making their contribution to the one great theme than to try to discern too close ties between sections. This seems to be what John is saying when he tells us why he has written this book (20:30–31)."[19] Yet, the prevalence of these features suggests that their appearing in sequences of seven might play a role in the subtle presentation of theology in John's Gospel.

## SEVEN "I AMS"

Another commonly recognized instance of John's sevens is his employment of Jesus's self-identification as "I am." We saw in chapter 5 that John presents two types of I am (ἐγώ εἰμί) statements, one without predicates and one with. It is the latter, of which there are seven, that interests us. Their purpose is to establish the identity of Jesus, both his nature and his function or mission. Although "I am" is found sparingly elsewhere in the Synoptics, Acts, and Revelation, it is John's employment that stands out, for it aligns clearly with the purpose of the Gospel to reveal the person and function of Jesus.[20] The first occurs in John 6:35, 48, 51, where Jesus says that he is the bread of life. The Passover is near, and in this self-identification, Jesus anticipates his death. He is the new Moses (the Prophet of Deut 18:15) who brings the manna of eternal life from heaven, not like the old that was gathered daily, but himself as the true manna from the Father offered once for all for them to eat.[21] In the second instance Jesus identifies

18. Morris, *Jesus*, 32–35, 38–39.

19. Morris, *Jesus*, 41.

20. Morris, *Jesus*, 106.

21. Morris (*Jesus*, 110) points out that, with respect to the use of the definite article, "The definite article with 'bread' ('the bread', not 'a bread' or simply 'bread') is perhaps unexpected because predicate

himself as the light of the world (8:12). For the Festival of Booths the menorahs illuminated the temple with light, after which the priests would perform torch dances and
would sing and play instruments. Jesus is the light of life, whose function is to lead us
to follow the light as the Israelites did in the desert and to give the light of sight to the
blind (9:5). Third, Jesus claims that he is the door of the sheepfold (10:7, 9), the gate
of life protection, the gate of salvation from death to life, and the doorway to green
pastures. Fourth, following from the previous, Jesus says that he is the good shepherd
who protects the flock, even to the extent of laying down his life for it (10:11, 14), and
is the giver of eternal life that cannot be taken away by another. Fifth, he is the resurrection and the life; those who believe in him will have eternal life (11:25). He has the
power to raise Lazarus, which is a foretaste not only of his own resurrection but that of
everyone. Sixth, he has come to reveal the Father, and in doing so he claims to be the
way to the Father, for in seeing Jesus one sees the Father, the truth of word and reality, and the giver of life (14:6). Finally, he is the true vine, through whom we get our
sustenance and the ability to bear fruit (15:1, 5). Each of these "I ams" connects with
life, and all together, they support John's contention that through believing that Jesus
is the Messiah, the Son of God, we have eternal life. At the same time, each of the "I
ams" calls for a response: to eat of him, follow him, enter the fold through him, believe
in him, come to the Father through him, and remain in him, and love both him and
others. It is not enough to identify Jesus; what is required is believing manifested in
true discipleship. In these seven "I ams" we understand that Jesus in these aspects is
all that we need.

The author's argument from Jesus's self-identification is complete. For John, they
are sufficient to establish who Jesus is and what he does. The number of "I ams" points
to this.

## SEVEN WITNESSES

Richard Bauckham affirms a view suggested by others that the Gospel of John takes
the form of a trial. It emulates the lawsuit brought by Yahweh "against the gods of the
nations and their supporters in order to determine the identity of the true God" (Isa
40–55). In a trial, producing reliable testimony is critical. Thus, we find the Beloved
Disciple, who himself is a witness (19:35; 21:24), introducing individual witnesses in
defense of Jesus's identity.

> In the first phase, which comprises the Gospel's own narrative scope, there are
> seven witnesses. (In view of other series of sevens in the Gospel, the number
> is surely not accidental. Seven witnesses add up to complete, indeed, super-
> abundant witness, exceeding the Mosaic law's minimal requirement of two

---

nouns usually do not take the article. A. T. Robertson pointed out that 'when the article occurs with
subject (or the subject is a personal pronoun or proper name) and predicate, both are definite, treated
as identical, one and the same, and interchangeable.'"

witnesses for adequate witness.) The seven witnesses, in order of appearance, are John the Baptist (1:7, etc.), Jesus himself (3:11, etc.), the Samaritan woman (4:39), God the Father (5:32), Jesus's works or signs (5:36), the Scriptures (5:39), and the crowd who testify about Jesus's raising of Lazarus (12:17).[22]

These seven occur in the first phase of the trial (chapters 1–12), when Jesus publicly defends his identity. Although, as Bauckham notes, John later adds the testimony of the Paraclete (15:26) and of the disciples (15:27), these are given not as part of Jesus's public ministry but for his ongoing mission. If this suggestion holds, it means that the Evangelist saw the presentation of the witnesses as sufficient and complete, not needing supplement.

As we observed in chapter 4, the narrator, as the Beloved Disciple, presents from the testimony of others that Jesus is the promised one sent from God, the Messiah and Son of God. Andrew (1:41), Nathanael (1:49), Moses (5:46), the blind beggar (9:33), Martha (11:27), and Mary by her action (12:7), all in one way or another testify. What Bauckham seems to suggest, although he does not say it, is that these are not part of the seven because John does not use the word for testify or witness (μαρτυρέω) in these cases, as he does in the seven noted above.

## SEVEN SCENES IN DIALOGUES

In chapter 7 we noted that John's dialogic scenes may imitate to some degree the Greek theater in their structure. Since many of those for whom the Gospel was written were probably illiterate, John crafts the dialogic structure to suit an oral presentation. Three of these dialogues interest us here because John presents them in dramatic acts that in each case have seven distinct scenes.[23]

I have treated John's dialogues with the blind man and others in chapter 7. Here I want to focus not on the contents of the dialogues but on John's structure. It is easy to discern the seven scenes in chapter 9 that give the complete transformation of the blind man from helplessness to discipleship and worship, and Jesus's pronouncement that in his place it is the Pharisees who are willfully blind.

> Scene 1: Jesus encounters the man born blind and finds himself in dialogue, first with his disciples about the reason for the man's blindness, and then with the blind man himself whom Jesus tells to wash in the Pool of Siloam. 9:1–7

> Scene 2: The formerly blind man dialogues with his neighbors, who clearly had little regard for him, and reveals his ignorance of the one who healed him. 9:8–12

22. Bauckham, *Eyewitnesses*, 387–88.
23. Koester, *Symbolism*, 312.

Scene 3: The formerly blind man converses with the Pharisees, who are more concerned about the Sabbath rules and the performer of the deed than the joyful restoration of his sight. 9:13–17

Scene 4: The Pharisees confront the formerly blind man's fearful parents, who are worried that they would be ostracized from the temple for acknowledging Jesus's act. 9:18–23

Scene 5: The attention returns to the dialogue between the Pharisees and the formerly blind man, who testifies to his new discipleship and shows his mettle in responding to the Pharisees. 9:24–34

Scene 6: Jesus, whom the formerly blind man does not know, returns and reveals himself to the man, who in turn worships him. 9:35–39

Scene 7: Jesus engages in a double-entendre dialogue with the Pharisees about their blindness and the reason for it. 9:40–41

These seven scenes, with their chiastic structure,[24] demonstrate the complete cycle of the rise of the blind man's believing, leading to his acceptance and worship of Jesus, and the steadfast refusal of the Pharisees to believe. John brings the story to a high point in 9:27, where the once blind man makes the astounding offer to the aghast Pharisees that they also ought to believe and become disciples. The succeeding scenes reveal the diametrically opposed responses to the offer of discipleship. The blind man believes, becomes Jesus's disciple, and worships him. He becomes sighted and whole. The Pharisees, on the other hand, reaffirm their blindness, so that they end up where the blind man began in scene one, in blindness, but with the difference that their blindness is willful and hence connects with their sin. They pass up the opportunity to become sighted and whole.

The narrative here conveys John's intent to completely reveal Jesus's identity. In the beginning of the story, Jesus is simply a "man they call Jesus" (9:11). He is human but possesses a special power. From here, subject to persistent questioning, the blind man identifies Jesus as a prophet, one with a special connection to God as referenced in the Old Testament (9:17). Later, the blind man, when pressed again, identifies Jesus as coming from God (9:33). From there Jesus reveals himself as the Son of Man, and with this recognition the formerly blind man prostrates before him, an action appropriately directed to God. The story, through its seven scenes, completely reveals the multiple aspects of Jesus's identity: He is God, the revealer of God sent by God with power and authority, the prophetic Word of God, and the sign giver who points back to the Father.

The second instance of seven scenes in a dialogic account occurs in the story of the resurrection of Lazarus (ch. 11). This account also exhibits a chiastic structure, although perhaps less obvious than the previous.

24. Ellis, "Inclusion," 308–10, treats this as a chiasm, although differing in structure from mine.

Scene 1: Many people cross the Jordan to hear Jesus. Jesus is informed about Lazarus's illness but only acts after four days. 10:40–11:16

Scene 2: Martha believes Jesus that Lazarus will rise. She goes beyond believing in a future resurrection to an affirmation of who Jesus is. 11:17–27

Scene 3: Martha goes to inform Mary of Jesus's presence. 11:28

Scene 4: Mary comes to Jesus with the same accusation as her sister: "If you had been here, our brother would not have died." Jesus is compassionately moved in Mary's presence. 11:29–35

Scene 5: Jews accompanying Mary to meet Jesus are both impressed with his compassion and skeptical. 11:36–37

Scene 6: Martha has doubts about the wisdom of raising Lazarus. 11:38–44

Scene 7: Jews who came to witness the event at Bethany express a divided opinion about Jesus, some believing, others reporting him to the authorities. 11:45–46

At the center of this chiasm one sees the heart of Jesus as he emotionally deals with the death of his friend.[25] Although he realizes that this was for the purpose of bringing about believing (11:15, 42), yet it is not without his own agony that the events unfold as they do. In the end, the seven scenes lead to Jesus's restoration of the family to wholeness: Lazarus to health, Martha to her ministry of entertaining and serving (12:2), and Mary to her worship (12:3). Not only does the story reveal the heart of Jesus, it also anticipates Jesus's own death and resurrection.

The third instance of seven scenes in a dialogical account occurs when the arrested Jesus is brought before Pilate. The scenes alternate between outside the palace (18:28–32, 38b–40, 19:4–8, 13–16), where Pilate confers with the Jewish leaders, and inside the palace (18:33–38a; 19:1–3, 9–12), where Pilate questions and deals with Jesus. Whereas in two scenes inside the palace Pilate discourses with Jesus, in the central scene Pilate says nothing to Jesus but has him flogged, tortured, and mocked.

Scene 1 outside: "What charge do you bring?" Jews seek execution. 18:28–32

Scene 2 inside: "Are you the king of the Jews?" "My kingdom is not of this world." 18:33–38a

Scene 3 outside: "I find no basis for a charge. Whom do you want me to release?" 18:38b–40

Scene 4 inside: Pilate has Jesus flogged. Jesus mockingly is hailed as a king. 19:1–3

25. Although Ellis ("Inclusion," 313–15) sees this as a series of chiasms, I prefer to treat it as a single extended chiasm.

Scene 5 outside: "I find no basis for a charge. You take him and crucify him." 19:4–8

Scene 6 inside: "Where do you come from? Don't you know I have power over you?" Power lies in God's kingdom. 19:9–12

Scene 7 outside: "Shall I crucify your king?" Execution granted. 19:13–16a

For John, the seven scenes show Pilate's dialectical struggle with the Jewish leaders and his efforts to understand this man brought before him.[26] "The movement of Pilate from inside the praetorium, where he speaks with Jesus, to outside, where he speaks with the Jews, dramatizes his attempt to control the action. While appearing to speak as Jesus's advocate, he actually is orchestrating the Jews' affirmation of the authority he represents."[27] Scenes 1 and 7 bring to the fore the Jewish ambiguity over the alleged kingship of Jesus. In scenes 2 and 6 Pilate struggles with trying to understand this person who claims to have a kingdom but bears no kingly trappings. In scenes 3 and 5, Pilate presses the matter of releasing versus condemning Jesus, wanting to take no responsibility for what happens. In the center of the chiasm, we encounter the real Pilate, the cruel representative of Caesar who serves only one ruler, and the ironic affirmation of Jesus's kingship.

At stake for the Jews and Pilate is the question of kingship. "As earlier Pilate moved into the Jewish worldview in calling Jesus 'king' (ὁ βασιλεὺς), now 'the Jews' move across into the world of Rome to name their ruler to be Caesar (Καίσαρα)."[28] They have turned their back on Yahweh a second time, first in soliciting Samuel to give them a king like the nations around them (1 Sam 8), and now in rejecting a king from their own people in favor of a foreign oppressor.

The seven scenes reveal the decisiveness of the trial, from the initial accusation to the final condemnation. At stake for Jesus is whether he would act in accord with the Father's will. To bring about God's salvific intention, both Jews and Pilate must unite in action. Jesus affirms that they do so through the will of God who gave Pilate and Jews power over Jesus (19:11). In reality, Jesus has the power to upend the situation but voluntarily refuses to use it to complete the task assigned to him.

Each of these three dialogues brings us to a more complete understanding of who Jesus is. He is the healer who brings light to the blind and blindness to those thought sighted. He is the resurrection and the life, who himself will experience the Father's resurrecting action. He is king from another place who, testifying to the truth, has the power to lay down his life for others, to bring them to eternal life.

26. A similar chiasm can be found in Coloe, *God,* 182; Brown, *Gospel xiii–xxi,* 858–59.

27. Brant, *Dialogue,* 30.

28. Coloe, *God,* 185.

## SIMON PETER'S SEVEN APPEARANCES

John details seven encounters with Simon Peter: six dialogues that Simon Peter has with Jesus and a seventh presentation in the race to the tomb. In his seven distinct appearances we begin to get a full picture of this future leader of the church. Each appearance adds to our understanding of who this leader is and how his friend, the Beloved Disciple, viewed him as he completed his journey with Jesus. (1) Strong, he is the rock who will provide a steady foundation for the developing church (1:42). (2) Courageous, he is the leader who resists the temptation of peer pressure to abandon Jesus, as other disciples did, but affirms his faith in the one sent from God (6:48). (3) Impulsive, he responds quickly and to an extreme but learns from Jesus's exhibition what it is to be a servant leader (13:6–17). (4) Curious, he wants to know what was going on with everyone else (13:24; 21:20–21), while at the same time proudly affirming his own faithfulness. (5) Apprehensive, he fears for his own safety (18:10, 17–18, 25–26). (6) Hopeful, he looks for some redemption (20:3–7). (7) Vulnerable, he can be hurt; as devoted, through it all, he reaffirms his love for his Lord (21:1–19). Of all the followers, John paints a more complete picture of Peter than of the other followers. He is the more complete leader who, despite all his faults, will carry forward Jesus's mission.

## SEVEN NAMED DISCIPLES

Of interest is John's naming of Jesus's disciples. In the Gospel, John treats the disciples in three ways: as unnamed, as a group, and as named persons. The unnamed disciples appear in several places. In John 1:37–38, one of the unnamed disciples, who is initially a disciple of John, becomes a follower of Jesus. In John 21 there are two groups of unnamed disciples: one group identified as two other disciples, the other as the sons of Zebedee. We would not know the names of the latter were it not for the Synoptic references to them as James and John (Mark 3:17; Matt 4:21; Luke 5:10). We also encounter the enigmatic disciple whom Jesus loved, who appears several times (John 13:23–25; 19:26; 20:2, 8–9; 21:7, 20), and whose identity is much debated. Elsewhere John refers to the entire group of followers as Jesus's disciples or, less frequently, as the Twelve (6:67, 70). However, those who are of interest to us are the named disciples and the fact that John names seven of them. Andrew (1:40–41, 44; 12:22); Simon Peter (1:40–42, 44; 6:68; 13:6–11, 36–37; 18:10, 15–18, 25–27; 20:2–6; 21:7–20); Judas Iscariot (6:71; 12:4–6; 13:27–30; 18:2–5); Philip (1:43–48; 12:21–22; 14:8–9); Nathanael (1:45–49; 21:2); Thomas (11:16; 20:24–28; 21:2); and Judas not-Iscariot (14:22). The number twelve, used to designate the disciples, is also significant for its numerological connections. Not only does it derive from three multiplied by four, as noted earlier, but it connects with Jacob, the father of Israel, who had twelve sons and subsequently with the tribes of Israel, and with the tabernacle utensils and worship

(Lev 7:84–87; Ezra 8:35). John alludes to the significance of "twelve" in the baskets of bread collected by disciples (6:13). However, it is the seven named disciples that continues our theme of John's emphasis on seven.

It is not merely the number of disciples named that is significant; it is also the way that they are treated. They are not merely listed, as in Matt 10:2–4. In each mention, though in some more than others, we learn about their character through their interaction or dialogue with Jesus. Andrew, a disciple of John the Baptizer, chooses to follow Jesus whom the Baptizer designates as the Lamb of God. In response to Jesus's query, "What do you want?" he indicates that he wants to have an intimate relation with Jesus ("Where are you staying?"). To stay with Jesus, as he does for an entire day, gives Andrew more opportunity to learn about this identified person. Apparently, Andrew is impressed with this discovery, so that next the Evangelist tells us about Andrew's initiative to go and find his brother Simon to bring him the good news of the discovery of the Messiah. He becomes the first disciple-evangelist.

Jesus summons Philip to discipleship, and once called, like Andrew he is eager to share his discovery about the identity of Jesus and his connection to Moses (1:43–45). He also is an enlister, inviting Nathanael to "come and see" and later enlisting Andrew to together take a message to Jesus (12:21–22).[29] Yet he is also critically inquisitive, not yet having understood who the one Moses spoke about really is (14:10). It is only later in the writing of Luke that we realize that Philip understands the true connection between the one spoken about in the Old Testament and Jesus (Acts 8:35). He becomes a proclaimer of the Messiah in Samaria (Acts 8:4) and an interpreter of Isaiah to the Ethiopian on the road in Gaza (Acts 8:32). Jesus's calling ultimately is carried beyond Jews through Philip.

We have spoken of Thomas and Nathanael in chapter 4 and Simon Peter in chapter 6 and above. Simon Peter is the leader of the Twelve who affirms who Jesus is ("the Holy One of God") and his function (the purveyor of the words of eternal life) (6:67–69). He is the leader who both adheres to traditional leadership/follower roles (13:6–9) and then goes all out to show his loyalty. He is the curious one (13:24, 36–37), who again exhibits his verbal commitment to his Lord. This commitment is later tested, first with failure, and then, when implicitly forgiven, with the prediction that it will be tested again. The dialogues reveal Simon Peter as a leader, someone who readily (sometimes perhaps too readily) speaks his mind, is fully devoted, yet plagued by his all too human fears when the chips are down.

The disciple Judas Iscariot receives significant billing in John. We are told early on what to expect from this disciple (6:70–71), which he exhibits later in his devilish deed (13:21–30). Dismissed from the person of light, he goes out into the darkness, a place that accords with his corrupt character. The scene where he first appears reveals

29. Philip had a Greek name and thus may have had some Hellenic connection. If so, it would be natural for the Greeks seeking to approach Jesus to come through him. Philip's cross-cultural ministry is emphasized in Acts 6 and 8. Anderson, "Philip," 178–81.

his greed. Watching with personal anguish Mary pour expensive perfume on Jesus, he criticizes her for her wastefulness (12:4–6). As the group's treasurer, he has his hand in the till and thus rues this missed opportunity when Mary anointed Jesus rather than sold the expensive perfume and contributed the money to the group to donate to the poor. To being a thief, he adds the trait of being a traitor, moving from disciple to defector, from association with the Son of God to being in league with Satan, for we find him not with the loyal disciples in the garden but leading the crowd of arresters waiting outside (18:3). Although John says nothing about any exchange of money for the betrayal as does Matthew (Matt 27:3–5), the hint of the reason is given in the scene with Mary. Judas in effect makes a pact with the devil and thus was of the devil (6:70; 8:44).

The question is: Given the presence of evil, whatever its origin, how will God and Jesus deal with it? As the story unfolds, Judas is of the devil, yet even though he foreknew Judas's action (6:64), Jesus chooses him along with the other disciples (6:70). The devil puts betrayal into Judas's heart, yet Jesus washes his feet (13:1–11, 21). Jesus gives Judas a piece of bread dipped in wine, inviting him into eucharistic fellowship, only to have Judas take the bread but refuse the fellowship. Having given Judas one last opportunity to change, Jesus permits the betrayer to leave (13:26–30). Having given himself over to Satan, who enters him (13:26–27), he departs into the darkness of Satan's realm. Rather than combating evil with force, Jesus meets it with gracious actions of servitude and invitation, finally turning the evil toward God's saving end of glorification (13:31). Judas provides the example of those who function as disciples, who take the Eucharist but do not really believe, who are lost in their own machinations (17:12). As Jesus says, "No one can come to me unless the Father has enabled him" (6:65). From Judas we learn that some seem enabled but are not really so.

Judas not-Iscariot might be the most enigmatic to be included among the named persons (14:22). He does not appear elsewhere in John. A Judas son of James is named in Luke's account (Luke 6:16), but his identity is disputed. Two questions arise: why include Judas not-Iscariot at all among the named disciples, and why have Judas not-Iscariot rather than someone else more prominent among the named raise the question, "Lord, why do you intend to show yourself to us and not to the world?"[30]

---

30. Barrett, *Gospel,* 388–89. Bultmann (*Gospel of John,* 622) states that this question is foolish. But it seems to be an important question to Jesus's and John's audience (Michaels, *Gospel of John,* 788–89). Jesus's brothers ask this question out of unbelieving (7:3–5). Jesus's response to them was that his time had not yet come. We don't know the attitude out of which Judas posed the question, but now Jesus's time had come. He replies by repeating himself rather than directly answering the question. But from what he says we might construct an answer. A general revelation to the world would not work, for the world (note the double meaning of "world") stands opposed to him (17:14) and would not recognize him, in the same way that the Jewish leaders and crowd did not recognize him. Recognition grows out of obedience to his word (λόγον σου), something not found in the world, and obedience in turn results in loving him and being loved by the indwelling Father. If the world is to see and believe in Jesus, it is through those who love and obey him (17:21).

This obscure Judas is perplexed about Jesus's claim about to whom he would reveal himself, since the disciples, along with the other Jews, were expecting the Messiah to reveal himself to everyone by bringing them liberation (6:15) and implementing a Moses-like feeding program (6:26). It would have been much simpler for John to keep him anonymous, like Andrew's friend, or even to name one of the other more prominent disciples that he has already referenced to express this question. After all, there were other candidates among the named disciples. In fact, a candidate lies ready at hand: the unnamed disciple who with Andrew left John the Baptizer and turned to Jesus. Or even the Beloved Disciple could have been chosen. Why introduce Judas not-Iscariot here by name? Two answers intrigue me. One is that Judas not-Iscariot is named because this complementarity between Judas Iscariot and Judas not-Iscariot repeats the theme of contrasting dualisms developed in John's Gospel. Judas Iscariot was of the devil (6:71); Satan entered him at the Passover meal (13:27), and before long he left the light and entered into the darkness of evil purpose. Judas not-Iscariot, however, precipitates a discourse about love, not betrayal, of belonging to the Father, not departure into darkness. It is the Counselor (παράκλητος), the Spirit, the opposite of the devil, who will indwell the disciples. A second answer, relevant to our thesis of completeness, is that this additional named disciple is added to make the number of named disciples seven. A bit player, yes; important to indicate that bit players like us can be disciples, yes; completeness of the disciple core, very possibly, for it extends the Evangelist's concern for completeness.

With each of these named disciples, we learn something about what it is to be a complete disciple. Disciples follow the Lord, invite others to encounter Jesus as the Messiah, move from being doubters to confessors, are loyal to their Lord despite temptation and persecution, and provide for manifestations of love and light in the lives of the community. Even the most obscure disciple is important and known by name in God's kingdom.

One might also note the number of disciples in the Galilee incident that forms the denouement of the Gospel. Although all the disciples present are not named, seven are fishing (21:2). Peter, Thomas, and Nathanael are named, two others are not named but referred to as the sons of Zebedee (James and John, Matt 4:21), and two disciples are not named, one of whom is the Beloved Disciple (21:20). "[S]even disciples have come together, doubtless a symbolical number, representing the whole disciple group, and indeed the whole Body of disciples, the Church."[31] Jesus's three-year ministry to his disciples is complete, except for the final matter dealing with the reinstatement of Peter, his commissioning, and the prophecy about his future. The future of the movement must be guaranteed. Whereas in the Prologue Jesus brings the ministry of God to his own, Peter now carries Jesus's ministry to his flock. The transfer from the Father to the Son to the evangelizing disciples is complete.[32]

31. Beasley-Murray, *John*, 399.

32. A much more speculative identification of "seven" concerns the appearances of the Beloved

## TWO WEEKS (SEVEN DAYS) BRACKET JESUS'S MINISTRY

In chapter 9 we detailed the two weeks that bracket Jesus's ministry. The first week of seven days sets the stage for Jesus's ministry. The last week of seven days concludes his ministry in his death and resurrection. Again, one might suggest that John indicates the completeness of Jesus's ministry by this seven-day bracketing. His ministry began and ended with his identification, his final glorification is portended in the sign at Cana and realized on the cross, and his mission was accomplished by his followers believing and being commissioned.

## SEVEN CLAIMS ABOUT THE RIGHT TIME

Of particular importance is Jesus's identification of personal time, when he speaks of the present moment as not being or being the right time for his glorification (see ch. 9). This occurs seven times. In the first four instances, the hour or time has not yet come (2:4; 7:6–8; 7:30; 8:20). In the transitional chapter 12 (vv. 23, 27), the hour is about to come. In the final two instances, Jesus knows that the hour has come (13:1), the hour to depart from the world (17:1).

The fact that these are grouped in the seven of completeness shows that John considers that Jesus's death is completely and perfectly fulfilled, not in the time that we might think would be appropriate (2:3), the time even those who might be closest to him might think (7:6), or even the time specified by his enemies (7:30; 8:20). Rather, it is the time of his own choosing. Jesus does not ask the Father to save him from this hour when the Son of Man is to be glorified; rather, he accepts it willingly. As revealed in his dialogue with Pilate, Jesus has the matters in his own hands and in the hands of his Father. No one, not even Pilate, has the power to determine the proper time of Jesus's being lifted up (19:11).

## SEVEN AS A COMPLETE MEAL

Followed by a great crowd, Jesus ascended a mountain, ostensibly to teach. In time, the need arose for the crowd to eat. Philip, in response to Jesus's rhetorical question, recognized the direness of the situation (6:7). Andrew introduced an apparently pathetic remedy: five loaves and two fish. From a human standpoint, it is enough to feed the boy but not enough to feed a large crowd. Jesus took what is complete for the individual and made it complete for the entire following, with twelve baskets

---

Disciple. Bauckham (*Eyewitnesses*, 554) sees him (1) as a disciple of the Baptizer, accompanying Andrew (1:37); (2) intimately leaning on Jesus (13:23); (3) escorting Peter into the courtyard of Annas (18:15); (4) standing at the foot of the cross (19:25); (5) racing Simon Peter to the tomb (20:3); (6) spotting Jesus on the Galilean shore (21:7); (7) the object of Peter's curiosity (21:20). In instances (1) and (3) the anonymous individual is not named as the disciple whom Jesus loved, and (3) is particularly speculative. For a contrarian view on (3), see Michaels, *Gospel of John*, 897–99.

(another symbolic number) left over. The physical bread, which provides temporary satisfaction, symbolically transmutes into the spiritual bread, which is Jesus himself, which ends forever the hunger of those who partake.

## PAIR OF SEVEN OLD TESTAMENT QUOTATIONS

We have already noted that the Evangelist is rooted in the Old Testament. From the outset he connects with the Genesis creation story and soon makes allusion to God's presence in the tabernacle (1:14) and giving the Law to Moses (1:17). Köstenberger notes that, in addition to the multiple Old Testament allusions throughout the Gospel, "[e]xplicit OT quotations in John's Gospel follow a symmetrical pattern. In the first half of the Gospel, variations of the introductory formula, 'It is written,' predominate; in the second half, starting at 12:38, John switches to fulfillment language. Each half contains seven quotations."[33] He goes on to remark that both sets of seven citations follow a similar pattern, not only beginning with a quote from Isaiah and concluding with a quote from Zechariah, but including the same number of references to the Psalms (four), Isaiah (two), and to Zechariah (one). The citations complete a testimonial cycle: they begin with the testimony of John announcing the coming of the Lord and end with the testimony of the Beloved Disciple at the cross.

## SIX AS INCOMPLETE

One of the more interesting exceptions to the use of seven occurs in John's account of the first sign, the changing water into wine at Cana (2:1–11). When John gives us details, there must be some reason for his doing so. For example, commentators suggest that the natural but specified size of the jars "suggests that the great quantity they contained reflected the fullness of Christ's grace, in contrast to the limitations of the old covenant (John 1:16–17)."[34] John informs us that the number of stone water jars is six and that Jews used these for ceremonial purposes, such as washing of hands and utensils for eating and cooking. However, why six rather than another number? Something more than abundance seems involved.[35] If "seven" indicates completeness, then "six" indicates that something is almost but not fully complete.[36] Something is lacking to bring what is referenced to full completion. Possibly John indicates something

---

33. Köstenberger, "Use of the Old Testament," 49. The first set is 1:23 (Isa 40:3); 2:17 (Ps 69:9a); 6:31 (Ps 78:24b); 6:45 (Isa 54:13a); 10:34 (Ps 82:6a); 12:13 (Ps 118:26a); 12:15 (Zech 9:9). The second set is 12:38 (Isa 53:1); 12:40 (Isa 6:10); 13:18 (Ps 41:9b); 15:25 (Ps 35:19; 69:4); 19:24 (Ps 22:18), 19:36 (Ps 34:20), 19:37 (Zech 12:10).

34. Beasley-Murray, *John*, 35. See Culpepper, *Gospel and Letters*, 131.

35. Lewis, *John*, 38–39.

36. Augustine, "Homilies," IX, 6. See Morris, *Gospel*, 160–61.

about the old order of ceremonial washing, namely, that it is incomplete.[37] Washing purifies the outside of things and of people but does not affect the inside. It fails to create the purity that really matters. The something more that is needed is found in the nature and function of the one who performs the sign, who completes the purification not by adding another jar to legalistic washing but by transforming the very content of the jars so that it purifies the inside when drunk.[38] As Jesus turns the water into wine, he turns his blood into a drink that gives life (6:56–57). The Law, John explains, came through Moses; but grace and truth come through Jesus Christ (1:17). The incompleteness is made whole in a totally unexpected way, presaging the new birth that Jesus discusses with Nicodemus.

In another instance, Jesus meets the Samaritan woman at the sixth hour (noon). She had had five husbands and now lives with a sixth man to whom she is not married. Her lifestyle has bestowed on her a social status that requires her to come to the well at the sixth hour and not when the acceptable village women draw water. She also is unfulfilled, still thirsty in life (laboring in the heat of the day) and in religious worship, until she meets Jesus. John has already referred to Jesus as the bridegroom through the Baptizer's allegory (3:29). So here it may be that symbolically the woman encounters the true bridegroom, the seventh man, who gives meaningful, qualitative (eternal) life. "After their discussion she returns to her village to speak of her encounter and, while there is no betrothal, there is an invitation to stay (4:40) and by the conclusion of this scene there is significant union between the Samaritan villagers and Jesus."[39]

According to John, the Jews state that the temple took forty-six years to build (2:20). In Scripture, forty often refers not to a specific number of years but stands for a very long time (Gen 7:4, 17; 25:20; Exod 24:18; Num 14:34; 1 Sam 4:18; 2 Sam 5:4; 15:7; 1 Kgs 2:11; 4:25; 11:22; 12:1; 2 Chr 24:1; Jonah 3:4; Matt 4:2). However, of significance for us is the "six." Perhaps John introduces it to emphasize that the temple reconstructed by Herod[40] was humanly built, temporary, and still incomplete. It is the culmination of Herod's construction projects, almost perfect. Yet, if something's identity is found in its origin, then the temple as a building symbolized imperfection, given the despotic and grossly immoral character of its builder. Jesus claims that this

---

37. It should be noted that this point about the significance of six jars, as with many symbols, is debated. Morris writes, "The Jews saw seven as the perfect number, and six accordingly was short of perfection and thus lacking, incomplete. The six pots are then held to symbolize Judaism as imperfect. There may be something in this, but a strong objection is that the narrative contains nothing that would symbolize completeness" (*Gospel*, 160–61). See Michaels, *Gospel of John*, 149n31 and Brown, *Gospel i–xii*, 100, 106.

38. Coloe, *God*, 69. Barrett notes that John does not add a seventh jar (*Gospel*, 160), but that is to be expected, since Jesus himself is the living water transforming the inside, not the outside.

39. Coloe, *God*, 98.

40. Begun in 20 BC, the entire temple complex apparently was not completed until shortly before its destruction in AD 70. However, it is thought that the temple proper was completed by priests in a year and a half.

temple, as temporary, would be destroyed and a new, perfect temple, not made with hands but come from God himself, would replace it (2:21; 4:20–24; see Heb 9:11).

A similar use of "six" inaugurates John's identification of the final week. Jesus arrives at Bethany "six days before the Passover." The Passover was the most important Jewish festival, celebrating liberation from Egyptian bondage. However, for John the Passover is not the final event, only the penultimate event, superseded by the resurrection. Thus, although Jesus's crucifixion and death are central to the story, as presaged elsewhere in John, and although John indicates that Jesus was killed at the very time that the Passover lamb was killed, yet that is not the complete story.[41] The salvation story is incomplete until the seventh day, when God raises Jesus from the dead.

Not only does John use sevens to establish the completeness of Jesus's ministry, he uses "six" to indicate where there is incompleteness and to anticipate Jesus bringing his unique "finish" to everything. Thus, Jesus asserts at a time *after* the sixth hour, when he was crucified (19:14), that the saga of salvation is now complete or finished. In this way, using his symbols, John constructs layer upon layer of meaning.

## JOHN AND GENESIS

The creation motif is prevalent in John.[42] "John had one eye fixed on the Genesis account of creation . . . and the other eye fixed on the stories about Jesus."[43] It is likely that John derived the significance of "seven" from Gen 2:2, where God resting on the seventh day indicates that his work is complete and finished. Indeed, the Sabbath provides the contentious context for John's treatments of Jesus's signs and dialogues in chapters 5, 7, and 9.

The Evangelist was quite familiar with the book of beginnings. As we noted in chapter 1, John's Prologue indicates to the readers the themes he believes to be important in the remainder of the book. He uses Gen 1:1—2:4a to thematically construct his Prologue. The opening of the book, "In the beginning" (Ἐν ἀρχῇ, 1:1), echoes the Septuagint of Gen 1:1. He sees the Word (ὁ Λόγος) as intimately connected to God (1:1–2) and as creator (1:3). In Genesis, God creates via his word, and although εἶπεῖν rather than λόγος is used in Gen 1 LXX, Ps 33:6 says that "By the word (λόγῳ) of the LORD the heavens were made (ἐστερεώθησαν)." The Prologue, as the rest of the Gospel, emphasizes life (ζωή) (as in Gen 1:20, 21, 24, 30; 2:7, 9, 19) and light (φῶς) (dualistically contrasted to darkness) (Gen 1:2, 3–5, 4–5, 18), central themes of Gen 1.

---

41. It is the sixth hour (noon) of the Preparation Day, when three things take place: Jews cease their work, leaven is gathered out of the houses and burned, and the slaughtering of the Passover lambs commences. The Passover festival, for all practical purposes, now begins. Beasley-Murray, *John*, 341.

42. Du Rand, "Creation Motif," 21–46.

43. Minear, *Christians*, 83.

Some have seen creation themes subtly present elsewhere in the Gospel. Jannine Brown points to the role of the garden both preceding the arrest (John 18:1) and in the resurrection account, where Jesus is buried in the garden tomb (19:41) and where Mary Magdalene encounters the gardener (20:15). Although John uses κῆπος (garden) rather than παράδεισος (paradise), which is used by the LXX of Genesis, J. Brown notes that this presents no obstacle, for the latter term in the New Testament context is more appropriate to the final state rather than for the arresting place of Jesus.[44] She also suggests that it is possible that Jesus is viewed not only as the gardener that Mary Magdalene mistakes him as, but as the new Adam, alluding to the first human in Genesis.[45] "Virtually all commentators understand John to be echoing the moment in Gen 2:7, when God breathes (LXX: ἐμφῦσάω) into Adam the breath of life (LXX: πνοήν ζωῆς). In John 20:22 the same verb is used (ἐμφῦσάω) to express Jesus's imparting of the Holy Spirit (πνεῦμα ἅγιον) to his disciples."[46] J. Brown later concludes that there is support for the view that John's emphasis on Jesus "completing God's work echoes the creation story of Genesis."[47]

Raymond Brown thinks that the theme of revelation supersedes the theme of creation in John. "Although not absent, . . . the theme of creation is subordinated to the theme of revelation in John."[48] In one sense this is so, for John tells us plainly that Jesus has come to reveal the Father to us. Yet, while revelation is the goal, creation provides the structural framework for the presentation of this revelation (1:3), and in this regard it is reasonable to think that the employment of seven days in Genesis influenced John's construction and composition.

John knows other parts of Genesis as well. He quotes Gen 28:12 in 1:51. "John 8:56 reflects a rabbinic interpretation of the clause in Gen 24:1, 'Abraham entered into the days' (= Abraham was advanced in years), as meaning that Abraham in vision entered the future, and so enjoyed a vision of the days of the Messiah (so R. Akiba . . . )."[49] The story of John the Baptizer referring to Jesus as the Lamb of God, echoes that of Abraham finding the ram provided by God to replace Isaac in his sacrifice (Gen 22:13).

## DEMURRERS AND RESPONSE

After looking at the evidence of the role of "seven" in John, some might still demur, and they would be in good company. Raymond Brown writes that "a closer look leads one to suspect that this ingenuity is being imposed on the evangelist, who never once

44. Brown, "Creation's Renewal," 280.
45. Brown, "Creation's Renewal," 281–82.
46. Brown, "Creation's Renewal," 282.
47. Brown, "Creation's Renewal," 285.
48. Brown, *Introduction*, 305.
49. Beasley-Murray, *John*, lxi.

gives the slightest indication that he has such numerical patterns in mind and never uses the word 'seven' (contrast Revelation). For instance, does the evangelist intend [the signs of feeding the five thousand and walking on the water] to be treated as two separate signs?"[50]

Although symbols are important, care should be taken about seeing symbols everywhere and in the process overlooking the strength of the narrative. For example, Koester cautions about an over-citation of numerical symbols. "Our interpretations of Johannine symbolism can impoverish the meaning by venturing to say too little, and they can empty it of meaning by trying to say too much. . . . Authentic freedom is enjoyed precisely within limits."[51] For him the test is whether interpreting the numbers symbolically contributes to the "symbolic significance of a passage."[52] This test is helpful, particularly when it is coupled with John's connection of a specific account or narrative with the Old Testament. In doing so, one can affirm a middle ground between seeing everything as symbolic and refusing to see the symbols. We have seen that the Gospel meets this test. "It is a text that constantly creates the impression that more is going on than immediately meets the eye. It is also a closely integrated whole, so that the more familiar readers become with the whole Gospel, the better they will understand the parts."[53] In effect, where John's numerology enhances the meaning rather than is taken to supplant it, we can reasonably hold that John gives the readers more than what is simply immediately apparent in the text.

## CONCLUSION

The analysis we have carried out in this Book of Completeness testifies to the creative literary construction of the Gospel of John. In the Gospel, aware of traditions about Jesus, the author weaves a narrative about events having theological and symbolic meanings. "The intended readers of the Fourth Gospel almost certainly would have assumed that the narrative depicted actual people and events from the past. At the same time, they were told that the evangelist selected and shaped his material to convey a coherent message (20:30–31). . . . A comparison of the four New Testament Gospels shows that none of the evangelists was content merely to repeat the tradition. . . . Each revered the tradition enough to preserve it, yet exercised the freedom to reshape it and make it his own."[54] We have observed that an important motif of reweaving is the traditionally symbolic number seven; this distinctly connects John to the Old Testament, and in particular, to the creation story. Recognizing his symbolism, we can

50. Brown, *Introduction*, 303.
51. Koester, *Symbolism*, 316.
52. Koester, *Symbolism*, 314.
53. Bauckham, *Gospel*, 132.
54. Koester, *Symbolism*, 38–39.

reasonably hold that John wants his readers to understand more than what he overtly gives in the text.

The presence of "seven" bookends the Bible and marks completeness. Genesis sees the wholeness of creation completed in seven days, setting the pattern for and justifying the Jewish treatment of the Sabbath. In the final book, Revelation, sevens have a symbolic, numerological function showing completeness or fulfillment. The author of the Gospel of John likewise subtly structures his narrative using sevens. Using the symbolism of seven adds to his literary, argumentative quiver to establish the identity of Jesus the Word as fully God (1:1) and the fulfillment of Jesus's mission to bring completeness and wholeness of (eternal) life.[55]

## QUESTIONS FOR REFLECTION AND DISCUSSION

1. What numbers were significant to ancient cultures, and what meaning did the respective numbers have?

2. What instances of the use of seven or seventh do you find in the Old Testament? What significance do you find where these are used?

3. Do you think that John was trying to convey any message by his indirect use of numbers like seven, three, and twelve, or do you think that this is reading too much into the text?

4. Which uses of a structure of sevens did you find most informative, significant, or persuasive?

5. Are there particular numbers that are important in today's culture? What are they and why are they significant? (Hint: Think about birthdays, anniversaries, special celebrations, national holidays.) How do they convey a qualitative significance more than just a numerical time measurement?

55. It might also be seen as providing some evidence that John, in focusing on a key mnemonic device, was writing for an oral society with whom he wanted to communicate in the best way possible to bring to believing. Seven is the perfect device for recollection (Miller, "Magical Number," 81–97). If John was written to be read and presented to an oral culture, the construction using sevens would facilitate remembrance of the themes and ideas. It is not that John was aware of this, but the fact that this book was written and read in an oral society gives this feature additional, practical relevance.

CHAPTER ELEVEN

# Book of Parentage

THE CLIMAX OF THE Gospel of John is Jesus's trial, crucifixion, and resurrection, as evidenced by the texts anticipating and the material devoted to presenting these events.[1] The Gospel is an extended drama. Its tempo, first quickly then in slower progression, leads up to these events and then ends with a final coda. Its melodic theme, the shadow of the cross, extends back through the length of the Gospel to the Baptizer's recognition of Jesus as the Lamb of God (1:29). Its thematic variations course through Jesus's hour (2:4; 7:6, etc.), his body (2:19), his being given and lifted up (3:14–15), his given flesh and blood (6:53–56), his glorification (8:27; 12:32), his sadness (11:35), Caiaphas's warning (11:51–52), Jesus's anointing (12:7), his acclamation (12:12–16), his production of "seed" (12:23–24), his acceptance of his forthcoming death (12:27–33), his coming betrayal (13:21), and the glorification prayer (17). Each melodic line adds color, texture, and significance to the entire piece. How, then, is the musical statement—that believing in Jesus as the Messiah, the Son of God enables eternal life—scored? What is it, as the Samaritans proclaimed, to be "the savior of the world" (4:42)?

Rather than "precise dogmatic formulations,"[2] multiple soteriological or salvation themes emerge from John's extended drama about Jesus. Salvation motifs are "taught implicitly through allusion, . . . expressed with more subtlety."[3] By considering John's narrative features,[4] we uncover the significant clues to a multifaceted soteriology scattered throughout the Gospel and consider how the fact and necessity of Jesus's death on the cross and resurrection fit into the picture. In addressing John's soteriology,

1. One might add his departure, though this is only alluded to rather than described.

2. Zimmermann, "Jesus," 95.

3. Gieschen, "Death of Jesus," 245.

4. "[T]he Fourth Gospel is not so much interested in precise dogmatic formulations, but rather Christology is made by means of literary devices like metaphors and narration" (Zimmermann, "Jesus," 95), though, we might add, rooted in traditions.

we will emphasize how the theme that salvation brings life, both qualitatively and quantitatively, underlies and unifies his Gospel.

In chapter 7 we saw that many of John's dialogues can be considered as dramas. If we take this as a clue, we can understand John's soteriology as arising from not only literary devices and individual dramas or dialogues, but from the entire Gospel as a drama of the cross. We are thereby presented not with an abstract, dogmatic account but with dramas of salvation.[5]

## BIRTH FROM ABOVE (1:12-13; 3:3-7)

The Gospel of John is a book about paternity or parentage. The narrator reveals Jesus's identity as found in his relationship with the Father. He comes from (is sent by) and goes to the Father, is testified to by the Father (8:18), does the Father's work (10:37), is taught by the Father (15:15), is loved by and obeys the Father (15:9–10), glorifies and is glorified by the Father (17:1), and is one with the Father (10:30). The Gospel's mission is to bring us to proper parentage, to "become children of God, children born not of natural descent, nor of human decision or a husband's will, but born of God" (1:12–13). John thus initiates in the Prologue discussion of salvation through the metaphor of birth.

As we have already noted, for John who we are depends on our origin. We have seen how Jesus's heritage preoccupies the Jews (1:46; 6:42; 7:27–29, 41, 52; 8:48), and Jesus responds (6:33, 50; 7:28–29; 8:23, 29, 42). Jesus's contemporaries affirm their earthly identity based on natural descent from Abraham (8:33) and, John adds, human decision (1:13). However, being born of faithful human lineage does not guarantee right believing and action (8:39–40). Through sin we easily can slip into having parentage of the devil (8:44). To be born of God we must rely not on human activity but on the work of God (1:13; 6:44), and to do the work of God is to believe in Jesus (6:29). Through believing and receiving Jesus (1:13), we become children of God through the Father's drawing grace facilitated through Jesus (1:16–17; 6:65).

After the Prologue, the Evangelist returns to and expands on the birth motif in Jesus's dialogue with Nicodemus. In the first scene of an extended three-act play (3:1–15; 7:45–52; 19:38–42), the theme of origins sets the narrative: Nicodemus comes *from* the Pharisees, acknowledging that Jesus comes *from* God. Jesus builds on origins. To be saved, to take on a new identity, to enter the kingdom of God (salvation), which is Jesus's kingdom from which he came (18:36) and which he intends to extend to the cosmos he created (1:3), one must have a different origin; one must be born again or from above (3:3; i.e., from heaven or God, 3:31). The phrase "to be reborn" is inherently ambiguous, a riddle to be solved, and Nicodemus does not solve it because he

5. "Johannine theology is, in some radical sense, far more *theo-logical* and more *theo-dramatic*. . . . Secondly, it is more *theo-dramatic*. The *Theos* is revealed in a divinely-authored drama of love" (Kelly and Moloney, *Experiencing God*, 83–84).

fails to pick up on the double meanings of γεννάω ἄνωθεν, meaning either physical rebirth or spiritual birth from God. From an earthly perspective, we cannot reenter our mother's womb and be reborn; rebirth cannot be brought about by our own effort or improvement. However, from the heavenly perspective we can be reborn when God gives us new parentage and identity. "God must become Father to those who would 'see the kingdom of God.'"[6]

Jesus proceeds to explain to Nicodemus his riddle, or better, to extend it. He supplements the double meanings on which the riddle rests by two other riddles. To be born from above is to be "born of water and wind" (3:5). Both "water" and "wind" have double meanings here. On the earthly level, "water" (ὕδωρ) here might mean water involved in diverse aspects of physical birth.[7] However, "water" understood from the heavenly or divine perspective connects to purification.[8] Similarly, πνεῦμα can mean either "wind" or "spirit." Jesus trades on this ambiguity, such that Nicodemus, from the earthly perspective, likely takes it as "wind," whereas Jesus, from the heavenly perspective, means it as "spirit." The proverb in 3:8,[9] which likewise trades on this ambiguity, further muddies the riddle. The obvious earthly meaning of the proverb is that we feel the wind but can neither trace its origin nor track where it goes. Similarly, from the heavenly or divine perspective, those born from above know that something

---

6. Michaels, *Gospel of John*, 180. "[M]an receives a new *origin*, and this is manifestly something which he cannot give himself. For everything [that] lies within his power to do is determined from the start by his old origin, which was the point of departure for his present life, and by the person he has always been. For it is one of the basic ideas of Johannine anthropology . . . that man is determined by his origin, and determined in such a way that, as he now is, he has no control over his life, and that he cannot procure his salvation for himself. . . . [I]t must start from another point, and man must be able to reverse his origin, and to exchange the old origin for a new one. He must be 'reborn'!" (Bultmann, *Gospel of John*, 137–38).

7. Thatcher, *Riddles*, 270; Bauckham, *Gospel of Glory*, 89–90.

8. Whether water also indicates baptism in this text is much disputed. On the one hand, "there can be little doubt that the Christian readers of John would have interpreted vs. 5, 'being begotten of water and Spirit,' as a reference to Christian Baptism; and so we have a secondary level of sacramental reference" (Brown, *Gospel i–xii*, 141–42). John hints that such an understanding is possible because in the story that immediately follows the Nicodemus story, we find Jesus and the Baptizer baptizing (3:22). It is also possible that John understood it as "Jewish proselyte baptism . . . , a custom wherein the baptized proselyte was compared to a new-born child" (Brown, *Gospel i–xii*, 142). Being reborn is a baptismal theme elsewhere in the NT (1 Pet 1:23). Thus, if it is a baptismal text, then Jesus is emphasizing the role of the Spirit in baptism and that baptism signifies God's role in rebirth ("from above"). On the other hand, in its historical context, it is unclear whether Nicodemus could have understood Jesus's riddle as referring to baptism, and certainly not to the Christian rite. Yet the baptismal interpretation for Nicodemus's understanding is not necessary. His knowledge of the Old Testament might have led him to recall that "many of the OT passages which mention the outpouring of the spirit also mention water; thus water and spirit do go together" (Brown, *Gospel i–xii*, 142). "In the Old Testament the washing of people in water and the outpouring of the Spirit will usher in the new age (Ezek 36:25–27; Isa 44:3)" (Gench, *Encounters*, 21). Indeed, the combination of water with spirit occurs elsewhere in John (7:38–39). In short, the passage is laden with ambiguity and double meanings.

9. Collins, *These Things*, 139.

has occurred but cannot explain how it came about. Using these double meanings, Jesus contrasts the earthly perspective (flesh, σάρξ) with the heavenly perspective (spirit, πνεῦμα) (3:6). Physically, we experience life in the waters of maternal birth. Spiritually, our rebirth is from above, such that purification or salvation is ultimately of the Spirit, from God (1:33). In short, salvation or the new birth, which gives us our new identity, comes from God, at his initiative, not ours. Yet, we acquire this changed identity, this new parentage and new life, through our believing (3:15).

But how does rebirth or salvation take place? Jesus suggests that, like determining the coming and going of the wind, its "how" is fundamentally inexplicable (3:8). Yet like our understanding of the wind, we know that rebirth occurs and has its effects. We can experience it. The point of the dialogue with Nicodemus is not to establish the precise mechanism of rebirth but rather the fact that in changing our origin we acquire a new identity: we become new persons, children of God through the Spirit. Rebirth makes entry into the kingdom possible. However, *how* does his death facilitate our new identity? The Nicodemus drama goes on to affirm that salvation comes to earth in the person of the Son of Man who came from heaven, and what happens to Jesus—being lifted up—in some way facilitates our rebirth and eternal life (3:13–14). John shifts the discussion of rebirth to another motif.

## THE LIFTED-UP ONE (3:14; 8:28; 12:32)

For John, Jesus came into the world to save it (3:17; 4:42; 12:47). This salvation becomes effective through believing in Jesus or believing in his name (which is the same thing) (3:16, 18; 12:46–47). John's double meanings appear again. To believe in Jesus is both *believing* that he is the word of God, that what he says and claims is true, and also *receiving* him as an existential event (1:12).[10] All of this comes about because God loves the world, which the Word created and that still rejects him. He does not give up on it but sends his unique (μονογενής) Son to it to save it (1:10–12; 3:16).

How is this world-saving brought about? The Evangelist analogizes the drama that will unfold of Jesus's crucifixion with that of Moses lifting up the bronze serpent in the wilderness (3:14–15; Num 21:8–9), the first mention of being lifted up. In the Moses story, the Israelites wandering through the Sinai grumble about their traveling experience: "There is no food. There is no water. And what food we have is detestable."

---

10. Michaels writes, "While the word order suggests that it is a matter of 'believing in' the Son of man, the verb 'to believe' (*pisteuein*) is never used with *en* (the preposition for 'in') in the Gospel of John, but always with *eis* (literally 'into,' as in 1:12; 2:11, 23) or with a noun in the dative case (meaning to accept something as true, 2:22). Jesus is not speaking explicitly of 'believing in him,' therefore, but simply of 'believing' (used absolutely)" (*Gospel of John*, 199–200). However, as Bultmann notes, although believing in Jesus is believing that what he (the Word) says is true, in that "to believe the words of Jesus is materially the same as 'to believe in Jesus,'" "'[t]o believe in Him' is 'to come to Him' (5:40; 6:35, 37, 44f, 65; 7:37), 'to receive Him' (1:12; 5:43), 'to love Him' (8:42; 14:15, 21, 23f., 28; 16:27)," ("πιστεύω," 203n221, n223).

In complaining not only against Moses but against God, they sin against God. God punishes them with a plague of venomous snakes, and they, confessing their sin, plead with Moses to intercede with God to remove their punishment. In response, the LORD instructs Moses to erect a bronze snake and place it on a pole, so that whoever looks on it will be healed. The bronze snake, in some mystical and ironic fashion, facilitates their healing.[11] The icon of deceit, temptation, and death becomes their healer and life-giver.[12] Jesus too will be raised on a pole so that sinners can believe in (look on) him and have eternal life (be healed) (3:15). The Gospel story does not parallel every element of the Mosaic story (for example, those who raise Jesus's cross are not like Moses), but John draws on the story's healing or life-giving essence. In both dramas, the source of healing is raised above them. By looking on (believing in) Jesus raised up, one moves from perishing to being given life.

For the Evangelist, "being lifted up" has multiple meanings. On the one hand, to be lifted up (ὑψωθῆναι) is to be honored or glorified, exalted and set on high—as done to a king (12:13). On the other hand, the Evangelist tells us that it refers to the cruel means by which Jesus will die, a stark, ironic contrast with the first meaning of glorification (12:33).[13] In both cases, Jesus's death is in view. But how being lifted up brings about salvation or becoming children of God through rebirth, Jesus (or the Evangelist) does not tell us. What he affirms is that believing in Jesus (3:15–18) and living by the truth (3:19–21) are necessary and sufficient for eternal life. Interestingly, John does not speak of repentance or confession here or elsewhere in the Gospel.[14] Rather, he presents a gospel of unambiguous choice. If one continues in doing evil out of love for darkness, one will both fear and miss the Light and the eternal life that the Light makes possible. Only by changing so that one lives by truth (understood both propositionally and as a person) can one enter the Light and have eternal life (3:19–21). The criteria for judgment are based on accepting Jesus and the discipleship deeds that follow therefrom. Nevertheless, John here does not directly discuss how being lifted up facilitates our rebirth or healing.

What purpose lies behind being lifted up? In a later dialogue, the second of three passages or scenes concerned with being lifted up, Jesus explains that by being lifted up the Jewish leaders will know his identity ("that I am") and that he has a special

11. Keener notes that "ancient Egyptians used images of snakes as magical protection against snakebites, which also cursed the snakes" (Keener, *John*, 30).

12. Second Temple authors were understandably uncomfortable with the irony of a healing serpent, particularly since Hezekiah destroyed the allegedly preserved bronze serpent (2 Kgs 18:4) because the people named and worshiped it as a graven image (prohibited in Exod 20:4–6). The author of the Wisdom of Solomon (16:5–12) attributed the healing to God, not the serpent.

13. "John did something theologically remarkable when he collapsed this sequence [death and exaltation] into what he can speak of as a single event of Jesus's exaltation ('lifting up') or glorification" (Bauckham, *Gospel of Glory*, 73).

14. Perhaps the closest the Evangelist comes to repentance is in his quote from Isaiah 6:10, where he speaks of a turning (ἐπιστρέψωσιν) or change that those who heard Jesus could not do (12:40). Even Simon Peter is not asked to repent, only to love him (21:15–19).

relationship to the Father (8:27–29). He was sent from and experiences the presence of the Father, who never abandons him (16:32).[15] He does and speaks what his Father tells him to do and say, which pleases the Father (8:28). That he was sent from the Father, emphasized in the first part of the Gospel, cannot be separated from his returning to the Father, emphasized in the second part and part of his exaltation.[16] In effect, it shows his parentage, in which we can partake. However, being lifted up in chapter 8 has nothing *directly* to do with salvation. In fact, it has nothing directly to do with anything Jesus *does* to bring about our reconciliation with God. Rather, it functions to affirm Jesus's self-testimony of identity.[17] He is the I am; to know him is to know the Father. His identity derives from the one he came from and on whose behalf he speaks and acts. When he is lifted up, people will see that his claims about his close relation to his Father are true. Any connection with salvation comes through establishing Jesus's connection with the Father and thus his power and authority to bring about our salvation. At the same time, John indicates that Jesus's identity is critical to his saving act by noting that his affirmation of his identity leads many to "put their faith in him" (8:30), and in this way connects with the next lifted-up passage that emphasizes drawing people to him.

The third discussion of being "lifted up" occurs at the end of Jesus's public ministry (12:32–33), this time with the crowd. Here again John employs double meanings. On the one hand, the narrator informs us by an aside that "being lifted up" signifies the kind of death—crucifixion—Jesus will die. On the other hand, being lifted up is to be exalted. For Jesus, it is his promised glorification (12:23, 28)—"exaltation in humiliation, since nothing could rid crucifixion of its meaning (for all citizens and subject of Rome) as the most abject humiliation."[18] "When I am lifted up from the earth, I will draw all men to myself" (12:32). This drawing, too, is ambiguous. On the one hand, by his death he will "produce many seeds" (12:24), for many will be drawn to him. Jesus invokes an agricultural analogy, already mentioned (4:34–38), to convey his point. As grains of wheat must first die before they produce a great crop, so he too must die before he produces a great crop of believing disciples (4:36). His death is necessary for his program of creating children of God coming to fruition. However, once he dies, his bounty will be part of his glorification. "All I have is yours, and all you

15. This may hint at what occurs at his arrest and crucifixion, when all the disciples but Simon Peter and the Beloved Disciple respectively are not present, as well as the possibility of hope in God's raising him from death.

16. Loader, *Jesus*, 247–48.

17. "'Lifted up' is a curious expression, but it must point to the cross here as in other places where it occurs in this Gospel. It is not a natural expression to use for crucifixion, and no other New Testament writer uses it with this meaning. Elsewhere it always means 'to exalt.' John probably uses it to convey a double meaning. Jesus was 'lifted up' on the cross, and he was also exalted in a deeper sense, for his greatest glory consists in accepting the shame and the humiliation of the cross in order that thereby he might bring salvation to sinners. Here he is saying that the Jews will not understand who he really is before they have crucified him" (Morris, *Gospel*, 401).

18. Bauckham, *Gospel of Glory*, 73.

have is mine. And glory has come to me through them" (17:10). Jesus's glorification thus has two sources: from the Father (17:1, 5, 24) and from those given to him by the Father who believe on and accept him. Believing readers of the Gospel thus contribute to Jesus's and God's glorifications. On the other hand, the drawing of people's attention will occur when those who see him lifted high above them and look up to him recognize and are attracted, even if in horror, to the one hanging on the cross. Attached to that cross is also his identification: "Jesus of Nazareth, the King of the Jews" (19:19). The kingship noted by Nathanael, in whom there is complete integrity, is confirmed by Pilate, who has no concern for the truth but unwittingly affirms the truth in his vengeance against the Jewish leaders. Being lifted up on the cross points beyond the horrific and tragic crucifixion to his kingship.

However, what lifting up has to do with atonement, salvation, and becoming people of a new origin or parentage and why this particular method is necessary to accomplish this, is not overtly stated. A possible hint, however, exists in Jesus's use of "being lifted up" (ὑψόω) and "glorified" (δοξάζω). These two words are used in Isaiah 52:13 LXX, where the prophet says that "my servant shall prosper; he shall be exalted and lifted up and shall be very high." This leads to describing the servant as being "despised and rejected," physically marred and suffering. The cup the Father gives Jesus (18:11), which is likely the cup of suffering, echoes Isa 53:3-4. The Isaiah passage continues with several salvation motifs. A healing view is described, where this servant takes up human infirmities in his death and heals us by his wounds (Isa 53:4-5). Isaiah also presents a vicarious atonement, where in his death the servant takes on our sins and endures punishment to bring us peace (Isa 53:5-12).[19] There is reason to believe a linkage exists between Jesus's use of "lifted up" and "glorify" and Isaiah 53, since in John the third lifted up/glorification passage is followed immediately by quotations from Isaiah, including 53:1. The Evangelist also identifies the Baptizer's self-understanding as announcing the coming of the Lord, which in Isaiah reveals the glory of the LORD (1:23; Isa 40:3, 5). In linking Jesus's use of these words to the Isaiah passage, John intimates though leaves undeveloped soteriological dimensions of substitution and healing, to which we turn shortly.

John treats being lifted up not merely as a description of fact but the expression of necessity: the Son of Man *must* be lifted up (ὑψωθῆναι δεῖ, 3:14 by Jesus; 12:34, by the crowd that hears him). It echoes 3:3-7: one *must* be born again. But why the "must," the necessity? The answer is unclear. The analogy with Moses's serpent does not answer this question, for it was not necessary that healing be accomplished by creating and erecting a bronze serpent. No reason is given why God chose and commanded this specific ironic method to heal those bitten by the snakes.

19. "Sacrificial language pervades the text: 'sprinkle' (Is 52:15), 'carried' (Is 53:4), "lamb that is led to the slaughter' (Is 53:7), 'offering for sin' (Is 53:10), 'bear' (Is 53:11, 12) [See Lev 16]. The sacrificial character of the text is particularly evident with the reference to the guilt offering in Isaiah 53:10" (Schreiner, "Penal," 86).

To explain crucifixion as the necessary method for salvation, one must understand the matter of God's will. It is necessary that Jesus die in this fashion because that is what the Father willed. John lays the groundwork for God's will in the Prologue. Through receiving the Word (Logos) and believing in his name, we obtain the right to become children of God, born not of human will but of God (1:12–13). God's will makes possible the status of being God's children.[20] Jesus's role or mission, then, is to facilitate our new parentage by doing God's will through finishing his work (4:34; 6:38–39). In doing the Father's will, he seeks the pleasure of the one who sent him (5:30). The necessity, then, is not of a specific act or manner of dying on the cross but in the obedience to the Father. Jesus thus willingly goes to the cross because that is what the Father wants (18:11), not because of any logical or metaphysical necessity. It is God's chosen way to show his love for the world and bring about his kingdom (18:36; 3:16–17).

The necessity is what Michaels refers to as "divine necessity." "The impersonal verb *dei*, 'it is necessary,' points to a divine necessity (in John's Gospel alone, see 3:14, 30; 4:4, 24; 9:4; 10:16; 12:34; 20:9). Yet the necessity is not an inevitability. . . . Rather, what 'is necessary' is what God has decreed *as the means* by which a person sees or enters the kingdom of God."[21] Similarly, the claim that Jesus *must* be lifted up or crucified means that God has decreed this as the means by which salvation is achieved.

## THE LAMB OF GOD (1:29, 36)

The Evangelist uses the symbol of a lamb to point to the atoning work of Jesus. In the Gospel's opening drama, the Baptizer twice identifies Jesus in this way: "Look, the Lamb of God" (1:29, 36). The first time, the exclamation is followed by a statement of Jesus's mission or function: as God's Lamb, he is the world's sin-remover, both corporately (κόσμος or world understood broadly) and individually (3:16–18; 4:42). In the second instance, the identification leads to discipleship. Once Jesus is identified, two of the Baptizer's disciples turn and follow Jesus.[22] The appellation "lamb" gives both identity and function, as we noted in chapter 2.

The lamb was a common sacrificial animal in the Old Testament.[23] Not only were lambs offered regularly, they also were offered to atone for sin. According to Leviticus,

20. Although "will" is not used of God here, one might see in this passage God's will as parallel to the human will spoken of. Elsewhere, the Gospel refers to God's will (7:17; 9:31).

21. Michaels, *Gospel of John*, 186.

22. "[N]o such title is attested in the Hebrew Bible or early Judaism" (Michaels, *Gospel of John*, 109). However, the lamb appears twenty-eight times in the book of Revelation. The lamb was slain (Rev 5:6) but is alive with eternal life and worshiped (Rev 5:8–13). "Salvation and victory come through the blood of the Lamb and by the word of their (our brothers') testimony" (Rev 12:11). The Lamb has his disciples who follow him (Rev 14:4).

23. Redemption of the first born (Exod 13:11–13); regular offerings (Exod 29:39–41); peace offering (Lev 3:7). For other regular offerings see Num 28–29.

the community member who sinned, whether intentionally or unintentionally, was to bring a lamb to the priest to make atonement for the offerer's sin, and "he will be forgiven" (Lev 4:32–35; 5:6). Likewise, a diseased community member was to bring two lambs to be slain, one as a guilt or sin offering (Lev 14:10–20).

Because of the Evangelist's knowledge of the Old Testament, it is difficult not to interpret this symbol in light of dramatic passages like Gen 22:8, 13; Exod 12:3–11; or Isa 53:7. In Genesis, Abraham receives God's command to travel to Moriah to sacrifice his son Isaac. Abraham obeys willingly but expresses his confidence to Isaac that God will provide a lamb in place of his son. God provides a ram, which Abraham sacrifices as a substitute for Isaac. Jesus becomes the ram figure exemplifying the substitutionary sacrifice of one life for another.

In Exodus, the drama involves a lamb that is slain for the protection of the Israelites from the destroying LORD who passes through the land (Exod 12:1–13). Seeing the blood, a sign that the inhabitants of the house are protected, the LORD passes over them. Where there is no sign, he brings death. The blood obtained by the death of the lamb and painted on the doorpost with hyssop (Exod 12:22) protects the inhabitants from death and thereby gives life: "for the life of a creature is in the blood" (Lev 17:11). The Passover, where an animal was to be slain (Deut 16:2; 2 Chr 30:15), was to be celebrated annually to remember salvation from death (Exod 12:14). "The Passover lamb was the cultic and liturgical symbol of Israel's deliverance. In Judaism, the Passover lamb was not viewed as a sacrifice for sin, but the early church quickly reinterpreted Passover symbolism in light of the Eucharist (e.g., 1 Cor 5:7–8)."[24] The centrality of the exodus in Jewish thought makes the slain Passover lamb an appropriate messianic symbol for John.[25]

The Passover plays a central role in John. John indirectly refers to the paschal lamb by reference to Jesus's legs not being broken at crucifixion as fulfilling a paschal Scripture (19:32, 36; Exod 12:46), and by the lifting the hyssop plant to Jesus's lips (19:29), the hyssop being used to sprinkle blood in an atoning ritual (Exod 12:22; Lev 14:4–7, 52–56). Although John does not elsewhere directly refer to a paschal lamb, salvation from death or perishing is a Johannine theme (3:16; 8:51–52; 10:28). As we noted in chapter 9, John mentions the Passover in three occasions as a festival in connection with Jesus (2:13, 23; 6:4; 11:55; 12:1; 13:1). In one instance, Jesus tells his audience to eat his flesh, for "whoever eats my flesh and drinks my blood has eternal life" (6:53). The statement echoes Moses's command to kill the lamb "roasted over the fire, along with bitter herbs, and bread made without yeast" and put its blood on the doorframe (Exod 12:7–8). Jesus ties the flesh of his incarnation and blood of his crucifixion together to be eaten in his proto-eucharistic discourse; the bread must die (be consumed, appropriated) to give life.

24. O'Day, *Gospel of John*, 528.
25. Ninow, *Indicators*, 98.

In Isa 53, the servant is "led like a lamb to the slaughter. . . . He is cut off from the land of the living; for the sins of my people he was stricken" (Isa 53:7–8). However, death is not his end; though he is crushed, bruised, and made to suffer, and though our sins are laid on him so that "his life is a guilt offering," yet in the end, he will see his offspring: a new lineage of children he sires (Isa 53:10). "He will see the light and be satisfied," for by his action he "will justify many" (Isa 53:10–11). By bearing "the sin of many, he is made intercessor for the sinners" (Isa 53:12). It is true that the lamb features particularly in maintaining silence, while the other features apply to the servant, such as bearing away sin.[26] Yet it is easy to see John through the Baptizer making a broader analogical linkage between the lamb and the sin-bearing servant.

The crucifixion scene contains several allusions to Isaiah 52–53. Jesus is raised up (19:18; Isa 52:13); is crucified with others (19:17; Isa 53:12); speaks briefly only three times but not in protest (19:26–27, 28, 30; Isa 53:7); is pierced (19:34; Isa 53:5); voluntarily gives up his life (19:30; presaged in 10:11, 15, 17; Isa 53:12).

In the lamb motif, we have a vicarious view of salvation from death (Genesis and Exodus) and sin (Isaiah). Cross and salvation are linked. It is not a mere accident that Jesus is killed on Passover, at the very time that the Passover lamb was slain (19:14). He is the unblemished sheep (8:46; Lev 1:3; 4:32) who, as Caiaphas prophesied, "dies for the people" (11:49–50).[27] An important difference between traditional sacrifice and Jesus's sacrifice is that in the former the sin-remover was passive; Jesus is actively and willingly engaged in sin removal. John does not tell us how substitutionary atonement works in terms of "taking away" or removing (αἴρων) sin. However, neither does the Old Testament develop the mechanism of atonement as removing sin except in symbolic drama. Both the cross and the cultic sacrifice are dramas of significance, enactments of salvation, not mechanical processes.

John makes no direct mention of the sin offering. "It is characteristic of this Gospel, however, that the emphasis in the passage [6:51–54] falls not on Christ's death *for sin* but on his death for *life*."[28] The Gospel is about life, which is in the blood (Lev 17:11), and in the shedding of blood, atonement is made and life given. John reiterates this link between blood and life. To drink Jesus's blood is to have eternal life (6:53–56). It creates a new identity, a shared life, for the participants are united with Jesus and Jesus with them. Participation in the death of Jesus on the cross, in which he gives his life for the life of the world (6:51), brings life. As in the Levitical offerings, the death of one being, there an animal, here Jesus, substitutes its life for another. Yet, for life to be given, sin and death must be dealt with, which is what the Lamb vicariously does

26. Zimmermann, "Jesus," 85.

27. "By this period, Passover lambs seemed to be viewed as sacrificial (cf. Josephus, *Antiquities* 3.248, 294; 11.110; *Jewish Wars* 6.423)" (Keener, *John*, 16).

28. Beasley-Murray, *John*, 94.

(1:29; 5:24; 8:51). Believing replaces the sin of unbelieving, leading to life overcoming death (8:21–24).[29]

In short, John symbolically tells us that Jesus engages in substitutionary atonement, and although John does not give the mechanism by which this act accomplishes salvation,[30] the underlying feature is that it brings life.[31]

## THE SHEPHERD (10:1-18)

The sheep motif returns with an emphasis on the shepherd of the sheep. The discourses on the good shepherd portray Jesus laying down his life for the sheep (10:11–18). He invests in his sheep, whether in his pen or outside, so that they know him and his voice and willingly follow him (10:3–4, 14). Contrary to the hired hand who tends but does not own the sheep, the good Shepherd voluntarily risks his life for *his* sheep: "No one takes (my life) from me, but I lay it down of my own accord" (10:17). It is not a matter of necessity, but a free act of obedience that becomes a reason why the Father loves him. It is not that the Father would not have loved the Son had he not willingly died. "John does not mean that the Father loved Christ because the crucifixion took place. However, the love of the Father for the Son is a love that is eternally linked with and mutually dependent upon the Son's complete alignment with the Father's will and his obedience even unto death."[32] Jesus does not seek to escape his death but willingly absorbs it as part of his mission (12:27–28).

Vicarious death is a central theme of the Gospel; Jesus dies for his friends out of love[33] (15:13), for the nation (11:50; 18:14), for those present and scattered (11:49–51), and for the world (3:16–17; 6:51). John makes other suggestions of vicariousness: in the garden Jesus offers himself for the freedom of his disciples (18:8–9); his life is exchanged for that of Barabbas (18:39–40).[34] Pilate is even rescued from his persistent antagonists by giving up "the man" (19:5).

Although 10:11–18 contains no explicit statement of an *atoning* death for sin on behalf of (ὑπέρ) others, vicariousness here can be understood as atonement. We must see the shepherd motif in light of the entire Gospel presentation, where death results from the sin of unbelieving (5:24; 8:51) while becoming children of God and having

29. The sacrifice for sin is not only found in 1:29, it is specifically reaffirmed in the Johannine literature (1 John 2:2; 4:10—αὐτὸς ἱλασμός ἐστιν περὶ τῶν ἁμαρτιῶν ἡμῶν) and in Paul (Rom 5:25).

30. "John's Gospel never articulates a real *doctrine* of atonement. In very general terms, we find recorded here the 'benefits of his passion,' but without specifying *how* Jesus's death 'gives life to the world' or *on what basis* he 'takes away sin'" (Michaels, "Atonement," 109).

31. Dennis, "Jesus's Death," 341; "John may not emphasize this explanation [about expiation and propitiation for us], but he can barely have failed to realize his readers were likely to assume it" (Turner, "Atonement," 122).

32. Barrett, *Gospel*, 377.

33. Bauckham, *Gospel of Glory*, 64–71.

34. Frey, *Glory*, 192.

eternal life grow from believing (1:12; 6:27–29, 40; 3:16; 10:27–28) and where the shepherd of the sheep motif links to the motif of the Lamb addressing sin (1:29). In short, the shepherd narratives must be seen in light of the entire Gospel characterization of Jesus's role in bringing salvation and life.

## DEFEATER OF THE ENEMY (12:31; 16:11)

The "dying on behalf of" (ὑπέρ) motif may have another interpretation.[35] Unlike hired shepherds who flee in the face of mortal danger, Jesus voluntarily dies defending the sheep (10:12–13). Interpreted this way, Jesus's death is a deadly battle with the enemy, the thieves and wolves, who threaten the flock. Vicarious death is in view in John 10, but not a death where the one killed carries away the sin of others. Rather, it is a sacrifice given by one who, like soldiers, dies defending others from the enemy.[36] The passage hints at a view of soteriology where in the context of being lifted up Jesus dies battling spiritual forces. The devil comes (14:30) but will be judged, condemned (16:11), and driven out (12:31).

Jesus says, "Take heart! I have overcome the world" (16:33). The world is under the influence of the devil, who is a murderer and father of lies (8:44) and who prompted Judas Iscariot to betray Jesus (13:2, 27). John sees the devil behind Jesus's death. By killing and thus eliminating Jesus, the evil one contemplated attaining victory. However, the crucifixion is not the end of the narrative; God has the last word by raising Jesus from the dead. The prince of the world is driven out (12:31), Judas disappears unheralded from the scene, and the Shepherd continues his mission via his proxies (21:15–17). Salvation frees us from the power of the devil to adopt the truth (with its double meaning of propositional truth and truth found in a person) that sets one free from sin (8:24, 32–34). The emphasis on truth at Jesus's trial speaks to this: truth conquers lies, betrayal, murder, and death.

In conquering the devil, John extends his soteriological themes to the conquest of sin. Jews are slaves of sin (8:34) and by extension slaves to the devil, whose desire is that they sin and not believe the Truth (8:44–47). Thus, Jews who owe their parentage to the devil, stand in opposition to Jesus, who not only traces his parentage to the Father whom he seeks to obey, but provides a new parentage for those who believe in and love him.

But how, one might ask, do Jesus's death and resurrection win the cosmic battle and subject the evil powers?[37] Part of the answer is that although Jesus died, his resurrection reveals that the devil "has no hold on" him (14:30). His death and

35. The application of this interpretation of ὑπέρ in 6:51, 11:50–52, and 15:13 would be more strained.

36. Michaels, "Atonement," 112.

37. "The cosmic significance of Christ's work is ontologically more fundamental than its soteriological significance" (Boyd, "Christus Victor," 33).

resurrection foretoken our own victory over the evil power and his works by our sharing in Jesus's victory and resurrection. "Because I live, you also will live. . . . I am in my Father, and you are in me, and I am in you" (14:19–20). Again, salvation for John addresses the theme of giving life (11:25–26).

## THE HEALER (4:46–54; 5:1–15; 9; 11)

From John's analogy of the lifting up of Jesus with Moses's raising the bronze serpent so that those who gaze on it are healed (3:14; Num 21:8–9), we glimpse salvation as healing, a view generally overlooked in formal treatments of salvation and atonement. Sickness and sin are connected in the Old Testament.[38] The psalmist writes, "Have mercy on me, LORD; heal me, for I have sinned against you" (Ps 41:4). Sin begets suffering, though not all suffering results from sin, as the book of Job makes clear. The Levitical laws did not require a sin offering for every illness, only for those that were prolonged or possibly contagious.[39] However, this connection continues into the New Testament worldview (5:14; 9:1–2; Jas 5:13–16).

Themes from Isa 52–53 again come into view. In being lifted up (12:32; Isa 52:13), Jesus takes on "our infirmities and carries our sorrows," to the extent that "we consider him stricken by God, smitten by him and afflicted. . . . By his wounds we are healed" (Isa 53:4–5; 19:1–3, 34). Isaiah's diagnosis is that we are without well-being, for we are a sinful people (Isa 1:2–4).

Sickness describes not only our spiritual condition but our physical, economic, political, social, and environmental conditions. In his dramatic stories, John gives a litany of persons lacking well-being: a wedding host, temple merchants, an ostracized woman, an official's son, an invalid, hungry listeners, terrified disciples, a blind man and blind Pharisees, Lazarus, betraying Judas, impetuously denying Peter, searching Mary, and doubting Thomas. The biblical view is that restoration is needed—of individuals, the people (Isa 10:21), their land (2 Chr 7:14; Joel 2:25), their institutions (Hos 6:6–7)—for their spiritual and physical health (Ps 41:3–4, 8). The sufficient condition is to turn to God who restores—"I am the LORD, your Healer" (Exod 15:26). When the LORD comes, "No one living in Zion will say, 'I am ill'; and the sins of those who dwell there will be forgiven" (Isa 33:24).

John develops the link between sickness, healing, and salvation in four healing stories. In the drama of Jesus and the official with the dying son, Jesus proclaims, "Your son lives" (4:50). John repeats the phrase two other times for a total of three (three being symbolic of completion). Here John bonds his central themes of believing, life, and salvation (3:16–17) with healing; Jesus gives life to the son through the official's believing response to Jesus's promise.

---

38. Brown, *Israel's Divine Healer*.

39. Anderson and Culbertson, "Inadequacy," 308–9.

In the second healing story (5:1–15), Jesus comes to a porticoed healing pool (probably an asclepion)[40] located near the temple, where he encounters a man paralyzed for thirty-eight years. Jesus asks the invalid if he wants to be made well or whole (ὑγιής), a term not ordinarily used for healing but whose double meaning manifests a typical Johannine play on words.[41] The invalid, understanding the question from the below-perspective of human experience, affirms his desire to become physically well. Jesus offers this and more: wholeness as salvation seen from above, for when the former paralytic returns, Jesus commands him to sin no more (5:14). Salvation as healing from sin restores to wholeness, but it requires persistent attention to prevent the sin that attacked the wholeness from returning (8:11).

The third healing story also conjoins healing with sin (9:1–3). On the one hand, the disciples initiate the discussion by asking whose sin precipitated the man's blindness, and the Pharisees accuse the formerly blind man of being conceived in sin (9:34). On the other hand, as the story goes from scene to scene, the Pharisees and people ponder whether the healer of the blind man is the sinner, since he healed on the Sabbath (9:16, 24–25, 31). Despite Jesus rejecting the view that his sin caused his blindness,[42] the relation between the two lies in the background. In the end, from the heavenly perspective, believing leads to sight and worship; disbelieving to spiritual blindness (9:40–41). The story finishes with Jesus doing God's work, the sin of unbelieving, and the possibility and actuality of healing.

In the final healing story, the disciples inquire whether Lazarus will be healed or saved (σωθήσεται), whether from the illness or from death is unclear (11:6, 11). The double meaning of from below and from above is again evident. Jesus, who is the resurrection and the life (11:25–26), brings physical and salvific life out of death.

Two other passages may allude to salvation by healing. In 13:10 the source of purification (καθαρός) is not given; in 15:3 purification comes through Jesus's word. In neither case does John make clear from what we are cleansed, although he gives its purpose as bearing fruit in 15:3. This same word (καθαρίζω) is used by Matthew to refer to the healing or purification/cleansing of lepers (Matt 8:2; 10:8; 11:5), whose unclean, diseased status prevents them from participating in religious rituals. Given John's penchant for double meaning, it is very possible that from the perspective-from-above, salvation as healing/purification/cleansing is in view in these verses.

---

40. An asclepion was a healing temple dedicated to Asclepius, the god of healing. The pool in Jerusalem had four covered porticos around the sides and one dividing the pool in two. The infirm, who at times were housed there, were encouraged to dream as receiving a visit from the god. The dream contents were interpreted by temple priests who prescribed a cure regimen that included cleansing baths. Jesus brought a different kind of faith healing, requiring an immediate response to his command.

41. Thomas, "Healing," 27.

42. Rightly so, since no longer were the sins of parents to be visited on their children (Ezek 18:4, 20), and for the blind man to have sinned required him to preexist, which was a Greek notion.

In the OT, although sickness was connected with sin, the Levitical system was not designed to provide healing for persons with infectious diseases (Lev 13–14), and the priests were not healers but rather certifiers that healing had occurred. When certified as healed, the ill were to return to the community with a burnt and a sin or guilt offering, which the priest used to atone for the sin related to their disease. The offering involved bodily washing and sprinkling with blood, which symbolically and ceremonially purified the impure person (Lev 14:7–8, 14). Thus, it is symbolic that on the cross, when Jesus was pierced, blood and water, both symbols of purification, flow from his body (19:34).

John does not theorize about salvation as healing. Rather, through careful construction of his four dramatic healing narratives he shows how Jesus's saving action brings healing, physical and spiritual. "His initiative to heal, restore, and give life dominates the narrative."[43] Although John speaks of healing in connection with the lifted-up motif, John leaves unclear how healing relates to Jesus's crucifixion. Ironically, in the Lazarus account John hints by Jesus weeping that the giver of life will himself need the Father's resurrection healing (11:35).

## A SALVATION DRAMA

As Alan Culpepper notes, it is important, in considering soteriology in the Gospel of John, that we don't import traditional or contemporary theories of salvation into the text. "Reading ancient texts faithfully, while reading with contemporary issues and sensitivities in mind, is always tricky. . . . The Gospel of John . . . is subtle and paradoxical, presenting differing perspectives without reconciling them."[44] Although the Evangelist does not directly exposit a theory of salvation, hints of what later theologians treat as soteriological theories run through the Gospel as the drama develops from seeing the Lamb to the Lamb's death. As the apostle Paul does not shy away from mixing soteriological motifs (Rom 5:9–11), so John dramatizes diverse ways of understanding salvation.

From statements about the Lamb of God, we glimpse salvation as vicarious substitution. "[T]he animal victim is a substitute for the worshipper, makes atonement for him, and thereby restores him to favour with God."[45] The lamb is sacrificed on our behalf for the removal of our sins, its death for our death, giving us life. Our sins are transferred in some way to the sacrificed animal and taken away. John also sees that salvation has a conquest dimension. The world, the place of lies, darkness, and death, is overcome (16:33). Although in one sense, on the cross (being lifted up) the battle is finished (12:31–32), in another sense it has just begun. It becomes the ongoing work of the Spirit to expose that the devil is condemned (16:11). The Gospel of John

43. Thompson, "Christus Victor," 10. I discuss the healing view in Reichenbach, "Healing."
44. Culpepper, "Inclusivism," 85.
45. Wenham, "Theology," 84.

portrays Jesus as a divine healer. Jesus takes on himself our sin and the sickness of the world and bears it, suffering, to the cross to bring about healing (1 Pet 2:24).

Although John does not reconcile these salvation motifs, what holds them all together is John's central concept of life. Salvation is giving life (3:16); it overcomes death (perishing) and the one who occasions death and resists the truth (8:44). Since sin is the sickness unto death, only (3:14; 12:34) by Jesus being lifted up (both crucified [12:32–33] and resurrected [10:17–18]) and by the world's believing in him can the sickness be removed and life (both qualitative and quantitative) restored (3:14–15).

However, how this is accomplished through Jesus's death John leaves unsaid. Thus, in the end we must move from theory and return to the dramatic narrative itself, which conveys John's testimonial argument for his thesis about Jesus's messianic mission. The story of the cross is the climax of Jesus's victory over sin, sickness, and the devil. In this John gives us not so much a theology as a drama of salvation. Through symbol, metaphor, and story, he affirms that we attain a new parentage, not from earthly parents but from above. God is our father, not the devil, and we carry out God's desires (8:44). In rebirth, we do not reenter the natural order, but by our believing in and receiving Jesus as the Messiah, the Son of God, we are united with Jesus in life and death, and thereby gain new parentage through a new origin from above, a new identity as children of God, abundant life, and a new mission of obedient discipleship (21:19, 22).

## QUESTIONS FOR REFLECTION AND DISCUSSION

1. Explain how John understands salvation as a new parentage. What texts in John support this idea? Does this give a new meaning to God as our Father?

2. If all who are saved have new parentage, what are the implications of this for treating Jesus as our brother, as John does in 20:17, and all believers as sisters and brothers?

3. John views Jesus as the Lamb of God, and lambs were part of ritual sacrifice. How do you understand this view of salvation in a society and culture where we do not practice animal sacrifice? In what ways is sacrifice still a relevant, contemporary concept with significant meaning for us?

4. How do the crucifixion and resurrection of Jesus show that the enemy is defeated? In what sense is the defeat of the enemy temporal and in what sense is it completed?

5. If salvation is understood as healing, what are the implications of this for our view of illness, healing, and the medical profession?

6. How do you theoretically or practically connect Jesus's death and resurrection with your salvation?

7. Salvation can be understood as salvation from and salvation to. Do you find these themes in John, and if so, how does John develop them? What are the implications of these themes for your own life and salvation?

CHAPTER TWELVE

# Concluding Thoughts

WE HAVE LOOKED AT the Fourth Gospel through the lenses of eleven "books." Of course, the Fourth Gospel is only one book, but its riches dazzle when reviewed and analyzed thematically. We might liken our experience to diving deeply into an old, preserved treasure ship, searching for and retrieving a gem from its cargo, and returning to the surface. Holding it to the light, its beauty shines when viewed from one perspective, but its fullness blazes when seen from multiple angles. Its beauty and value come alive in the light. Likewise with the Fourth Gospel, where Jesus who is the Life comes alive as Light for those he encounters. Each theme we considered adds a new and diverse perspective to the arguments that advance the Evangelist's goal of revealing Jesus's identity and mission and function to bring about believing leading to eternal life.

The Evangelist realizes that none of the jeweled facets is sufficient in and of itself to convey the Word to us, let alone to convince us. The signs can be ignored, explained away, or deflected by other concerns, as the Pharisees did by focusing not on the sign of restored sight and its *signi*ficance but on Jesus's apparent breaking of the Law by healing on a Sabbath. The testimonies of those who encountered Jesus can be rejected, as the Pharisees rejected the testimony of the formerly blind man to his healing or Thomas rejected the testimony of the other disciples to Jesus's resurrection. The testimonial claims of Jesus himself can be brushed aside as products of self-aggrandizement or self-delusion; anyone can make baseless claims about themselves without confirmation or attending witnesses, the Pharisees argued. As the Pharisees contended, testimony needs complementary affirmation. Or Jesus's eccentric, self-testimonial claims can be rejected because they are so radical and contrary to a person's worldview that they are difficult if not impossible to believe; after all, how could the eternal God become incarnate as a human being. As the Jewish leaders maintained, for a human to claim identity with God is not only outrageous, it is blasphemous. One can also be suspicious of someone who claims to be sent from and returning to God, who predicts being lifted up and ultimately being raised up. Someone making these claims must either be crazy or completely misunderstood.

Furthermore, the symbols Jesus uses in his dialogues and discourses exude ambiguity; earthly realities are insufficient to fully represent and help us comprehend deeper heavenly realities. Even if they could so function, those who listen to Jesus's use of ambiguous language often are more confused than convinced by the double meanings, irony, riddles, and symbols. What does it matter, one might argue, that Jesus can cleverly create riddles, outwit the Pharisees, or claim time as his own? What does it matter, one might argue, that the author can wrap events and lists up into symbolic sevens or create character-evoking dialogues? It simply makes Jesus a clever arguer or the Evangelist a clever author or editor. How does the ability to construct triadic, chiastic discourses demonstrate that Jesus's identity is from above and not from Galilee?

The Evangelist knows all this and takes it into account in his elaborate defense. It is evident that John constructed a careful defense of his thesis about Jesus's identity and mission. One piece of evidence showing that John is aware of potential pitfalls in his project is that he marshals all these facets or dimensions to construct a case to bring about believing. He does not place all his faith in the convincing power of one aspect of his account or argument. Like any good courtroom lawyer, he persuades not by invoking one piece of evidence but by the weight and unified message of the totality of claims. We are to look at the whole picture John presents, not just at each individual book of the eleven. Furthermore, the Evangelist shows us both the successes and failures of Jesus's ministry. He points to the few whom Jesus persuades and to the many who either remain unpersuaded or who once were persuaded but could not sustain their apparently tenuous believing and wandered off, or, like Judas and Simon Peter, at some point overtly rejected their commitment to their Lord. John is a realist: Jesus, he reports, did not trust himself to those who believed simply based on signs, for he knew that the hearts and minds of people are easily swayed by the amazement and wonder of the moment (2:24). Some of those who hailed Jesus at the beginning of Passover week as he entered Jerusalem could well have been those who demanded crucifixion early on Passover Friday.

Yet, the Evangelist is a person of hope, for when he wrote, the church had already been planted. Granted, struggles loomed, as the Johannine Epistles unabashedly inform us. However, he has an opportunity to contribute to the growth and success of the church through presenting Jesus and his mission through irony, symbols, signs, testimony, self-identification claims, character studies of those who believed, and effective dialogues and discourses. Each of the facets of the jewel tells a story and may catch the eyes of the readers, the ears of the hearers, and the minds of those who attend to the reasoning, ultimately leading to further believing.

For the open-minded, the Gospel is mysterious, even magical, both dark and light, shallow and deep. Nothing is straightforward, but twists and turns, giving levels of meanings, where subtle messages abound to tease the curious mind and challenge

the struggling spirit. The Word reveals the hidden God without losing God's myste-
riousness and transcendence. God's creative speech, the Word, provides the key to
understanding God, for God himself exists, purposes, creates, promises, covenants,
and acts in and through his word. The word spoken to and through the prophets, the
word of judgment and love, of grace and truth, becomes real in flesh and bone in the
Gospel of John. God's persistent love for his own as his children is deepened, for even
though they have repeatedly rejected him and his pleas, God returns and tries again to
establish the covenant, even to the extent not only of sending his Word in the flesh, but
sending him to the cross in his own time. In the very beginning of his Gospel, John
takes us from creation to the anticipated sacrifice of the Lamb. From the Prologue that
sets forth creation and incarnation, the book marches inexorably in time and structure to the death and resurrection of the Son. The very theology of this sequence is put
not in Jesus's mouth but in that of his enemy: "one man must die for the people, and
not only for the nation but also for the whole world, to bring them together and make
them one" (11:50–53). The salvation event reveals not the condemnation or death of
persons or the nation but the deep love of God for the world (3:16–17). This entering
Word of light shatters the darkness of the cosmos, opens blind eyes and blinds others.
Ultimately, he births new children, parented not of ancient lineage or of human will,
but of God.

The revealer of God is as mysterious as the God he reveals. Jesus is an enigma,
for how could the eternal come in time? How could the creator of light and life find
his way into darkness and death? How could spirit become mortal flesh? How could
the Son of Man be God? The divine Word is itself ambiguous, speaking with double
meanings that instead of creating clarity elicit misunderstanding, accusations, anger,
and in the end deadly violence. Jesus speaks his own language that, on the one hand,
sounds very much like our language, but really can be understood only from above,
and even then, not without ambiguity, irony, and confusion. The audience itself must
change its perspective to grasp his message; it must, like Mary Magdalene, turn to
grasp, only perhaps to let go. It comes encapsulated in a language with secret, special,
multiple meanings that must be penetrated to exploit its richness and overcome its
offensiveness. "They are hard sayings; who can accept them?" (6:60). Jesus is not soft
but sharp-edged, defiant, combative, and at times judgmental. He can speak about
love to his followers, encouraging them to love each other as the Father loves him and
he loves them, while bluntly accusing his adversaries of coming from the devil whose
deeds and deceits they emulate. He is no humble babe; children are absent from the
Gospel's adult world of identity and mission conflict. He is who he is: take him or leave
him. Pursue him to slay or to pray.

Yet, unless his words and message are heard, penetrated, and imbibed into one's
very bones, flesh, and spirit, what is portended is only death, not merely eternal death,
but the death of a meaningless existence here and now. For only in Jesus do we have
the way out of death to life, out of darkness to light; only in him is there living water

in the human desert of wandering existence, bread of life in our spiritual famine, truth amid a sea of lies and falsity, light to shine on dangers and for direction on the dark path, a door to open abundant possibilities that appeared dead ends, a reliable shepherd among pretenders and soul thieves, a vine to sustain and nourish us branches, a resurrector to lead us to fuller life. Understanding the significance of Jesus, his mission, and his claims, we can only affirm with Simon Peter: "Lord, to whom else can we go? You alone have the words of eternal life" (6:68).

The Gospel never forthrightly responds to many of the difficult questions we raised in this book of books. Yet ultimately the Evangelist responds in his own way, for the answers are to be found in our very encounter with Jesus. Testimony, signs, symbols, ambiguous answers, dialogues and discourses, numbers, all have their place. However, when all are stripped away, what brings about believing and becoming God's children is the personal encounter with Jesus. Not argument, not ambiguity or cleverness, not long sermons, and not miracles, but Jesus himself. Nicodemus eventually comes to faith because he meets the rabbi; the Samaritan woman and her townspeople become believers when they come out to meet, hear, and spend time with Jesus. The royal official believes when he encounters the healer who restores his son. The blind man is lost in darkness until Jesus comes and not only heals his infirmity but reveals to him who this healer truly is; with that revelation true worship begins. Despite their affirmation that Jesus is the Messiah, Martha and Mary are without hope until Jesus comes to them. The very presence of Jesus changes the attitudes of the Jews when they see for themselves how much he loves his friend Lazarus. Thomas comes to faith when he fingers the wounds of the Jesus with whom he lived for many years. Touching radically alters the perspective of this skeptic whose worldview could not encompass the idea of resurrection from the dead. Mary Magdalene is restored to hope when she turns, sees, and embraces her Lord. Simon Peter jumps out of the boat and hurries to shore when he realizes Jesus has come to them on the beach. Meeting Jesus is what changes people. For John, it is the unforgettable relationships that people have with Jesus that now define the character and persons of those to whom Jesus reaches out. The good Shepherd knows us by name and leads us out to his abundant, life-giving pastures, even willingly dying along the way to defend and free his flock.

But how can we touch and be touched by Jesus who lived two thousand years ago? That is, ultimately, the point of the Fourth Gospel. Having been with him, grazing through the green but rocky pastures of this Gospel, we recognize the Shepherd's voice. "Because you have seen me, you have believed; blessed are those who have not seen and yet have believed," Jesus says to Thomas, and John says to his audience (20:27). The purpose of this Gospel is to encounter God through encountering Jesus, for we are who we are because we experience him. Thus, we return to the Evangelist's mission: to reveal to us the identity of Jesus. Who is this wandering, wise, provocative, frustrating, confrontational, cold, caring, puzzling teacher from Galilee, who willfully refuses in the end to defend himself and be rescued from a painful, humiliating crucifixion? John's answer is that he is the one sent from and by God to demonstrate God's sacrificial saving and healing love for us by voluntarily dying on the cross. Only as we encounter and obediently hear Jesus through the Gospel can Jesus have meaning and significance for us. Only by penetrating the testimonies, signs, symbols, ambiguity, dialogues, and discourses, and only by moving through and beyond them to meet Jesus himself, can we inculcate believing and the eternal life it brings. The Evangelist's narrative devices are not ends in themselves but *signifiers* of Jesus's identity and function or mission. They do more than point; they reveal the living Savior, sent by the Father, who continues to be testified to by this Gospel and the Spirit who brings all into our remembrance. The argument of the Gospel, in effect, boils down to the person of the Gospel: encountered, heard, queried, killed, raised, and believed in.

My hope is that by diving into and penetrating in new and insightful ways the Gospel of John, by engaging, even swimming, with John in his arguments and insights, you will encounter afresh Jesus, the creating and revealing Word, the Resurrection and the Life, the Bread and the Water, the Light and the Way, the Wine and the Vine, the Lamb and the Shepherd, paradoxically the Son of Man and Son of God, and in doing so will have found or renewed your faith. The Evangelist writes with a mission and invites his audience to participate in it. If this happens for you, if you truly experience Jesus, believe, and come alive in him and his love, your perspective will change and John's Gospel and this book about it will have been successful.

## QUESTIONS FOR REFLECTION AND DISCUSSION

1. How has this book changed your view of the Gospel of John?

2. What three things that are meaningful for your life are you taking away from this book?

3. The author of the Gospel links believing with life. How has believing in Jesus as the Messiah given you life?

# Bibliography

Abrams, M. H. *A Glossary of Literary Terms*, 3rd ed. New York: Holt, Rinehart & Winston, 1921.

Akala, Adesola Joan. *The Son-Father Relationship and Christological Symbolism in the Gospel of John*. Library of New Testament Studies 505. London: Bloomsbury, 2014.

Allen, Garrick V., et al. *Son of God: Divine Sonship in Jewish and Christian Antiquity*. University Park, PA: Eisenbrauns, 2019.

Anderson, Megory, and Philip Culbertson. "The Inadequacy of the Christian Doctrine of Atonement in Light of Levitical Sin Offering." *Anglican Theological Review* 68 (1986) 303–28.

Anderson, Paul N. "From One Dialogue to Another: Johannine Polyvalence from Origins to Receptions." In *Anatomies of Narrative Criticism: The Past, Present, and Futures of the Fourth Gospel as Literature*, edited by Tom Thatcher et al., 93–119. Resources for Biblical Study 55. Atlanta: Society of Biblical Literature, 2008.

———. "Philip: A Connective Figure in Polyvalent Perspective." In *Character Studies in the Fourth Gospel: Narrative Approaches to Seventy Figures in John*, edited by Steven Hunt et al., 168–88. 2013. Reprint, Grand Rapids: Eerdmans, 2016.

———. *The Riddles of the Fourth Gospel: An Introduction to John*. Minneapolis: Fortress, 2011.

———. "Why the Gospel of John is Fundamental to Jesus Research." In *Jesus Research: The Gospel of John in Historical Inquiry*, edited by James H. Charlesworth et al., 7–46. Jewish and Christian Texts. London: T. & T. Clark, 2019.

Anderson, Paul N., et al. *John, Jesus, and History*, Vol. 2: *Aspects of Historicity in the Fourth Gospel*. Society of Biblical Literature Symposium Series 44. Atlanta: Society of Biblical Literature, 2009.

Arndt, W. F., and F. W. Gingrich. *A Greek-English Lexicon of the New Testament and Other Early Christian Literature*. Chicago: University of Chicago Pres, 1957.

Asiedu-Peprah, Martin. *Johannine Sabbath Conflicts as Juridical Controversy*. Tübingen: Mohr Siebeck, 2001.

Augustine. *The City of God*. In *Basic Writings of Saint Augustine*, edited by Whitney J. Oates, 2:2–661. Grand Rapids: Baker, 1948.

———. "Homilies on the Gospel of John." In *Nicene and Post-Nicene Fathers* 7, edited by Philip Schaff, 1–452. Grand Rapids: Eerdmans, 1997.

Bacher, Wilhelm, and Max Landsberg. "Night." In *Jewish Encyclopedia*, 9:303–4. New York: Funk & Wagnalls, 1904.

Barclay, William. *Gospel of John*. 2 vols. Rev. ed. Daily Study Bible. Philadelphia: Westminster, 1975.

Barrett, Charles K. *Essays on John*. Philadelphia: Westminster, 1982.

———. *The Gospel According to St. John*. London: SPCK, 1955.

Bauckham, Richard. *Gospel of Glory: Major Themes in Johannine Thought*. Grand Rapids: Baker, 2015.

———. *Jesus and the Eyewitnesses: The Gospels as Eyewitness Testimony*, 2nd ed. Grand Rapids: Eerdmans, 2017.

———. *The Testimony of the Beloved Disciple: Narrative, History, and Theology in the Gospel of John*. Grand Rapids: Baker, 2007.

Bauer, Walter. "οὖν." In *A Greek-English Lexicon of the New Testament and Other Christian Literature*, 597. Translated by William F. Arndt and F. Wilbur Gingerich. Chicago: University of Chicago Press, 1957.

Beasley-Murray, George R. *John*. 2nd ed. Word Biblical Commentary 36. Dallas: Word, 2002.

Beilby, James, and Paul R. Eddy, eds. *The Nature of the Atonement: Four Views*. Downers Grove, IL: InterVarsity, 2006.

Bekken, Per Jarle. *The Lawsuit Motif in John's Gospel from New Perspectives: Jesus Christ, Crucified Criminal and Emperor of the World*. Novum Testamentum Supplements 158. Leiden: Brill, 2014.

Bennema, Cornelis. *Encountering Jesus: Character Studies in the Gospel of John*. Peabody, MA: Paternoster, 2009.

———. "Judas (the Betrayer): The Black Sheep of the Family." In *Character Studies in the Fourth Gospel: Narrative Approaches to Seventy Figures in John*, edited by Steven Hunt et al., 360–72. 2013. Reprint, Grand Rapids: Eerdmans, 2016.

Bernard, John Henry. *A Critical and Exegetical Commentary on the Gospel according to John*, 2 vols. International Critical Commentary. Edinburgh: T. & T. Clark, 1928.

Beutler, Johannes. *A Commentary on the Gospel of John*. Grand Rapids: Eerdmans, 2017.

Beutler, Johannes, and Robert Fortna, eds. *The Shepherd Discourse of John 10 and Its Context*. Cambridge: Cambridge University Press, 1991.

Birch, Bruce C. "Number." In *The International Standard Bible Encyclopedia*, 3:556–61. Grand Rapids: Eerdmans, 1986.

Black, David Alan. "Introduction." In *Linguistics and New Testament Interpretation*, edited by David Alan Black et al., 10–13. Nashville: Broadman, 1992.

Black, David Alan, et al., eds. *Linguistics and New Testament Interpretation*. Nashville: Broadman, 1992.

Blaine, Bradford B., Jr. *Peter in the Gospel of John: The Making of an Authentic Disciple*. Academia Biblica 27. Atlanta: Society of Biblical Literature, 2007.

Boda, Mark. *Haggai, Zechariah*. NIV Application Commentary. Grand Rapids: Zondervan, 2004.

Boismard, Marie E. "L'Evangile a Quatre Dimensions." *Lumiere et Vie* 1 (1951) 94–114.

Boring, M. Eugene. *Hearing John's Voice: Insights for Teaching and Preaching*. Grand Rapids: Eerdmans, 2019.

Borchert, Gerald L. *John 1–11* and *12–21*. New American Commentary 25A and B. Nashville: Broadman & Holman, 1996.

Bourgel, Jonathan. "John 4:4–42: Defining a Modus Vivendi between Jews and the Samaritans." *Journal for Theological Studies* ns 69 (2018) 39–65.

Bovon, François. "Names and Numbers in Early Christianity." *New Testament Studies* 47 (2001) 267–88.

Boyd, Gregory A. "Christus Victor View." In *The Nature of the Atonement: Four Views*, edited by James Beilby et al., 23–49. Downers Grove, IL: InterVarsity, 2006.

Brant, Jo-Ann A. *Dialogue and Drama: Elements of Greek Tragedy in the Fourth Gospel*. Peabody, MA: Hendrickson, 2004.

Breck, John. *The Shape of Biblical Language*. Crestwood, NY: St. Vladimir's Seminary Press, 1994.

Brinton, Laurel J. "Historical Discourse Analysis." In *The Handbook of Discourse Analysis*, edited by Deborah Tannen et al., 138–60. Hoboken, NJ: Wiley, 2015.

Brockmuehl, Markus N. A., and James Carleton Paget, eds. *Redemptions and Resistance: The Messianic Hopes of Jews and Christians in Antiquity*. Edinburgh: T. & T. Clark, 2007.

Brown, Jannine K. "Creation's Renewal in the Gospel of John." *Catholic Biblical Quarterly* 92 (2010) 275–90.

Brown, Michael L. *Israel's Divine Healer*. Grand Rapids: Zondervan, 1995.

Brown, Raymond E. *The Death of the Messiah: From Gethsemane to the Grave*. 2 vols. Garden City, NY: Doubleday, 1994.

———. *The Gospel According to John I–XII*. Anchor Bible. Garden City, NY: Doubleday, 1966.

———. *The Gospel According to John XIII–XXI*. Anchor Bible. Garden City, NY: Doubleday, 1970.

———. *An Introduction to the Gospel of John*. New York: Doubleday, 2003.

———. "Roles of Women in the Fourth Gospel." *Theological Studies* 36 (1975) 688–99.

Bruner, Frederick D. *The Gospel of John: A Commentary*. Grand Rapids: Eerdmans, 2011.

Bruns, J. Edgar. "The Use of Time in the Fourth Gospel." *New Testament Studies* 13 (1966–1967) 285–90.

Bultmann, Rudolf. *The Gospel of John: A Commentary*. Translated by G. R. Beasley-Murray et al. 1971. Reprint, Johannine Monograph Series. Eugene, OR: Wipf & Stock, 2014.

———. "The History of Religions Background of the Prologue to the Gospel of John." In *The Interpretation of John*, edited by J. A. Ashton, 18–35. Philadelphia: Fortress, 1986.

———. *Theology of the New Testament*. 2 vols. Translated by Kendrick Grobel. New York: Scribners, 1951.

———. "ἀλήθεια, ἀληθής, κτλ." In *Theological Dictionary of the New Testament*, edited by Gerhard Kittel and Gerhard Friedrich, translated by Geoffrey W. Bromiley, 1:232–51. Grand Rapids: Eerdmans, 1964.

———. "ἀφίημι, ἄφεσις, κτλ." *Theological Dictionary of the New Testament*, edited by Gerhard Kittel and Gerhard Friedrich, translated by Geoffrey W. Bromiley, 1:509–12. Grand Rapids: Eerdmans, 1964.

———. "ζάω, ζωή, κτλ." *Theological Dictionary of the New Testament*, edited by Gerhard Kittel and Gerhard Friedrich, translated by Geoffrey W. Bromiley, 2:832–72. Grand Rapids: Eerdmans, 1964.

———. "πιστεύω, πιστός, κτλ." *Theological Dictionary of the New Testament*, edited by Gerhard Kittel and Gerhard Friedrich, translated by Geoffrey W. Bromiley, 6:174–228. Grand Rapids: Eerdmans, 1968.

Burridge, Richard A. *What Are the Gospels? A Comparison with Graeco-Roman Biography*. 2nd ed. Grand Rapids: Eerdmans, 2004.

Carmichael, Calum M. *The Story of Creation: Its Origin and Its Interpretation in Philo and the Fourth Gospel*. Ithaca, NY: Cornell University Press, 1996.

Carson, Donald A. "Understanding Misunderstandings in the Fourth Gospel." *Tyndale Bulletin* 33 (1982) 61–91.

Carter, Warren. *John: Storyteller, Interpreter, Evangelist*. Peabody, MA: Hendrickson, 2006.

———.*Pontius Pilate: Portrait of a Roman Governor*. Interfaces. Collegeville, MN: Liturgical, 2003.

Charlesworth, James H., ed. *The Messiah: Developments in Earliest Judaism and Christianity*. Minneapolis: Fortress, 1992.

Chevalier, Jean, and A. Gheerbrant. *Dictionary of Symbols*. Translated by John Buchanan-Brown. Oxford: Blackwell, 1994.

Childs, Brevard S. *The New Testament as Canon: An Introduction*. Philadelphia: Fortress, 1984.

Christensen, David. "Atonement in John: The Death of Jesus in Light of Exodus Typology." MA thesis, The Southern Baptist Theological Seminary, 2017. https://repository.sbts.edu/handle/10392/5476.

Clark, Douglas K. "Signs in Wisdom and John." *Catholic Biblical Quarterly* 45 (1983) 201–9.

Clark-Soles, Jaime. "Mary Magdalene: Beginning at the End." In *Character Studies in the Fourth Gospel: Narrative Approaches to Seventy Figures in John*, edited by Steven A. Hunt et al., 626–40. 2013. Reprint, Grand Rapids: Eerdmans, 2016.

Collins, Adela Yarbro, and John J. Collins. *King and Messiah as Son of God: Divine, Human, and Angelic Messianic Figures in Biblical and Related Literature*. Grand Rapids: Eerdmans, 2008.

Collins, John. "Pre-Christian Jewish Messianism." In *The Messiah in Early Judaism and Christianity*, edited by Magnus Zetterholm, 1–20. Minneapolis: Fortress, 2007.

Collins, Raymond F. *These Things Have Been Written: Studies on the Fourth Gospel*. Leuven: Peeters, 1990.

Coloe, Mary L. *God Dwells with Us: Temple Symbolism in the Fourth Gospel*. Collegeville, MN: Liturgical, 2001.

———. "The Mother of Jesus: A Woman Possessed." In *Character Studies in the Fourth Gospel: Narrative Approaches to Seventy Figures in John*, edited by Steven Hunt et al., 202–13. 2013. Reprint, Grand Rapid: Eerdmans, 2016.

Connick, C. Milo. "The Dramatic Character of the Fourth Gospel." *Journal of Biblical Literature* 67 (1948) 159–69.

Cronin, Sonya. *Raymond Brown, 'the Jews,' and the Gospel of John: From Apologia to Apology*. Library of New Testament Studies 504. London: Bloomsbury T. & T. Clark, 2015.

Crowe, Brandon D. "The Chiastic Structure of Seven Signs in the Gospel of John: Revisiting a Neglected Proposal." *Bulletin for Biblical Research* 28 (2018) 65–81.

Cullmann, Oscar. *The Johannine Circle*. Translated by John Bowden. Philadelphia: Westminster, 1975.

Culpepper, R. Alan. *Anatomy of the Fourth Gospel: A Study in Literary Design*. Foundations and Facets. Philadelphia: Fortress, 1983.

———. *The Gospel and Letters of John*. Interpreting Biblical Texts. Nashville: Abingdon, 1988.

———. "Inclusivism and Exclusivism in the Fourth Gospel." In *Word, Theology, and Community in John*, edited by John Painter et al., 85–108. St. Louis: Chalice, 2002.

———. "Nicodemus." In *Character Studies in the Fourth Gospel: Narrative Approaches to Seventy Figures in John*, edited by Steven Hunt et al., 249–59. 2013. Reprint, Grand Rapids: Eerdmans, 2016.

———. "Peter as an Exemplary Disciple in John 21:15–19." *Religious Studies* 37 (2010) 165–78.

———. "Reading Johannine Irony." In *Exploring the Gospel of John: In Honor of D. Moody Smith*, edited by R. Alan Culpepper et al., 193–207. Louisville: Westminster John Knox, 1996.

———. "Symbolism and History in John's Account of Jesus' Death." In *Anatomies of Narrative Criticism: The Past, Present, and Futures of the Fourth Gospel as Literature*, edited by Tom Thatcher et al., 39–54. Resources for Biblical Study 55. Atlanta: Society of Biblical Literature, 2008.

Culpepper, R. Alan, and C. Clifton Black, eds. *Exploring the Gospel of John: In Honor of D. Moody Smith*. Louisville: Westminster John Knox, 1996.

Davies, Margaret. *Rhetoric and Reference in the Fourth Gospel*. Journal for the Study of the New Testament Supplements 69. Sheffield: JSOT Press,1992.

de Boer, Martinus C. *Johannine Perspectives on the Death of Jesus*. Contributions to Biblical Exegesis and Theology 17. Kampen: Pharos, 1996.

de Jonge, Marinus. *Jesus, Stranger from Heaven and Son of God: Jesus Christ and the Christians in Johannine Perspective*. Sources for Biblical Studies 11. Atlanta: Society for Biblical Literature, 1977.

———. "Jewish Expectations about the 'Messiah' according to the Fourth Gospel." *New Testament Studies* 19 (1971) 246–70.

Denaux, Adelbert. "The Twofold Purpose of the Fourth Gospel: A Reading of the Conclusion to John's Gospel (20,30–31)." In *Studies in the Gospel of John and Its Christology*, edited by Joseph Verheyden et al., 519–36. Leuven: Katholieke University, 2014.

Dennis, John. "Jesus' Death in John's Gospel: A Survey of Research from Bultmann to the Present with Special Reference to the Johannine Hyper-Texts." *Currents in Biblical Research* 4 (2006) 331–63.

———. "The 'Lifting up of the Son of Man' and the Dethroning of the 'Ruler of this World': Jesus' Death as the Defeat of the Devil in John 12,31–32." In *The Death of Jesus in the Fourth Gospel*, edited by G. Van Belle, 677–91. Leuven: Leuven University Press.

Dodd, Charles H. "The First Epistle of John and the Fourth Gospel." *Biblical Journal of Religious Literature* 21 (1937) 144–45.

———. *Historical Tradition and the Fourth Gospel*. Cambridge: Cambridge University Press, 1963.

———. *The Interpretation of the Fourth Gospel*. Cambridge: Cambridge University Press, 1953.

Dodson, Bob. "Before the Rooster Crows." *Acts 242 Study*. (March 11, 2022). http://acts242study.com/category/general/.

Domeris, William R. "The Johannine Drama." *Journal of Theology for Southern Africa* 42 (1983) 29–35.

Draper, Jonathan A. "The 'Theatre of Performance' and 'The Living Word' of Jesus in the Farewell Discourse(s) in John's Gospel." *Journal of Early Christian History* 1 (2001) 26–43.

Duke, Paul D. *Irony in the Fourth Gospel*. Atlanta: John Knox, 1985.

Du Rand, Jan A. "The Creation Motif in the Fourth Gospel: Perspectives on Its Narratological Function within a Judaistic Background." In *Theology and Christology in the Fourth Gospel: Essays by the Members of the SNTS Johannine Writings Seminar*, edited by G.

Van Belle et al., 21–46. Bibliotheca Ephemerideum Theologicarum Lovaniensium 184. Leuven: Leuven University Press, 2005.

———. "A Syntactical and Narratological Reading of John 10." In *The Shepherd Discourse of John 10 and its Context*, edited by Johannes Beutler et al., 94–115. Cambridge: Cambridge University Press, 1991.

Edward, Ruth B. *Discovering John: Content, Interpretation, Reception*. 2nd ed. Grand Rapids: Eerdmans, 2014.

Ellis, Peter F. *The Genius of John: A Composition-Critical Commentary on the Fourth Gospel*. Collegeville, MN: Liturgical, 1984.

———. "Inclusion, Chiasm, and the Division of the Fourth Gospel." *St. Vladimir's Theological Quarterly* 43 (1999) 269–338.

Emerton, John A. "The Hundred and Fifty-Three Fishes in John 21:11." *Journal of Theological Studies* 9 (1958) 86–89.

Estes, Douglas. *The Temporal Mechanics of the Fourth Gospel: A Theory of Hermeneutical Relativity in the Gospel of John*. Leiden: Brill, 2008.

Eusebius. *Historia Ecclesiastica*. Translated by Paul L. Maier. Grand Rapids: Kregel, 2007.

Evans, Craig A. "On the Prologue of John and the *Trimorphic Protennoia*." *New Testament Studies* 27 (1981) 395–401.

Fitzmyer, Joseph A. *The One Who is to Come*. Grand Rapids: Eerdmans, 2007.

Fortna, Robert T. *The Gospel of Signs: A Reconstruction of the Narrative Source Underlying the Fourth Gospel*. Society for New Testament Studies Monograph Series 11. Cambridge: Cambridge University Press, 1970.

Frey, Jörg. "Dualism and the World in the Gospel of John." In *The Oxford Handbook of Johannine Studies*, edited by Judith M. Lieu et al., 274–91. Oxford: Oxford University Press, 2018.

———. *The Glory of the Crucified One: Christology and Theology in the Gospel of John*. Translated by Wayne Coppins and Christoph Heilig. Waco, TX: Baylor University Press, 2018.

Frey, Jörg, et al., eds. *Imagery in the Gospel of John: Terms, Themes, and Theology of Johannine Figurative Language*. Wissenschaftliche Untersuchungen zum Neuen Testament 200. Tübingen: Mohr Siebeck, 2006.

Freyne, Sean. "The Herodian Period." In *Redemption and Resistance: The Messianic Hopes of Jews and Christians in Antiquity*, edited by Markus Bockmuehl et al., 29–43. London: T. & T. Clark, 2007.

Freyne, Sean, and Tom Thatcher, eds. *Jesus in Johannine Tradition*. Louisville: Westminster John Knox, 2001.

Gench, Frances Taylor. *Encounters with Jesus: Studies in the Gospel of John*. Louisville: Westminster John Knox, 2007.

Giblin, Charles H. "Suggestion, Negative Response, and Positive Action in St John's Portrayal of Jesus (John 2:1–11; 4:46–54; 7:2–14; 11:1–44)." *New Testament Studies* 26 (1979–1980) 197–211.

Gieschen, Charles A. "The Death of Jesus in the Gospel of John." *Covenant Theological Quarterly* 72 (2008) 243–61.

Givón, Talmy. *Syntax and Semantics Volume 12: Discourse and Syntax*. New York: Academic, 1979.

Hagner, Donald A. *Matthew 14–28*. Word Biblical Commentary 33B. Dallas: Word, 1998.

Haiman, John. *Talk is Cheap: Sarcasm, Alienation, and the Evolution of Language.* Oxford: Oxford University Press, 1998.

Harner, Phillip B. "Qualitative Anarthrous Predicate Nouns: Mark 15:39 and John 1:1." *Journal of Biblical Literature* 92 (1973) 75–87.

Harris, Elizabeth. *Prologue and Gospel: The Theology of the Fourth Evangelist.* Journal for the Study of the New Testament Supplements 107. Sheffield: Sheffield Academic, 1994.

Harris, William V. *Ancient Literacy.* Cambridge: Harvard University Press, 1989.

Hartley, John E. *Leviticus.* Word Biblical Commentary 4. Dallas: Word, 1992.

Harvey, Anthony E. *Jesus on Trial: A Study in the Fourth Gospel.* London: SPCK, 1976.

Hedner-Zetterholm, Karin. "Elijah and the Messiah as Spokesmen of Rabbinic Ideology." In *The Messiah in Early Judaism and Christianity*, edited by Magnus Zetterholm, 57–78. Minneapolis: Fortress, 2007.

Hick, John. *God and the Universe of Faiths.* London: Macmillan, 1977.

Hobbs, T. Ray. *2 Kings.* Word Biblical Commentary 13. Dallas: Word, 1985.

Horsley, Richard A. "Like One of the Prophets of Old: Two Types of Popular Prophets at the Time of Jesus." *Catholic Biblical Quarterly* 47 (1985) 435–63.

———. "Popular Messianic Movements around the Time of Jesus." *Catholic Biblical Quarterly* 46 (1984) 471–95.

Horsley, Richard A, and Tom Thatcher. *John, Jesus, and the Renewal of Israel.* Grand Rapids: Eerdmans, 2013.

Hudgins, Thomas W. "An Application of Discourse Analysis Methodology in the Exegesis of John 17." *Eleutheria* 2 (2012) 24–57.

Hunt, Steven A. "The Roman Soldiers at Jesus' Arrest: 'You Are Dust, and to Dust you Shall Return.'" In *Character Studies in the Fourth Gospel: Narrative Approaches to Seventy Figures in John*, edited by Steven Hunt et al., 554–67. 2013. Reprint, Grand Rapids: Eerdmans, 2016.

Hunt, Steven A., et al., eds. *Character Studies in the Fourth Gospel: Narrative Approaches to Seventy Figures in John.* 2013. Reprint, Grand Rapids: Eerdmans, 2016.

Hurley, James B. *Man and Woman in Biblical Perspective.* Grand Rapids: Zondervan, 1981.

Hyers, Conrad. *The Meaning of Creation: Genesis and Modern Science.* Atlanta: John Knox, 1984.

Hylen, Susan. *Allusion and Meaning in John 6.* Beihefte zur Zeitschrift für die neutestamentliche Wissenschaft und die Kunde der älteren Kirche 137. Berlin: de Gruyter, 2005.

Jeremias, Joachim. *The New Testament Theology.* New York: Scribner, 1967.

———. "ποιμήν, ἀρχιποίμην, κτλ." *Theological Dictionary of the New Testament*, edited by Gerhard Kittel and Gerhard Friedrich and translated by Geoffrey W. Bromiley, 6:485–502. Grand Rapids: Eerdmans, 1968.

Jordaan, Pierre J. "Ritual, Rage and Revenge in 2 Maccabees 6 and 7." *HTS Teologiese Studies* 68 (2012). http://www.hts.org.za.

Keener, Craig S. *The Gospel of John: A Commentary.* Peabody, MA: Hendrickson, 2004.

———. *John.* Grand Rapids: Zondervan, 2019.

Kelly, Anthony J., and Francis J. Moloney. *Experiencing God in the Gospel of John.* Mahwah, NJ: Paulist, 2003.

Kierkegaard, Søren. *The Concept of Irony: With Constant Reference to Socrates.* Translated by Lee M. Capel. London: Collins, 1966.

Kim, Jintai. "The Concept of Atonement in the Gospel of John." *Faculty Publications and Presentations.* Paper 250 (2009). http://digitalcommons.liberty.edu/lts_fac_pubs/250.

Kim, Sang-Hoon. *Sourcebook of the Structures and Styles in John 1–10*. Eugene, OR: Wipf & Stock, 2014.

Koester, Craig R. *Symbolism in the Fourth Gospel: Meaning, Mystery, and Community*. 2nd ed. Minneapolis: Fortress, 2014.

———. "Theological Complexity and the Characterization of Nicodemus in John's Gospel." In *Characters and Characterization in the Gospel of John*, edited by Christopher W. Skinner, 163–79. Library of New Testament Studies 461. London: Bloomsbury, 2013.

———. "Topography and Theology in the Gospel of John." In *Fortunate the Eyes That See: Essays in Honor of David Noel Freedman in Celebration of His Seventieth Birthday*, edited by Astrid B. Beck, 436–48. Grand Rapids: Eerdmans, 1995.

Köstenberger, Andreas J. *John*. Baker Exegetical Commentary on the New Testament. Grand Rapids: Baker Academic, 2004.

———. *A Theology of John's Gospel and Letters*. Grand Rapids: Zondervan, 2009.

———. "The Use of the Old Testament in the Gospel of John and the Johannine Epistles." *Southwestern Journal of Theology* 64 (2021) 41–55.

Labahn, Michael. "Simon Peter: An Ambiguous Character and His Narrative Career." In *Character Studies in the Fourth Gospel: Narrative Approaches to Seventy Figures in John*, edited by Steven Hunt et al., 151–67. 2013. Reprint, Grand Rapids: Eerdmans, 2016.

Ledonne, Anthony, and Tom Thatcher, eds. *The Fourth Gospel in First-Century Media Culture*. Library of New Testament Studies 426. London: T. & T. Clark, 2011.

Levinsohn, Stephen H. "Member Reference in Koine Greek Narrative." In *Linguistics and New Testament Interpretation*, edited by David Alan Black et al., 31–44. Nashville: Broadman, 1992.

Lewis, Karoline. *John*. Fortress Biblical Preaching Commentary. Minneapolis: Fortress, 2014.

Lieu, Judith M. "The Messiah and Resistance in the Gospel and Epistles of John." In *Redemption and Resistance: The Messianic Hopes of Jews and Christians in Antiquity*, edited by Markus Bockmuehl et al., 97–108. London: T. & T. Clark, 2007.

———. "The Mother of the Son in the Fourth Gospel." *Journal of Biblical Literature* 117 (1998) 61–77.

Lieu, Judith M., and Martinus C. de Boer. *The Oxford Handbook of Johannine Studies*. Oxford Handbooks Online. Oxford: Oxford University Press, 2018.

Lincoln, Andrew T. *Truth on Trial: The Lawsuit Motif in the Fourth Gospel*. Peabody, MA: Hendrickson, 2000.

Loader, William. *Jesus in John's Gospel: Structure and Issues in Johannine Christology*. Grand Rapids: Eerdmans, 2017.

Longman, Tremper, III. "The Messiah: Explorations in the Law and Writings." In *The Messiah in the Old and New Testaments*, edited by Stanley Porter, 13–34. Grand Rapids: Eerdmans, 2007.

Maccini, Robert G. *Her Testimony Is True: Women as Witnesses according to John*. Journal for the Study of the New Testament Supplements 125. Sheffield: Sheffield Academic, 1996.

MacGregor, George H. *The Gospel of John: Its Significance and Environment*. London: Hodder and Stoughton, 1928.

Martyn, James Lewis. *The Gospel of John in Christian History*. New York: Paulist, 1978.

———. *History and Theology in the Fourth Gospel*. 3rd ed. Louisville: Westminster John Knox, 2003.

Matson, Mark A. "The Temple Incident: An Integral Element in the Fourth Gospel's Narrative." In *Jesus in Johannine Tradition*, edited by Robert T. Fortna et al., 145–53. Louisville: Westminster John Knox, 2001.

Maynard, Arthur H. "Peter in the Fourth Gospel." *New Testament Studies* 30 (1984) 531–48.

McGrath, James F. "The Gospel of John as Jewish Messianism: Formative Influences and Neglected Avenues in the History of Scholarship." In *Reading the Gospel of John's Christology as Jewish Messianism*, edited by Benjamin E. Reynolds and Gabriele Boccaccini, 43–65. Ancient Judaism and Early Christianity 106. Leiden: Brill, 2018.

Mead, A. H. "The βασιλικος in John 4.46–53." *Journal for the Study of the New Testament* 23 (1983) 69–72.

Menken, Maarten J. "'The Lamb of God' (John 1,29) in the Light of 1 John 3,4–7." In *The Death of Jesus in the Fourth Gospel*, edited by Gilbert Van Belle, 581–90. Bibliotheca Ephemeridum theologicarum Lovaniensium 200. Leuven: Leuven University Press, 2007.

———. *Numerical Literary Techniques in John: The Fourth Evangelist's Use of Numbers of Words and Syllables.* Novum Testamentum Supplements 55. Leiden: Brill, 1985.

Michaels, J. Ramsey. "Atonement in John's Gospel and Epistles." In *The Glory of the Atonement*, edited by Charles E. Hill et al., 106–18. Downers Grove, IL: InterVarsity, 2004

———. *The Gospel of John.* New International Commentary on the New Testament. Grand Rapids: Eerdmans, 2010.

———. "The Invalid at the Pool." In *Character Studies in the Fourth Gospel: Narrative Approaches to Seventy Figures in John*, edited by Steven Hunt et al., 337–46. 2013. Reprint, Grand Rapids: Eerdmans, 2016.

Miller, George A. "The Magical Number Seven, Plus or Minus Two: Some Limits on our Capacity for Processing Information." *Psychological Review* 63 (1956) 81–97.

Minear, Paul Sevier. *Christians and the New Creation: Genesis Motifs in the New Testament.* Louisville: Westminster John Knox, 1994.

Moloney, Francis. "The Fourth Gospel and the Jesus of History." *New Testament Studies* 46 (2000) 42–48.

———. *Glory not Dishonor: Reading John 13–21.* Minneapolis: Fortress, 1998.

———. *The Gospel of John.* Sacra Pagina 4. Collegeville, MN: Liturgical: 1998.

———. *Johannine Studies 1975–2017.* Wissenschaftliche Untersuchungen zum Neuen Testament 372. Tübingen: Mohr Siebeck, 2017.

———. *Love in the Gospel of John: An Exegetical, Theological, and Literary Study.* Grand Rapids: Baker, 2013.

———. *Signs and Shadows: Reading John 5–12.* Minneapolis: Fortress, 1996.

Morris, Leon. *The Gospel according to John.* Rev. ed. Grand Rapids: Eerdmans, 1995.

———. *Jesus is the Christ: Studies in the Theology of John.* Grand Rapids: Eerdmans, 1989.

———. *Studies in the Fourth Gospel.* Grand Rapids: Eerdmans, 1969.

Moulton, Richard G. *The Literary Study of the Bible.* Boston: Heath, 1989.

Myers, Alicia D. *Characterizing Jesus: A Rhetorical Analysis on the Fourth Gospel's Use of Scripture in its Presentation of Jesus.* Library of New Testament Studies 458. London: T. & T. Clark, 2012.

Neirynck, Frans. "The Signs Source in the Fourth Gospel: A Critique of the Hypothesis." In *Evangelica* 2.7 (TU 126) 359–63.

Neyrey, Jerome H. *The Gospel of John in Cultural and Rhetorical Perspective.* Grand Rapids: Eerdmans, 2009.

———. "The Noble Shepherd in John 10: Cultural and Rhetorical Background." *Journal of Biblical Literature* 120 (2001) 267–91.

Ninow, Friedbert. *Indicators of Typology within the Old Testament: The Exodus Motif.* Friedensauer Schriftenreihe, Theologie 4. Frankfurt: Lang, 2001.

Novenson, Matthew V. *The Grammar of Messianism: An Ancient Jewish Political Idiom and Its Users.* New York: Oxford University Press, 2017.

O'Day, Gail. *The Gospel of John: Introduction, Commentary, and Reflections.* New Interpreter's Bible 9. Nashville: Abingdon, 1995.

Painter, John. "The Prologue as an Hermeneutical Key to Reading the Fourth Gospel." In *Studies in the Gospel of John and Its Christology*, edited by Joseph Verheyden et al., 37–60. Bibliotheca Ephemeridum theologicarum Lovaniensium 265. Leuven: Peeters, 2014.

———. *The Quest for the Messiah: The History, Literature and Theology of the Johannine Community.* Edinburgh: T. & T. Clark, 1991.

———. "Theology, Eschatology and the Prologue of John." *Scottish Journal of Theology* 46 (1993) 27–42.

———. "Tradition, History and Interpretation in John 10." In *The Shepherd Discourse of John 10 and its Context*, edited by Johannes Beutler et al., 53–74. Society for New Testament Studies Monograph Series 67. Cambridge: Cambridge University Press, 1991.

Parsenios, George L. "'No Longer in the World' (John 17:11): The Transformation of the Tragic in the Fourth Gospel." *Harvard Theological Review* (2005) 1–21.

Parsons, Mikeal C. "Exegesis 'By the Numbers': Numerology and the New Testament." *Perspectives in Religious Studies* 35 (2008) 25–43.

Peppard, Michael. *The Son of God in the Roman World: Divine Sonship in Its Social and Political Context.* New York: Oxford University Press, 2011.

Peterson, Michael, et al. *Reason and Religious Belief.* 5th ed. New York: Oxford University Press, 2013.

Popp, Thomas. *Grammatik des Geistes: Literarische Kunst und Theologische Konzeption in Johannes 3 und 6.* Leipzig: Evangelische Verlagsanstalt, 2001.

Porter, Stanley E., ed. *The Messiah in the Old and New Testaments.* Grand Rapids: Eerdmans, 2007.

Powell, Mark Allan. *Loving Jesus.* Minneapolis: Fortress, 2004.

Reed, Jeffrey T. "Discourse Analysis as New Testament Hermeneutic: A Retrospective and Prospective Appraisal." *Journal of the Evangelical Theological Society* 39 (1996) 223–40.

Reichenbach, Bruce R. *Divine Providence: God's Love and Human Freedom.* Eugene, OR: Cascade Books, 2016.

———. *Evil and a Good God.* New York: Fordham University Press, 1978.

———. "Genesis 1 as a Theological-Political Narrative of Kingdom Establishment." *Bulletin for Biblical Research* 13 (2003) 47–69.

———. "Healing View." In *The Nature of the Atonement: Four Views*, edited by James Beilby et al., 117–42. Downers Grove, IL: InterVarsity, 2006.

Resseguie, James L. *Narrative Criticism of the New Testament: An Introduction.* Grand Rapids: Baker, 2005.

Reynolds, Benjamin E. "The Gospel of John's Christology as Evidence for Early Jewish Messianic Expectations: Challenges and Possibilities." In *Reading the Gospel of John's Christology as Jewish Messianism*, edited by Benjamin E. Reynolds and Gabriele Boccaccini, 13–42. Ancient Judaism and Early Christianity 106. Leiden: Brill, 2018.

Reynolds, Benjamin E., and Gabriele Boccaccini, eds. *Reading the Gospel of John's Christology as Jewish Messianism: Royal, Prophetic, and Divine Messiahs.* Ancient Judaism and Early Christianity 106. Leiden: Brill, 2018.

Richard, Earl J. "Expressions of Double Meaning and Their Function in the Gospel of John." *New Testament Studies* 31 (1985) 96–112.

Riesenfeld, Harald. "ὑπέρ." *Theological Dictionary of the New Testament,* edited by Gerhard Kittel and Gerhard Friedrich and translated by Geoffrey W. Bromiley, 8:507–16. Grand Rapids: Eerdmans, 1972.

Robinson, John A. *Historical Character of St. John's Gospel.* London: Longmans, Green, 1908.

Robinson, John A. T. *The Priority of John.* London: SCM, 1985.

Rowe, Eric, and Jerome Neyrey. "'Telling Time' in the Fourth Gospel." (June 19, 2007) 1–40. https://www3.nd.edu/~jneyrey1/telling-time.pdf.

Ruckstuhl, E., and P. Dschulnigg. *Stilkritik und Verfasserfrage im Johannesevangelium: Die johanneischen Sprachmerkmale auf dem Hintergrund des Neuen Testaments und des zeitgenössischen hellenistischen Schrifttums.* Novum Testamentum et Orbis Antiquus 17. Göttingen: Vandenhoeck & Ruprecht, 1991.

Rylaarsdam, J. C. "Booths, Feast of." In *Interpreter's Dictionary of the Bible* 1, edited by George Arthur Buttrick, 456. Nashville: Abingdon, 1962.

Sanders, Joseph N. *A Commentary on the Gospel according to St. John,* edited and completed by B. A. Mastin. London: Black, 1968.

Sasse, Herman. "κοσμέω, κόσμος, κτλ." In *Theological Dictionary of the New Testament,* edited by Gerhard Kittel and Gerhard Friedrich and translated by Geoffrey W. Bromiley, 3:867–98. Grand Rapids: Eerdmans, 1965.

Schaper, Joachim. "The Persian Period." In *Redemption and Resistance: The Messianic Hopes of Jews and Christians in Antiquity,* edited by Markus Bockmuehl James Carleton Paget, 3–14. Edinburgh: T. & T. Clark, 2007.

Schnackenburg, Rudolf. *The Gospel according to John.* 3 vols. Translated by K. Smith et al. New York: Crossroad, 1982.

Schnelle, Udo. "The Person of Jesus Christ in the Gospel of John." In *The Oxford Handbook of Johannine Studies,* edited by Judith M. Lieu et al., 311–30. Oxford Handbooks Online. Oxford: Oxford University Press, 2018.

Schreiner, Thomas R. "Penal Substitution View." In *The Nature of the Atonement: Four Views,* edited by James Beilby et al., 67–98. Downers Grove, IL: InterVarsity, 2006.

Schuchard, Bruce G. "Temple, Festivals, and Scripture in the Gospel of John." In *The Oxford Handbook of Johannine Studies,* edited by Judith M. Lieu et al., 381–95. Oxford Handbooks Online. Oxford: Oxford University Press, 2018.

Segovia, Fernando F. "The Theology and Provenance of John 15:1–17." *Journal of Biblical Literature* 101 (1982) 115–28.

Senior, C. P. Donald. *The Passion of Jesus in the Gospel of John.* Leominister, UK: Gracewing, 1991.

Shepherd, David. "'Do You Love Me?' A Narrative-Critical Reappraisal of ἀγαπάω and φιλέω in John 21:15–17." *Journal of Biblical Literature* 129 (2010) 777–92.

Sheridan, Ruth. "The Testimony of Two Witnesses: John 8:17." In *Abiding Words: The Use of Scripture in the Gospel of John,* edited by Alicia D. Myers et al., 161–84. Resources for Biblical Study 81. Atlanta: Society of Biblical Literature, 2015.

Sherwin-White, A. N. "Pilate." *The International Standard Bible Encyclopedia,* edited by Geoffrey W. Bromiley, 3:867–69. Rev. ed. Grand Rapids: Eerdmans, 1986.

Siliezar, Carlos Raúl Sosa. *Creation Imagery in the Gospel of John*. New York: Bloomsbury T. & T. Clark, 2015.

Skinner, Christopher W. *Characters and Characterization in the Gospel of John*. Library of New Testament Studies 461. New York: Bloomsbury T. & T. Clark, 2013.

———. "The World: Promise and Unfulfilled Hope." In *Character Studies in the Fourth Gospel: Narrative Approaches to Seventy Figures in John*, edited by Steven Hunt et al., 61–70. 2013. Reprint, Grand Rapids: Eerdmans, 2016.

Smalley, Stephen. *John: Evangelist and Interpreter*. Exeter: Paternoster, 1978.

Smith, D. Moody. *John*. Philadelphia: Fortress, 1986.

Stählin, Gustav. "φιλέω, κτλ." In *Theological Dictionary of the New Testament*, edited by Gerhard Kittel and Gerhard Friedrich, translated by Geoffrey W. Bromiley, 9:113–46. Grand Rapids: Eerdmans, 1974.

Staley, Jeff. "The Structure of John's Prologue: Its Implications for the Gospel's Narrative Structure." *Catholic Biblical Quarterly* 48 (1986) 241–64.

Strachan, Robert H. *The Fourth Evangelist: Dramatist or Historian?* New York: Doran, 1925.

Stauffer, Ethelbert. "ἀγαπάω, ἀγάπη, κτλ." *Theological Dictionary of the New Testament*, edited by Gerhard Kittel and Gerhard Friedrich and translated by Geoffrey W. Bromiley, 1:21–55. Grand Rapids: Eerdmans, 1964.

Stibbe, Mark W. G., ed. *The Gospel of John as Literature: An Anthology of Twentieth-century Perspectives*. New Testament Tools and Studies 17. Leiden: Brill, 1993.

———. *John as Storyteller: Narrative Criticism and the Fourth Gospel*. Society for the New Testament Studies Monograph Series 73. Cambridge: Cambridge University Press, 1992.

———. *John's Gospel*. London: Routledge, 1994.

———. "Magnificent but Flawed: The Breaking of Form in the Fourth Gospel." In *Anatomies of Narrative Criticism: The Past, Present, and Futures of the Fourth Gospel as Literature*, edited by Tom Thatcher et al., 149–65. Resources for Biblical Study 55. Atlanta: Society of Biblical Literature, 2008.

Stovell, Beth M. "Son of God as Anointed One?: Johannine Davidic Christology and Second Temple Messianism." In *Reading the Gospel of John's Christology as Jewish Messianism*, edited by Benjamin E. Reynolds and Gabriele Boccaccini, 151–77. Ancient Judaism and Early Christianity 106. Leiden: Brill, 2018.

Stuckenbruck, Loren T. "Messianic Ideas in the Apocalyptic and Related Literature of Early Judaism." In *The Messiah in the Old and New Testaments*, edited by Stanley E. Porter, 90–115. Grand Rapids: Eerdmans, 2007.

Swidler, Leonard. *Women in Judaism: The Status of Women in Formative Judaism*. Metuchen, NJ: Scarecrow, 1976.

Talbert, Charles H. *Reading John: A Literary and Theological Commentary on the Fourth Gospel and the Johannine Epistles*. New York: Crossroad, 1992.

Tannen, Deborah. *Gender and Discourse*. New York: Oxford University Press, 1994.

Tenney, Merrill C. *John: The Gospel of Belief*. Grand Rapids: Eerdmans, 1976.

Thatcher, Tom. "Antinomies of the Fourth Gospel: Past, Present, and Future Probes." In *Anatomies of Narrative Criticism: The Past, Present, and Futures of the Fourth Gospel as Literature*, edited by Tom Thatcher et al., 1–35. Resources for Biblical Study 55. Atlanta: Society of Biblical Literature, 2008.

———. "Aspects of Historicity in the Fourth Gospel: Phase Two of the John, Jesus, and History Project." In *John, Jesus, and History*, Vol. 2: *Aspects of Historicity in the Fourth*

*Gospel*, edited by Paul Anderson et al., 1–8. Symposium Series 44. Atlanta: Society of Biblical Literature, 2009.

————. *Jesus the Riddler: The Power of Ambiguity in the Gospels.* Louisville: Westminster John Knox: 2006.

————. *The Riddles of Jesus in John: A Study in Tradition and Folklore.* SBL Monograph Series 53. Atlanta: Society of Biblical Literature, 2000.

————. "Riddles, Repetitions, and the Literary Unity of the Johannine Discourses." In *Repetitions and Variations in the Fourth Gospel: Style, Text, Interpretation,* edited by Gilbert Van Belle et al., 357–77. Bibliotheca Ephemeridum theologicarum Lovaniensium 223. Leuven: Peeters, 2009.

————. "Riddles, Wit, and Wisdom." In *Handbook for the Study of the Historical Jesus*, edited by Tom Holmén and Stanley E. Porter, 4:3349–72. Leiden: Brill, 2019.

————. *Why John Wrote a Gospel: Jesus–Memory–History.* Louisville: Westminster John Knox, 2001.

Thatcher, Tom, and Stephen D. Moore, eds. *Anatomies of Narrative Criticism: The Past, Present, and Futures of the Fourth Gospel as Literature*: Resources for Biblical Study 55. Atlanta: Society of Biblical Literature, 2008.

Thomas, John Christopher. "Healing in the Atonement: A Johannine Perspective." *Journal of Pentecostal Theology* 14 (2005) 23–39.

Thompson, Marianne Meye. "Christus Victor: The Salvation of God and the Cross of Christ." *Theology, News and Notes* 59 (2012) 8–11.

Thyen, Paul. "Aus der Literatur zum Johannesevangelium." *Theologische Rundschau* 39 (1975) 1–69, 222–52, 289–330.

Tovey, Derek. *Narrative Art and Act.* Sheffield: Sheffield Academic, 1997.

Turnage, Marc. "Sometimes a Rooster is not a Rooster." (March 11, 2022). https://news.ag.org/features/sometimes-a-rooster-is-not-a-rooster.

Turner, Max. "The Atonement and the Death of Jesus in John—Some Questions to Bultmann and Forestell." *Evangelical Quarterly* 62 (1990) 99–122.

Van Belle, Gilbert. "Repetitions and Variations in Johannine Research: A General Historical Survey." In *Repetitions and Variations in the Fourth Gospel*, edited by Gilbert Van Belle et al., 33–85. Bibliotheca Ephemeridum theologicarum Lovaniensium 223. Leuven: Peeters, 2009.

————. "Theory of Repetitions and Variations in the Fourth Gospel: A Neglected Field of Research?" In *Repetitions and Variations in the Fourth Gospel*, edited by Gilbert Van Belle et al., 23–32. Bibliotheca Ephemeridum theologicarum Lovaniensium 223. Leuven: Peeters, 2009.

Van Belle, Gilbert, et al., eds. *Repetitions and Variations in the Fourth Gospel: Style, Text, Interpretation.* Bibliotheca Ephemeridum theologicarum Lovaniensium 223. Leuven: Peeters, 2009.

Van Der Watt, Jan G. "Repetition and Functionality." In *Repetitions and Variations in the Fourth Gospel: Style, Text, Interpretation*, edited by Gilbert Van Belle et al., 87–108. Bibliotheca Ephemeridum theologicarum Lovaniensium 223. Leuven: Peeters, 2009.

————. "Salvation in the Gospel According to John." In *Salvation in the New Testament: Perspectives on Soteriology*, edited by Jan G. van der Watt, 101–31. Novum Testamentum Supplements 121. Leiden: Brill, 2005.

Verheyden, Joseph, et al., eds. *Studies in the Gospel of John and Its Christology: Festschrift Gilbert Van Belle*. Bibliotheca Ephemeridum theologicarum Lovaniensium 265. Leuven: Peeters, 2014.

Verman, Mark. "The Power of Threes." *Jewish Bible Quarterly* 36 (2008) 171–81.

Voight, Andrew G. "The Discourses in the Gospel of St. John." *Lutheran Church Review* 43 (1924) 214–27.

Wallace, David H. "Nazarene, of Nazareth." In *The International Standard Bible Encyclopedia*, edited by Geoffrey W. Bromiley, 3:499–50. Rev. ed. Grand Rapids: Eerdmans, 1986.

Wenham, Gordon J. "The Theology of Old Testament Sacrifice." In *Sacrifice in the Bible*, edited by Roger T. Beckwith and Martin J. Selman, 75–87. 1995. Reprint, Eugene, OR: Wipf & Stock, 2004.

Whitenton, Michael R. "The Dissembler of John 3: A Cognitive and Rhetorical Approach to the Characterization of Nicodemus." *Journal of Biblical Literature* 135 (2016) 141–58.

Williams, Catrin H. "'I Am' or 'I Am He'?: Self-declaratory Pronouncements in the Fourth Gospel and Rabbinic Tradition." In *Jesus in the Johannine Tradition*, edited by Robert T. Fortna et al., 343–52. Louisville: Westminster John Knox, 2001.

———. "John (the Baptist): The Witness on the Threshold." In *Character Studies in the Fourth Gospel: Narrative Approaches to Seventy Figures in John,* edited by Steven Hunt et al., 46–60. 2013. Reprint, Grand Rapids: Eerdmans, 2016.

———. "Judas (not Iscariot): What's in a Name?" In *Character Studies in the Fourth Gospel: Narrative Approaches to Seventy Figures in John*, edited by Steven Hunt et al., 550–53. 2013. Reprint, Grand Rapids: Eerdmans, 2016.

Yeung, Maureen W. *Faith in Jesus and Paul: A Comparison with Special Reference to 'Faith that Can Remove Mountains' and 'Your* Faith *Has Healed/Saved You.'* Wissenschaftliche Untersuchungen zum Neuen Testament 2/147. Tübingen: Mohr Siebeck, 2002.

Zetterholm, Magnus, ed. *The Messiah in Early Judaism and Christianity*. Minneapolis: Fortress, 2007.

Zimmermann, Ruben. "Eschatology and Time in the Gospel of John." In *The Oxford Handbook of Johannine Studies*, edited by Judith M. Lieu et al., 292–309. Oxford Handbooks Online. Oxford: Oxford University Press, 2018.

———. "Jesus—the Lamb of God (John 1:29 and 1:36)." In *The Opening of John's Narrative (John 1:19–2:22)*, edited by R. Alan Culpepper et al., 79–96. Tübingen: Mohr Siebeck, 2017.

———. "The Jews: Unreliable Figures or Unreliable Narration?" In *Character Studies in the Fourth Gospel: Narrative Approaches to Seventy Figures in John*, edited by Steven A. Hunt et al., 71–109. 2013. Reprint, Grand Rapids: Eerdmans, 2016.

———. "Symbolic Communication between John and His Reader: The Garden Symbolism in John 19–20." In *Anatomies of Narrative Criticism: The Past, Present, and Futures of the Fourth Gospel as Literature*, edited by Tom Thatcher et al., 221–35. Resources for Biblical Study 55. Atlanta: Society of Biblical Literature, 2008.

Zumstein, Jean. "The Purpose of the Ministry and Death of Jesus." In *The Oxford Handbook of Johannine Studies*, edited by Judith M. Lieu, 331–46. Oxford Handbooks Online. Oxford: Oxford University Press, 2018.

# Index of Biblical Names

mother of Jesus, 49n46, 56, 57n19, 59–60, 87, 98, 101, 126, 145–48, 152, 156, 158, 224

Nathanael, 11, 22–23, 30, 49n46, 65n46, 81, 83, 86, 88–91, 93–94, 99–100, 130, 146, 158, 160, 174, 183, 220–22, 234, 238, 239, 241, 255

Nicodemus, 11, 19, 22, 27, 95, 98, 105n9, 129–36, 156, 159, 160, 169, 177, 214–15, 221, 231, 244, 250–52, 269

paralytic, 53, 56, 58, 61–62, 69, 72, 101, 152, 159, 216, 231–32, 262

Paul, Apostle, 104, 105, 125, 136n31, 149n69, 225, 228, 259n29, 263

Peter, Simon, 10, 18, 27–28, 31, 49n46, 66, 68, 73, 81, 85, 86, 87–88, 97–98, 112, 121, 129–30, 136–45, 149, 156, 158, 167–70, 172n45, 215, 220, 238–39, 241–42, 253n14, 254n15, 261, 267, 269

Pharisees, 9–11, 14, 19, 22–23, 27–29, 36, 63, 70, 72, 79n11, 80, 95, 100, 101, 108, 120, 129–30, 133–35, 159, 162–67, 172n40, 177–84, 185, 187, 194–95, 196–97, 214, 216, 232, 234–35, 250, 261–62, 266–67

Philip, 22–23, 30, 64, 73, 81, 85, 88–91, 92, 99, 101, 220, 238–39, 242

Pilate, 24n19, 34, 47, 90, 129, 131, 134n23, 160, 170–80, 185, 221, 224, 236–37, 242, 255, 259

Samaritan woman, 10, 16–17, 19, 30, 61, 81–85, 99, 117n36, 129, 131, 134, 146, 159, 160, 214, 231, 234, 244, 269

Samuel, 77, 237

Scribes, 95, 180–82

Simon of Samaria, 73

Thomas, 70, 72, 88, 92–94, 100, 113, 129–30, 134, 221–22, 238–39, 241, 261, 266, 269

# Index of Biblical Citations